# teach yourself
## MCSE Windows NT® Server 4.0
## IN 14 DAYS

**David G. Schaer, MCT, MCSE,**
**Walter J. Glenn, MCSE,**
**Marcus W. Barton, MCT,**
**Theresa A. Hadden, MCSE, MCSI**

**SAMS**
PUBLISHING

201 West 103rd Street
Indianapolis, Indiana 46290

# teach yourself
# MCSE
# Windows NT®
# Server 4.0
# IN 14 DAYS

*For Josie and Morgan.*
*—David G. Schaer*

*For Susan and Liam.*
*—Walter J. Glenn*

*For my wife, Alba.*
*—Marcus W. Barton*

*—For Ron*
*Theresa A. Hadden*

# Copyright © 1998 by Sams Publishing

FIRST EDITION

International Standard Book Number: 0-672-31128-3

Library of Congress Catalog Card Number: 97-67204

01  00  99  98          4   3   2   1

Interpretation of the printing code: the rightmost double-digit number is the year of the book's printing; the rightmost single-digit, the number of the book's printing. For example, a printing code of 98-1 shows that the first printing of the book occurred in 1998.

*Composed in AGaramond, Poppl-Laudatio, and MCPdigital by Macmillan Computer Publishing*

*Printed in the United States of America*

**Senior Vice President of Publishing**   Richard K. Swadley
**Publisher**   David Dwyer
**Executive Editor**   John Kane
**Managing Editor**   Sarah Kearns
**Vice President, Brand Management**   Jim Price
**Brand Marketing Director**   Alan Bower
**Brand Associate**   Kim Spilker
**Brand Coordinator**   Linda B. Beckwith

**Acquisitions Editor**
Cari Skaggs

**Development Editors**
Jeff Koch
Robert L. Bogue

**Project Editor**
Tonya R. Simpson

**Copy Editors**
Sean Dixon
Kate Givens
Susan Moore

**Indexing Manager**
Ginny Bess

**Indexer**
Ginny Bess

**Technical Reviewer**
Vincent Averello III

**Editorial Coordinators**
Mandie Rowell
Katie Wise

**Technical Edit Coordinator**
Lynette Quinn

**Editorial Assistants**
Carol Ackerman
Andi Richter
Rhonda Tinch-Mize
Karen Williams

**Cover Designer**
Sams Design Team

**Cover Illustrator**
Aren Howell

**Book Designer**
Gary Adair

**Copy Writer**
Eric Borgert

**Production Team Supervisor**
Brad Chinn

**Production**
Marcia Deboy
Michael Dietsch
Cynthia Fields
Maureen West

# Overview

# Contents

# Acknowledgments

I would like to thank my family, my students, and everyone at Knowledge Alliance for their support.

—David G. Schaer

I'd like to thank my family, most of all my parents for getting me started with computers and then in business; my wife for supporting me and indulging me in all my toys; and my son, for reminding me how much fun learning can be.

—Walter J. Glenn

I would like to thank my kids, Ashley, Aaron, and Jesslyn for being so patient while Dad was inaccessible while writing.

—Marcus W. Barton

I would like to thank my family and my students for their patience during this project.

—Theresa A. Hadden

# About the Authors

**David G. Schaer** is certified as both a Microsoft MCSE/MCT and a Novell MCNE/CNI. He has attended over 30 certified courses on computer topics offered by Novell and Microsoft and has provided training sessions throughout the United States, Germany, Italy, and Central America. He has contributed several technical articles to corporate newsletters. In recent years he has lectured at COMDEX/Hispania, received a certificate of award from US Army Europe and trained several hundred professionals on Microsoft and Novell products.

**Walter J. Glenn** is an independent networking consultant and a Microsoft Certified Systems Engineer working in Huntsville, Alabama. He has been working in the computer industry for about 13 years as a PC technician, trainer, and consultant. He has a wife, Susan, and a one-year-old son, Liam.

**Marcus W. Barton** is a Microsoft Certified Trainer currently employed by PC Productivity, a training and consulting firm. In addition to training the MCSE track, he consults on the deployment, integration, and migration to Windows NT and other Microsoft BackOffice products. Marcus first started with networks while serving on active duty in the United States Air Force.

**Theresa A. Hadden**, MCSE, MCSI, has over 10 years of System Administration experience using Novell, UNIX, and Windows NT. She is presently teaching in the MCSE program at a local college where she teaches Windows NT 4.0, Networking Essentials, TCP/IP, and Internet-related products, both in the classroom and on a one-on-one basis. She is actively involved in the design and implementation of online courses that include instructor access utilizing audio conferencing via the Internet. She is the mother of two sons and presently is living in New Mexico.

**Russell P. Mickler** has over five years of networking and PC-related experience and works as an Information Systems Manager for a durable medical equipment company out of Portland, Oregon. Mickler is pursuing his Masters degree in Applied Information Management from the University of Oregon. As both an MCP for Windows 95, NT 4.0, NT 4.0 Enterprise, Networking Essentials, and CNA for Windows 3.1*x*, Mickler is planning to earn his MCSE by the end of 1997. He can be contacted at `mickler@paclink.com`.

**James F. Causey** is an Intel Systems Specialist for Indiana University Computing Services. He performs high-level support, development, and administration tasks for NT-centric networks, with clients ranging from NT and 95 to DOS/Windows and MacOS. He also teaches courses on networking and the Microsoft suite of operating systems, as well as doing freelance software development. Originally trained as a Military Historian, his interests include music, sports cars, history, and any other recreational task which takes him as far from computers as possible. He has occasionally been known to pine for the days when VMS was king and Commodores were cool from his home in Bloomington, Indiana. He lives with his partner, Tina, and his cat, Gabby. James can be reached via e-mail at `jcausey@bluemarble.net`.

# Tell Us What You Think!

As a reader, you are the most important critic and commentator of our books. We value your opinion and want to know what we're doing right, what we could do better, what areas you'd like to see us publish in, and any other words of wisdom you're willing to pass our way. You can help us make strong books that meet your needs and give you the computer guidance you require.

Do you have access to the World Wide Web? Then check out our site at http://www.mcp.com.

> **Note**  If you have a technical question about this book, call the technical support line at 317-581-3833 or send e-mail to support@mcp.com.

As the team leader of the group that created this book, I welcome your comments. You can fax, e-mail, or write me directly to let me know what you did or didn't like about this book—as well as what we can do to make our books stronger. Here's the information:

Fax:      317-817-7448

E-mail:   jkane@mcp.com

Mail:     John Kane
          Executive Editor
          Macmillan Computer Publishing
          201 W. 103rd Street
          Indianapolis, IN  46290

# Introduction

If you do not want to pass Microsoft Examinations 70-67 (Implementing Microsoft NT Server 4.0) or 70-68 (Implementing Microsoft NT Server 4.0 in the Enterprise) put this book back on the shelf. If you plan to take the exams, and if you want to pass the first time, then this is the book for you.

Microsoft Certified Trainers and Microsoft Certified Systems Engineers who have already passed the exams wrote this book. This is not a book of answers; it is not a cheat sheet. It is a guide designed to ensure that you have the tools to prepare for the examinations. An effort has been made to provide technical information at a similar depth to that of the actual exams.

## How to Use This Guide

Read this section at least once in its entirety before moving on to the technical chapters. Answering test questions is easier when you understand how they are written. This introduction will show you how it's done.

Success comes through comprehension, not merely memorization. The Microsoft exams are designed to ensure that the people who pass have a full understanding of the software implementation. Too often, people believe that they can pass the exams simply by cramming facts about the software into their brains. The topics in this book are arranged to let you form links between subject matter.

Each chapter contains review questions written in a similar fashion to those on the actual exams. Complete the reading in a given chapter before attempting to answer the review questions. The review questions include answers that detail the correct answer. Don't be satisfied with merely answering a question correctly; make sure you understand the answer in full before moving on.

Relax, no one is grading you...yet.

### Dissect Each Exam Question

Exam questions are written to test several levels of knowledge. On the most basic level you might be asked a question that requires you to recall a simple command. A more complex question, popular with Microsoft but seemingly less so with test takers, is the comprehensive scenario question. In this type of question you are presented with a problem scenario, sometimes incorporating exhibits. A proposed solution is offered along with a listing of required and desired effects. You will be required to determine which combination of required and desired results, if any, is achieved by the solution.

There are no trick questions. Microsoft invests a significant amount of time to ensure that questions are not ambiguous. This does not mean that they are obvious. The skill being tested might not be apparent from the question. Often the main objective of a question is to test your knowledge of how different areas of NT work together.

Don't be concerned about finding the right answer, worry about selecting the wrong one. Each question can be answered correctly by eliminating the wrong answers. Don't select your answer until you've eliminated all the other possible choices. Then make sure that the answer you select is accurate in the context of the question.

# Exam Day

The following is a quick guide to what you must do to prepare for exam day.

## How to Schedule Your Exams

Microsoft MCSE testing is currently provided through Sylvan/Prometric. In the United States they can be reached at (800) 755-EXAM. At the time of writing the cost of the exams was set at $100 per exam. It might be possible to schedule your exam the day of the call; however, it is better to schedule a week in advance.

## What to Bring With You

In addition to this guide, which you can bring to the testing site but not into the examination room, you will need to bring the following:

- One picture ID (such as a driver's license or passport)
- One other form of ID with name and signature (such as a credit card or ATM card)
- Your favorite pencil
- Coffee cup (personal preference)

## One Exam or Two?

Before you schedule your exams, decide whether you want to take them both on the same day. There is significant overlap between the topics of both exams. By scheduling early you should be able to take your exam at the site of your choice and at the time of your choice. If possible, schedule your first exam about an hour before lunch and your second one following. This will give you time to come down from the rush. Use the time between tests to review the topics in the final checklist.

Sign in early for your exam. You want to get the formalities of the testing over with as soon as you get to the testing center so that you have time to review your last-minute checklist.

You might want to bring this guide with you to the exam center for a last-minute review. A final checklist with referenced pages is included in the appendixes. However, do not bring this book, or any other reference material, in the testing room with you. The test should come as a natural review of the topics you have studied in this guide.

# Day 1

# How to Become an MCSE

*by David Schaer and Theresa Hadden*

## 1.1. Overview of the MCSE Process

There are many avenues you can follow toward becoming a Microsoft Certified
Systems Engineer (MCSE). As you prepare to take the examinations you can elect to
attend classes or follow a course of self-study. This book is aimed toward helping you
prepare whichever route you decide to take. This chapter provides an overview of the
MCSE certification tracks and the testing process and shows you how to prepare for
each of them.

### 1.1.1. Charting Your Course

At this time, there are two MCSE certification tracks, one based on NT 4.0 and the
other on the older NT 3.51. You can find the most current MCSE requirements on
Microsoft's training and certification Web site at `http://www.microsoft.com/`
`Train_Cert/mcp/certstep/mcse.htm`.

The following charts outline the required exams for the NT 4.0 track. You are not
required to take the exams in any specific order.

All MCSE candidates must take the following two exams:

| | |
|---|---|
| Implementing and Supporting Microsoft NT Server 4.0 | 70-067 |
| Implementing and Supporting Microsoft NT Server 4.0 in the Enterprise | 70-068 |

If you are a Novell CNE, MCNE, or CNI, or a Banyan CBS or CBE, you are exempt from having to take the following core exam. All others must pass this exam.

| | |
|---|---|
| Networking Essentials | 70-058 |

The fourth core operating exam can be any one of the following:

| | |
|---|---|
| Implementing and Supporting Microsoft NT Workstation 4.0 | 70-073 |
| Implementing and Supporting Microsoft Windows 95 | 70-063 |
| Microsoft Windows for Workgroups 3.11 | 70-048 |
| Microsoft Windows 3.1 | 70-030 |

The final step is to pass two electives. As the following chart shows, there are several different choices. You must pass only two of the following exams:

| | |
|---|---|
| Internetworking with Microsoft TCP/IP on Microsoft Windows NT 4.0 | 70-059 |
| Internetworking with Microsoft TCP/IP on Microsoft Windows NT (3.5–3.51) | 70-053 |
| Implementing and Supporting Microsoft Exchange Server 4.0 | 70-075 |
| or | |
| Implementing and Supporting Microsoft Exchange Server 5.0 | 70-076 |
| Microsoft SQL Server 4.2 Database Administration for Windows NT | 70-021 |
| Microsoft SQL Server 4.2 Database Implementation | 70-022 |
| System Administration for Microsoft SQL Server 6.5 | 70-026 |
| Implementing a Database Design on Microsoft SQL Server 6.5 | 70-027 |
| Implementing and Supporting Microsoft SMS 1.2 | 70-018 |

1

| | |
|---|---|
| Implementing and Supporting Microsoft Internet Information Server 3.0 and Microsoft Index Server 1.1 | 70-077 |
| Implementing and Supporting Microsoft SNA Server 3.0 | 70-013 |
| or | |
| Implementing and Supporting Microsoft SNA Server 4.0 | 70-085 |
| Implementing and Supporting Microsoft Proxy Server 1.0 | 70-078 |
| Implementing and Supporting Microsoft Proxy Server 2.0 | 70-088 |
| Microsoft Mail for PC Networks 3.2 Enterprise | 70-037 |
| Implementing and Supporting the Microsoft Internet Explorer Administration Kit for Microsoft Internet Explorer 4.0 (to be released in beta December 1997) | 70-079 |

You might want to consider taking a beta exam as they become available. They consist of 150 to 200 questions that you have three hours to complete. This enables you to see all of the proposed questions. It is also only $50 instead of $100. The drawback is that it will take 6 to 8 weeks before you get your results.

Although there is no imposed time frame within which you must meet all of the MCSE requirements, as the products are updated there always is a chance that an exam might be retired and no longer count toward new or continued certification. The Microsoft Web site contains the latest certification news at http://www.microsoft.com/Train_Cert/mcp/.

## 1.1.2. Registering for the Exams

Microsoft MCSE testing currently is provided through Sylvan/Microsoft. You can reach Sylvan in the United States at (800) 755-EXAM. At the time of this writing, the cost per exam was $100 U.S. dollars. It often is possible to schedule your exam on the day of the call; however, it is better for you to schedule a week in advance to ensure that you get the time slot you want.

In order to locate a Sylvan testing center in the U.S. or internationally, go to http://www.microsoft.com/Train_Cert/mcp/certstep/sylvan.htm.

Testing is offered at a majority of the Microsoft Authorized Training Centers (ATEC) and also at most of the Novell Authorized Education Centers (NAEC). The testing centers all have minimum equipment requirements that a site must meet to host the exams. Unfortunately, some of the sites meet the requirements better than others. One site in your area might use 486-based systems, whereas another might offer Pentiums. Because the exam is heavily graphical and also timed, you might want to ensure that the site you will use offers equipment beyond the minimum.

Make sure you give the proper test number(s) when you call. Check the Microsoft Web site if you are unsure about a test number.

# 1.2. How to Pass MCSE Exams

There often is debate over which are more difficult, the Microsoft or the Novell exams. The truth is that the hardest exam you will ever take is the one for which you are not prepared. If you properly prepare for the MCSE examination, you can pass it. To prepare for the MCSE exams, you must follow a few basic rules and understand a few standard testing principles.

## 1.2.1. Identifying Exam Topics

Microsoft provides a list of the examination topics for each of the MCSE and MCSD exams on its Web site at http://www.microsoft.com/Train_Cert. The first step in preparing for an examination is to print out a copy of the appropriate guide. Use this to focus your studying; these topics are what you will be tested on. You might also want to think of possible questions that address each of these topics as a way for a last-minute review.

### Not Just Bells and Whistles

The exams are designed to ensure that the Microsoft Certified Systems Engineers (MCSE) who pass the exams understand how to implement the products under the most common circumstances. Focus your study on the major functions of the product for which you are testing. For example, on the NT examinations it will be infinitely more important for you to understand how to establish printer priorities than to know where in the registry to configure script mapping for Perl.

1

### Remember Who Wrote the Questions

Microsoft exams are written by people employed to do so by Microsoft. It is in Microsoft's best interest that the exams highlight the strong points of its products. You will never find a question on a Microsoft exam that asks "When would it be better to implement a product from Netscape or Novell…."

Microsoft contracts people who implement the products to write the exams. Groups of MCSEs and Microsoft employees sample the exam questions from several authors to determine the validity of the questions. If a significant number of the testers in the sample group feel a question is without merit, is ambiguous, or is technically inaccurate, it will be rewritten or discarded. A final beta exam is compiled from the remaining questions. Microsoft offers the beta exam to groups of MCSEs at a discount rate. Based on the performance of the beta group, questions are deemed valid or discarded and a passing score is established.

For more information on how exams are written, or even how to participate as a contract writer, visit `http://www.microsoft.com/Train_Cert/mcp/examinfo/iwrite.htm`.

### Your Topics Are Their Topics

If you were writing the exams, what questions would you ask? The concept is simple enough. If the exams were about cars you wouldn't ask questions only about the engine. The engine might be the primary focus, but you would also ask about the transmission, wheels, steering, and perhaps basic accessories, such as air conditioning. Apply the same logic as you prepare for the Microsoft examinations.

The exam topics are chosen based upon the importance of the requirement that a system engineer recall the information necessary to make proper decisions during the planning, installation, maintenance, and troubleshooting of NT Server. Because you will not be allowed to bring reference material into the exam room, you will not be expected to recall overly obscure information. As you review for the exam, think of when and why you would ever need to know the information in the "real" world. This will help you to apply your knowledge when you walk through your answers.

## 1.2.2. Dissecting Exam Questions

Dissecting the exam questions enables you to separate the scenarios into those areas you know are true, those you know are false, and those that are suspect. Also, you will be able to discern what a particular question actually is asking.

## Questions Can Have Many Levels

Exam questions are written to test several levels of knowledge. On the most basic level, you might be asked a question that requires only that you recall a simple command to answer. A more complex kind of question, popular with Microsoft but seemingly less so with test takers, is the comprehensive scenario question. In this type of question you are presented with a problem scenario, often one that incorporates exhibits. A proposed solution is offered along with a listing of required and desired effects. You will be required to determine which combination of required and desired results, if any, the solution achieves.

## Write Your Own Exam Questions

This is perhaps the most important segment of this chapter. As you study the technical summaries in this book, you should try to formulate questions of your own. If you create your own questions, you will force yourself to fully comprehend the material. When you get to the review questions, hopefully some of the questions will match closely with the ones you have written.

First, read the technical summary in full. As you are reading the summary note the key words. Try to establish a mental image of how the information in the summary could apply to a physical network.

Second, before you reread the material, create a list of what you consider to be the most important points to recall. Doing this before you reread the material will help you establish your list of primary topics.

Third, reread the material. As you do, look for the detail items within your primary topic list. The details will become your secondary topic list. The points that you select might seem relatively minor until you put them into the context of your question.

Fourth, create your scenarios. It often is helpful to draw a diagram of the network on which you are basing your scenarios.

Fifth, write your questions based on the scenarios. When you write scenario-based questions, you will be able to look at the topics from several different angles. You will find that as you write the scenario-based questions, the answers can change based on minor adjustments in the exhibits. For example, you may write a question that tests someone's knowledge in protocol selection on a LAN. You then could rewrite the same question with the addition of a router between the client and server. Choosing the proper answer then would depend on a greater depth of understanding.

Finally, reread your questions. Look for areas in your questions that might be ambiguous. Is the question technically accurate? Does it test for knowledge in the proper area? Why is it important?

1

There are only so many topics for which questions can be asked on an examination. Your goal in reviewing the study material through writing your own questions is not to create the questions as they will appear on the exam verbatim. Your goal is to ensure that you have considered each of the potential primary and secondary topics from all possible angles.

## The Question Within the Question

There are no trick questions. Microsoft invests a significant amount of time in ensuring that questions are not ambiguous. This does not mean that they are obvious. It might not be apparent from a question what skill it is testing. Often, the main objective of a question is to test your knowledge of how different areas of NT work together.

Don't be concerned about finding the right answer; worry about selecting the wrong one. You can answer each question correctly by eliminating the answers that are wrong. Don't select your answer until you've eliminated all the other possible choices. Then, make sure that the answer you select is accurate within the context of the question.

## Formulating a Hypothesis

Never leave an answer purely to chance. If you feel that you must guess on a question, guess wisely. In other words, formulate a hypothesis, an educated guess with a basis in fact. Carefully read the question that you are trying to answer, select the answer that looks most reasonable, mark the question by checking the box in the upper-left corner, and then move on. As you go through the exam, you will find that many questions are similar in content. Keep the question of which you were unsure in the back of your mind, and when you find a question or scenario that is similar, try to confirm your previous selection by extracting the answer from this new question.

You often can deduce the answer to a question from another question by means of comparison. For example, if a question were to ask, "NT Server 4.0 can provide file-level security when using which of the following file systems: FAT, HPFS, or NTFS?" Another question might ask, "What occurs to the file permissions when a file is copied from an NTFS partition to a FAT partition?" From the second question you learn that NTFS supports file permissions. Because the first question is looking for only one answer, it is obvious that NTFS is the correct response. The second question also now becomes easier, because NT supports file-level security only on NTFS partitions; moving the file to a FAT partition results in the permissions being lost.

## 1.2.3. The Day of the Exam

The day of your exam inevitably will bring with it a few anxieties. The best response is to relax and make sure that you have everything you need before going to the testing center.

## At the Testing Center

Arrive at the testing center well in advance of your exam's scheduled start time. Sign in with the proctor as soon as you arrive to ensure that there are no last-minute distractions before you go into the test room.

It might seem unsociable, but try to avoid talking with other testing candidates who also are waiting. Use the time remaining before your exam to review the fast facts and compose yourself for the exam.

## What to Bring to the Testing Center

In addition to this guide, which you may bring to the testing site but not into the examination room, you will need to bring the following:

- One picture ID (such as a driver's license or passport)
- One other form of ID with your name and signature (such as a credit card or ATM card)

## Last-Minute Reviews

No matter how well you are prepared, you might feel that you have forgotten everything the moment you get to the testing center. Don't worry, you have plenty of time to get your mind back on track before the exams begin. Use the fast facts for that last-minute review in the parking lot before going in to take your test. Reviewing the fast facts will bring what you learned in each chapter of this book to the forefront.

Relax: by this time you've seen the questions in this book enough to know the answers as soon as you begin reading the questions. When you take the actual exam, the questions should be an extension of your review.

Try to close your book at least five minutes before the exam begins. Meditate on the things you have reviewed and simply relax.

## Shoot for the Moon

Passing the exam is certainly a goal you can obtain. Don't go in with just the hope to pass; shoot for the moon. You could be the next one to get a perfect score.

# 1.3. How to Pass This Test

Exams 70-067 and 70-068 are two of the core exams required to become an MCSE. The success you have on these exams will set the stage for your performance on the electives. Unlike elective exams, which are narrowly focused on a specific topic or feature set, these exams take more of a shotgun approach to testing your knowledge.

1

### 1.3.1. Exam 70-067, Implementing and Supporting NT Server 4.0

This exam tests your knowledge of NT Server 4.0 in a single-domain environment. You should understand how to manage the individual server and its supporting services. Also be very familiar with managing users and groups as well as providing access to resources. You can download details of the exam and sample exams from Microsoft at `http://www.microsoft.com/Train_Cert/mcp/exam/stat/SP70-067.htm`.

### 1.3.2. Exam 70-068, Implementing and Supporting NT Server 4.0 in the Enterprise

This exam is geared toward managing the heterogeneous environment including elements such as integrating UNIX and NetWare servers. The key elements in this exam are multiple domains and WAN links. Be very familiar with the issues pertaining to domains and trusts. You can find a complete list of the exam topics at `http://www.microsoft.com/Train_Cert/mcp/exam/stat/SP70-068.htm`.

# Day 2

# Windows NT Architecture and Domain Design

*by David Schaer, Walter Glenn, and Theresa Hadden*

This chapter introduces two concepts very important to Windows NT. *Windows NT architecture* describes the way in which Windows NT itself runs on a particular machine and the way in which applications interface with the operating system. *Domain design* concentrates on the way in which computers running Windows NT interact with one another, as well as how entire Windows NT-based networks interact with one another.

## 2.1. Overview

In order to understand Windows NT thoroughly, you must understand the underlying system architecture. This chapter will present you with a detailed explanation of the Windows product line, including Windows NT Server, Windows NT Workstation, and Windows 95. There are distinct differences in these operating systems, and understanding those differences is essential to understanding how they operate together on a network. You will also learn how applications run on each of these operating systems and how the internal processes of the operating systems themselves function.

After you have developed an understanding of how the operating system works on a single machine, you will be introduced to the concepts behind networking. On a Microsoft-based network, computers are organized into logical groupings called domains. This chapter details the workings and interoperability of domains and provides insight into domain design.

## 2.1.1. Objectives

The basic Windows NT Server exam tests the concepts of Windows NT architecture, and the enterprise-level exam covers the concepts only tangentially. The Microsoft Preparation Guide for the Windows NT Server exam lists the following objectives concerning Windows NT architecture:

- Managing the operations of 32-bit and 16-bit applications in a Windows environment
- Configuring application priority

The concepts of domain design are tested in the Windows NT enterprise-level exam and are not covered in the scope of the Windows NT Server exam. The Microsoft Preparation Guide for the enterprise-level exam lists the following objectives about domain design:

- Plan the implementation of a directory services architecture, including selecting the appropriate domain model, supporting a single logon account, and letting users access resources in different domains.
- Manage user and group accounts, including managing Windows NT user accounts, managing Windows NT user rights, managing Windows NT groups, and administering account policies.

This list might seem short, but keep in mind that trust relationships also affect how you think about almost every other thing you learn about implementing a Windows NT-based network.

## 2.1.2. Fast Facts

The following list of facts is a concise picture of the information presented in this chapter. It acts as both an overview for the chapter and as a study aid to help you do any last-minute cramming.

- Windows 95 has excellent backward compatibility because it supports both 32-bit protected mode and older real-mode DOS drivers. It does not provide the same level of operating system protection as NT.
- Both Windows NT and Windows 95 run NetBEUI, TCP/IP, and IPX/SPX protocols.
- The most important service provided by NT Directory Services is the capability to log on to the network from any location with a single user name and password.

- Pass-through authentication occurs when the domain in which you are logging on cannot verify your user account and must pass the verification process on to a trusted domain.

- Trust relationships require a permanent link between two NT servers that are Primary Domain Controllers (PDCs). Trust relationships cannot exist over a RAS dial-up link.

- Trust relationships also require a common protocol between the two PDCs.

- When logging on to a network with trust relationships, user location is irrelevant, but user account location is important.

- Remember the acronym AGLP. Accounts are placed into Global groups, which are placed into Local groups, which are assigned Permissions.

- Global groups are defined in the trusted domain.

- Local groups are defined in the trusting domain.

- Trusts are established with User Manager for Domains. A trust relationship must be defined on both the trusting and trusted PDCs.

- Trusts are non-transitive. Just because Domain A trusts Domain B and Domain B trusts Domain C does not mean that Domain A trusts Domain C.

- The only effective way to repair a trust is to break it on both ends and re-establish the trust.

- The NetLogon service validates logon requests, synchronizes the PDC with the BDCs, and provides pass-through authentication.

- The NetLogon service is dependent on the Workstation and Server services.

- The single domain model contains only one PDC and is the easiest to administer.

- The master domain model consists of a master domain that contains all the user accounts and multiple resource domains that contain all computer accounts and resources. The resource domains trust the master domain.

- The multiple master domain model contains more than one master domain containing user accounts and multiple resource domains, each of which trusts all master domains.

- In the complete trust model, each domain trusts every other domain.

- Each single domain can contain up to approximately 20,000 users. This includes user accounts, groups, and computer accounts.

- Each master domain can contain up to approximately 40,000 users. This includes user and group accounts only.

**2**

■ The NT Directory Services database size is limited to 40MB. A user account takes up 1KB. Computer accounts take up 0.5KB. Global group accounts take 512 bytes plus 12 bytes per user. Local group accounts take 512 bytes plus 36 bytes per user.

■ There should be one backup domain controller for every 2,000 user accounts.

■ The following are minimum installation requirements to install various operating systems on Intel-based systems:

|            | NT Server | NT Workstation | Windows 95 |
|------------|-----------|----------------|------------|
| **Processor**  | 486DX/33  | 486DX/33       | 386DX/20   |
| **Memory**     | 16MB      | 12MB           | 4MB        |
| **Disk Space** | 130MB     | 120MB          | 40MB       |

■ The basic differences in Microsoft's major operating systems are summarized in Table 2.1.

**Table 2.1. Basic differences between major operating systems.**

|                                    | NT Server                    | NT Workstation               | Windows 95          |
|------------------------------------|------------------------------|------------------------------|---------------------|
| Supported platforms                | Both Intel and RISC based    | Both Intel and RISC based    | Intel-based only    |
| Maximum number of processors supported | Four. Up to 32 with OEM versions | Two. Up to 32 with OEM versions | One.            |
| Disk file systems                  | NTFS, FAT                    | NTFS, FAT                    | FAT, FAT32          |
| Fault Tolerance                    | RAID1, RAID5                 | No                           | No                  |

■ Table 2.2 compares the functions of the various roles that an NT server can play on a network.

**Table 2.2. Comparison of NT Server roles in the domain.**

|                   | PDC | BDC | Member | Standalone |
|-------------------|-----|-----|--------|------------|
| Domain Validation | Yes | Yes | No     | No         |
| Domain Member     | Yes | Yes | Yes    | No         |

# 2.2. Major NT Design Components

Windows NT has the capability to act as both a client and a server. Because a system running Windows NT can share files, it can function as a file server; because it can share print devices, it can also be a print server. Additionally, high-level applications such as Microsoft SQL Server and Microsoft Exchange Server run on the NT platform; this means NT can also be an application server.

## 2.2.1. The Function of the HAL

Windows NT is considered to be hardware independent. A portion of the network operating system known as the Hardware Abstraction Layer (HAL) is responsible for managing hardware. The other pieces of the network operating system communicate with HAL, which then communicates with the hardware on their behalf. This provides two very important features. It makes Windows NT independent from the actual hardware on which it runs, meaning that NT can be rapidly deployed on newer and faster processors as they are developed. Already, versions of NT are available for the Intel (CISC) and the DEC Alpha, PowerPC, and MIPS (RISC) processors.

Using HAL makes Windows NT very stable. Because no other part of Windows NT, or any application running on it, can access the hardware directly, crashes are extremely rare. When they do occur, they affect only the application or process that caused the error, and no other part of the operating system.

Early operating systems were written in assembly code, and their growth was limited to the hardware platforms for which they were designed. Microsoft overcame this by writing a majority of the NT source code in C and C++. Because these are high-level languages, the code developed can be quickly recompiled to run on other platforms. However, some of the code must be written to talk directly to the processor in the language it understands, without interpretation. This small percentage of the code is contained within a module called the Hardware Abstraction Layer (HAL).

## 2.2.2. Multiple Processor Support

Microsoft designed NT to take advantage of multiprocessor systems. NT Workstation 4.0 can take advantage of two processors, and NT Server 4.0 can take advantage of four processors. OEM versions of NT can reach up to 32 processors. You can easily track processor performance by using the Performance Monitor tool included with NT. In Figure 2.1 Performance Monitor is being used to track the overall percentage of processor utilization.

**Figure 2.1.**

*You can track processor utilization by using Performance Monitor.*

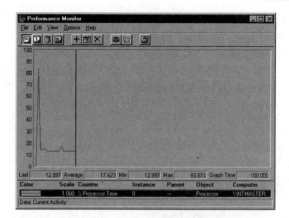

### 2.2.3. Spreading the System Code

There are two major types of multiprocessing systems: *asymmetric multiprocessing* (ASMP) and *symmetric multiprocessing* (SMP). In asymmetric processing, a processor is dedicated to the system code. In symmetric multiprocessing, the operating system can "spread" the system code across all the available processors. Microsoft has implemented the more efficient symmetric multiprocessing.

When choosing between a single, high-power, processor and a multiprocessor system it is important to consider the type of services to be provided by the server. In general, a system used primarily as a file server or print server will benefit little from multiple processors. Multiple processors often can enhance performance of application servers, such as Microsoft Exchange and Microsoft SQL Server, because they are multithreaded applications.

### 2.2.4. Multithreaded Applications

A *multithreaded application* has multiple executable entities called *threads*, each of which can be prioritized. For example, a word processor could have one thread to monitor the input from the user at the keyboard and another that performs spell checking. By prioritizing the thread that monitors user input higher than the thread that performs the spell checking the user never feels a response delay. The spell checker thread would receive processor time when the processor is not handling a thread of higher priority.

Because NT is both multitasking and multithreaded, several processes can pass multiple threads to the processor queue at the same time. The microkernel passes the threads to the processors based on their priority, not on their order of arrival.

The priority assigned to a process determines the priority range a thread can utilize. A normal thread within a normal priority class process is assigned a base priority of 8 on a scale of 1 to 31. By raising the priority class to high, the base priority raises to 13. Figure 2.2 shows `Winword.exe` as a multithreaded application (four threads) with a normal priority base.

**Figure 2.2.**
`Winword.exe` *is running in normal priority with four threads.*

### 2.2.5. See How They Run

In order to provide support for legacy, or older, applications, Windows NT was designed to run several types of applications. NT provides support for DOS, 16-bit Windows, 32-bit Windows, 16-bit OS/2 character-based apps, and POSIX applications. The 32-bit Windows applications are considered native applications because they can talk directly to the client/server subsystem (Win32 subsystem).

Non-native application support is provided by a set of operating system emulators or environment subsystems. The environment subsystem makes the application believe it is running in its native environment. By default, the only environment subsystem initially launched by NT is the Win32 subsystem.

When you launch an application that requires a different subsystem, the appropriate subsystem is launched. The other environment subsystems are not initiated on the startup of NT to prevent needless memory use. After a subsystem is initialized it will remain active until NT is restarted. The default subsystem entry in the registry (see Figure 2.3) controls which subsystems will be launched by default.

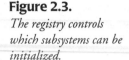

**Figure 2.3.**

*The registry controls which subsystems can be initialized.*

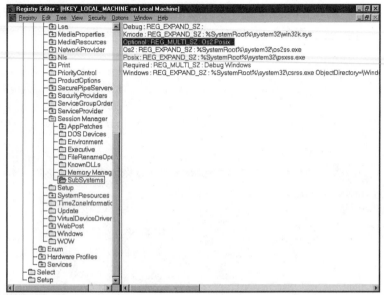

All environment subsystems operate in user mode of NT. Security subsystems operate in kernel mode.

## 2.2.6. Protecting NT from Itself

When you go through the drive through at a bank you do not have direct access to your money straight from the vault. You simply fill out a withdrawal slip and send it up the tube to the cashier with your credentials. Upon receiving your request the cashier then can request the services of others to help complete the transaction. Whether the money is retrieved from the cash drawer or the vault does not concern you.

Transactions occur in a similar way within NT. On one side of the environment subsystem is user mode and on the other side is kernel mode. (Sometimes, kernel mode is referred to as privileged processor mode.) The applications launched by the user all reside in user mode along with the environment subsystems. The applications make their requests to the subsystems, which do not have direct access to the hardware.

The requests made by the applications are passed by the subsystem to a set of executive services running in kernel mode. The credentials of the application requesting a service to be performed are validated, and if sufficient privileges are present the service is performed on behalf of the application.

The user mode applications are unaware of the functions performed by the executive services. They communicate only with their appropriate subsystems, never with the services or hardware directly.

By separating applications from the executive services the operating system has greater stability. An application running in user mode will not directly bring down the operating system.

Because some DOS applications and utilities such FDISK.EXE try to directly access the hardware, they will not perform properly within NT. Figure 2.4 shows the error message received when you try to run FDISK from within NT.

**2**

**Figure 2.4.**
*Windows NT does not allow applications, such as* FDISK.EXE, *to directly access hardware.*

One of the goals of the NT developers was to enable applications designed for a wide variety of operating systems to run unchanged on top of NT. As shown in Figure 2.5, the NT Task Manager shows EDIT.EXE, HYPERSNAP.EXE, and WINWORD.EXE running simultaneously.

**Figure 2.5.**
*The Task Manager can be used to view application status.*

Neither DOS nor 16-bit Windows applications require a new subsystem to be launched; instead, the NT Virtual DOS Machine (NTVDM) provides support for DOS applications. The NTVDM captures the interrupt calls made by the DOS application. The calls are interpreted and passed to the Win32 subsystem.

16-bit window applications run by default in a single process space within an NTVDM. NT runs Windows on Windows (WOWEXEC) on top of the NTVDM to convert Win16 API calls to Win32 API calls before passing them to the Win32 subsystem.

## 2.3. Windows 95 Versus Windows NT

Both Microsoft Windows 95 and Microsoft NT are among the most popular operating systems today. Both products were designed with a specific market in mind. The NT platform was intended to be the platform for high-level business applications, whereas Windows 95 was geared more toward the home market. Although the home market might have been the primary audience for Windows 95 it is certainly prolific in the business community as well. It is important to be aware of the similarities and differences between the two products.

When presented with scenarios in which you must decide which operating system is the better choice, make sure you begin your evaluation at the lowest level and work up. At the lowest level you will want to consider the hardware and whether it meets the minimum requirements. Next, confirm that the file system trying to be accessed is compatible with the operating system. Is high-level security required? Is full compatibility with real-mode drivers important? What applications will be run? Will the machine function primarily as a client or as a server?

## 2.4. NT Server 4.0 Versus NT Workstation 4.0

Remember that the term *server* refers to services that a system provides. Both NT Workstation and NT Server can provide file and print sharing and can be used as application servers and network clients. On the surface the two products appear almost identical; however, there are significant differences:

- Domain validation can be performed only by NT servers, and then only when they are installed as domain controllers. An NT workstation can be a member of either a domain or a workgroup. This is also true of an NT server installed as a stand-alone server.

■ Although NT Server can support unlimited client connections, NT Workstation has a fixed limit of 10 simultaneous client connections.

■ Several of the high-end services, including the DHCP server, WINS Server, and DNS Server, run only on the NT Server product. NT Workstation can take advantage of the services from a client's perspective but cannot be the one providing these services. When running the directory replicator service, NT Server can be configured as both an import and export server; NT Workstation can act only as an import server. The function and configuration of each of these services is detailed in Chapter 11, "Configuring and Optimizing NT 4.0 Services."

■ Only NT Server can provide disk fault tolerance, which is provided through the use of RAID technology. RAID uses redundant arrays of inexpensive disks. There are five common levels of RAID implementations. NT Server supports RAID0, RAID1, and RAID5; NT Workstation supports only RAID0. Think of the 0 in RAID0 as zero redundancy. RAID0 is striping without parity. RAID1 is disk mirroring and disk duplexing. RAID5 refers to striping with parity. Chapter 5, "Managing Local File Systems," details how to implement RAID on NT.

# 2.5. NT Directory Services

NT Directory Services provide a secure, distributed directory database to manage user accounts, resources, and network access on an NT network. The essence of the NT Directory Services is that every user on a network has one user account. This allows for a single logon from anywhere on the network and for centralized administration of users and resources.

## 2.5.1. Single Logon

With the single logon feature, a user must remember only one password to be able to log on to the network from either the home domain or a trusting domain and still access those resources to which she has been assigned permissions. For example, a worker who is normally based in Chicago logs on to the network while visiting the Fargo office. Assuming that Chicago and Fargo are separate domains in which Fargo trusts Chicago, the domain controller will forward the logon request to the Chicago domain, which then will verify the user. This process is known as pass-through authentication.

## Pass-Through Authentication

Pass-through authentication provides two very important features:

- The capability to log on from a domain in which you have no user account (providing that the domain trusts the domain where your user account resides)
- The capability to access resources in a domain other than the one in which your user account resides (also providing that the resource domain trusts the domain where your user account resides)

In either case, the logon request is passed to the primary domain controller (PDC) of the domain in which the resource you are accessing resides, which in turn passes the request to the PDC in the domain in which your user account is defined (see Figure 2.6).

**Figure 2.6.**

*Pass-through authentication.*

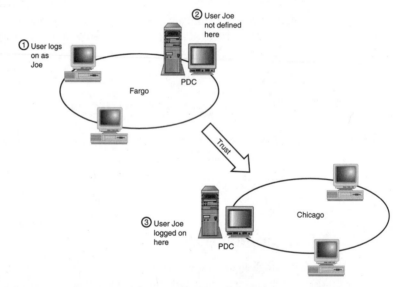

Whenever a user logs on, the logon dialog box asks to which domain she would like to log on. The user must log on to the domain on which her user account resides in order to be able to access resources. On the exam, pay close attention. The domain to which a user logs on will make a difference in the answer you choose.

### The NetLogon Service

The NetLogon service governs authentication interactions within the domain as well as between trusting domains. It is primarily responsible for

- Validating logon requests
- Synchronizing the NT directory database between the PDC and BDCs of a domain
- Pass-through authentication between trusting domains

The NetLogon service must be running on any NT computer acting as a domain controller, or that computer cannot provide the functions just listed. Because the NetLogon service depends on the Workstation and Server services, they also must be running.

You can pause the NetLogon service using the Services Control Panel. When it is paused, no logon requests will be validated, but synchronization can still occur.

## 2.5.2. Centralized Administration

NT Directory Services also provides for centralized administration. As the administrator of a network, you may log on from any computer in your domain and administer the resources of that domain. You may also log on from a trusting domain to administer your home domain. Centralized administration enables you to administer an entire network no matter where the members of that domain are physically located.

Before you can administer a domain, your account must be a member of the Domain Admin group. When a Windows NT computer joins a domain, the global group Domain Admin is automatically added to the local Administrator group on that computer.

# 2.6. Domain Design and Implementation

The most basic Windows NT-based network is a single domain with a primary domain controller and one or more backup domain controllers. In some situations, however, you might be forced to consider using more than one domain on your network. Understanding how domains interact with each other is the basis of enterprise-level networking.

A *domain* is a logical grouping of users, computers, and resources. It is tempting to think of a domain in physical terms, but this is misleading. A domain is not necessarily described by the geography of its users and resources or the architecture on which the network is built. Depending on the situation, however, you might choose to define domains by either the geography or architecture of your network.

*Trusts* are used to define the relationships between domains. If one domain trusts another domain, it enables the user accounts in the domain it trusts to access its local resources (see Figure 2.7).

**Figure 2.7.**

*Domain A trusts Domain B.*

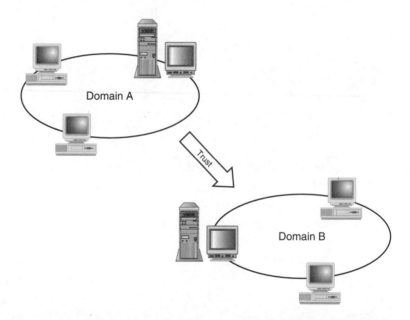

The concept of trusts is a tough one for many people. A good way to think about trusts is that *resources trust people.* If Domain A trusts Domain B, then Domain A's resources trust Domain B's users. User accounts in Domain B can be assigned permissions to the resources in Domain A.

You will find that a solid understanding of trust relationships, and how they affect other aspects of Windows NT networking, is essential to passing the Windows NT Enterprise exam. Almost every question presents trusts in some way.

### 2.6.1. Who's on the Team?

Every team has a captain. Within a domain the primary domain controller (PDC) is the captain. The PDC holds the original copy of the SAM database, which is like a team roster. The SAM database includes the names of all the team members, including users, local groups, global groups, NT workstations, NT Member Servers (stand-alone servers), and NT backup domain controllers (BDC). When deploying NT Server it is important to understand the purpose of each of the server types.

### 2.6.2. The Role of the PDC

Grouping systems into a domain makes controlling logon security easier. This is vastly different from a workgroup that does not have centralized security.

The primary domain controller (PDC) is like the head bouncer at a club. As users log on to the domain, it is the responsibility of the domain controllers to validate the users' credentials by comparing the user names and passwords provided against the SAM database. Each domain has only one PDC; it is the first computer installed within a domain.

Several hardware factors govern the number of users a PDC can support. Microsoft's official guidelines are shown in Table 2.3.

**Table 2.3. Choosing the size and speed of your PDC.**

| SAM file size | Number of accounts | Minimum CPU required | RAM required |
| --- | --- | --- | --- |
| 10MB | 7,500 | 486DX/66 | 32MB |
| 15MB | 10,000 | Pentium or RISC-based | 48MB |
| 20MB | 15,000 | Pentium or RISC-based | 64MB |
| 30MB | 20,000–30,000 | Pentium or RISC-based | 96MB |
| 40MB | 30,000–40,000 | Pentium or RISC-based | 128MB |

During the installation of the PDC the security ID (SID) for the domain is created. The SID is a unique identifier, similar in concept to your social security number. You can change your name, but your social security number remains the same. This is how it works with a domain: Although you can rename a domain, as shown in Figure 2.8, the SID associated with it does not change.

**Figure 2.8.**

*Renaming the KNOWLEDGE domain to MASTERDOM.*

 **Note** Although renaming a domain is possible, this will require you to enter the new name at each client computer and break and re-established any trusts.

### 2.6.3. The Role of the BDCs

The job of the BDCs is to validate logon requests. The SAM database held by a BDC is simply a copy of the one maintained by the PDC and is kept synchronized with that of the PDC by the NetLogon service.

The general guideline is that you must have one domain controller for every 2,000 accounts. It is also recommended that you always have at least one BDC, regardless of the number of accounts in your domain. For example, a domain with 10,000 accounts would need 5 domain controllers: one PDC and four BDCs.

 **Note** These calculations assume that no extra burdens are placed upon your domain controllers. BDCs are commonly used as application, mail, or print servers. This increases the demand on the machines' resources and increases the number of domain controllers you will need to support your domain.

There is no limit to the number of BDCs you can install within a domain. BDCs are placed strategically throughout the physical network to ensure efficient logon and provide fault tolerance to the NT Directory Services. If the PDC crashes or is brought down for an extended period of time, it is possible to promote a BDC to take over the role of the PDC. If a PDC is not available, it will not be possible to make any changes to the SAM database.

In Figure 2.9, NTBACKUP is being promoted to the role of primary domain controller. NTMASTER, the current PDC, will be automatically demoted to the role of BDC. This is can be done by a member of the Domain Admins group using Server Manager.

**Figure 2.9.**
*NTBACKUP is being promoted to the role of PDC.*

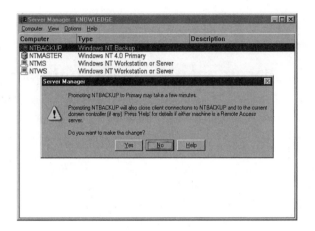

When installing a backup domain controller it is important to ensure that the BDC can communicate with the PDC. This means that the systems must have at least one protocol in common. If the BDC cannot contact the PDC during the BDC's installation, the installation will fail.

At the time of installation, the PDC provides the BDC with the SID unique to that domain. Because the domain SID is assigned to a BDC only during installation, moving a BDC to another domain will require reinstallation.

## 2.6.4. Stand-Alone and Member Servers

A stand-alone server has all of the features of Windows NT Server available to it. Unlike domain controllers, a stand-alone server does not participate in user account validation or directory replication. Stand-alone servers are useful for providing file/print sharing and applications services because the computer they are on does not also have to provide other services. A stand-alone server can be a member of a domain or just a workgroup. A stand-alone server that participates in a domain is also called a *member server.*

Neither a stand-alone nor member server can serve as a logon server. Each server maintains an independent security account manager database. The SAM database held at the servers is identical in structure to that of an NT Workstation but different from that of a domain controller. This is one of the reasons why it is possible to upgrade an

NT Workstation to become a member server but not a domain controller. Upgrading a stand-alone or member server to become a domain controller is not possible; instead, you must reinstall the system.

Stand-alone and member servers are not interrupted by clients requesting to be validated on the domain. These systems are, therefore, better suited than domain controllers to be application servers.

## 2.6.5. Placement of Domain Controllers

Proper placement of the domain controllers is central to controlling network traffic and providing adequate response during periods of high activity. The most common method of designing a domain is to do so geographically. That is, a domain might be created for each building in a complex or each city in which the company has offices. Placing the domain controllers that are meant to do the most logon validation activity closest to the most users on your network is often helpful. Placing certain resource servers on subnets in your network to reduce the traffic load on other subnets is also helpful.

However, structuring a domain geographically is not always advantageous or practical. Often, planning a domain based on function or department makes more sense. For example, your sales department might have its own domain, even if that sales department resides in several different geographic locations. This can be especially helpful if that department has its own management or special resources that it must administer itself.

Domains are abstract; your network is not. It is helpful when planning placement of domain controllers to think of your network in its physical terms. In other words, your network is probably a group of individual, well-connected LANs that are connected to each other over various types of slower WAN links. The domains on your network sit on top of this architecture, but often not neatly. It might be nice in some aspects if each of these well-connected LANs were a domain, but this is not always the most practical approach.

There can be only one PDC in a domain, which means that parts of a domain will be located on the other side of a slower WAN link from the PDC. Consider Figure 2.10.

In this figure, the PDC for the Chicago domain exists in Building One. Another section of the Chicago domain exists in Building Two. Buildings One and Two are connected by a 56kbps WAN link, which is much slower than the networking cable within the two LANs. The PDC and a BDC exist in Building One. Users in Building Two must log on across the WAN link. If many users are logging on, the WAN link becomes a bottleneck, slowing the logon process for the users in Building Two. Consider what would happen if we moved the BDC from Building One to Building Two, as shown in Figure 2.11.

**Figure 2.10.**
*The Chicago domain exists over a WAN link.*

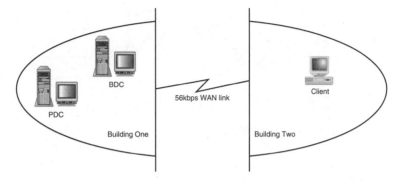

The Chicago Domain

**Figure 2.11.**
*Moving the BDC in the Chicago domain to the other side of the WAN link.*

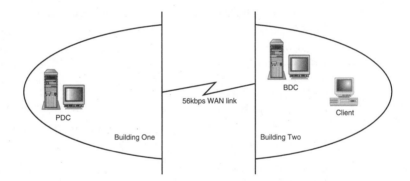

The Chicago Domain

Now, when users in Building Two log on to the domain, the process happens much more quickly because the BDC is now on their own LAN. It seems we have solved the problem of the WAN bottleneck with this move, but we have created another problem. Now, synchronization of the directory database between the PDC and the BDC must occur over the WAN link. Depending on the size of the database, the WAN link might be tied up for some time, making it much more difficult for users to access resources across the WAN link. Again, the WAN link has become a bottleneck. Unfortunately, there is no ideal solution to this problem. It becomes, instead, a matter of weighing the costs of logging on versus the costs of synchronization and making the best decision possible.

Understanding the effects on network traffic of placing BDCs locally or on the other side of a WAN link is important. Basically, having a BDC local means that synchronization traffic doesn't occur over the WAN link, but logon traffic does. Moving the BDC to the other side of the WAN link reverses this. Logon traffic doesn't occur over the WAN link, but synchronization traffic will.

## 2.6.6. Synchronization

When a user logs on to a domain, they do not request a specific controller to perform the logon validation. The first controller to respond to the request performs the logon validation. This could be either the PDC or any of the BDCs. The one that processes the request is often the one physically closest to the user.

All updates to the SAM database occur only at the PDC. This means that if you were sitting at the BDC and creating a new user, the new user would be entered into the SAM database at the PDC. The changes are then replicated to the BDCs via the NetLogon service. Communication between the PDC and BDCs within a domain is performed through the use of remote procedure calls (RPCs).

In order for backup domain controllers to validate user logons, the BDCs must have an up-to-date copy of the directory database, the master copy of which is stored on the primary domain controller. This is accomplished through synchronization. Synchronization is governed by the NetLogon service and occurs in the following manner.

At a predetermined interval called a pulse, the PDC checks its directory services database to see whether a change has occurred and sends a message to the BDCs that need the change. These BDCs then contact the PDC and download the information.

Two types of synchronization can occur: full synchronization, in which the entire directory services database is sent to a BDC, and partial synchronization, in which only changes in the database since the last synchronization are sent. This process can be fine-tuned using registry parameters found in HKEY_LOCAL_MACHINE\SYSTEM\ CurrentControlSet\Services\NetLogon\Parameters. These parameters are summarized in Table 2.4.

**Table 2.4. Registry parameters governing synchronization.**

| Parameter | Description |
| --- | --- |
| ReplicationGovernor | This parameter governs the total percentage of bandwidth that can be used by the synchronization process. The default is 100%. This parameter does not exist by default in the registry, but can be added as a REG_DWORD type. |
| Pulse | This parameter controls how often the PDC checks its directory database for changes. The default value is five minutes, and this can be increased to a maximum of 48 hours. |
| PulseMaximum | This parameter controls how often the PDC will send messages to each BDC, even if that BDC's database is current. The default value is two hours, and this can be increased to a maximum of 48 hours. |
| PulseConcurrency | This parameter controls the maximum number of BDCs the PDC will send synchronization messages to simultaneously. The default value of this parameter is 10. |
| ChangeLogSize | This parameter controls the number of changes to the database that must occur before a full synchronization is triggered. The default value for this parameter is 64KB, or about 2,000 changes. |

Synchronization traffic can quickly grow out of control on large networks, making the capability to control the process important. Controlling the process of synchronization becomes especially vital when it must occur over a slow WAN link, especially if that WAN link must also handle the traffic of user logons and pass-through authentications.

In addition to controlling synchronization using the registry parameters mentioned in Table 2.4, another useful technique is pausing the NetLogon service. While paused, synchronization can still occur but validation of logon requests and pass-through authentication does not.

Experiment with pausing the different services on your NT Server. Pausing different services causes different effects, some of which can be quite useful.

It is possible to request the synchronization between a single BDC and the PDC, as shown in Figure 2.12, by selecting the BDC in Server Manager and selecting the option to synchronize with the primary domain controller. You might choose to synchronize a single BDC if you have recently added several user accounts that will be validated by a specific server because of physical proximity. You might also do this if a WAN link has been down and the BDC on the other end must be brought up to date.

**Figure 2.12.**

*Server Manager synchronizing a single BDC with the PDC.*

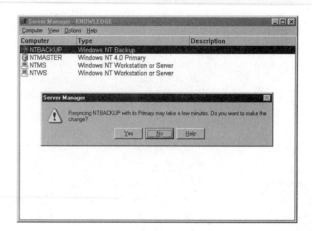

Forcing synchronization between the PDC and BDCs only speeds up the process of what would occur automatically anyway. Force synchronization only when having the SAM databases updated immediately is necessary. Chapter 8, "Managing Network Resources," takes a closer look at domain models and the controlling synchronization.

A request to synchronize the entire domain can also be performed through Server Manager as shown in Figure 2.13. The PDC must be the selected computer in order to synchronize the entire domain. Because synchronizing the entire domain can place high stress on the network it is better to synchronize only a specific BDC if it will be sufficient.

**Figure 2.13.**

*Server Manager synchronizing the KNOWLEDGE domain.*

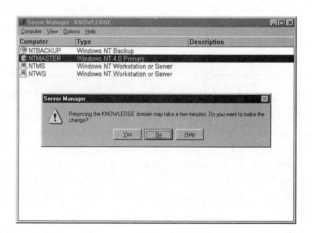

## 2.7. Trust Relationships

Without a trust relationship, two domains, even if connected by physical medium, can have no regular communications. Trust relationships provide a secure channel for users and resources from different domains to interact.

A domain that trusts another domain is called a *trusting* domain; the domain being trusted is the *trusted* domain. The trusting domain is entrusting its resources to the users from the trusted domain. Diagrammatically, trusts are always defined by an arrow pointing from the trusting domain to the trusted domain (see Figure 2.14).

**2**

**Figure 2.14.**
*Fargo trusts Chicago.*

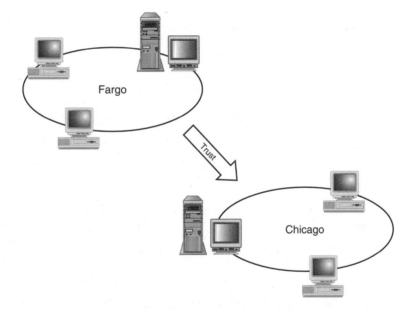

> Trusts by themselves do not provide any permissions. The administrator of the trusting domain still controls access to resources. The administrator of a trusting domain can grant access to any user or group account in its own domain or to any global user or global group account in any domain that it trusts.

### 2.7.1. Implementing a Trust Relationship

Implementing and managing a trust relationship is a fairly simple task. The following are the requirements for a trust relationship:

- The domains in the relationship must share a permanent connection.
- The domains must also share a common networking protocol.
- Only the PDCs of the domains can establish the trust.
- Only members of the Administrators group can establish a trust.

### Setting Trusts

The procedure for setting trusts is quite straightforward, but must be set up on both the PDC of the trusting domain and the PDC of the trusted domain. To establish a trust, use User Manager for Domains. Choose Trust Relationships from the Policies menu to bring up the Trust Relationships dialog box shown in Figure 2.15.

**Figure 2.15.**

*Setting up trust relationships.*

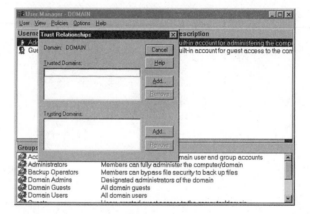

This dialog box enables you to choose what domains the PDC you are administering trusts, as well as which domains are permitted to trust it. To give permission to a domain to trust your domain, select the Add button next to the Trusting Domains window. Simply type the name of the domain to which you want to give the permission, as shown in Figure 2.16.

Note that you can also assign a password to this permission. This is not the same as the administrator's logon password. It is simply a password protecting against an unauthorized link.

**Figure 2.16.**

*Allowing other domains to trust your domain.*

The procedure for choosing which domains your domain trusts is quite similar. From the Trust Relationships dialog box shown in Figure 2.15, select Add next to the Trusted Domains window to bring up the dialog box shown in Figure 2.17.

**Figure 2.17.**

*Trusting other domains.*

Simply enter the domain that you want to trust and a password, if there is one. If your domain is permitted to trust the domain you have entered, the relationship will be successfully established.

> Which end of a trust relationship you set up first is not critical. It is usually better, however, to configure the trusted domain first. This way, the new trust relationship takes effect immediately. If the trusting domain is configured first, it can take up to 15 minutes before the trust relationship takes effect.

After you have established the trust relationship, global users and global groups from the trusted domain can be granted resource privileges or local group membership in the trusting domain.

Often, you will see a type of trust named a two-way trust, in which two domains trust one another. Two-way trusts are simply two separately established one-way trusts, and you would follow the procedure above to establish each trust.

Another important point to be aware of when planning trust relationships is that trusts are non-transitive. That is, the trusts do not flow through the network. Consider Figure 2.18. Domain A trusts Domain B. Domain B trusts Domain C. However, Domain A does not trust Domain C unless an additional trust relationship is established between Domains A and C.

**Figure 2.18.**

*Trusts are non-transitive.*

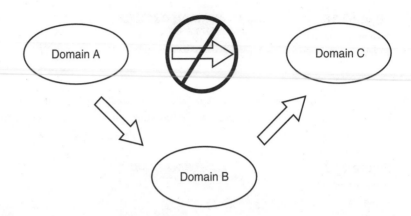

Be careful about this when you are taking the exam. Often a situation will be presented that looks great in other ways (for example, user account and groups are handled appropriately, permissions are assigned, and trusts look right), but a user should not be able to access a resource because the domain in which her user account is located is not directly trusted by the resource domain.

## Group Strategies

The strategy for using users and groups in a multiple domain environment is essentially the same as in a single domain environment. User accounts should be placed into appropriate global groups in the trusted domain. These global groups should then be placed into local groups in the trusting domain. You should then assign these local groups the permissions to use the appropriate resources. Remember, only global should cross trust relationships. They serve as the vehicle that carries user accounts across the trust.

Technically, it is possible to grant a user account from a trusted domain membership in a local group of a trusting domain. However, putting the users in global groups then granting the global groups the appropriate memberships in local groups is a better long-term methodology.

Remember that local groups cannot cross trusts. There are several questions on the exam where this knowledge is essential.

This strategy is built into the function of Windows NT. For example, when a user account is created on a PDC, that account is automatically made a member of the Domain Users global group. This Domain Users global group is, by default, a member of the local group Users. This means that any new user account created is automatically made a member of the local Users group. Many of the built-in global and local groups in Windows NT exhibit this functionality.

**2**

The basic group strategy can be summed up by the acronym AGLP: put user Accounts into Global groups, which should go into Local groups, and assign these Permissions. Many of the questions on the exams will test your knowledge of this procedure in different ways.

Interestingly, the relationships between the computers themselves within a domain are trust relationships. Windows NT computers participating in the domain trust the domain controllers. Because all users and global groups are managed on the PDC, these can cross the trust relationships to be placed into the local groups on the client computers.

## Managing Trusts

Administration of a trust account is really limited to the establishment of the trust. There are, however, situations in which a trust relationship can fail. The primary domain controllers maintain the trust. If one of the PDCs is unavailable, the trust will be broken. A PDC might become unavailable when there is a break in the physical network infrastructure, when the PDC is brought down for maintenance, or when the domain is renamed. The only effective way to repair a broken trust is to complete the break on both ends and re-establish it.

The NT 4.0 Resource Kit includes a utility called Domain Monitor, which can confirm the status of trust relationships.

### 2.7.2. Trusts and Security

The trust relationships themselves do not imply any specific rights. When a trust relationship is established between domains, the administrator of the trusting domain can grant access to its resources to global users and global group accounts from the trusted domain. Unless rights are granted there will be no specific rights.

When a user who is logged on with an account from the trusted domain attempts to access a resource in the trusting domain, the trusting domain passes the supplied logon credentials to the PDC in the trusted domain for verification. Even after the account is validated, the actual rights are dependent on those that have been assigned by the administrator of the trusting domain.

If part of a question on the exam states that a user cannot access a resource across a trust, go back to the basics. Make sure that the trust is established in the right direction. The trusting domain should contain the resource, and the trusted domain should contain the user. Keep in mind that trusts are non-transitive. If all this is correct, check the group assignments. The user should be put into a global group in the trusted domain. That group should be put into a local group in the trusting domain. The local group should be assigned permissions to access the resource. This basic guide will be useful to you on almost every question on the test that involves trusts—and that is most of them!

## 2.8. Domain Models

Proper use of trust relationships enables you to construct a network of almost any size that still maintains the single logon capability. There are various constructs of domain/trust interaction, known as domain models. Microsoft defines four basic types of domain models:

- Single domain model
- Single master domain model
- Multiple master domain model
- Complete trust model

## 2.8.1. Single Domain

The single domain model is a network consisting of only one domain. This is the model that is used mainly in small to medium-sized networks. With only one domain, user accounts and resources are centralized, and administration is a fairly simple task (see Figure 2.19).

**Figure 2.19.**

*A single domain model.*

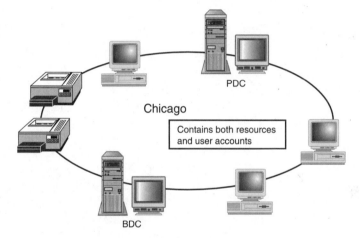

As your organization grows, however, moving to a multiple domain model might become necessary. For example, Microsoft indicates that the maximum size for an NT Directory Services database not exceed 40MB, approximately 20,000 users along with groups and computer accounts. If your database grows larger than this, splitting your network into two or more domains will become necessary.

There are several good things about the single domain model:

- Managing user and group accounts is easier because they are all in one place.
- Administering resources is easier because they are centrally located.
- Security is centralized.

It might be time to consider another model in the following circumstances:

■ The size of your NT Directory Services database grows to more than 40MB or you have more than 20,000 users.

■ You must divide the management of resources by department or geographical location for administrative purposes.

## 2.8.2. Master Domain

In the master domain model, multiple domains are defined and linked by trust relationships. One domain, the master domain, contains all the user accounts. Other domains are configured as resource domains and contain the various resources used on the network. This model is represented in Figure 2.20.

**Figure 2.20.**

*The master domain model.*

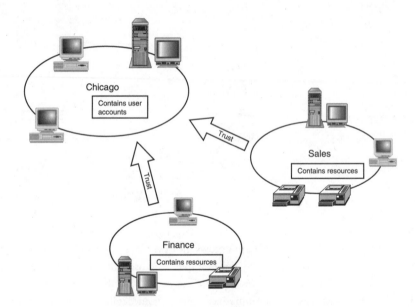

In this example, all network users log on to the Chicago master domain because all user accounts reside there. When a user is logged on to the Chicago master domain, she can access any resources located in any domain that trusts the Chicago master domain. For example, a user in Fargo can log on to the Chicago master domain and access the color plotter in the Sales domain.

**Note** Remember that a user's physical location is unimportant in this process. A user always logs on at a computer in a domain that trusts the Chicago master domain to log on to the Chicago master domain via pass-through authentication.

**2**

In this model, the resource domains are divided by department, each of which trusts the Chicago domain. This model assumes that the Chicago domain is sufficiently secure that the resource domains can entrust their resources to it. This model gives the advantage of having the user accounts administered centrally, while each department manages its own resources.

Managing groups becomes a little more complex in this model because of the way in which trust relationships work. Remember that user accounts in the trusted domain must be put into global groups. The global groups must then be put into local groups in the trusting domains. These local groups are then assigned permissions to use resources, as shown in Figure 2.21.

**Figure 2.21.**

*Managing groups in a master domain model.*

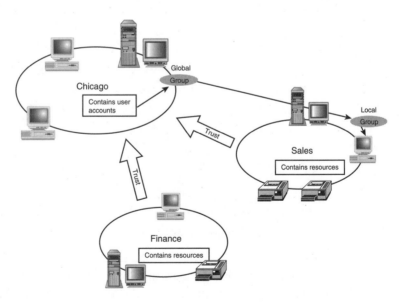

In this figure, user accounts in the Chicago domain must be put into a global group in the Chicago domain. That global group can then be placed into a local group in the Sales (or Finance) domain. That local group can then be assigned permissions to access resources.

The master domain model is good because

- Security management is centralized. Only one user account database exists.
- Resource domains can be used to organize resources by department or by geographical location.

You might have to consider another model when the size of your NT Directory Services database grows to more than 40MB or you have more than 40,000 users.

## 2.8.3. Multiple Master Domain

The multiple master domain model takes the concept of the master domain model one step further. In this model, multiple domains contain the user accounts for the network. These are the master domains. There are also multiple resource domains, each of which trust every master domain. Consider the example in Figure 2.22.

**Figure 2.22.**

*The multiple master domain model.*

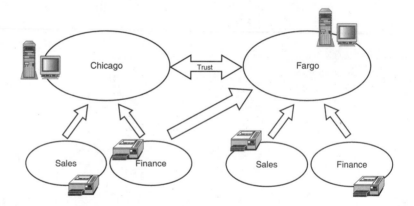

In this example, all users log on to either the Chicago domain or the Fargo domain, depending on where their user account is located. When they are logged on, these users can access the resources on any domain that trusts the domain on which they are logged.

This model makes managing groups even more complex. Now, in order for any user to be able to access resources, the same global groups must be created in each master domain, and each of these global groups must be placed into local groups in the resource domains. Consider the example in Figure 2.23.

**Figure 2.23.**

*Managing groups in the multiple master domain model.*

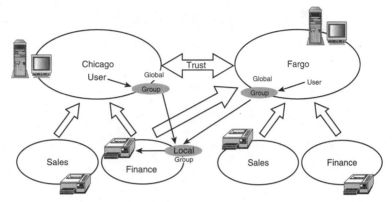

In this example, things are a little more complex than in the master domain model. Users in both the Chicago and Fargo master domains must access a resource in the Finance resource domain in Chicago. The first step is to create appropriate global groups in both the Chicago and Fargo master domains. Each of these global groups must then be placed into the local group in the Finance domain. Permissions are then assigned to that local group. You can see that group management in the multiple master domain model can quickly grow quite time-consuming as more master domains are introduced.

The multiple master domain model is good because

- Security management is centralized.
- Resource domains can be used to organize resources by department or by geographic location.

The following are the disadvantages of the multiple master domain:

- The number of groups and trust relationships rises dramatically with each new master domain that is added.
- User accounts are not centrally located, forcing many groups to be duplicated among master domains and increasing the complexity of user account management.

The formula for calculating the number of trusts in a relationship is M(M−1) + (RM). In this formula, M is the number of master domains and R is the number of resource domains.

### 2.8.4. Complete Trust Domain

In the complete trust domain model, each domain on the network is a single domain and each of the domains trust all the other domains (see Figure 2.24).

**Figure 2.24.**

*The complete trust domain model.*

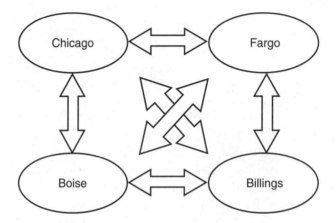

In this model, each user logs on to the domain on which her user account resides and can then access any resource in any domain that trusts the domain onto which she logged. This model lacks centralized security. Each domain relies on the other domains' administrators to manage their users and resources securely enough to trust. The one advantage to this model is that no centralized department must manage the network. Each domain's department is responsible for management.

The complete trust model is good because

- Each domain maintains its own users. There is no need for a centralized MIS department to manage network security and resources.
- This is a useful model to implement when two or more existing smaller networks must join, such as in the merging of two companies.

The following are the disadvantages of the complete trust model:

- No centralized security exists.
- The number of trust relationships that must be implemented grows dramatically as the number of domains increases.

The formula for calculating the number of trusts in a relationship is d(d−1), where d is the number of domains.

# 2.9. Lab

This lab will aid in your learning by testing you on the information presented in this chapter, as well as by giving you exercises to hone your skills. Answers to the review questions can be found in Appendix B, "Answers to Review Questions."

## 2.9.1. Review Questions

### Question 1

Corporation A is planning to add a Microsoft NT Server to a network consisting of several Microsoft Windows 95 systems. The system administrator decides to install the NT Server as a stand-alone server so that it can be placed in the same workgroup as the Windows 95 systems. Later, the system administrator decides to implement user-level security on the Windows 95 systems.

Which of the following steps must the system administrator complete to implement user-level security?

A. Convert the Windows 95 file system to NTFS

B. Specify the name of the NT Server as the security host

C. Promote the NT Server to a primary domain controller

D. Reinstall the NT Server as a primary domain controller

E. Upgrade the Windows 95 systems to NT Workstations

### Question 2

Corporation B has offices in Miami, New York, and Los Angeles. A T1 line connects the offices between Miami and New York. A T1 line has been ordered but not yet installed to link Miami and Los Angeles. The system administrator has created a domain called VALIDATE and placed the PDC in the Miami office and a BDC at the office in New York. Users in Los Angles are anxious to begin using the network.

In order to expedite the users in Los Angeles coming online, the system administrator proposes the following: As a temporary solution, a PDC will be installed in Los Angeles. The SA will install the system with the domain name of VALIDATE. TCP/IP will be installed on all controllers to ensure a common protocol for when the link becomes active. When connectivity between the sites has been established, the SA will demote the PDC in Los Angeles to a BDC.

Which of the following objectives will be met by the system administrator's solution?

A. A controller will be available to validate users in Los Angeles.

B. User accounts created in Miami will be merged into the SAM database in Los Angeles.

C. User accounts created in Los Angeles will be merged into the SAM database in Miami.

D. The users will have no interruption of services when the domains are merged.

## Question 3

The system administrator for Corporation B recently added a BDC to domain MASTERDOM. The BDC is located on the same physical segment as the PDC. The system administrator is planning to promote the new BDC to become the PDC. Which of the following steps must the system administrator perform?

A. Change the name of the BDC to match the name of the PDC.

B. Install NetBEUI on both the BDC and PDC.

C. Log on as Administrator.

D. Log on using an account that is a member of Domain Admins.

E. Reinstall the BDC.

## Question 4

The system administrator for Corporation B is planning to install Microsoft SQL. The SA wants to take advantage of the integrated security feature of Microsoft SQL, which enables NT user accounts to be mapped to logon IDs on the SQL Server. The users that will be accessing the SQL Server are all members of the GENIUS domain.

The GENIUS domain consists of the PDC, one BDC, one member server, and 20 users. The client machines run Microsoft Windows 95. Which of the machines would be capable of running the SQL server application?

A. The PDC

B. The BDC

C. The member server

D. The Windows 95 clients

## Question 5

As the number of domain members increases, so does the size of the SAM database at the PDC. Which other systems on the network will receive a copy of the SAM database from the PDC?

A.  Windows 95 clients

B.  NT stand-alone servers

C.  NT member servers

D.  Backup domain controllers

**2**

## Question 6

The system administrator of Corporation B learned that only backup domain controllers receive a copy of the account database from the PDC. Wanting to centralize account management, he has installed all the clients as BDCs. Now, 5,010 clients act as BDCs. Users are complaining that the system is often very slow when validating logons after their passwords have been changed. Sometimes they cannot be validated at all by providing their new password. This is especially true when switching between machines during the day.

What is causing the problem the users are experiencing?

A.  The PDC is unavailable

B.  The SAM database is not synchronized

C.  Fault tolerance is not enabled

D.  The maximum number of BDCs per domain is 5,000

## Question 7

The system administrator of Corporation B has mistakenly installed a new backup domain controller into the wrong domain. He has used the Network Neighborhood properties to rename the domain to match the proper one. The user accounts are not being synchronized properly with the PDC. What must the system administrator do to properly move the system into the correct domain?

A.  Register the BDC with the WINS Server

B.  Change the domain SID manually in the registry

C.  Synchronize the entire domain from Server Manager

D.  Reinstall the BDC

## Question 8

True or False: Betty's user account resides in Domain A. She attempts to log on to a computer in Domain B. Domain B trusts Domain A. Betty is still able to log on to the network.

## Question 9

What requirements are there for setting up a trust relationship between two domains? (Choose two.)

A. Both domains involved in the trust must share a common architecture.

B. Both PDCs involved in the trust must share a common protocol.

C. Both domains involved in the trust must share a common protocol.

D. There must be a permanent link between the two involved PDCs.

## Question 10

True or False. Domain A trusts Domain B. Your user account resides in Domain A and you want to print to a printer in Domain B. Because of the trust relationship, you will be able to do this.

## Question 11

True or False: Domain A trusts Domain B. Your user account resides in Domain B. You must be able to back up a server in Domain A. The administrator places your user account into the Backup Operators local group in Domain A. You are now able to back up the server.

## Question 12

True or False: Domain A trusts Domain B. Domain B trusts Domain C. Your user account resides in Domain C. You must be able to back up a server in Domain A. The administrator places your user account into the Backup Operators local group in Domain A. You are now able to back up the server.

## Question 13

True or False: If you pause the NetLogon service, users will not be able to log on to the domain.

### Question 14

What is the maximum size that an NT Directory Services database can reach?

A. 20MB

B. 40MB

C. 75MB

D. 128MB

2

### Question 15

If your domain has 16,000 users, how many BDCs will you need?

A. 16

B. 8

C. 7

D. 4

## 2.9.2. Exercises

### Exercise 2.1

Your company has 40,000 employees. Everyone has his or her own desktop computer running NT Workstation. Your company is based in Chicago and has a complex of six buildings. Each building houses a different department, and these buildings are connected by 256kbps dedicated WAN links. These departments are Sales, Finance, MIS, Management, Engineering, and Training. Each of these departments must maintain control of its own resources, but the MIS department wants to administer all user accounts centrally. The MIS department also wants to be responsible for backing up data in all departments. Sketch out your design for this network, answering the following questions:

- What will be the size of the directory database? Remember to take into account users, computers, and groups.
- What domain model should you implement?
- How many master domains will you need to govern the number of users you have. What do you think is the best way to divide those user accounts up?

- How powerful will the PDC in each of the domains have to be to support this number of users?
- How many BDCs will be needed in each domain to provide a reasonable level of redundancy?
- Where would you place the BDCs in each domain for optimum network performance? Keep in mind that the BDCs are involved in both user logon validation and directory replication.
- How would you configure the trust relationships on this network?
- How would you set up user accounts and global groups so that the MIS department can perform the backups for all the departments?

# Day 3

# Installing NT Server 4.0

*by David Schaer and Theresa Hadden*

## 3.1. Overview

Questions about installing NT Server can be as basic as reviewing your knowledge of hardware requirements to as complex as questions on automated setup options. This chapter guides you through each step of the installation and upgrade process of NT Server 4.0. The questions that follow act as a review on areas of installation, upgrades, and operating system coexistence.

This chapter leads you through the multiple phases of an NT installation. The exam tests your ability to select equipment that is capable of running NT Server 4.0, install it both locally and from across the network, upgrade it from previous operating systems, and troubleshoot common installation problems.

### 3.1.1. Objectives

The information in this chapter provides a basis for properly understanding how to install Windows NT. The following Microsoft objectives as stated in the Preparation Guide are addressed in this chapter:

- ■ Choose a protocol for various situations.
- ■ Install, configure, and troubleshoot various protocols including TCP/IP, NWLink, and NetBEUI.
- ■ Install Windows NT Server on Intel-based platforms.
- ■ Install Windows NT to perform various server roles including primary domain controller, backup domain controller, member server, and stand-alone server.

- Install Windows NT using various methods including CD-ROM and over the network, and by using Network Client Administrator.
- Configure protocols and protocol bindings.
- Configure network adapters.
- Choose the appropriate course of action to take to resolve installation failures.

## 3.1.2. Fast Facts

The following list of facts is a concise picture of the information presented in this chapter. It acts as both an overview for the chapter and as a study aid to help you do any last-minute cramming.

- Minimum requirement for NT Server 4.0 is 486DX/33, 12MB RAM (16MB RAM is recommended), and 125MB free disk space on an Intel-based computer.
- Minimum requirement for NT Server 4.0 on a RISC-based computer is 16MB RAM and 160MB free disk space.
- RISC-based machines can be installed only from a SCSI CD-ROM.
- Multiple copies of NT can be installed on the same partition provided they are in separate directories.
- There is no automatic upgrade option from Windows 95 to NT 4.0; you must reinstall all common applications.
- The BOOT.INI file is a text file that contains the operating system boot choices.
- The BOOTSECT.DOS file contains the original boot sector code before NT is installed.
- The logic might sound backward, but you boot from the system partition and system files are held on the boot partition.
- The boot and system partitions can be the same.
- WINNT32.EXE is used to upgrade when NT is already installed on the computer.
- You can set up Intel-based computers using either a local CD-ROM or from over the network. Floppy disks are not an option in NT 4.0.
- The minimum video configuration is VGA.
- Passwords are case sensitive, user names are not.
- You can create an NTHQ diagnostic disk by running MAKEDISK.BAT to test the system for compatibility.

- RDISK is the repair disk utility. It is used to both create and update emergency repair disks.
- The emergency repair disk is not bootable.
- The NT Setup Manager is used to create hands-free installation scripts.
- You use hands-free scripts with over-the-network setup by specifying the /b, /u, /udf, and /s switches.
- The /udf switch is used with a file containing overrides to the unattended script file called with the /u switch.
- The SYSDIFF.EXE utility is helpful for installing large numbers of systems with preinstalled software requirements.
- TCP/IP and NWLink IPX/SPX-compatible transport are both routable protocols.
- TCP/IP is the default protocol.
- Automatic detection of network adapter cards locates only the first network card. Select the Find Next button to detect additional network cards. Only one card at a time is detected.
- Computer names can be up to 15 characters and must be unique across the network.
- NetBEUI is non-routable; it requires bridging.

3

# 3.2. Choosing the Right Equipment

As operating systems become more complex, the level of equipment required increases dramatically. You can personally cut corners to try to squeeze out a little more power for your money when purchasing your personal system. However, for purposes of the test, money is not the object; when choosing equipment, compatibility is the major criterion.

## 3.2.1. The Hardware Compatibility List (HCL)

The equipment that you use must be supported on the HCL. The latest copy of the HCL, shown in Figure 3.1, can be found at http://www.microsoft.com/hwtest/hcl or downloaded from ftp://ftp.microsoft.com/bussys/winnt/winnt-docs/hcl/HCL40.

**Figure 3.1.**

*Microsoft's Web site provides the latest HCL information.*

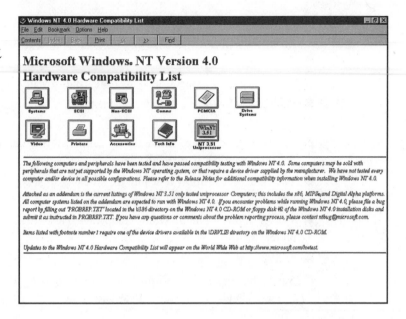

When troubleshooting a new system, one of the first things to confirm is that all of the equipment being used is supported on the HCL. The HCL contains listings of supported systems and accessories such as mice, SCSI cards, modems, network adapters, tape drives, and video cards.

NTHQ is an NT diagnostic tool that can help detect hardware conflicts. You create the bootable NTHQ disk by running `makedisk.bat` from the NT Server CD's `/support/hqtool` directory. The NTHQ diagnostics are run automatically when you boot from the disk. Booting from the disk enables the utility to interact more closely with the hardware than diagnostics run from within NT.

A specific piece of hardware may be found compatible, but not necessarily across all hardware platforms. For example, the same network card that might be approved for use on an Intel x86-based system might not be approved on a DEC Alpha, MIPS, or PowerPC.

## 3.2.2. Hardware Requirements

The hardware requirements for NT will vary based on what the system will be used for. A system running Microsoft SQL and servicing 500 users has greater hardware requirements than a system that is being used solely to provide file and print services to a few dozen people. Because hardware requirements can vary so drastically based on function, the tests are forced to focus on minimum requirements.

### Intel x86 Installation Requirements

The Intel x86-based systems (80486, Pentium) are the most common systems used to run NT Server 4.0. Because of this it is reasonable to expect the exam to place more attention on this platform than on the RISC.

Be sure to know the minimum installation requirements for an x86 system. They are

- A 486DX/33 or above
- 16MB of RAM
- 130MB of free disk space
- VGA or better video capabilities
- CD-ROM or access to files via a network
- A FAT or NTFS partition for installation

**Processor Requirements**   NT requires a 486DX/33 or above. NT also supports systems with multiple processors. NT Workstation supports two, and NT Server supports four. Various OEM versions of NT running on specialized hardware have been designed to support up to 32 processors.

**Memory Requirements**   The minimum amount of memory you can have is 16MB. The terms random access memory (RAM) and physical memory will be used interchangeably.

RAM is the focus of many performance issues in Chapter 11, "Configuring and Optimizing NT 4.0 Services." A system with a slower processor yet a large amount of RAM can often outperform systems with faster processors and less memory.

**Hard Disk Space Requirements**   The minimum hard disk space requirement, 130MB, is listed for a system with 16MB of physical memory. Certain configurations of NT require additional hard disk space. Configuring a large paging file for emulating physical memory on a hard disk requires a hard disk of greater capacity. The default pagefile size is the amount of RAM plus 12MB—the minimum pagefile size is 2MB. Configuring the recovery option of writing system memory to a dump file (%SystemRoot%\MEMORY.DMP) when a system failure occurs requires a pagefile on the system partition at least equal to the amount of RAM in the computer.

**Video Requirements**   The system must support VGA or greater resolution. You will be asked to test the video driver and resolution during the installation.

It is better to install the standard VGA driver during installation. After you have finished the installation, then you can install the specific drivers for your video adapter card.

You must use the video drivers for NT 4.0. Video is handled differently in NT 4.0 than in previous versions of NT, and video drivers from NT 3.x are not compatible. This is true also of Windows 95 drivers; they cannot be used as the drivers for NT 4.0 systems.

**Installation Media Requirements**   There are only two installation methods for NT 4.0, CD-ROM or via a network. The CD-ROM drive may use either a SCSI or supported IDE controller.

In certain systems that support booting from the CD-ROM you might not need to boot from a floppy disk to begin the installation. Because a majority of systems do not support this feature, NT Server comes with three floppy disks that are used to initialize the CD-ROM under a limited character-based version of NT.

Installation from a shared network device is supported for systems that do not have a local CD-ROM drive. Performing multiple installations or upgrades is often easier using the across-the-network method.

The fastest method for installing NT is via a network share. In fact, you can point to multiple shares to speed the installation even more.

**Primary File System Requirements**   On an Intel x86-based machine the system partition can be either FAT or NTFS. Either file system is supported because the NTLDR file initializes the mini-file system drivers to provide support for both on bootup.

### RISC-Specific Issues

The same hardware requirements as for x86-based computers must be met when installing NT Server 4.0 on a RISC-based computer with the addition of a SCSI CD-ROM and a 2MB FAT partition.

Because RISC-based computers do not include the NTLDR file found on x86-based NT installations, the mini-file system drivers required for NTFS access are not initialized at boot time.

> A RISC-based computer requires the following additional items:
>
> - SCSI CD-ROM
>
> - A minimum of a 2MB FAT partition

**Installation Media Requirements**   You have only one option here, a SCSI CD-ROM. Because RISC machines boot off of firmware, only devices initialized by the system directly will be available to perform the installation.

**Primary File System Requirements**   FAT is the only file system initialized by a RISC system's firmware. The FAT partition must be at least 2MB in size. This gives the partition room to hold the OSLOADER.EXE, HAL.DLL, and any *.PAL (DEC Alpha-specific) files to continue initializing NT. RISC-based systems use the Arcinst.exe utility to create and format partitions which may be NTFS.

On RISC-based machines the system administrator can secure the FAT partition through the Secure System Partition command on the Partition menu of Disk Administrator. This security feature is unique to the RISC platform and should not mislead you into thinking that FAT offers any file-level security.

## 3.3. Planning for Multiple Operating Systems

You might need or want to boot into a different operating system to perform certain functions. The operating systems that you want available to boot into in addition to NT will normally be installed before installing NT. Usually you will want to install the operating systems in the order of DOS, Windows 95, then NT.

3

You can install your operating systems in any order. Just repair the NT installation to return to a multiboot environment.

Don't confuse the concept of multiple operating systems with environment subsystems. Environment subsystems let NT emulate an operating system so that applications written for those systems can run unchanged under NT. Because not all applications will run properly under the operating system emulators, NT provides the capability of booting into other operating systems. Only one operating system can be active at a time.

You can select the default operating system to start at boot time through the Startup/Shutdown tab in the System Properties dialog box under Control Panel, as shown in Figure 3.2.

**Figure 3.2.**

*Setting the default operating system.*

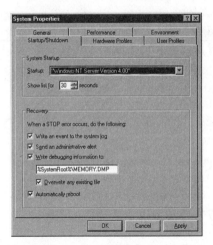

You also can adjust the time allowed to select an operating system boot choice before the default is loaded. The default loads immediately if the time-out value is set to 0.

Because FAT is the only file system supported by DOS, Windows 95, OS/2, and NT, FAT must be the file system on the system partition on dual-boot systems. Other partitions that contain file systems or configurations unique to a particular operating system are available only when the supported operating system is active.

### 3.3.1. Coexistence with DOS

When DOS is installed on a computer, the boot sector is modified to call the DOS initialization files. When NT is installed to the same partition, the NT installation program copies the boot sector information to a file called BOOTSECT.DOS. The information is saved before NT overwrites the boot sector so that it is available to be called later.

The operating system that is selected and booted is the actual operating system. It is in no way different in function because the boot process began with the NT loader. The installation and configuration of common devices must be performed under each operating system.

If the BOOTSECT.DOS file ever is deleted or corrupted or the NT boot sector is accidentally overwritten, the NT boot sector can be replaced. To do this, you must inspect the NT boot sector through the emergency repair options. Boot from NT Server Setup Disk 1—the emergency repair disk is not bootable—and select the option to repair. Under the repair options, clear all options except to inspect the boot sector. Simply insert other required disks as prompted. This process repairs both the boot sector and creates the BOOTSECT.DOS file if required.

### 3.3.2. Coexistence with Windows 95

Dual booting between Windows 95 and Windows NT is supported in the same way as dual booting NT and DOS. If dual booting is already configured for DOS, boot into DOS and run the Windows 95 setup. You must take care to ensure that you do not accidentally install Windows 95 in the same directory as Windows NT; this would overwrite the NT system files.

You must configure devices and software once under each operating system. Be especially careful when changing network settings; changing the IP address under NT will have no effect on the IP address under Windows 95. The same is true of physical hardware configuration settings; if a network card is moved to a different IRQ the change must be adjusted under both operating systems.

The only file system fully supported between NT and Windows 95 is FAT. However, not all FAT is created equal. Systems installed with OEM versions of Windows 95 might come installed with partitions formatted with an incompatible version of FAT called FAT32. FAT32 partitions would be accessible only under Windows 95.

Windows 95 cannot understand partitions formatted with NTFS. Partitions created as volume or stripe sets under NT are not accessible under Windows 95 even if formatted as FAT. Disks that were mirrored under NT do not appear or function as mirrored sets under Windows 95.

### 3.3.3. Coexistence with OS/2

Coexistence with OS/2 would be desirable for people who have an installed base of Microsoft LAN Manager or IBM LAN Server, both of which were designed to run on OS/2.

#### OS/2 1.x

Integrating OS/2 1.x is fairly simple. Before you load NT, simply install and configure OS/2 1.x to allow for dual booting of OS/2 and DOS. To boot between OS/2 1.x and DOS, select DOS from the options offered during the NT boot. When the system loads to the command prompt you can type boot /os2 or boot /dos to enable the proper operating system.

#### OS/2 2.x

Like NT, OS/2 supports booting into multiple operating systems. If you plan to support additional operating systems besides NT, you should first configure NT to boot as described previously.

After installing NT, you can install OS/2 on the same system. A different partition must be used for the OS/2 boot partition. The OS/2 BOOTLOADER can be used to select the operating system boot choice of OS/2 or NT. If NT is selected, the system will call the NTLDR that in turn reads the BOOT.INI to present the user a choice of operating systems to boot into.

## 3.4. Upgrading Existing Operating Systems

The issues with upgrading are slightly different than issues with coexistence. When upgrading it is important to confirm that NT will support all hardware required.

A system might have run without problems on Windows 95 or even NT 3.x but might not work with NT 4.0. You should check the hardware against the HCL before beginning the upgrade, and confirm the availability of drivers. Back up all data before you begin the upgrade process.

### 3.4.1. Upgrading from OS/2 to NT 4.0

Although NT can be installed on a machine running OS/2 it does not upgrade the operating system. NT will be installed as a separate operating system on the machine. In previous versions of NT the High Performance File System (HPFS) was supported. In NT 4.0 the OS/2 subsystem no longer supports HPFS.

### 3.4.2.  Upgrading from Windows 95 to NT 4.0

This is a manual upgrade process. Although both NT and Windows 95 use a registry to store configuration information, the two registries are incompatible.

> Do not install Windows NT into the same directory as Windows 95. You would be unable to boot either operating system due to registry incompatibilities.

You do the upgrade as a new installation of NT. You can perform the installation from the local CD-ROM or from across the network. When you use the across the network installation method you must execute WINNT.EXE. Even though Windows 95 supports 32-bit applications you cannot use the WINNT32.EXE utility to perform your upgrade because it requires NT-specific support files.

> You can install Windows NT from the RUN prompt under Windows 95 by using WINNT.EXE with the /w switch. This also requires that you manually perform the first reboot.

It is necessary to reinstall all applications under NT. Install each application into the same directory to save disk space. If you are installing a member server, it will only contain default users, groups, and policies. A BDC will receive a copy of the domain SAM database.

> It is possible to get around reinstalling certain programs by using the System applet on the Control Panel to add the location of the needed DLLs to the Windows NT path.

### 3.4.3.  Upgrading from NT 3.*x* to 4.0

The preferred method of upgrading a system that already has a version of NT loaded is to use the WINNT32.EXE executable. This method can also be used to install additional copies of NT on the same machine.

3

### 3.4.4. Updates and Service Packs

Periodically, Microsoft releases service packs to correct bugs or enhance the released product. To install a service pack, run the UPDATE.EXE utility from the source directory. Check with the hardware vendor before applying service packs to machines with proprietary hardware. When applying service packs to machines with multiple processors, special instructions are required.

# 3.5. Initiating NT Server 4.0 Setup

There are two basic setup methods: installation from a local CD-ROM and installation from a source on the network.

## 3.5.1. Initiating NT Server 4.0 Setup from a Local Source

When you set up a single system, using a local CD-ROM as the setup source is usually simplest. Having the source files held locally, on the CD-ROM, or even copied to a directory on the hard disk can aid in later repairing the system files if necessary. However, don't assume that all systems will have a CD-ROM drive or the extra hard disk capacity to hold a copy of the source files.

You normally begin local installation by booting from the NT Server Setup Disk 1. This initializes a basic version of NT, which loads the drivers necessary to access hardware including the CD-ROM drive. Figure 3.3 shows the installation at the point of initializing SCSI and IDE controllers.

If NT does not support the local CD-ROM drive it can still be used as a local source for the NT server installation files. An unsupported CD-ROM that is accessible under DOS can be treated as a network device for installation purposes. The installer would activate the CD-ROM under DOS and follow the directions for an over-the-network installation.

 When dealing with a non-supported CD-ROM, you can copy the installation files to the hard drive and install from there.

Local installation is the only option for RISC machines. You must install them by using a supported SCSI CD-ROM. RISC machines boot from firmware and do not require the NT Server Setup disks.

**Figure 3.3.**

*Local setup initializing SCSI and IDE controllers.*

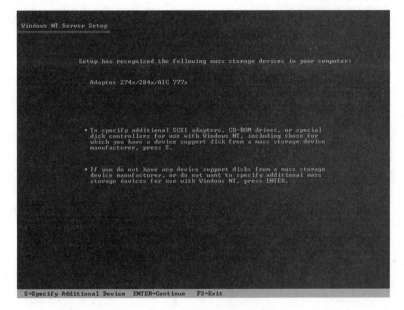

3

## 3.5.2. Initiating NT Server 4.0 Setup from a Network Share Point

Over-the-network setup from a share point on the server allows the system administrator to centrally control the installation files. The SA can either share the appropriate directory (such as I386) on the NT CD-ROM or copy the source files to a shared directory on the server.

The target machine must be connected to the file server via the network. If the operating system on the target machine is DOS-based, the executable will be WINNT.EXE. If the target machine is installed with an existing copy of NT, then WINNT32.EXE can be utilized.

### WINNT.EXE and WINNT32.EXE

You can use both WINNT.EXE and WINNT32.EXE to perform either local or over-the-network installations.

After executing the file appropriate to the client's operating system, the installation copies source files to a partition on the target computer. The basic installation creates a temporary directory called $WIN_NT$.~LS to hold the source files. If the /b option is used with WINNT.EXE or WINNT32 an additional directory, $WIN_NT$.~BT also is created.

This directory provides temporary storage for the information normally held on the three setup floppies. Because the /b option alleviates the need for the floppy disks, it is a common option to choose.

Other common switches to use with WINNT.EXE and WINNT32.EXE are as follows:

| | |
|---|---|
| /s | This switch enables you to specify the source directory that contains the installation files. |
| /o or /ox | Use these switches when you must rebuild the three NT setup floppies for use with the CD-ROM. |
| /u | This switch activates unattended setup mode. You must specify the name of the unattended script file created using the Setup Manager from the NT 4.0 Resource Kit. The Setup Manager is shown in Figure 3.4. Unattended mode also requires using the /s switch to provide the source path. |
| /udf | This switch loads a file that supersedes section values in the unattended script file. Common override values can be assigned, or sections can be applied only to individual machines based on their ID. |

**Figure 3.4.**

*The entry screen for the Setup Manager.*

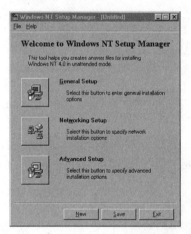

The unattended script file is a text file that provides the answers to the common setup questions. The system administrator controls the degree of user interaction.

After executing WINNT.EXE or WINNT32.EXE the initial files are copied to the temporary directories as described earlier. As the final step of phase one the system is rebooted.

## Phase Two of NT Server 4.0 Setup

The installation setup screen is shown in Figure 3.5.

**Figure 3.5.**

*The installation welcome screen.*

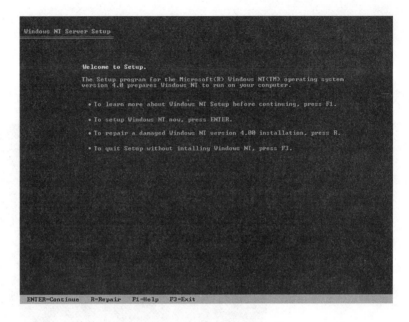

Using the unattended script files as described previously would alleviate you from needing to respond to some or all of the screens that follow.

As seen in Figure 3.6, you have the option of specifying SCSI or IDE devices that are not detected automatically.

**Figure 3.6.**

*You can select additional SCSI or IDE devices.*

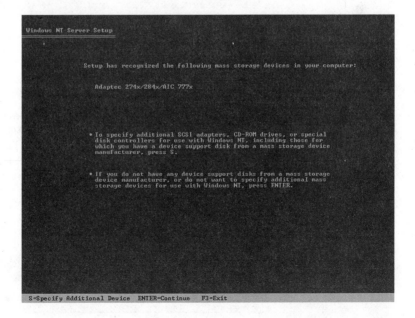

The license agreement is then displayed. You must agree to the license agreement to continue installation.

A screen appears, as shown in Figure 3.7, showing the hardware believed to be present in the system. You can override the hardware detected by the installation program. You must confirm the hardware before continuing.

**Figure 3.7.**

*You are required to confirm detected hardware.*

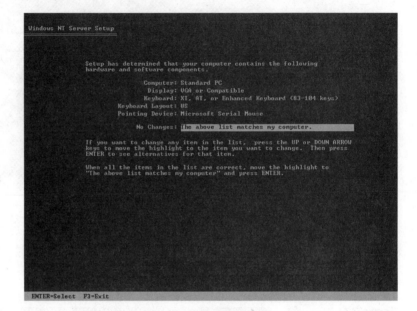

You must then choose a partition on which to place the installation, as seen in Figure 3.8. Many installations of NT can reside on the same partition as long as they are installed in separate directories. If extended DOS partitions exist, there will be a separate listing for each logical drive.

**Figure 3.8.**

*Choose the installation partition.*

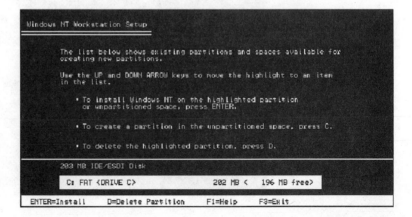

You can create and delete partitions at this point of the installation. You next determine whether the partition should be formatted or converted. If you format the partition, all data on that partition will be lost.

In the example in Figure 3.9 the C drive will be converted to NTFS. This will render all operating systems but NT from accessing the drive. The data will still remain on the drive, but it will not be accessible to any operating system but NT. If you planned on dual-booting the system the file system must be left intact as FAT.

**Figure 3.9.**

*Choosing to convert the C drive.*

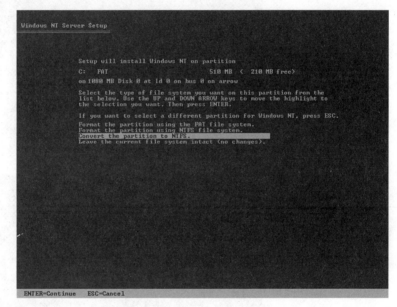

The default installation directory as shown in Figure 3.10 can be overridden. Notice that the drive is not specified, only the directory; this is because the partition has already been selected.

The system offers to perform a check of the hard disk for bad blocks, as shown in Figure 3.11. If the hard disk is old or suspect in any way it is especially important to allow the secondary test to be performed.

**Figure 3.10.**
WINNT *is the default installation directory.*

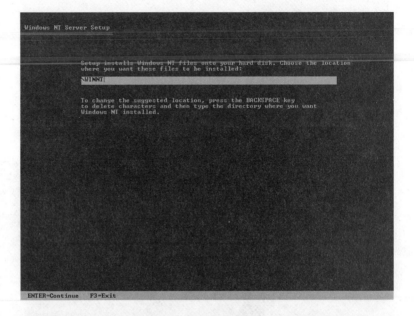

**Figure 3.11.**
*The system can perform a check for bad blocks on the hard disk.*

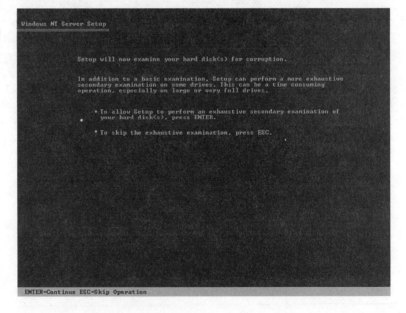

Following the hard disk check, the setup program states it is copying files, as shown in Figure 3.12. In the over-the-network setup the files are really being expanded from the temporary directory to the selected installation directory. The network is not accessible at this point of the installation.

**Figure 3.12.**
*When the copying is complete you are prompted to reboot the system.*

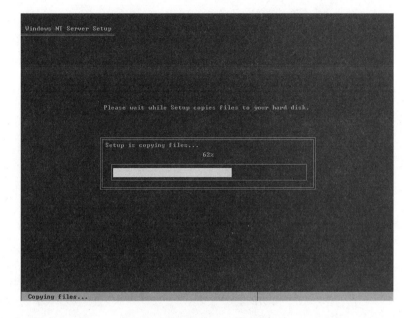

Figure 3.13 shows that the second phase of installation is complete.

**Figure 3.13.**
*The second phase of installation completes.*

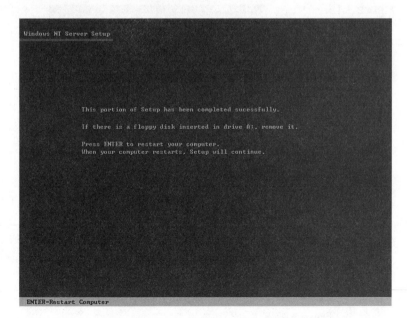

## Phase Three of the NT Server 4.0 Setup

The NT Setup Wizard prompts you through the remainder of the installation referred to as the GUI portion. Figure 3.14 shows the first screen of the third installation phase.

**Figure 3.14.**

*The third phase of installation begins.*

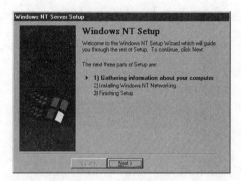

The registered user information is requested in Figure 3.15. This information is for registration purposes only and will not affect the user, computer, workgroup, or domain names.

**Figure 3.15.**

*Registration informa-tion is requested.*

The license information must be completed before continuing. Figure 3.16 shows the two licensing options.

Licensing requirements can vary significantly. In general, if you have only one server, choose server-based licensing; if you have more than one server, it would be better to select the Per Seat option.

The computer name, or NetBIOS name, of up to fifteen characters is requested in Figure 3.17.

**Figure 3.16.**
*NT licensing options.*

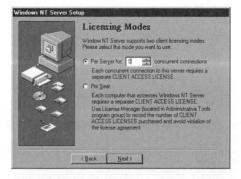

**Figure 3.17.**
*The computer name is requested.*

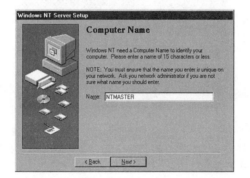

Two systems on the same network cannot have the same computer name. If two computers are installed with the same computer name on separate unconnected network segments they will function properly until the segments are connected. The first system to register the NetBIOS name with the network will be the system that functions. The second receives a failure when attempting to register the NetBIOS name, and its network capabilities are rendered inoperative.

You must select the server type. The three server type options are displayed in Figure 3.18.

**Figure 3.18.**
*The three NT server types.*

If you fail to select the function of the system properly you might need to reinstall. NT does not provide a method of changing a stand-alone server into a domain controller (PDC or BDC) or in the other direction.

The administrator password is case sensitive, as are other user passwords in NT. Enter and confirm the administrator password as in Figure 3.19.

**Figure 3.19.**

*The administrator password is case sensitive.*

Creating an emergency repair disk is optional, as seen in Figure 3.20. The repair disk holds copies of the configuration information that might be required to troubleshoot the system. You can create or update the emergency repair disk by using the Repair Disk Utility, RDISK.EXE, at any time. Updating the repair disk whenever significant changes to hardware, software, or users have been performed is good practice.

**Figure 3.20.**

*The emergency repair disk is optional.*

Each of the optional components to install can be specified. Not all components of each category must be selected, as shown in Figure 3.21.

The network portion of the installation commences. The system may communicate with the network by using a standard network adapter card or may attach by using remote access services. If neither of the selections, as shown in Figure 3.22, are selected the system will not be able to run any of the network services.

**Figure 3.21.**
*Not all components must be selected.*

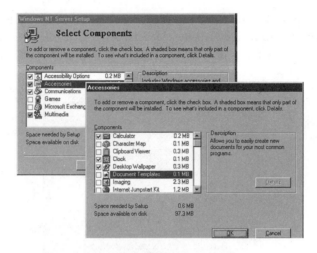

**Figure 3.22.**
*Specify the type of network connection.*

The Internet Information Server, commonly known as a Web server, can be installed now or added later. Figure 3.23 shows the IIS Server installation option.

**Figure 3.23.**
*IIS can be added now or later.*

The network adapter card can be detected automatically, as in Figure 3.24. If multiple adapter cards are present, only the first one is detected. If the system is configured to serve as a BDC it is important to confirm the card is attached to a segment that allows connectivity to the PDC.

**Figure 3.24.**

*Installation of the network adapter cards.*

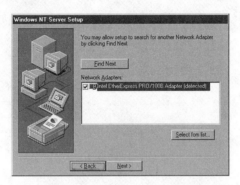

If the network adapter card being used is not located automatically or is improperly identified, you can select it manually from the list. If the card is not listed, the driver might be available from the manufacturer, and you can add it as an unlisted adapter.

You can select one or multiple protocols at this time. Figure 3.25 shows the protocol selection screen.

**Figure 3.25.**

*Initial protocol selection is made.*

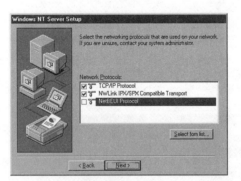

Select TCP/IP when there is a need for connection to the Internet or when systems must communicate over an IP-routed network. NWLINK, or NetWare Link, is compatible with Novell's IPX/SPX protocol. It can be used on a routed network whether or not a NetWare server is present. NetBEUI (Network Basic Enhanced User Interface) is a very fast protocol for use on single segments of a network. NetBEUI is not a routable protocol; it can, like all other protocols, be bridged. If the computer being installed is a BDC you must select at least one protocol that is also in use on the PDC.

In addition to the basic network services shown in Figure 3.26, you can also select to install advanced services at this time. Advanced services include DHCP Server, Remote Access Server, DNS server, and others, which are discussed in Chapter 11.

**Figure 3.26.**
*Selecting the basic network services.*

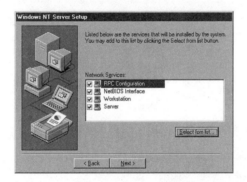

After you select the services you must configure protocol settings for TCP/IP or IPX/SPX, if either were selected. If you have selected to install the DHCP Server service on the system you must configure TCP/IP manually; a DHCP server cannot be a DHCP client. NetBEUI is self-configuring.

The protocol bindings are displayed in Figure 3.27. You can change the binding order and thus the priority of the protocols relative to specific services.

**Figure 3.27.**
*The protocol binding order.*

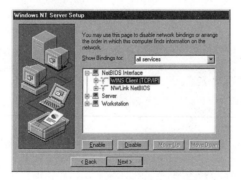

The system now initializes the network.

When installing a PDC the name of the domain being created is required. Figure 3.28 shows NTMASTER being installed as the PDC for the KNOWLEDGE domain.

**Figure 3.28.**
*NTMASTER is configured as the PDC for KNOWLEDGE.*

Enter the appropriate time zone. Figure 3.29 shows the system configured for GMT+01:00.

**Figure 3.29.**
*Enter the time zone information.*

The system displays the video information and requires that you test the video configuration before continuing. In Figure 3.30 the video configuration is displayed.

**Figure 3.30.**
*Configuring the system video.*

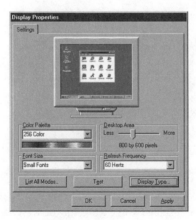

If the video does not appear properly during the test mode simply wait until the test completes and try a different configuration.

The final step is to create the emergency repair disk if the option was selected. The emergency repair disk only reflects the system configuration at the time of installation unless it is periodically updated using the Repair Disk utility, RDISK.EXE. The emergency repair disk should be updated following any major system change including hardware, software, and user configuration.

The BOOT.INI is updated to reflect the new installation of NT as the default boot selection.

The installation is now complete.

## 3.6. Hands-Free Installations

3

Several methods are available to perform hands-free installations. The most common method is by utilizing the NT Setup Manager to create text-based answer files. The answer files are called during over-the-network installation when the /u and /s switches are employed.

The NT installation can also be activated through Microsoft Systems Management Server or by something as simple as a batch file called in a logon script.

Microsoft System Management Server can be used to force or push the installation of various software packages to the target system. For example, a package containing Microsoft Office 97 could be distributed and installed on the client machine. Not all software packages provide a script that lets SMS perform an automated installation.

The sysdiff.exe utility allows an installation of NT to be enhanced by including additional software. The software installed using sysdiff.exe does not have to support scripting. In essence, the sysdiff.exe utility creates a file containing system differences between a clean target machine and the same machine after desired software has been installed. The difference file can be applied to other target machines to lay down the software and update the registry. Hardware and software resellers use the sysdiff.exe utility most commonly.

## 3.7. Uninstalling Windows NT

If you loaded NT for trial purposes, or if you want to turn a stand-alone or member server into a controller, removing it at some point might be necessary. Uninstalling NT, without losing other applications or data, requires only a few simple steps.

If NT was installed on a FAT partition, simply boot into DOS or Windows 95 either from a system disk or by selecting the other operating system on multiboot machines. A system disk is a better choice because it is often necessary to SYS the drive.

Next, delete the entire Windows NT directory structure from the %SYSTEM_ROOT% down.

Finally, delete the file pagefile.sys and all system files in the root of the system partition, including NTLDR, NTDETECT.COM, BOOTSECT.DOS, BOOT.INI, and—if it exists—NTBOOTDD.SYS.

If NT is installed on an NTFS partition and another copy of NT is installed in another directory, delete the unwanted NT installation manually. The BOOT.INI file must be manually updated to note the removal.

If NT is installed as the only operating system on an NTFS partition, remove it by deleting the partition (the setup disks can be used for this).

# 3.8. Selecting Network Protocols

The exams will test your knowledge of four basic network protocols: TCP/IP, NWLink (IPX/SPX), NetBEUI, and DLC. Remember to focus on what each protocol has in common and at the same time what features make each protocol unique.

## 3.8.1. TCP/IP

TCP/IP has been popularized within NT and Microsoft exams. TCP/IP has gained so much popularity over the years for several reasons:

- TCP/IP is a routable protocol.
- TCP/IP is the protocol the Internet uses.
- TCP/IP is a common protocol implemented by all major network manufacturers.

## 3.8.2. NWLink (IPX/SPX)

NWLink is Microsoft's implementation that is compatible with Novell's implementation of IPX/SPX. Although the name implies that the sole purpose of NWLink is to connect to NetWare servers, that is not the case. In fact, NWLink may be the protocol running on a pure NT network. Also, NWLink without either Client Services for NetWare (CSNW) or Gateway Services for NetWare (GSNW) loaded would allow access to a NetWare application server (such as Oracle or Sybase running as an NLM).

NWLink has several powerful features:

- NWLink is a routable protocol.
- NWLink alone can allow NetWare clients access to an NT application server.
- NWLink alone can allow NT clients access to a NetWare application server.

### 3.8.3. NetBEUI

NetBEUI lacks the routing capability of TCP/IP and NWLink. The disadvantages of NetBEUI on a WAN are often never seen by the small network administrator. In fact, there are several times when NetBEUI may be the protocol of choice:

- NetBEUI is completely self-tuning.
- NetBEUI is the fastest protocol to use across RAS.
- NetBEUI is the only RAS dial-in protocol to support the NetBIOS gateway feature.

### 3.8.4. Data Link Control (DLC)

The Data Link Control (DLC) is a nonroutable protocol used in NT for some specific purposes, such as the following:

- DLC is commonly used with a 3270 or 5250 emulator to talk directly to IBM mainframes and IBM AS/400 computers.
- DLC is used with Hewlett-Packard print devices that connect to the network via JetDirect cards.

You should know that DLC cannot be used by clients to attach to a Microsoft NT network.

# 3.9. Lab

This lab aids in your learning by testing you on the information presented in this chapter, as well as by giving you exercises to hone your skills. Answers to the review questions can be found in Appendix B, "Answers to Review Questions."

## 3.9.1. Review Questions

### Question 1

The system administrator for Corporation B recently received a new RISC-based machine. He is planning to install NT Server on the machine. Which of the following installation methods are available to him?

A. Floppy disk

B. IDE CD-ROM

C. SCSI CD-ROM

D. Shared network directory

### Question 2

Corporation B has received 50 new Pentium computers capable of running Windows NT. You want to install Windows NT on each of the systems with as little human intervention as possible. You know that the installed video cards provide at least VGA resolution but are of different brands on several machines. Which of the following steps must you perform to automate the installations?

A. Create a differences file using `sysdiff.exe`

B. Create an unattended installation answer file

C. Use the over-the-network installation method

D. Install Microsoft System Management Server

### Question 3

The system administrator of Corporation B is evaluating an x86-based Pentium clone for use as the company's Web server. Which of the following are bootable disks that will allow the system administrator to confirm NT Server compatibility?

A. The emergency repair disk

B. The NTHQ diagnostic disk

C. The Windows NT Server Setup Disk #1

D. A Windows 95 Start disk

## Question 4

The primary domain controller for Corporation B is configured with TCP/IP, NetBEUI, and DLC. A BDC is planned to be installed on the other side of a router. The router is configured to allow NetBIOS broadcasts to pass on UDP Port 137. Which of the following could be used as the sole protocol on the BDC during installation?

A. NWLink (IPX/SPX)

B. NetBEUI

C. DLC

D. TCP/IP

## Question 5

The administrator of Corporation B created an emergency repair disk when he installed NTSRVX. After the installation the administrator created a volume set on the computer. Which of the following steps must the administrator perform to ensure that the emergency repair disk reflects the new configuration?

A. Create a new emergency repair disk

B. Run the NT Server Setup Manager

C. Update the emergency repair disk

D. Run the repair disk utility

## Question 6

A computer consultant wants the ability to demonstrate both NT Workstation, NT Server, and Windows 95 on the same computer. What is the minimum number of hard disks that will be required to load all of the desired operating systems and also allow the consultant to demonstrate NTFS-specific features?

A. One

B. Two

C. Three

D. The three operating systems cannot coexist

## Question 7

Which of the following installations will fail if a PDC is not accessible during installation?

A. Stand-alone server

B. Backup domain controller

C. Primary domain controller

D. All of the above

## Question 8

Which of the following parameters are the minimum required when configuring TCP/IP on an NT Server?

A. IP address

B. Subnet mask

C. Default gateway

D. Bridge address

## Question 9

Which of the following protocols are required to use a Hewlett-Packard JetDirect print device?

A. HPDLC

B. NWLink

C. DLC

D. NetBEUI

## Question 10

Which of the following are routable protocols?

A. TCP/IP

B. NWLink

C. DLC

D. NetBEUI

## Question 11

Which of the following protocols can be bridged?

A. TCP/IP

B. NWLink

C. DLC

D. NetBEUI

## Question 12

Which of the following protocols can be used with RAS to act across the NetBIOS gateway?

A. DLC

B. IPX

C. TCP/IP

D. NetBEUI

## Question 13

To allow NetWare clients to access a Microsoft SQL server, which protocol(s) must be loaded on the NT Server?

A. DLC

B. TCP/IP

C. NWLink

D. ISAPI

## Question 14

Which of the following must be loaded on an NT server to allow access to files on a NetWare file server?

A. GSNW

B. NWLink

C. NetBIOS

D. SQL

## 3.9.2 Exercise

Your company has acquired 50 new desktop computers and 20 laptops; you must install Windows NT on each of them. How are you going to do the installations? How would you create an unattended answer file?

# Day 4

# Configuring the Environment

*by David Schaer and Theresa Hadden*

## 4.1. Overview

This chapter will familiarize you with how to configure the most common services and drivers used in Windows NT 4 and the role the registry plays in configuring your environment. Understanding the registry is a required element in understanding how services and applications are implemented in NT Server.

Think of services as applications that perform certain duties. For example, the Alerter service is used to generate notification of significant system events.

A restaurant has waiters and cooks, and although each performs a specific service, one is dependent on the other. If the cooks don't prepare something to eat, the waiters will have nothing to serve. The waiters are dependent on the cooks. In a similar fashion some of the NT services are dependent on other services that must be running for them to perform their functions.

On the other hand, the registry, which records how these services are configured, is one of the most complicated areas of the NT operating system. Fortunately, when the registry is broken down into a few basic components, the veil is lifted and the overall structure becomes rather simple. The exam focuses on the areas listed in the following MCSE QuickFACTS.

### 4.1.1. Objectives

The information in this chapter is provided mainly as a basis for properly understanding how to configure services and the use of the registry. This chapter addresses how to

- Configure Windows NT Server core services
- Use the registry editor to configure your computer
- Configure peripherals and devices
- Choose the appropriate course of action to take to resolve configuration errors

## 4.1.2. Fast Facts

The following list of facts is a concise picture of the information presented in this chapter. It acts as both an overview for the chapter and as a study aid to help you do any last-minute cramming.

- Services can run with permissions independent of the logged-on user.
- A user does not need to be logged on for services to be running.
- Services can be controlled through Service in the Control Panel, Server Manager, or from the command line with the Net Start command.
- A service can be set as disabled, manual, or automatic.
- REGEDT32.EXE or REGEDIT.EXE can be used to modify the registry.
- By default, only members of the administrators group are assigned permissions to modify the registry.
- The LastKnownGood control set is located in HKEY_LOCAL_MACHINE.
- Service parameters are stored in the registry HKEY_LOCAL_MACHINE\SYSTEM\CurrentControlSet\Services.
- The SAM and SECURITY hives cannot be modified directly.
- Changes to HKEY_LOCAL_MACHINE affect all users of the system.
- If a series of services fails to start it is normally because of the failure of a service on which they depend.
- The Workstation service is independent of the Server service.
- The Alerter service generates alert messages; the Messenger service delivers messages.
- The Server Manager is used to configure alerts.
- The AT.EXE and WINAT.EXE applets are dependent on the Schedule service.
- The Netlogon service synchronizes the SAM database between the PDC and BDCs.
- If the Netlogon service is paused at the PDC, synchronization will continue to be performed.

- Pausing the Server service does not disconnect currently attached users.
- Tape drivers are installed through the Tape Devices applet in Control Panel.
- The UPS service can monitor a UPS with a serial cable attached to a COM port.
- Changing a driver, such as the mouse driver, affects all users of the system.
- If a driver or service has been configured improperly, the LastKnownGood control set can be used to return to the previous settings.
- The right to log on as a service is granted through User Manager for Domains.
- Service accounts should not be required to change their password.
- A service that has been paused can be continued.
- Errors that occur when a service starts will be recorded in the Event Viewer.
- The LastKnownGood control set is created when you log on.
- The HARDWARE key is a volatile key that contains the hardware information provided by NTDETECT.COM on x86-based machines.
- Modify the registry directly only if no applet exists that can make the changes for you.
- To prevent mistakenly modifying a parameter you can put REGEDT32.EXE in read-only mode.
- The REGEDT32.EXE Find Key feature, located under Tools, can search only for keys and subkeys; REGEDIT.EXE, however, can also search for values.
- To back up the registry you must select at least one file on the drive that contains the registry.

# 4.2. Services Versus Applications

A service is different from an application in many respects. The user always interfaces directly with applications, such as a word processor, but this is not true of all services. Applications are dependent on the logged-on user; when the user logs off, the applications are closed. Services can be active with or without a user logged on to the system.

Services can act independently of the user account that is logged on. The capability to let a service run under a separate account enables the service to perform its operations even if they exceed the rights granted to the logged-on user. Figure 4.1 shows the Directory Replicator configured to start automatically using the rights of the user account DRservice.

4

**Figure 4.1.**

*The Directory Replicator using the DRservice account.*

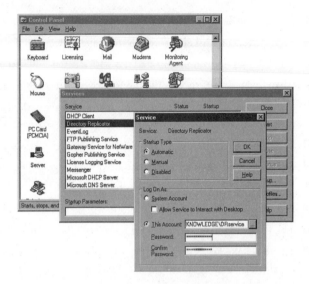

To quickly see which services are active on a system, type Net Start at the command prompt.

The user account that a service logs on as can be from the local SAM database, the SAM database from the local domain, or the SAM database of a trusted domain. The SRVANY.EXE utility included with the NT 4.0 Resource Kit enables any application to run as a service.

# 4.3. Purposes of the Registry

If you remember back to earlier versions of Windows, you no doubt can recall the various INI files. The INI, or initialization, files provided basic parameter values for the operating system and Windows applications. The parameters in the various INI files, such as WIN.INI and SYSTEM.INI, were provided in a flat structure, with individual section headings followed by the parameters and their respective values. Any one of the users sitting at the computer could modify the settings in the INI files. The settings made to the INI files would be common to all users of the system.

Although the NT registry does away with the need for INI files in general, NT maintains a limited WIN.INI and a SYSTEM.INI for older Windows applications that cannot interpret registry values.

If you took all of your INI files and structured them into a set of nested databases, you essentially would have the registry.

Unlike INI files, which can be modified by using a text editor, the registry can be modified only through applets or registry editing tools. The two tools provided with Windows NT for modifying the registry are REGEDT32.EXE and REGEDIT.EXE.

When the registry is viewed through REGEDIT.EXE, it appears to be a single database. In reality, the registry is a collection of several files, each controlling the parameters for separate registry subtrees, as demonstrated in Figure 4.2. The five major subtrees include HKEY_LOCAL_MACHINE, HKEY_CURRENT_CONFIG, HKEY_CURRENT_USER, HKEY_USERS, and HKEY_CLASSES_ROOT.

**Figure 4.2.**

*The registry viewed using* REGEDT32.EXE.

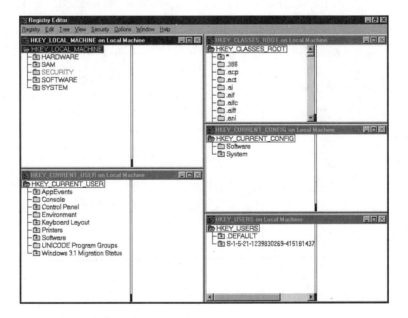

Each of the various subtrees contains a set of *hives*, sometimes called keys and subkeys. The hives each provide the controls for subsections of the subtrees.

HKEY_LOCAL_MACHINE controls the areas of NT initialized during the boot process.

HKEY_LOCAL_MACHINE contains five hives: HARDWARE, SOFTWARE, SYSTEM, SECURITY, and SAM. The names of the hives, with the exception of HARDWARE, each correspond to files located in the \%SYSTEM_ROOT%\SYSTEM32\CONFIG directory.

Each hive, with the exception of HARDWARE, has two files with corresponding names: the registry file and the log file.

The HARDWARE key does not have a corresponding file, because it is built dynamically during the boot process. Hardware detection is performed by NTDETECT.COM on x86-based systems and provided by firmware on RISC-based computers. Figure 4.3 shows the information recorded in the HARDWARE key on the author's machine.

**Figure 4.3.**

*Identified hardware is recorded in the* HARDWARE *key.*

Remember that the HARDWARE key is volatile. No file corresponds with the information held in the HARDWARE key.

The SOFTWARE hive contains the information used to control applications loaded on the system. Among the software that has settings in the registry is Windows NT itself.

The SYSTEM hive is the most critical to the proper operation of NT. The parameters assigned to services and drivers are recorded to and read from the SYSTEM hive.

A series of control sets are located within the SYSTEM hive. The SELECT key, as shown in Figure 4.4, handles the selection of the control set that is used by the system during the boot process. Whichever control set corresponds to the Current value is used in the boot process.

**Figure 4.4.**

*The* SELECT *subkey shows the use of each control set.*

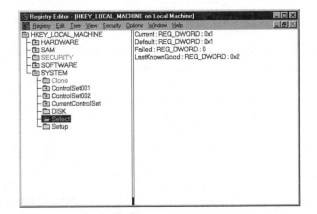

In Figure 4.4, both the Current and Default values are set to 0x1; this means they both correspond to ControlSet001. Any changes made to service or device settings will be recorded in ControlSet001.

The LastKnownGood control set has a value of 0x2 (in this case) and therefore corresponds to ControlSet002. If the system does not start properly after modifying services or drivers, the LastKnownGood control set can be used to revert to the former settings.

After you have logged on, the settings used during that system boot are recorded into the LastKnownGood. This is true even if services or drivers fail to start. To boot using the LastKnownGood control set, simply press the spacebar after selecting NT as your operating system.

The HKEY_CURRENT_CONFIG key displays the information contained in the hardware profile used during boot. Don't confuse this with the HARDWARE hive, which reflects the actual hardware configuration for the system.

Neither the SECURITY nor SAM hives can be directly modified. User Manager or User Manager for Domains is used to manage account information. The SECURITY hive controls system policies; for example, who has the right to log on as a service. The SAM (Security Account Manager) hive also includes user and group account information.

HKEY_CURRENT_USER displays the profile for the user who is currently logged on to the system locally. Changes that the user makes to areas of preference, such as colors and swapping mouse buttons, are recorded in the profile. The profile is contained in \%SystemRoot%\PROFILES\%USERNAME%\NTUSER.DAT and NTUSER.DAT.LOG. Each user who logs on locally to the machine will have a profile. Figure 4.5 shows the location of the profile that corresponds to the administrator on the author's system.

**Figure 4.5.**

*Preferential settings made by users can be stored in individual profiles. The* NTUSER.DAT *and* NTUSER.DAT.LOG *files in the Administrator directory represent the administrator's profile.*

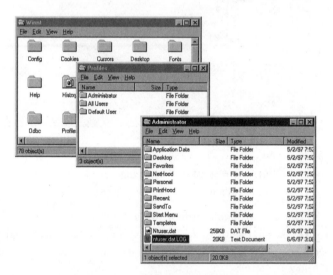

HKEY_USERS displays all active profiles. By default, only the DEFAULT profile and the profile of the user locally logged on will be displayed. Additional profiles can be loaded and modified by selecting Registry | Load Hive.

HKEY_CLASSES_ROOT maintains file associations and OLE settings. For example, when you double-click a file with an extension of .TXT it is opened within Notepad. Figure 4.6 shows the association of text files with Notepad.

**Figure 4.6.**

HKEY_CLASSES_ROOT *maintains file associations, such as text files opening with Notepad.*

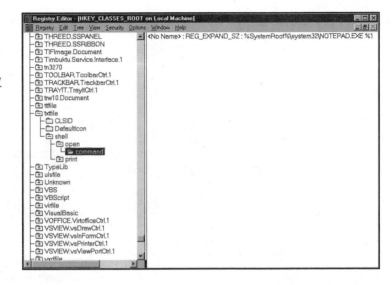

## 4.3.1. Maneuvering Through the Registry

The registry is like a labyrinth. Finding what you're looking for can seem impossible and, once you do, finding your way back to where you started can seem impossible. You access the Find Key tool in REGEDT32.EXE from the View option. As the name implies, the Find Key tool can locate only keys, not values. Use REGEDIT.EXE to search for values. In the example shown in Figure 4.7, the Winlogon service is being searched for within HKEY_LOCAL_MACHINE. The results of the search are shown in Figure 4.8.

**Figure 4.7.**

*The Find Key tool searches only for keys, not values.*

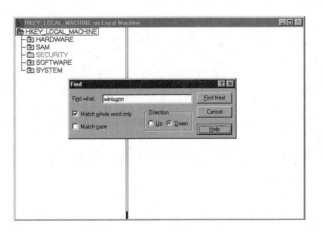

**Figure 4.8.**

*The results of the search for Winlogon.*

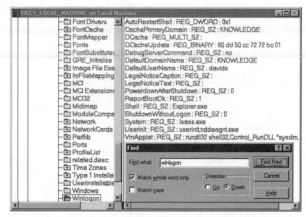

## 4.3.2. Backing Up the Registry

You can back up and restore individual areas of the registry by using the Save Key and Restore Key features in REGEDT32.EXE. This is an effective means of copying only a single area from one person's profile to another.

You can back up to tape the entire registry using the NTBACKUP utility. This, along with OEM backup systems, is the most effective means of backup, because the restoration can be performed for the entire system while online. In order to back up the registry using the NTBACKUP utility, it is necessary to back up at least one file on the same drive on which the registry resides. You select from the Backup menu the option to back up the registry.

# 4.4. Basic NT Services

Service entries are held in the registry in the subkey HKEY_LOCAL_MACHINE\SYSTEM\CurrentControlSet\Services. Figure 4.9 shows the users and groups with the rights to modify this area of the registry. The fact that they are held under HKEY_LOCAL_MACHINE indicates that all users of the system will be affected by their settings.

## 4.4.1. The Workstation Service

The Workstation service gives both NT Workstation and NT Server the capability to act as network clients and is sometimes referred to as the redirector. The Workstation service on the client is responsible for providing Server Message Block (SMB) connectivity to the Server service on the remote computer.

**Figure 4.9.**

*The users and groups with access rights to the* Services *subkey.*

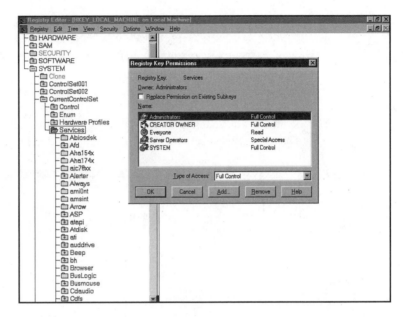

The Workstation service is configured by default to automatically start when NT is booted. Although the user can stop the Workstation service, it is important to understand that stopping the Workstation service will result in all dependent services stopping as well. Figure 4.10 shows the services dependent on the Workstation service.

**4**

**Figure 4.10.**

*Stopping the Workstation service results in the dependent services stopping as well.*

The Workstation service provides the network client capability for all NT computers regardless of whether they are running the workstation or server operating systems.

You modify the workstation parameters through the registry editor, as shown in Figure 4.11. The `LanmanWorkstation` subkey controls the Workstation service settings.

**Figure 4.11.**

*Workstation parameters are modified by editing the registry.*

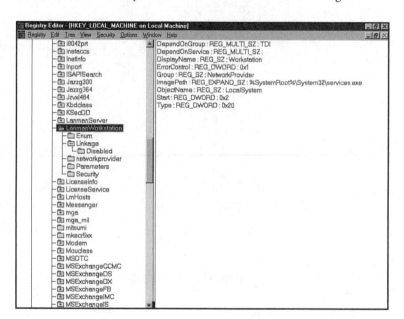

You can retrieve from the command prompt statistics of the Workstation service by running Net Statistics Workstation or Net Statistics RDR. Figure 4.12 shows the workstation statistics on `NTMASTER` redirected to a file by executing `net statistics workstation > Wsstats.txt` from the command prompt.

## 4.4.2. The Server Service

The Server service provides the capability to provide file and print services to SMB-based clients. The Server service is referenced in the registry as the `LanmanServer` and provides network services to legacy clients, such as Microsoft's LanMan.

**Figure 4.12.**

*Workstation statistics on* NTMASTER.

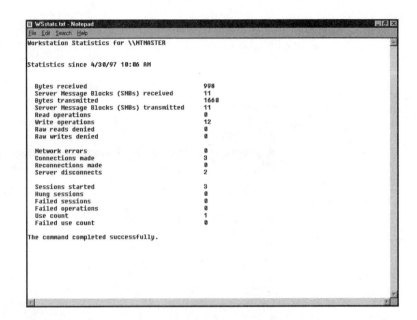

 The Server service runs on NT workstations as well as on NT servers.

**4**

Some of the basic Server service settings can be configured through the network properties. In Figure 4.13, the Server service is configured to maximize system resources as a file server.

**Figure 4.13.**

*Configuring the Server service.*

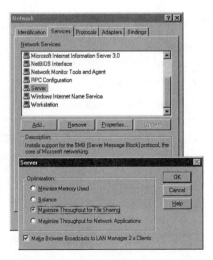

The Server service acts independently of the Workstation service on the same machine. A machine with the Server service stopped can still act as a network client; the reverse is also true.

The server statistics can be viewed in the same fashion as the workstation. Figure 4.14 shows the server statistics on NTMASTER redirected to a file by executing net statistics server > Srvstats.txt from the command prompt.

**Figure 4.14.**

*Server statistics on* NTMASTER.

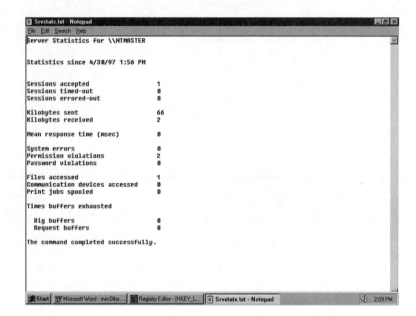

### 4.4.3. The Schedule Service

The Schedule service enables applications to be executed at scheduled times. The Schedule service works in conjunction with the AT.EXE command or the WINAT.EXE utility found on the NT 4.0 Resource kit.

A common usage of the Schedule service in conjunction with the AT.EXE command is to launch the NT backup program, NTBACKUP.EXE. Figure 4.15 shows the AT.EXE command being used to launch a user-created batch file that will execute the NT backup program with the necessary parameters. The execution of the batch file will be repeated every Monday through Friday.

**Figure 4.15.**

*The* AT.EXE *command being used to execute a batch file.*

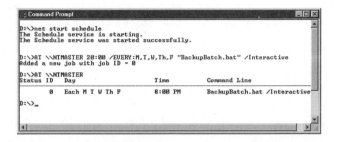

**Test Tip**

The NT 4.0 Resource kit includes a graphical version of the AT.EXE command called WINAT.EXE.

## 4.4.4. The Alerter Service

The Alerter service is used to generate administrative notifications. The Alerter service can generate alerts based on events, such as a disk nearing capacity, a printer running out of paper, or a shutdown request being issued to the server.

Server Manager or Performance Monitor is used to define which users or computers will receive the administrative alerts. Figure 4.16 shows the Server Manager configured to send the alerts to the user DAVIDS and the computer NTMASTER.

**4**

**Figure 4.16.**

*Using Server Manager to configure where to deliver alerts.*

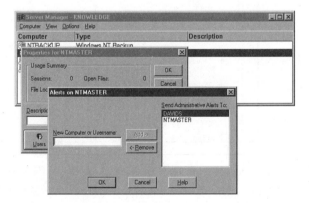

**Test Tip**

The Alerter service generates the alert but depends on the Messenger service to perform the delivery.

# 4.5. Understanding Registry Entries

NT uses the settings in the registry to control how each of the individual services is configured. The registry lets NT know where the executable is located, initialization settings, dependencies, and error reporting levels.

> Viewing the registry with REGEDIT.EXE instead of REGEDT32.EXE lets you search on values as well as on keys and subkeys.

The configuration settings for the Alerter service are provided in Figure 4.17 as an example.

**Figure 4.17.**

*The Alerter service settings in the registry.*

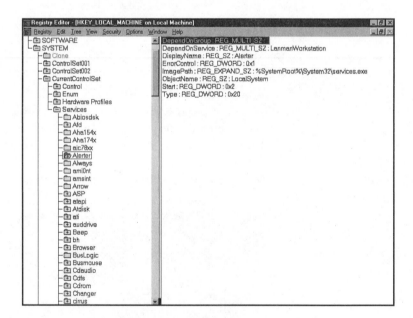

The Alerter service does not have an entry in the DependOnGroup setting. Services with an entry in DependOnGroup require that at least one of the services listed in the DependOnGroup setting start before the service starts.

The DependOnService entry shows that the LanmanWorkstation service must be started before the Alerter service is started.

The DisplayName entry value is set to Alerter. This is how the service name will appear when viewed through the applets.

The ErrorControl value is set to 0x1. If the Alerter service failed to start, an entry would be recorded in the event log, but the system would continue to initialize. Services with an ErrorControl value of 0x0 report no errors. Those with ErrorControl values of 0x2 or 0x3 will record the error and also attempt to reinitialize the system using the LastKnownGood configuration. A value of 0x2 will continue on error while a value of 0x3 will cause a bug check to be run.

The ImagePath entry tells NT where the actual executable is located. In the case of the Alerter it is one of many commands that are internal to SERVICES.EXE.

The StartValue of 0x2 shows that the Alerter is set to automatically start. Values lower than 0x2 are usually reserved for drivers; for example, the driver needed to access the boot partition would be assigned a value of 0x0 and be called by the NTLDR file during the boot phase. Those with a value of 0x1, such as the video driver, will be called during the initialization phase. Services with a StartValue of 0x3 require a manual start by the user or another process. Disabled services and drivers receive a StartValue of 0x4.

The TypeValue is set to 0x20. This means that the service will be capable of launching within the same Win32 process space as other services. A service like the Domain Name Server has a value of 0x10 and runs in its own process space. An advantage to having a service run in its own process space is that it can be tracked independently in Performance Monitor, as shown in Figure 4.18. Services internal to SERVICES.EXE are tracked collectively under services.

**Figure 4.18.**
*Performance Monitor set up to track services.*

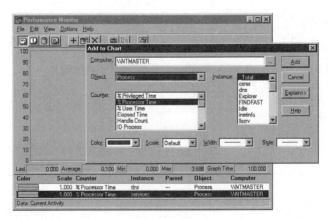

## 4.5.1.  The Messenger Service

The Messenger service is used to send and receive network messages. For example, the administrator might want to send a message to all users on the server before shutting it down. The administrator can send a message using the options in Server Manager, as shown in Figure 4.19.

**Figure 4.19.**

*Server Manager can be used to generate a message.*

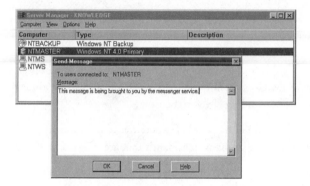

The message that is delivered to the users by the Messenger service is shown in Figure 4.20. The computer on which a message is to be received must also be running the Messenger service.

**Figure 4.20.**

*The message as it appears to the user.*

## 4.6. Configuring Services

The Services applet under the Control Panel enables the administrator to control the startup of services. Figure 4.21 shows the status of services on NTMASTER.

**Figure 4.21.**

*The status of services on NTMASTER.*

Server Manager can also be used to configure services on remote computers.

## 4.6.1. Start Options

The system administrator can define which services will be initialized when NT boots. There are three service start options: automatic, manual, and disabled.

A service that is configured to start automatically will be launched when NT boots. The user does not need to log on to the computer to activate the service. The Server service is an example of a service that is configured to start automatically. Figure 4.22 shows the configuration of the startup parameters.

**Figure 4.22.**

*The Server service is configured to start automatically.*

**4**

The settings made through the Services applet are recorded in the registry, as shown in Figure 4.23. The start value set to 0x2 shows the service will be started automatically. A value of 0x3 represents manual, and 0x4 represents disabled.

Services that are set to start manually can be started by the user or by another service that calls it as a dependency. A disabled service cannot be started manually by the user or called by another service. An administrator can choose to disable a restricted service on an NT workstation to prevent the user from activating it manually.

**Figure 4.23.**

*The registry holds the service initialization settings.*

## 4.6.2. Configuring Service Accounts

Because NT supports discretionary access control, even the actions of services are governed by system security. By default, most services are configured to run with the security of the system account. The system account is not a configurable user account.

Some services will require access beyond just the local system and as such require an account that can have privileges on more than just the local computer. The Directory Replicator service requires an account to be used that has privileges at both the Import and Export servers.

The account to be used as a service account requires special configuration. The account must be granted the right to log on as a service. This is an advanced right granted through policies in User Manager. Figure 4.24 shows the configuration of the DRservice account.

Be sure to clear the Change Password at Next Logon checkbox that requires the user to change the password at next logon and check the Password Never Expires checkbox.

**Figure 4.24.**

*Assigning the DRservice account the right to log on as a service.*

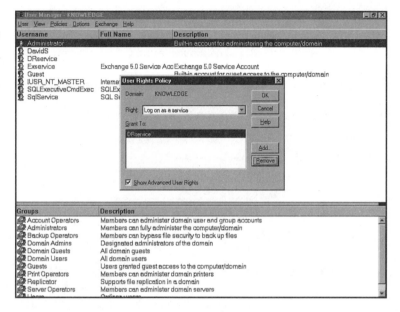

Instead of granting to each individual service account the right to log on as a service, a better administrative practice is to grant the right to a group and then make each service account a member of the group.

Some services require that a common service account be assigned on all servers. For example, when configuring MS Exchange Server, all servers within the same site or grouping must share a common service account name and password. When a common account is required it is necessary to choose a global account instead of a local one.

## 4.6.3. Starting, Stopping, and Pausing Services

There are several ways to start, stop and pause services. There are two occasions on which it might be necessary to manually start a service that was configured to start automatically:

- If a service configured to start automatically was dependent on a member of a dependency group that failed to start, the administrator must manually start the service after correcting the dependency service.

- If the administrator has modified the configuration of a service, she could stop and start that service manually in order to apply the new values.

Starting, stopping, and pausing services can be performed from the command prompt or from within several applets. Figure 4.25 shows the Netlogon service being stopped, started, paused, and continued from the command prompt.

**Figure 4.25.**

*Controlling the Netlogon service from the command prompt.*

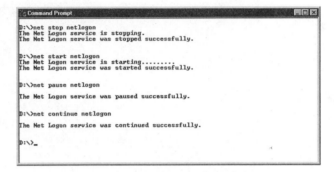

```
Command Prompt                                                    _ □ ✕
D:\>net stop netlogon
The Net Logon service is stopping.
The Net Logon service was stopped successfully.

D:\>net start netlogon
The Net Logon service is starting.........
The Net Logon service was started successfully.

D:\>net pause netlogon

The Net Logon service was paused successfully.

D:\>net continue netlogon

The Net Logon service was continued successfully.

D:\>_
```

Pausing a service is significantly different from stopping it. A paused service continues to perform some of its basic functions. When the Netlogon server on the PDC is paused it continues to provide update notification to the BDCs but does not validate user requests. When the Server service is paused, the users who are currently logged on remain attached but new users cannot attach to the server. Because some services would provide no benefit in a paused condition not every service can be paused.

> The Netlogon service on the PDC can be paused to let it catch up on synchronizing the BDCs.

You return a paused service to its active state by continuing the service. The Server Manager is being used to continue the Server service in Figure 4.26.

If a service is set to a disabled state, it cannot be started or continued. In Figure 4.27, the Messenger service cannot be started because it has been disabled on NTMASTER. It must be returned to a start value of automatic or manual before it can be started.

## 4.6.4. Services in the Registry

Service entries are held in the registry in the subkey HKEY_LOCAL_MACHINE\SYSTEM\ CurrentControlSet\Services. Figure 4.9, earlier in the chapter, shows the users and groups with the rights to modify this area of the registry.

**Figure 4.26.**
*The Server service can be continued through Server Manager.*

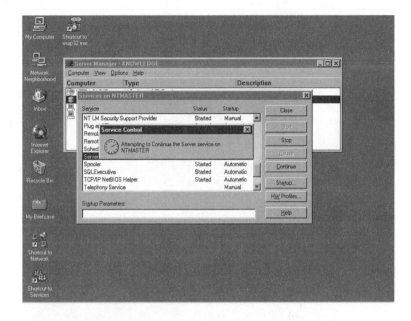

**Figure 4.27.**
*Disabled services cannot be manually started.*

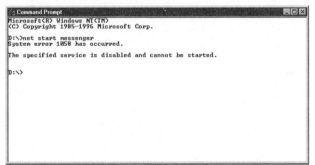

## 4.6.5.  Identifying Service Dependencies

A *dependency* is a service or driver that must be started in order to allow another to initialize. The Alerter service has as a dependency service the LanmanWorkstation. If the Workstation service were to fail to start, the Alerter service could not be started.

The Workstation service also has dependencies. The Workstation service dependencies are slightly different however; it has a value for the DependOnGroup setting but not for the DependOnService. Figure 4.28 shows the registry settings for the Workstation service.

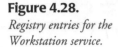

**Figure 4.28.**

*Registry entries for the Workstation service.*

The DependOnGroup value is set to TDI. At least one member of the TDI group must initialize successfully before the Workstation service can be started. The TDI group includes the set of network protocols, such as TCP/IP and NWLink, that interface with the Session layer.

Obviously, the failure of a single service or driver could affect several other services.

# 4.7. Configuring Hardware Drivers

The best way to configure drivers for new hardware or to update drivers for existing hardware is to use the applets provided for this use in the Control Panel.

## 4.7.1. SCSI Drivers

You can add and remove SCSI drivers through the SCSI Adapters applet in the Control Panel. The SCSI applet can also be used to add IDE CD-ROM controllers or removable media controllers that qualify as mass storage devices. Figure 4.29 shows the configured SCSI drivers on NTMASTER.

If an additional SCSI adapter were installed on NTMASTER it would be necessary to install the appropriate driver. In Figure 4.30, an additional SCSI driver is being installed on NTMASTER.

**Figure 4.29.**
*SCSI drivers configured on NTMASTER.*

**Figure 4.30.**
*An additional SCSI driver is installed on NTMASTER.*

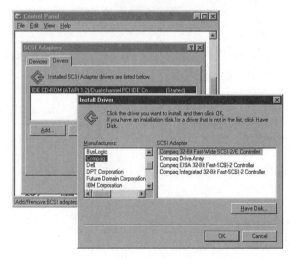

The driver configuration is saved in the `Services` subkey of the CurrentControlSet in the registry. In Figure 4.31, the `cpqfws2e` key holds the values for the Compaq 32-Bit Fast-Wide SCSI-2/E driver that was just added. The Start value of `0` shows that the driver will be initialized at boot time.

**Figure 4.31.**

*The registry holds the driver configuration settings.*

**Test Tip**

If the system fails to start because of an improperly configured driver, you can revert to the older configuration by choosing the Last Known Good configuration.

## 4.7.2. Tape Drivers

Tape drivers are installed through the Tape Devices applet in the Control Panel. The NT Backup utility is dependent on a tape device being installed, but it cannot install the driver itself.

If the tape device that is installed on your computer is on the HCL, it is possible to have the applet detect the tape device automatically. Tape device drivers can also be installed manually, as shown in Figure 4.32.

As with the SCSI adapter drivers, tape driver settings are recorded in the registry.

## 4.7.3. Configuring Mouse Drivers

The mouse applet in Control Panel enables the user to install and configure the pointing device. Individual users can personalize mouse functions, such as left-right buttons; however, the driver will be the same for all users of the same system. If the mouse type is not automatically detected, as in Figure 4.33, the system administrator can select the driver manually.

**Figure 4.32.**
*Manually installing a tape device driver.*

**Figure 4.33.**
*Configuring the mouse driver.*

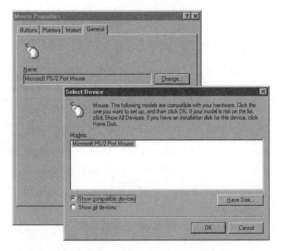

4

## 4.7.4. Configuring the UPS Service

The UPS, or Uninterruptible Power Source, service provides the capability of monitoring a UPS by means of a serial cable connected to a COM port. The administrator must configure the UPS settings based on the hardware configuration.

The UPS service has the capability to execute a command file before performing a shutdown of the system. The command must complete within 30 seconds. Figure 4.34 shows the UPS service configured to be monitored on COM2 and a command called GoingDown.bat being executed on shutdown.

**Figure 4.34.**
*UPS configuration dialog box.*

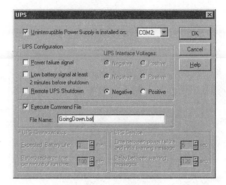

Use the NOSERIALMOUSE parameter in your boot.ini file to prevent NT from scanning the port attached to your UPS during the boot process.

## 4.7.5. Diagnosing Service Start Failures

The Event Viewer is an excellent tool for diagnosing the cause of service failures. The Event Viewer enables the administrator to view the service startup events in the system log. One of the most common reasons for a service failing to start is because the service account password is wrong. Figure 4.35 shows the message that is received when the Directory Replicator service is configured with an incorrect password.

**Figure 4.35.**
*An incorrect service account password.*

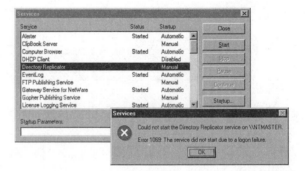

The information in the error message is also recorded in the system log, as shown in Figure 4.36.

**Figure 4.36.**

*Service start failures are recorded in the system log.*

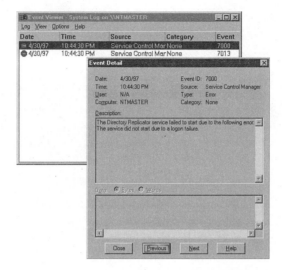

There's an old adage: "Don't kill the messenger for the message." It's a good thing to keep in mind when diagnosing service failures. Sometimes, one or more services fail to start when a single dependency service fails to start. Too frequently, administrators begin by trying to reconfigure the wrong service. If more than one service has failed to start, tracing the dependencies to the root cause of failure is important.

In Figure 4.37 the Alerter service failed to start because a dependency service, the workstation, failed to start. The workstation failed because all protocol bindings to the Workstation service were disabled.

**Figure 4.37.**

*The Alerter service reports a dependency failure.*

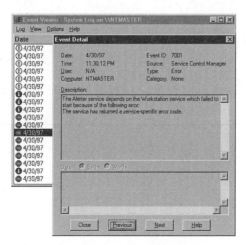

4

The Alerter service is dependent on the Workstation service starting successfully. The administrator should now investigate why the Workstation service failed to start rather than waste time troubleshooting the Alerter service.

When searching for the lowest-level dependency, go to the first failure after the Event Log service was started.

# 4.8. Lab

This lab will help in your learning by testing you on the information presented in this chapter, as well as by giving you exercises to hone your skills. You can find answers to the review questions in Appendix B, "Answers to Review Questions."

## 4.8.1. Review Questions

### Question 1

Based on Figure 4.38, on which of the following services is the Messenger service dependent?

A. Alerter

B. Workstation

C. NetBIOS

D. Server

**Figure 4.38.**

*Exhibit for Question 1.*

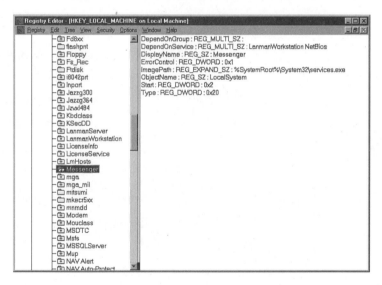

### Question 2

Which of the following StartValue settings would be used to designate a service as disabled?

A. 0x0

B. 0x1

C. `0x2`

D. `0x3`

E. `0x4`

## Question 3

Which of the following statements are true regarding pausing the Server service?

A. All users will be immediately disconnected from the server.

B. The Alerter service will generate a message telling all users to disconnect from the server.

C. Additional users will not be allowed to attach to the server.

D. The Workstation service will be paused automatically.

## Question 4

The administrator of Corporation B has paused the Server service on NTMASTER. Which of the following methods can be used to continue the Server service without disconnecting users?

A. Continue the service through Server Manager.

B. Continue the service using the Services applet.

C. Continue the service by typing `Net Start Server` from the command prompt.

D. Continue the service from the command prompt by typing `Net Continue Server`.

## Question 5

Corporation B has a total of three domains: DomainA, DomainB, and DomainC. Both DomainA and DomainB trust DomainC. When configuring Microsoft SQL Server on an NT Member Server in DomainC, the administrator is asked to provide a service account name and password.

Given the domain configuration described above, in which of the domains can the service account exist?

A. DomainA

B. DomainB

C. DomainC

D. Any of the domains

## Question 6

Which of the following services is required to run NTBACKUP.EXE at specified times using AT.EXE or WINAT.EXE from the resource kit?

A. Directory Replicator

B. Alerter

C. Messenger

D. Schedule

## Question 7

Using Server Manager, the administrator of NTBACKUP has configured alerts to be sent to NTMASTER. Alerts that should have been received appear not to have been sent. Which of the following services should the administrator confirm are running?

A. Messenger

B. Schedule

C. Signal

D. Alerter

4

## Question 8

The account assigned to the directory replicator service requires the right to log on as a service. Where does the administrator confirm that the account has the right to log on as a service?

A. Server Manager

B. Control Panel, Services

C. User Manager for Domains

D. Any of the above methods will work

## Question 9

The administrator has loaded a new service, WEBNET, on the server. After rebooting the server, the administrator notices that the service did not start. No error messages were displayed or recorded in the event log. The administrator next attempts to start the service from the command line by typing Net Start WEBNET at the command prompt. The service starts without error.

Why did the service not initialize when the server rebooted?

A. The service was set to Disabled.

B. The service was set to Manual.

C. The service was set to Automatic.

D. The service account was not properly configured.

## Question 10

Which of the following procedures would best enable the PDC to concentrate efforts on synchronizing the SAM database with the Backup Domain Controllers?

A. Stopping the Server service

B. Pausing the Server service

C. Stopping the Netlogon service

D. Pausing the Netlogon service

## Question 11

Which of the following Windows NT registry subkeys manages the association of files and applications?

A. `HKEY_CURRENT_CONFIG`

B. `HKEY_CURRENT_USER`

C. `HKEY_LOCAL_MACHINE`

D. `HKEY_CLASSES_ROOT`

## Question 12

When is the LastKnownGood control set created?

A. During the installation of NT Server

B. When the first user logs on to NT Server

C. When a user logs on following a reboot of the system

D. When the repair disk is updated

## Question 13

What is the fastest, most effective means of backing up the entire registry?

A. Using the Save Key feature in REGEDT32

B. Mirroring the registry by implementing the NT Directory Replicator

C. The repair disk utility

D. The NTBACKUP tape utility

## Question 14

Which of the following registry hives referenced from within `HKEY_LOCAL_MACHINE` do not correspond with a physical file in `\%SYSTEM_ROOT%\SYSTEM32\CONFIG`?

A. `HARDWARE`

B. `SOFTWARE`

C. `SYSTEM`

D. `SECURITY`

E. `SAM`

## Question 15

The administrator of an NT Server is changing the system's mouse and mouse driver. Where will this change be recorded and who will it affect?

A. `HKEY_CURRENT_USER`

B. `HKEY_LOCAL_MACHINE`

C. Only the administrator will be affected

D. All users of the system will be affected

## Question 16

The administrator of an NT Server is left-handed and prefers to have functions of the right and left mouse buttons reversed. If the administrator swaps the mouse button functions, where will the change be recorded and who will be affected?

A. `HKEY_CURRENT_USER`

B. `HKEY_LOCAL_MACHINE`

C. Only the administrator will be affected

D. All users of the system will be affected

## Question 17

A user named Rumplestiltskin logs on at the NT 4.0 Server. Which of the following files would represent the profile created automatically when the user changes his preferences?

A. `RUMPLE000` and `RUMPLE000.LOG`

B. `NTUSER.DAT` and `NTUSER.DAT.LOG`

C. `RUMPLESTILTSKIN.DAT` and `RUMPLESTILTSKIN.LOG`

D. `PROFILE.DAT` and `PROFILE.LOG`

## Question 18

After logging on at a BDC, the administrator receives a message that at least one service or driver failed to start. In response, she shuts down the system and boots using the LastKnownGood configuration.

Upon reboot the administrator receives the same error message. Why did the LastKnownGood control set not fix the problem?

A. The LastKnownGood control set is only valid on the PDC.

B. The rdisk utility must be run before using the LastKnownGood control set.

C. The LastKnownGood control set contained the improperly configured settings.

D. The LastKnownGood control set could not be located.

## Question 19

After the administrator has updated the network card parameters for the NT Server, the system fails to start. The administrator must get the system back up in the shortest amount of time. The administrator boots from the NT Setup Disk and initializes the option for Repair. The administrator then uses the Emergency Repair Disk to restore the settings in the `HARDWARE` key.

Which of the following best describes the administrator's solution?

A. The solution is excellent. It is the fastest way to restore the system settings.

B. The solution is good. It will work; however, it is not the fastest way to restore the settings.

C. The solution is poor. The solution will not work.

## Question 20

What is the mostly likely cause of several services failing to start properly?

A. The user logging on to the system lacks proper rights.

B. The services are all members of the same DependOnGroup.

C. The services are in a chain of services dependent on a single service that has failed.

D. The SYSTEM hive cannot be accessed.

## 4.8.2. Exercises

### Exercise 4.1

Using a networked computer running Windows NT Workstation or Server, go to Control Panel, Services, and pause the Server service. From another computer on the network, try to access a shared resource on the first computer. Can you access it? Why not? Can you access other computers from the first computer?

Explanation: You will not be able to access any resources located on the first computer from another computer on the network. The Server service is necessary to provide network access. You will still be able to access network resources from the first computer because this ability is provided via the Workstation service.

### Exercise 4.2

Open the registry using REGEDT32.EXE. Create a logon message to be displayed whenever anyone logs on to your computer. Enter a value for both LegalNoticeCaption and LegalNoticeText of type REG_SZ.

Explanation: Under HKEY_LOCAL_MACHINE\Software\Microsoft\Windows NT\ CurrentVersion\Winlogon, enter the following for the title of your logon message box:

```
Name:    LegalNoticeCaption
Type:    REG_SZ
Value:    Enter the text you wish displayed
```

Now enter the value for the logon text message itself as

```
Name:    LegalNoticeText
Type:    REG_SZ
Value:    Enter the text of the message to be displayed
```

### Exercise 4.3

Use Server Manager to configure your computer to send you alerts. Be sure to use the Services applet to verify that both the Alerter and Messenger services are started.

Explanation: Under Server Manager, select the computer you want to generate the alert messages by double-clicking it. Then select the Alerts button and enter the destination for the alert. If either the Alerter service or the Messenger service is not running, alert messages will not be sent.

4

## Exercise 4.4

Use the registry editor of your choice to configure autologon on your computer.

HINT: Be sure to enter domain name, username, and password for this to work.

Explanation: Under `HKEY_LOCAL_MACHINE\Software\Microsoft\Windows NT\`
`CurrentVersion\Winlogon`, enter the following for the title of your logon message box:

```
Name:    AutoAdminLogon
Type:    REG_SZ
Value:   1
Name:    DefaultDomainName
Type:    REG_SZ
Value:    Enter the name of your domain
Name:    DefaultUserName
Type:    REG_SZ
Value:    Enter the name of the user to be logged on
Name:    DefaultPassword
Type:    REG_SZ
Value:    Enter the password of the user to be logged on
```

# Day 5

# Managing Local File Systems

*by David Schaer and Theresa Hadden*

## 5.1. Overview

The choice of which file system or systems to use on a computer will be determined by many factors. These factors include the role of the computer, available disk space, desired disk performance, and whether you have a dual-boot machine.

### 5.1.1. Objectives

Operating systems use file systems to store and retrieve files in an ordered fashion. NT 4.0 supports three file systems: FAT, NTFS, and CDFS. In addition to choosing a file system, you must also understand how to manage your hard disk partitions. This chapter covers the following topics:

- Choice of file system
- Configuring fault tolerance
- Understanding the role of RAID and volume sets

### 5.1.2. Fast Facts

The following list of facts is a concise picture of the information presented in this chapter. It acts as both an overview for the chapter and as a study aid to help you do any last-minute cramming.

- NT Server supports FAT, NTFS, and CDFS file systems.
- NTFS is the only file system to provide local security.
- The default Access Control List (ACL) is initially set to Everyone Full Control.

- FAT is the only file system accessible to DOS, Windows 95, OS/2, and NT.
- FAT does not provide any form of local security.
- Long and short filenames can be created on both FAT and NTFS when NT is the active operating system.
- Compression can be applied only to files and directories on NTFS volumes.
- RISC-based computers require a minimum of a 2MB FAT system partition.
- Intel-based machines can run with NTFS as the only file system.
- No Access invalidates any other rights that a user is granted individually or through group membership.
- When files are moved between folders on the same NTFS partition they maintain their security settings (ACL).
- By default, compressing a directory compresses the files within it but not the subdirectories.
- The HPFS file system is not supported in NT 4.0.
- The Convert.exe utility converts only from FAT to NTFS. It is a one-way procedure.
- To convert the system or boot partition you must schedule the conversion for the next reboot of the system.
- Implementing file-level security or compression on FAT is not supported.
- LIST is the minimum set of NTFS permissions required to share a directory.
- DIR /X displays both the long and short filenames.
- A single physical disk can have a maximum of four partitions.
- Only one partition can be marked as active. Only primary partitions can be set as active.
- Partitions can be formatted as either FAT or NTFS.
- Up to four logical drives can be created within a single extended partition.
- Only one extended partition can exist per physical disk.
- The Disk Administrator is the major NT tool for managing disks and partitions.
- Large cluster sizes are a benefit when using large files.
- A 2TB partition is the theoretical maximum size with NTFS.
- When you change the assigned drive letter for a volume or CD-ROM the change takes place immediately.
- Configuration changes must be committed before you format new partitions.
- Volume sets do not increase performance.

- Volume sets can be extended only if they are formatted as, or converted to, NTFS.
- Volume sets can reside on 1 to 32 physical disks.
- The system or boot partitions cannot be part of a stripe or volume set.
- When you lose a single disk containing any portion of a volume set the data is lost across the entire volume set.
- Stripe sets cannot be extended.
- Stripe sets must be created from equal amounts of free space from two or more physical disks.
- Stripe sets without parity can be created from portions of 2 to 32 physical disks; stripe sets with parity require at least 3 physical disks to a maximum of 32.
- Stripe sets provide the best read/write disk performance.
- Stripe sets without parity do not provide fault tolerance.
- Data in stripe sets is written 64KB at a time.
- The disk configuration can, and should, be saved to floppy disk.

# 5.2. File System Basics

It is important not to confuse file systems with operating systems. Not all file systems are supported by all operating systems. For example, the DOS and Windows 95 operating systems support only the FAT file system, and OS/2 supports FAT and HPFS. The NTFS file system is supported only by the NT operating system.

5

Don't confuse file system with operating systems. FAT is the only file system that is supported across DOS, Windows 95, OS/2, and NT.

Applications running in environment subsystems under NT will be able to access files on FAT, NTFS, and CDFS. When you format a partition from within NT it defaults to the FAT file system unless you specify otherwise.

## 5.2.1. Sometimes FAT Is Good

You might have heard people say that a little fat is a good thing. The same can often be said of a little FAT, or more specifically, a little FAT partition for storing the NT boot and system files. Formatting the boot and system partitions with FAT in order to simplify the repair of corrupted files is sometimes advantageous.

FAT is the only file system that is accessible to DOS, Windows 95, NT, and OS/2. By booting from a DOS system disk you can access the FAT partitions that were formatted under OS/2 and NT. This is one of the reasons why the FAT file system is not recommended for partitions that require high security levels.

When compared with NTFS, the FAT file system structure has very little overhead. If none of the special features of NTFS are required, FAT is recommended for partitions of 400MB or less. By design, a FAT volume cannot exceed 4GB.

Although a DOS-based workstation can only access the FAT file system locally the file system in use at the file server can be NTFS.

Sometimes FAT is not only good it is necessary. This is true for RISC computers. The system partition on RISC computers must be formatted with FAT because RISC computers boot from firmware and only initialize the drivers for FAT. Only the system partition on RISC-based computers must be FAT; the boot partition and partitions holding programs and data can be NTFS.

It might sound backward at first but NT boots from the system partition and then accesses the boot partition.

## 5.2.2. Long and Short FAT Filenames

Even though NT uses the same 16-bit FAT structure as DOS, it is capable of supporting long filenames. When a file is created on a FAT volume under NT both a long and short filename can be created. The short filename follows the standard 8.3 character naming conventions, whereas the long filename can be up to 256 characters including multiple spaces and periods. A file called It is great to be an MCSE created through NT on a FAT volume would have a short filename of ITISGR~1.

To display both long and short filenames from the command prompt type
DIR /X.

The short filename would take up one directory entry and the long filename would take up two directory entries, one for every 13 characters. When the system is booted into DOS or when a DOS-based application is running in NT only the short filename is displayed.

> DOS-based file repair utilities can incorrectly identify, or fail to identify, the long filenames and potentially corrupt data.

A short filename created automatically from a long filename can become difficult to properly identify. Creating the file It is green eggs and ham for breakfast in the same directory as It is great to be an MCSE would yield the short filename ITISGR~2 because the first six legal characters of both filenames are identical. Correlating the short filename to the long filename becomes more difficult following the fourth file that results in the same six-character short name. After the fourth iteration with the same results the system hashes characters to form a unique short name. If the file ITISGR~4 already existed, creating a file called It is Greek to me in the same directory would generate IT558B~1. Figure 5.1 demonstrates how short filenames can become cryptic.

**Figure 5.1.**

*Short filenames can become cryptic.*

```
D:\demodir>dir /x
 Volume in drive D is NTSRV40
 Volume Serial Number is 1753-19FF

 Directory of D:\demodir

05/03/97  11:38p    <DIR>                     .
05/03/97  11:38p    <DIR>                     ..
05/03/97  11:39p              1 ITISGR~1      It is great to be an MCSE
05/03/97  11:39p              1 ITISGR~2      It is green eggs and ham
for breakfast
05/03/97  11:40p              1 ITISGR~3      It is growing by leaps an
d bounds
05/03/97  11:43p              1 ITISGR~4      It is grilled not fried
05/03/97  11:44p              1 IT558B~1      It is Greek to me
              7 File(s)          5 bytes
                      80,879,616 bytes free

D:\demodir>_
```

5

> You won't be expected to be able to convert long filenames beyond the fourth iteration.

The ability to create long filenames on FAT volumes can be toggled off in the registry. By setting the value of the HKEY_LOCAL_MACHINE\System\CurrentControlSet\ Control\Win31FileSystem subkey to 1, no additional long filenames could be generated on the FAT partitions.

### 5.2.3. FAT Deficiencies

One reason not to use FAT is because the FAT file system provides no form of local security. This means that you cannot selectively control access to files and directories on FAT partitions. Anyone who can log on to the machine locally will have full control of all files and directories. In addition, if you move files from an NTFS partition to a FAT partition, the file loses its permissions.

If you use compression methods, such as DoubleSpace and DiskSpace, NT will not be able to access the volume. When you move files from NTFS volumes to FAT volumes the files are no longer compressed.

# 5.3. NTFS Overview

The New Technology File System (NTFS) provides a significant improvement over the FAT file system. Under NT 4.0 NTFS provides both long and short filenames, security, file compression, speed, and recoverability. NTFS can be used exclusively on x86-based systems that will run only NT. RISC-based computers require at least a 2MB FAT partition to hold the boot files. Computers configured to dual boot DOS or Windows 95 must have at least one FAT volume.

> Regardless of third-party products that might make NTFS volumes accessible under DOS, for purposes of the exam NT is the only operating system that can access NTFS volumes.

### 5.3.1. Long and Short NTFS Filenames

Long filename support is also provided on NTFS volumes. Like those on FAT partitions they can contain up to 256 characters and contain multiple spaces and periods.

Short filenames are generated automatically in order to allow DOS- and OS/2-based computers to access the same data. The short filenames are generated based on the same rules as those of FAT volumes. Although it is possible to disable the short filename generation on NTFS volumes this would render filenames created outside the 8.3 character structure invisible to DOS and OS/2 applications. Long filenames would be visible from a Windows 95-based computer from across the network.

The short filename generation would not enable DOS, Windows for Workgroups, or OS/2-based systems to access the NTFS partition on a local basis. Short names generated on FAT volumes would be locally accessible to these machines; the short filenames generated on NTFS partitions would be available only from across the network.

# 5.4. Managing NTFS Security

One of the major benefits of using NTFS is that it makes available the capability of local security. By implementing NTFS security you can control which users and groups have access to files and directories on local NTFS volumes.

Each of the objects (files, directories) that can be protected through local security will receive an access control list (ACL). The ACL contains the listing of users and groups allowed to access an object, along with the specific rights they have been permitted. The individual user and group names in the ACL are called access control entries (ACEs).

The local security provided by NTFS can augment the network security implemented on shared directories. Chapter 9, "NT Server 4.0 Network Clients," details the integration of network security.

## 5.4.1. NTFS File Permissions

The default permissions on NTFS files are Everyone, Full Control. This means that by default the NTFS security is set to be most permissive. Figure 5.2 shows the default permissions assigned to NTFSfile.txt.txt.

**Figure 5.2.**
*The default permissions assigned to* NTFSfile. txt.txt.

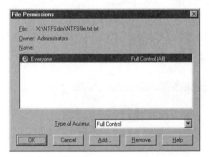

The right of Full Control encompasses all six file access rights. The six rights can also be assigned individually by selecting Special Access as shown in Figure 5.3.

**Figure 5.3.**

*Assigning Special Access file rights.*

The six rights displayed in Figure 5.3 provide the user or group with a different capability. A user or group can be assigned all, none, or any combination of the rights.

Read (R):               Grants the right to view the contents of a file.

Write (W):              Grants the right to change the contents of a file.

Execute (X):            Grants the right to launch an executable file.

Delete (D):             Grants the right to delete the entire file.

Change Permissions (P): Grants the right to modify the access control entries in the file's ACL.

Take Ownership (O):     Grants the right to assign oneself as the owner of the file. The owner has the right to change permissions. The Administrators group has the global right to take ownership regardless of assignments.

In order to simplify administration, predefined groupings of file rights can be assigned. As shown in Figure 5.4, granting Read access from the File Permissions screen also assigns the right to Execute. Granting Change access permits Read, Write, Execute, and Delete access.

**Figure 5.4.**

*Granting Read access also grants Execute access.*

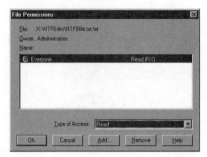

NTFS security supports the No Access right. When No Access is assigned it supersedes all other rights. Even if users have been granted rights individually or based upon group membership the rights will be fully revoked if they or a group of which they are members has been assigned No Access.

Figure 5.5 demonstrates how an administrator can assign Full control to Everyone but still restrict guests of the KNOWLEDGE domain from having access to the file NTFSfile.txt.txt.

**Figure 5.5.**
*Members of KNOWL-
EDGE/GUESTS will
be explicitly denied
access to the file*
NTFSfile.txt.txt.

Granting the No Access right for a file to Everyone will prevent all users from accessing the file. This will preclude even the administrators from accessing the file.

As an alternative to using the GUI interface to assign file permissions, you can use the command-line utility cacls both to display the access control list (ACL) for a particular file or to change it. You may specify more than one file or user in the command, making this a useful tool to be used in login scripts.

## 5.4.2. NTFS Directory Permissions

When an NTFS volume is created the root directory is given an ACL that gives Everyone full control. When a new subdirectory is created, it receives, or inherits, a copy of the ACL from the parent directory. If the default permission of Full Control has not been changed, then the new subdirectory receives all of the rights shown in Figure 5.6. Although the names of permissions are the same as those granted to files, the function of each is different.

**Figure 5.6.**

*The folder rights encompassed by Full Control.*

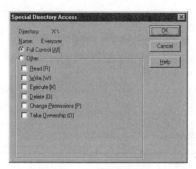

The options available when granting Special Directory Access are

| | |
|---|---|
| Read (R): | Grants only the right to view the name of the directory and the names of files within the directory. It does not grant the ability to read contents of files within the directory. |
| Write (W): | Grants the right to add files to the directory. It does not grant the ability to write to the files within the directory. |
| Execute (X): | Grants only the right to maneuver through the directory to subdirectories below. If you have rights to a subdirectory but not to a directory in its path you will not be able to switch to the subdirectory without typing its entire path. |
| Delete (D): | Grants the right to delete the directory itself. This right will not be permitted if you do not have the right to delete the files within the directory. |
| Change Permissions (P): | Grants the right to modify the access control entries in the directory's ACL. |
| Take Ownership (O): | Grants the right to make oneself the owner of the directory. |

You can individually select the directory rights by selecting Special Directory Access or by selecting any of the predefined groups of rights under the Security tab of the directory's properties. Setting Special File Access modifies the default access control list generated for files copied into or created in the directory. In Figure 5.7 the directory NTFSdirx is marked as Full Control on the directory and RX as the default file ACL. Notice how the rights are now reflected as Everyone, Special Access (ALL)(RX). The (ALL) represents the right of Full Control on the directory, and the (RX) represents the default file ACL settings.

**Figure 5.7.**

*The default ACL for files created in or copied to NTFSdirx will now reflect Everyone, (RX).*

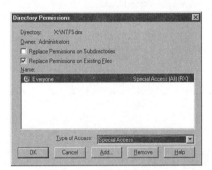

If the administrator does not clear the Replace Permissions on Existing Files box in Figure 5.7, all files in the directory will have their ACLs overwritten with the new ACL settings. By default, the Replace Permissions on Existing Files option is selected but the Replace Permissions on Subdirectories option is not. If both of the options are selected, all files in the current directory and subdirectories will be updated; the ACLs of the subdirectories will also be updated to reflect the change.

The predefined directory permissions are

Full Control (ALL)(ALL):   Encompasses all of the rights plus a special hidden right to delete files. In order to maintain POSIX compliance, if you have Full Control to a directory then you may delete any file within the directory regardless of file rights. This is the one difference between granting Full Control and granting all of the rights through Special Directory Access.

List (RX)(Not Specified):   The least permissive set of directory rights. It enables the name of the directory and names of files within the directory to be read but not to read the file contents. This is the minimum permission that you

*continues*

**5**

| | must have on a directory in order to make it shared. Granting List modifies the default ACL on new files to be blank. |
|---|---|
| Read (RX)(RX): | Permits RX to the directory and RX in the default file ACL. This is the set of permissions that is commonly assigned to application directories. |
| Add (WX)(Not Specified): | Permits WX to the directory but does not grant file permissions in the default file ACL. |
| Add and Read (RWX)(RX): | Permits RWX to the directory and RX in the default file ACL. |
| Change (RWXD)(RWXD): | Permits RWXD to the directory and RWXD to the file. This is the set of permissions that is commonly assigned to data directories. |
| No Access: | Can be applied to directories in the same fashion as files. |

# 5.5. Managing Files

When moving or copying files from one directory to another, the ACLs may or may not be altered. The rules of how the ACL is affected are relatively simple and are dependent upon whether a copy is being made. Remember, if a new file is created, it inherits the permissions of the folder where it is created. Moving may or may not involve making a copy.

## 5.5.1. Moving Files

When people move they usually take what they can with them. If their belongings can't be brought along they replace them when they get there. Moving files works the same way. When a file on an NTFS volume is moved to another directory on the same partition it can take its access control list with it. This is because when you move a file to another folder on the same partition, you are only changing the pointer in the file allocation table. Figure 5.8 shows the present permissions on the file NTFSfile.txt located in the NTFSdir. Figure 5.9 shows the permissions of the OTHERdir. As you can see in Figure 5.10, the file NTFSfile.txt has retained the same permissions even after being moved to the OTHERdir.

**Figure 5.8.**

*The access control list of* NTFSfile.txt.txt *before being moved. The file gives Domain Users Read permission and gives Domain Admins Full Control permission.*

**Figure 5.9.**

*The ACL applied to files created in or copied to* OTHERdir *is set to Everyone – Change.*

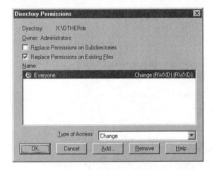

**Figure 5.10.**

*After* NTFSfile.txt.txt *is moved to* OTHERdir *the file still retains its ACL from before being moved.*

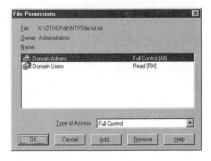

5

NTFS file permissions are maintained only when they are moved between directories on the same NTFS partition. A new ACL is generated if the file is moved to a directory on a different NTFS partition. Moving between partitions is actually a copy and delete. When you move a file to a FAT volume the ACL is lost. When a file is moved from a FAT volume to an NTFS volume the file will inherit an ACL from the destination directory.

When you move a file you must have the right to delete it from the source directory and the right to add files to the destination directory.

## 5.5.2. Copying NTFS Files

When you copy a file to an NTFS directory you must create a new file in the destination directory. When files are created in directories on NTFS volumes they receive an ACL from the destination directory. When copying a file you must have at a minimum the right to read the source file and the right to add in the destination directory.

## 5.5.3. Compressing Files and Directories

NTFS volumes support the compression of files and directories. In order to enable compression on a directory you must check the Compress attribute as shown in Figure 5.11.

**Figure 5.11.**

*The NTFS Compress attribute.*

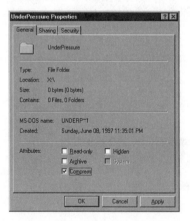

The compression status of a file is shown on the General tab of the Properties dialog box. Assigning the Compress attribute to a directory will automatically compress all files in the directory but not in subdirectories. In order to enable compression of the subdirectories you must also mark the Also Compress Subfolders option box shown in Figure 5.12.

**Figure 5.12.**
*Enabling the compression of subfolders.*

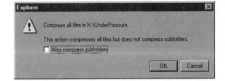

In addition to using the GUI interface, you can compress files and directories by using the command-line utility COMPACT. When used without any parameters, COMPACT will display the current compression status for the file or directory. It can also be used to uncompress files and directories. If a directory is not specified, then the current directory will be compressed or uncompressed.

## 5.5.4. Converting File Systems

The CONVERT.EXE utility can convert FAT volumes to NTFS volumes while preserving the data. There are two major reasons why you might want to convert a FAT volume to NTFS. The most common reason is that you want to implement the security or compression features of NTFS. The second reason involves the fact that only NTFS volume sets can be extended in size. Extending partitions by means of a volume set is detailed later in this chapter in Section 5.7.3.

Use of the CONVERT utility is a one-way procedure. The CONVERT utility can convert only from FAT to NTFS. To convert an NTFS volume to FAT you must back up the data, format the volume as FAT, and then restore the data from the backup.

You initialize the conversion process from the command prompt as demonstrated in Figure 5.13 by typing CONVERT *<drive letter>* /FS:NTFS. The present file system is determined as well as available space needed for the conversion.

**Figure 5.13.**
*Using the CONVERT utility to change the file system of the F drive from FAT to NTFS.*

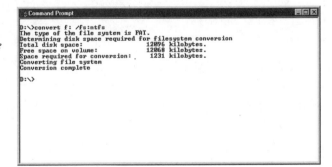

5

Converting the system partition on dual boot systems will prevent DOS from properly initializing.

If the system is unable to gain exclusive control of the drive to be converted you can schedule the conversion to occur at the time of the next reboot. In the case of the system or boot partitions and of drives that are in use, conversion must occur during the boot process. NT determines whether scheduling the conversion is necessary and if so prompts the user.

# 5.6. Understanding Partitions

Before you format a hard drive you must partition it to create logical boundaries. A single hard drive can contain up to four partitions; either four primary partitions or three primaries and one extended partition.

## 5.6.1. Primary Partitions

Only primary partitions can be used as system partitions. The *system partition* is the partition that holds the files required to boot NT. These files are `boot.ini`, `ntldr`, and `ntdetect.com` on x86-based systems. On x86-based systems only one primary partition can be marked as active; it will be the partition from which the system will attempt to boot. RISC-based computers do not require you to mark the system partition as active because they boot from firmware.

On x86-based computers the system and boot partitions can be formatted as either FAT or NTFS.

The system partition on RISC-based computers must be formatted with FAT. A special option in Disk Administrator for RISC-based computers enables you to secure the system partition even though it is FAT. This right is granted only to members of the administrators group.

Because NT will support a maximum of four partitions per physical disk it is important to plan space usage properly. It is possible to reach the four-partition maximum before you use all the free space on a drive. Figure 5.14 shows the error that is returned by the Disk Administrator when you try to exceed the four-partition maximum.

**Figure 5.14.**

*Attempting to exceed the four-partition maximum on physical disk 0.*

A total of four partitions are allowed per physical disk.

## 5.6.2. Extended Partitions

Notice that in Figure 5.14 two areas of free space still exist, a 98MB area and a 551MB area. The 551MB area is wasted space because no additional partitions can be created. The 98MB area is contained within an extended partition and can still accommodate logical drives as shown in Figure 5.15.

**Figure 5.15.**

*Extended partitions can contain multiple logical drives.*

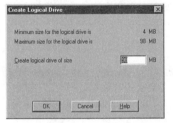

Only one extended partition is allowed per physical disk. A single logical drive can use the entire extended partition or up to four logical drives can receive portions of the area.

Only one extended partition is allowed per physical drive but it can hold multiple logical drives.

Regardless of the number of logical drives created on an extended partition, the entire extended partition is counted as one of the four potential partitions per physical disk. Each logical drive will, however, receive a partition number for identification purposes during the boot phase. NT identifies each partition and logical drive on extended partitions with a partition number. Physical partitions are numbered beginning with 1 before the logical drives are assigned numbers. In Figure 5.16 the logical drive D is assigned a partition number of 2 because it is the second partition on the drive.

**5**

**Figure 5.16.**

*Disk Administrator showing the partitions on Disk 0.*

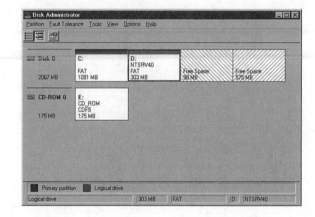

Be especially careful when the NT boot files have been installed on a logical drive. Adding additional primary partitions on the same physical disk will change the partition number assigned to logical drives. The boot.ini file in the root of the system partition identifies the boot partition by number. The boot.ini file of NTMASTER currently identifies the boot partition as partition 2 as shown in Figure 5.17; this is logical drive D.

**Figure 5.17.**

*The boot.ini file shows that the boot files are on partition 2, which is a logical drive.*

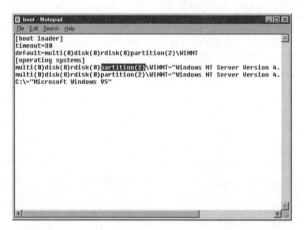

When an additional physical partition is added as in Figure 5.18 the logical drive is reassigned the partition number of 3. If you fail to edit the boot.ini file, the system will not boot.

**Figure 5.18.**

*The addition of another primary partition changes the number of the extended partition from 2 to 3.*

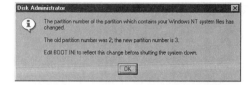

# 5.7. The Disk Administrator

You use the Disk Administrator tool to manage physical disks and partitions on NT. It is used to add, delete, and format partitions. It is also used to create mirrors, striping sets, and volume sets.

## 5.7.1. Adding Partitions

Partitions can be defined using the Disk Administrator program from areas of free disk space. By selecting an area of free space and right clicking on it you are given the option to create a primary or extended partition as shown in Figure 5.19.

**Figure 5.19.**

*Partitions are created from areas of free space.*

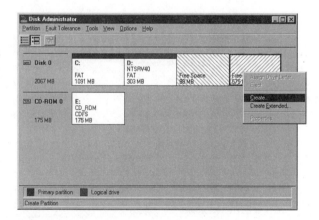

5

The partition does not have to utilize the entire amount of free space available as shown in Figure 5.20, although it can. The maximum size of the partition will be governed by the amount of free space available on a given disk.

Test Tip

The maximum size of a single partition theoretically is 2TB.

**Figure 5.20.**

*Selecting the size of the new partition.*

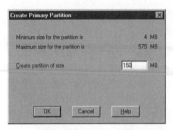

In Figure 5.20 the administrator has selected to create a primary partition of 150MB. The partition is assigned a drive letter; however, the file system type will be unknown until the partition is formatted. After the partition has been formatted it is commonly referred to as a *volume.*

Before formatting the partition the administrator must commit the changes to the disk configuration. The option to commit the changes immediately is shown in Figure 5.21. After the administrator has committed to the changes simply canceling from the program cannot reverse them. If changes are made and not committed, then quitting the Disk Administrator returns the system to its original configuration.

**Figure 5.21.**

*The option to commit changes now.*

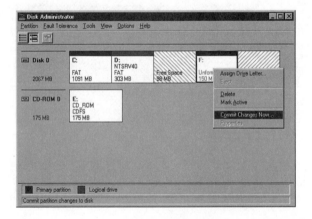

After the changes have been committed the administrator can format the partition by selecting the Format option under Tools. The partition can be formatted as either FAT or NTFS from the command prompt or through the Disk Administrator as shown in Figure 5.22.

**Figure 5.22.**

*Formatting the new partition as an NTFS volume.*

Although formatting from the Disk Administrator is more convenient, formatting from the command prompt enables the administrator to select cluster sizes greater than 4KB to be specified for the volume. The Disk Administrator limits the allocation unit size to 4KB because this is the maximum size cluster that can be used with NTFS compression. From the command prompt the cluster, or allocation unit, size can be set from 512 bytes to 64KB for NTFS. FAT can support clusters up to 256KB.

A volume on which you plan to hold mainly large database files would benefit from a large cluster size.

5

The drive letter automatically assigned the volume can be changed through the Disk Administrator. In Figure 5.22 the volume was assigned drive letter F. The administrator can change the drive letter assignment to any available letter. In Figure 5.23 the drive letter is modified to be drive X.

**Figure 5.23.**

*Modifying the drive letter through the Disk Administrator.*

Changing the drive letter associated with a volume or CD-ROM takes effect immediately if no program is accessing the drive.

## 5.7.2. Deleting Partitions

When a partition is deleted all data held on the partition is lost. The Disk Administrator will not enable you to delete the boot or system partition.

If you accidentally delete a partition before the changes have been committed you can cancel out of the Disk Administrator. The drive will still be intact.

## 5.7.3. Volume Sets

Volume sets are combinations of 2 to 32 segments of disk space from 1 to 32 physical disks. The segments do not have to be identical in size. The collective area forms a volume set that is represented by a single drive letter. The areas used to create the volume set can be from an existing NTFS partition and an area of free space or from separate areas of free space.

In Figure 5.24 the free spaces are selected and the size of the volume set determined (see Figure 5.25). You must restart your computer (Figure 5.26) before you can format the new volume set (Figure 5.27). The volume set is treated as a single partition even though it is composed on noncontiguous sections.

**Figure 5.24.**

*Areas of free space are selected to form a volume set.*

**Figure 5.25.**
*The volume set could be as large as the collective areas of free space selected.*

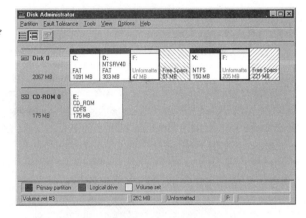

**Figure 5.26.**
*You must restart the computer before you reformat the volume set.*

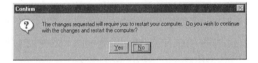

Know This: The volume set can be formatted as either FAT or NTFS.

**Figure 5.27.**
*The volume set is formatted as FAT. Either FAT or NTFS can be used as the file system for volume sets.*

5

You can incorporate into the volume set additional areas of free space to increase the total size. The space used can be from the same disk or from any other physical disk in the system. In order to be extended the volume set must have NTFS as its file system as shown in Figure 5.28.

**Figure 5.28.**

*A volume set formatted as FAT cannot be extended.*

Only volume sets with the NTFS file system can be extended.

In order to extend a volume set formatted with FAT you must first change the file system to NTFS by either formatting or converting the volume. Converting the file system using the convert program from the command prompt is normally the optimal solution because this will preserve the data on the volume.

Know this: The system and boot partitions cannot be part of a volume set regardless of the file system used.

Volume sets do not provide fault tolerance disk access improvements. Remember that they provide zero redundancy and therefore zero fault tolerance. Volume sets do not increase performance because they do not balance the reads and writes between the areas of space used. The first area of space incorporated into the volume set is filled completely before the next area is written to. If any of the disks containing any part of the volume set fail, the data across the entire volume set is lost. The data can be recovered only from backup.

Volume sets do not increase system performance regardless of how many physical disks are used.

Using volume sets is not a means of establishing fault tolerance.

## 5.7.4. Stripe Sets

You use stripe sets to increase disk performance. A stripe set is created from areas of free space on 2 to 32 physical disks. The largest amount of space that can be taken from a single disk in creating the stripe set is equal to the smallest area selected from any disk in the set. If two physical disks contained areas of 100 and 200MB of free space, respectively, the largest stripe set that could be created would be 200MB.

Remember that the exam often tries to test for more than cursory knowledge on a given question. For example, given a disk configuration of three disks, disk 1 with 210MB of free disk space, disk 2 with 410MB of free space, and disk 3 with 600MB of free space, what would be the largest stripe set that could be created?

On the surface it might appear that the largest stripe set that could be created is 630MB by combining the smallest common area between all three disks—210MB from each disk. It is true that you could create a 630MB stripe set by using all three disks, but a stripe set can be created from as few as two physical disks. By using space only from disks 1 and 2 you could create a stripe set of 820MB—410MB from each disk.

Stripe sets cannot be extended. Performance increases are gained by writing 64KB segments of data across the array of disks, one disk at a time. Generally, the more disks used to create the stripe set the better the performance.

Stripe sets are used to enhance disk performance.

Be careful not to confuse *stripe sets* (RAID0) and *stripe sets with parity* (RAID5). Stripe sets do not provide fault tolerance; they can be created on both NT workstation and server. Stripe sets with parity provide fault tolerance and can be created on NT server only.

Although the data is written across a series of disks, stripe sets without parity do not provide fault tolerance. If one of the disks used to create the stripe set fails you must restore the data from a tape backup.

## 5.7.5. Stripe Sets With Parity

Stripe sets with parity not only increase disk performance, but also provide fault tolerance. A stripe set with parity is created from areas of free space on 3 to 32 physical disks. The size of your stripe set with parity is equal to the number of disks times the smallest selected area. Parity information is written on one disk for each stripe. This parity information rotates across the disks.

When reading the exam questions, be sure to note whether the question asks for the size of the stripe set or the amount of usable space. Because parity information takes up one section of each stripe, the total space that is contained in the stripe set is the number of disks times the size of the smallest section. To determine the total space available for data, you must subtract the area that is used for parity. So, if you have the configuration explained earlier, you could create a stripe set with parity of 630MB. However, the amount of space available for data would be (630MB)(630/3) or 420MB.

## 5.7.6. CD-ROM Drives

CD-ROM drives are read-only devices. The Compact Disc File System (CDFS) is used in conjunction with CD-ROMs. You can change the drive letter assigned to a CD-ROM drive by using the Disk Administrator, and the change takes place immediately.

## 5.7.7. Saving the Disk Configuration

The Disk Administrator includes an option for saving the disk configuration to a floppy disk. The saved configuration will contain information on drive letters, partitions, volume sets, stripe sets, mirror sets, and stripe sets with parity.

If multiple copies of NT exist on the same machine they will be unaware of how the disk configuration has been modified while the system was booted under a different copy of NT with the exception of drive letter assignments. You can restore the configuration under each copy of NT to update the disk configuration settings. Alternatively, the Disk Administrator can be told to search the system to determine the disk configuration. If multiple copies of NT exist on the same machine determining which is the proper configuration can be difficult.

If the Disk Administrator displays Unknown for any disk areas it is a sign that the configuration might be out of synch.

# 5.8. Lab

This lab will aid in your learning by testing you on the information presented in this chapter, as well as by giving you exercises to hone your skills. Answers to the review questions can be found in Appendix B, "Answers to Review Questions."

## 5.8.1. Review Questions

### Question 1

The system administrator of Corporation B is installing NT Server on a x86-based computer with a single hard disk. Which of the following disk configurations can be established on the computer?

A.  Both NT system and boot files can be installed on a single primary partition formatted with NTFS.

B.  The NT system files can be installed on a FAT partition, and the NT boot files can be installed on an NTFS partition.

C.  The administrator can increase disk performance by installing the system files on a stripe set.

D.  The administrator can increase performance by installing the system files on a volume set.

### Question 2

The system administrator is planning to load applications to the hard disk of an NT server accessed by DOS-based network clients. Which of the following file systems can be used on the hard disk?

A.  FAT

B.  NTFS

C.  CDFS

D.  HPFS

### Question 3

A user on an NT workstation has saved a file to an NTFS partition of the server's hard disk. The file is named 1997 Accounting Files.doc. When the file is seen from a DOS-based network client how will the filename appear?

A. `1997 Accounting Files.doc`

B. `1997Acco.doc`

C. `1996.doc`

D. `1997AC~1.doc`

## Question 4

Under what circumstances is it necessary to have a FAT partition on a machine running NT Server?

A. When it is a RISC-based computer

B. When it will be accessed by DOS clients

C. When it will also boot into DOS

D. When disk compression will be used

## Question 5

An NT server has two partitions, both of which are formatted with NTFS. NTFS permissions have been set to allow Change to the Accounting group. A share has been created on the directory that allows Change to Accounting and Full Control to Administrators. Which steps must the administrator take after moving the accounting folder to a different partition?

A. Reset the NTFS permissions.

B. Reshare the new folder.

C. Assign permissions to the share.

D. No additional steps will be required.

## Question 6

An NT server has two partitions, both of which are formatted with NTFS. A share has been created on the directory that allows Change to Accounting and Full Control to Administrators. NTFS permissions have been set on the directory to allow Change to the Accounting group. What are the effective rights for members of the Administrators group when accessing the directory from across the network?

A. Change.

B. Full Control.

C. None.

## Question 7

When is it possible to delete a file to which you have been denied access?

A. When you have the Delete permission in the directory

B. When you have Full Control in the directory

C. When you are a member of the Network group

D. When you have Change permissions in the directory

## Question 8

Which of the following rights would enable you to modify the permission list (ACL) of a file?

A. Write

B. Change

C. Change Permissions

D. Take Ownership

## Question 9

The access control list for directory XYZ is configured as

Everyone: (RX)(RX)
Administrators: (ALL)(ALL)

The file ABC is located within directory XYZ and permitted as follows:

Everyone: (RWXD)

UserX has been neither granted nor denied permissions directly. What are UserX's effective rights on file ABC?

A. RX

B. RWXD

C. ALL

D. NONE

5

## Question 10

What is the default access control list for the root folder of a new NTFS partition?

    A. Administrators: (ALL)(ALL)

    B. Everyone: (RX)(RX)

    C. Everyone: (ALL)(ALL)

    D. Administrators: (ALL)(ALL); Everyone (RX)(RX)

## Question 11

NTSRVX has one physical disk with three primary partitions and one extended partition. What is the maximum number of partitions that can be marked active simultaneously?

    A. One

    B. Two

    C. Three

    D. Four

## Question 12

What is the minimum number of disks required when creating a volume set?

    A. One

    B. Two

    C. Three

    D. Four

## Question 13

A computer is configured as follows:

    Physical disk 0: 100MB free space

    Physical disk 1: 200MB free space

    Physical disk 2: 300MB free space

What is the largest stripe set that can be configured given this disk configuration?

    A. 100

    B. 200

    C. 300

D. 400

E. 600

## Question 14

Which of the following configurations would be valid on a single physical drive?

A. Four primary partitions

B. One primary partition, three extended partitions

C. Two primary partitions, two extended partitions

D. Three primary partitions, one extended partition

## Question 15

Which of the following statements about a volume set are true?

A. A volume set increases disk performance by spreading data evenly across multiple disks.

B. A volume set requires from 2 to 32 physical disks.

C. A volume set can be formatted as either FAT or NTFS.

D. The system partition can be part of a volume set.

## Question 16

The NT server CRASHNBURN contains a 350MB-volume set spanning disks 0, 1, and 2. If disk 2 fails, what steps would the administrator take to restore the data?

A. Select the option to regenerate the volume set.

B. Restore from tape backup.

C. Replace the failed disk.

D. Re-create the volume set.

**5**

## Question 17

When is it advantageous to have a cluster size larger than 4KB on an NTFS partition?

A. When storing large database files

B. When initiating NTFS compression

C. When storing several small files

D. When planning to convert to FAT

## Question 18

Which of the following is true regarding stripe sets?

    A.  Stripe sets are used to increase performance.

    B.  Stripe sets must be formatted as NTFS.

    C.  Stripe sets cannot be extended.

    D.  Stripe sets require a minimum of three physical disks.

## Question 19

When the drive letter associated with a CD-ROM drive is changed, when does it take effect?

    A.  At the next logon

    B.  When the system is rebooted

    C.  Immediately

    D.  CD-ROM drive letters cannot be manually assigned

## Question 20

The NT server NTSRVX has two physical disks. Disk 0 has two partitions. The first 200MB partition is formatted as NTFS and contains the system and boot files. The second 100M partition is formatted with FAT and contains data and applications. The remainder of the disk, 100MB, is free space. Disk 1 contains 500MB of free space. What is the largest volume set that the administrator can create?

    A.  200MB

    B.  600MB

    C.  700MB

    D.  800MB

# 5.8.2. Exercise

You have a new computer that will be used as an application server. It has five 1GB drives. You must plan for fault tolerance. The computer must not be down for more than one-half hour at a time. How would you manage the disks?

# Day 6

# Data Protection: Fault Tolerance and NT Backup

*by David Schaer and Theresa Hadden*

## 6.1. Overview

This chapter provides you with the necessary knowledge to configure and maintain a fault-tolerant NT Server 4.0 installation.

### 6.1.1. Objectives

This chapter gives an overview of RAID technology and describes when and how to implement RAID1 and RAID5 in NT Server 4.0. Additionally, you also learn the methodology for recovering data for a system equipped with RAID technology. The following are the objectives for the Windows NT Server and Enterprise exams:

- Choose a fault-tolerant method.
- Choose the appropriate course of action to resolve fault-tolerance failures.
- Implement an appropriate backup methodology.

### 6.1.2. Fast Facts

The following list of facts is a concise picture of the information presented in this chapter. It acts as both an overview for the chapter and as a study aid to help you do any last-minute cramming.

- NT Server 4.0 supports RAID1 (mirroring or duplexing) and RAID5 (stripe sets with parity).
- Disk mirroring requires a single controller and two physical disks.
- Disk duplexing requires two separate controllers and two physical disks.
- The system and boot partitions can be members of a mirror set but not of a RAID5 stripe set with parity.
- Stripe sets (RAID0) are not the same thing as stripe sets with parity (RAID5).
- The overhead of mirroring is equal to 1/2 the amount of disk space used.
- Performance is superior with stripe sets with parity than with mirror sets.
- A stripe set with parity is created from equal segments of free space from between 3 to 32 physical disks.
- If a single member of a stripe set with parity fails, the lost data can be regenerated from parity information held on the remaining members.
- If two or more members of a stripe set fail it is not possible to regenerate the lost data. The data must be restored.
- Breaking a mirror set does not delete the data.
- To back up the registry you must select at least one file on the partition on which the registry resides.

## 6.2. Redundant Arrays of Inexpensive Disks (RAID)

RAID technology was first proposed at the University of Berkeley to rectify the negatives of SLED or Single Large Expensive Drives. There are two specific areas in which the use of multiple drives would be better suited than a single drive: performance and fault tolerance.

Theoretically, a single drive would reach its maximum performance capacity and become a bottleneck before two less-expensive, albeit slower, drives working together to perform the same work. This concept forms the general basis of stripe sets, or RAID0.

The second, and primary area of concern relative to the examination is fault tolerance. Regardless of how fast a drive is performing, if the disk crashes the data is lost. RAID technology can change the "all the eggs in one basket" method by duplicating data across two drives (RAID1) or by spreading data and parity information across from 3 to 32 disks (RAID5). None of the RAID methods circumvent the need to back up the system to tape.

## 6.2.1. RAID Basics

The exam will test your knowledge of how RAID technology is provided by and implemented in NT Server 4.0. Fault tolerance can be provided by NT Server 4.0 in the form of either RAID1 (mirroring or duplexing) or RAID5 (stripe sets with parity).

RAID implementations can be either hardware- or software-based. Although both NT Workstation and NT Server can take advantage of hardware-level RAID such as those provided by Compaq and Hewlett Packard, software RAID0, RAID1, and RAID5 are available on the NT Server platform but only RAID0 is supported on the NT Workstation platform.

> Neither NT Workstation nor Windows 95 can provide software-based fault tolerance.

Hardware RAID solutions offload the management of the RAID array to a special controller. By providing their own processing and caching capability, hardware solutions almost always outperform software RAID. Additionally, if the disk fails, hardware solutions allow the failed disk to be substituted without bringing the system down. Many hardware solutions even offer a *hot-spare*, a disk that automatically takes the place of a failed disk in the array. The information that was held on the failed disk is calculated from the parity information in the array and written to the hot-spare in the background.

Software RAID is implemented by the operating system. The same processors and memory used to control the operating system are used to manage the RAID array. If a disk fails it is necessary to bring the system down to substitute the disk. NT Server provides software-based RAID.

## 6.2.2. When RAID Has No Redundancy (RAID0)

Remember that RAID was designed to provide for two primary functions, fault tolerance and performance. RAID0 provides increased performance but not fault tolerance. There is no fault tolerance because there is no redundancy of data. Think of the zero in RAID0 as zero redundancy. RAID0 can be implemented in both NT Server and NT Workstation in the form of *stripe sets*. Stripe sets are described fully in Chapter 7, "Managing Users and Groups."

6

RAID0 is used to provide performance improvements only. A common implementation is using stripe sets to hold read-only databases.

# 6.3. Configuring RAID1

RAID1 is implemented in NT Server 4.0 as either *disk mirroring* or *disk duplexing*. Two disks work in a pair to provide redundancy. All data written to a mirrored partition on one disk is simultaneously written to the other. The original Berkeley RAID specifications outlined the mirroring of entire disks, hence the term *disk mirroring*. The actual implementation is really partition or volume mirroring.

Both disk mirroring and duplexing are considered expensive in terms of overhead. Because all data written to one partition is written to the mirror, there is a 50 percent loss of available space. Mirroring two 100MB partitions yields an available space of 100MB.

Any NT partition, including the boot and system partitions, can be part of a mirror set.

RAID1 results in increased read performance because data is read from both disks but generally results in a decrease in write performance because all data is written twice.

## 6.3.1. Disk Mirroring

Disk mirroring is really just partition mirroring. Any NT partition can be used in a mirror set regardless of the file system. This includes the boot and system partitions. The most common areas to mirror are the system and boot partitions. This is important because neither the system nor boot partition can be members of a fault-tolerant stripe set with parity.

All data is written to both partitions in a mirror set. Should one of the disks fail, the system will continue to run, providing the data from the remaining member of the set. The users will be unaware of the disk failure. The administrator will see the failure noted in the event log. Mirroring requires two physical disks and a single controller as shown in Figure 6.1.

**Figure 6.1.**

*Mirroring requires two disks and a single controller.*

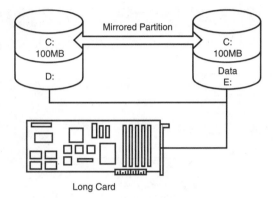

The controller is the single point of failure in disk mirroring. If the controller fails, neither member of the mirror set will be accessible.

### 6.3.2. Establishing a Mirror Set

Follow these steps to establish a mirror set:

1. From within Disk Administrator simply select the partition you want to mirror.

2. Holding the Ctrl key, select an area of free space on a separate physical disk equal to or greater than the mirrored partition.

3. Select Establish Mirror from the Fault Tolerance menu. (See Figure 6.2.) The resulting mirror set is shown in Figure 6.3.

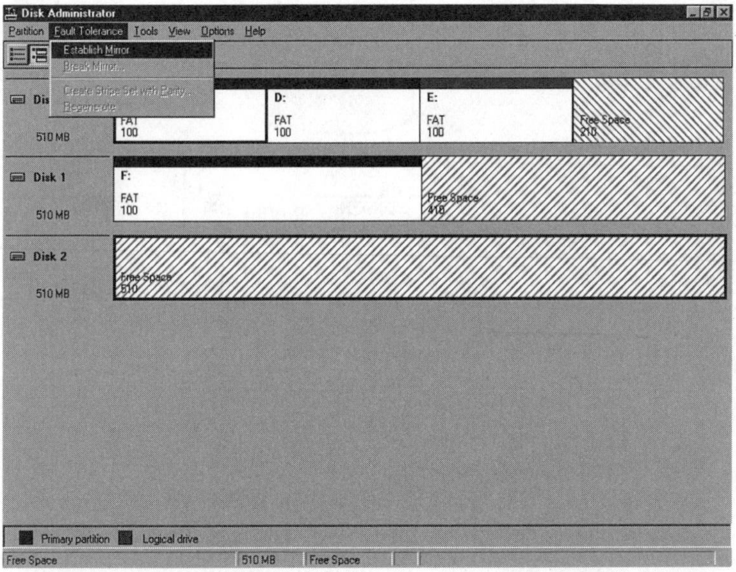

**Figure 6.2.**

*Mirroring the C drive from disk (0) to disk (2).*

**6**

**Figure 6.3.**

*The resulting mirror set.*

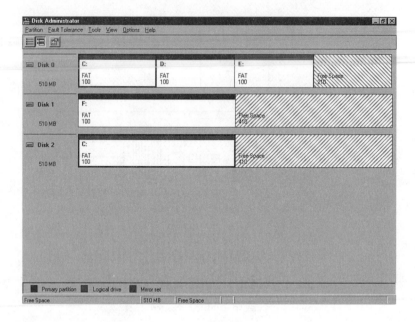

### 6.3.3. Disk Duplexing

Disk duplexing is really just disk mirroring with one special difference: the physical disks are each attached to a separate controller. Disk duplexing requires two physical disks and two separate disk controllers, as shown in Figure 6.4.

**Figure 6.4.**

*Disk duplexing requires two physical disks and two controllers.*

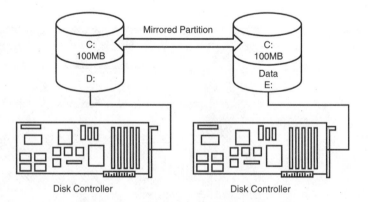

The addition of the second controller will reduce bus traffic, generally increasing the performance over that of mirroring alone. As with mirroring there is a cost of 50 percent of the disk space used.

# 6.4. Configuring RAID5

RAID5 is implemented on NT Server in the form of stripe sets with parity. It is the *with parity* that differentiates this implementation from simple RAID0 or stripe sets. A stripe set with parity is created from areas of free space from 3 to 32 physical disks. The greater the number of disks included in the array, the greater the performance and less the overall cost. In order to provide redundancy, parity information is spread across all disks in the array. In earlier RAID implementations such as RAID4, a single disk was used to hold the parity information. If a disk in the array fails, the data can be regenerated from parity information.

Overall, the performance of stripe sets with parity is greater than that of mirror sets. If a disk fails, however, read performance will be degraded because the data must be regenerated.

The overall space attributed to the parity stripe is equal to the space of one partition in the stripe. For example, a stripe set with parity created from equal 100MB areas of space from three drives would yield a total usable area of 200MB. If a total of five disks were used, the usable space would equal 400MB.

## 6.4.1. Creating a Stripe Set with Parity

The stripe set with parity is created from areas of free space on a minimum of three physical disks.

1. Using Disk Administrator, simply hold the Ctrl key while selecting the areas of space to combine into the stripe set with parity. The largest common denominator across the areas of space selected determines the maximum amount that each area can contribute, in this case 210MB.

2. Select Create Stripe Set With Parity from the Fault Tolerance menu (see Figure 6.5).

3. Specify the desired size of the stripe set up to the maximum value based on the smallest common area (see Figure 6.6).

4. The resulting stripe set with parity is 630MB (see Figure 6.7). After subtracting the overhead for the parity stripe the usable space will be 420MB.

**6**

**Figure 6.5.**

*Disk Administrator to establish a stripe set with parity.*

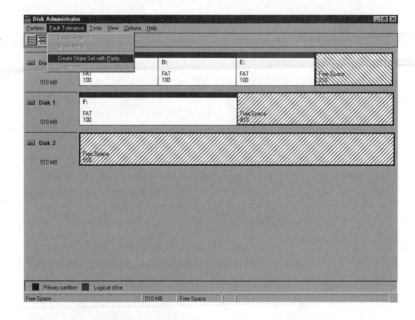

**Figure 6.6.**

*Sizing the stripe set with parity.*

## 6.4.2. Performance Considerations of RAID Technology

In the area of performance you must except some basic generalities. The exams do not provide a level of depth that will require advanced calculations to determine which RAID solution is best suited for a given situation.

In general, read performance is better on stripe sets with parity than on mirror sets. Reading data from the stripe set will slow if a member of the set fails because the data must be regenerated. Mirrored partitions do provide a modest increase in read performance, but this is countered by slower write performance. The write performance of mirrored sets is considered superior to that of stripe sets with parity. Duplexing provides the best write performance and good read performance.

**Figure 6.7.**

*A Stripe Set with Parity as shown in Disk Administrator.*

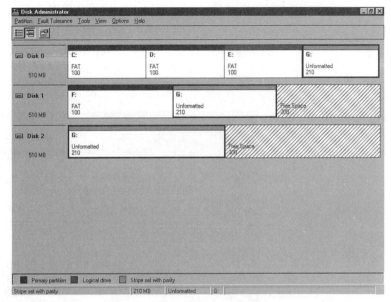

# 6.5. Recovering from Hard Disk Failure

Hard disk failure can occur for many reasons. This section of the exam will test your knowledge of how to recover the system given single- or multiple-disk failures.

## 6.5.1. When a Mirror Set Fails

If one of the disks in a mirror set fails, the system simply takes the failed disk out of the equation. The system will continue to run without a suspension of services. Because mirror sets commonly include the system or boot partitions, it's considered good practice to have a fault-tolerant boot disk on hand. The disk essentially takes the place of the system partition. To create the disk, follow these steps:

1. From within NT, format a floppy disk. Perform a full, not a quick, format.

2. Copy from the root of the system partition to the floppy NTLDR, NTDETECT.COM, and BOOT.INI. You will also require NTBOOTDD.SYS if you are using a SCSI controller and the BIOS is not enabled.

3. Modify the BOOT.INI file on the floppy disk to point to the mirrored copy of the boot partition.

6

To restore the mirror you must first "break" the mirror set. Using Disk Administrator, simply select Break Mirror from the Fault Tolerance menu as shown in Figure 6.8. Breaking the mirror set will expose the failed partition, enabling it to be deleted. If an area of free space of sufficient size is available, the mirror set can be reestablished into that area.

**Figure 6.8.**

*Breaking the mirror set to expose the partitions.*

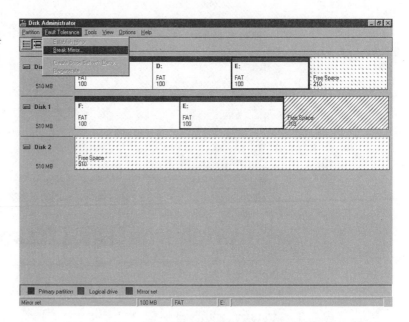

Breaking a mirror set does not delete the data on either member. It simply ends the relationship between the two, now independent, partitions.

## 6.5.2. When a Stripe Set with Parity Fails

If a single disk in a stripe set with parity fails, the system will continue to function with no loss of data. Of course, because this is an implementation of software RAID5, there could be a significant reduction in system performance until the lost member is recovered. So you will want to regenerate the stripe set as quickly as possible to avoid an excessive amount of system memory and processor time being dedicated to calculating data requests on the fly.

**Test Tip**

> A significant amount of memory and processor time can be required to calculate data when a member of a stripe set with parity fails.

There are two primary causes why a member of a stripe set with parity would fail. The first is a power loss to the specific drive and the second, more severe, is a head crash.

### Restoring a Single Lost RAID5 Member

When a power loss to a single drive causes a member to fail, simply bring the system down, reestablish the proper power, and restart the system. After the system has been restarted with power restored to the member disk, the stripe set with parity can be regenerated using the original members.

If the member set was lost due to a disk crash, you must replace the physical disk before you regenerate the stripe set with parity.

### Restoring a Stripe Set with Parity Following the Loss of Multiple Members

If multiple members of a stripe set with parity fail at the same time, simply regenerating the stripe set will not be possible. When multiple members fail simultaneously the set will not have sufficient information to regenerate the lost data. The solution is to use a tape backup unit. If multiple disks fail, the stripe set must be re-created—not just regenerated. After the stripe set has been re-created the data that was lost can be restored from tape.

> If more than one member of a stripe set with parity fails, the data cannot be regenerated. You must re-create the stripe set and restore from tape.

**6**

# 6.6. NT Backup Procedures

Backing up the NT server should be treated as a mandatory task. Even if mirroring, duplexing, or stripe sets with parity have been implemented your system is still susceptible to a system crash. Even if your system never crashes, a user may inadvertently delete or corrupt his data.

Because the details of the backup program are stressed on the NT 4.0 Workstation exam (70-63), only the key points of how NTBACKUP functions are covered here.

Although it might seem obvious, NTBACKUP was designed to back up to and restore from tape devices only.

## 6.6.1. Types of Backups

You can perform five different backup types. The key difference between the backup types is how they handle the archive bit. The archive bit for each file can be toggled on or off (cleared). If it is on, the file is considered to have been modified since the last full backup.

### Normal

A normal backup, sometimes called a full backup, copies all selected files and directories. The archive bit is cleared as the files are backed up. Although this is the longest backup to perform, it will restore the entire system the fastest.

### Copy

A copy is simply that—a copy. The copy option was included to let a user back up a set of files without effecting a standardized backup schedule. The archive bit is not cleared on modified files.

### Differential

If you can think of the D in Differential as standing for Different, this type of backup is easy to remember. All the files that have been modified since the last Normal backup can be selected. The archive bit is not cleared during the backup. If you were to perform a normal backup on Monday and a differential on each successive day, after a crash you must install the normal and then apply the latest differential backup.

### Incremental

An incremental backup is the fastest backup to perform but the longest to restore. Selected files that have been modified since the last backup are included in the backup. Because an incremental backup clears the archive bit, a series of incremental backups each will not necessarily back up the same information. If you were to perform a normal backup on Monday and an incremental backup each successive day, after a crash you would need to restore the normal and then apply each incremental backup in successive order.

### Daily

In a daily backup, only the files modified that day will be included in the backup set. The archive bit is not cleared during the backup.

## 6.6.2. Performing the Backup

Before starting the backup program it is a good practice to ensure that all files which must be included in the backup set are accessible. This includes establishing a connection to any remote computers that you will be backing up.

After launching the Backup program (see Figure 6.9), simply select the directories and files you want to include in the backup set. If multiple tapes are required to perform the backup they will be incorporated into a tape set. When a tape set is created, the tape catalog or listing of backups is stored on the final tape.

**Figure 6.9.**

*You can select files and directories to be backed up individually.*

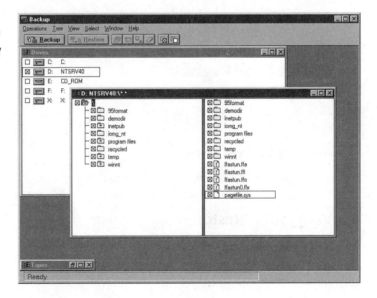

NTBACKUP provides several options that can be used to customize your backup as well as how the files will be restored.

### Backup Registry

The registry of the local, not remote, machine can be backed up to tape as long as at least one file from the drive containing the registry has been selected.

### Restrict Access to Owner or Administrator

If this option is selected, only the person who performed the backup or an administrator will be able to restore the data.

6

## Restoring a Tape Backup

NT must be running in order to restore a tape. This is not an issue unless the disk containing the NT system or boot files has failed. In that case it is necessary to reinstall a minimal copy of NT in order to be able to launch the backup program.

After the specific backup set has been selected from the tape catalog, a series of restore options are offered.

## Restore to Drive

The location to which the data will be restored must be identified. The data can be restored to either a FAT or NTFS partition, regardless of what file system was used during the backup. If files are restored to a FAT partition, then any NTFS permissions will be lost.

## Restore Local Registry

Selecting this option will restore the registry information on the backup set to the local computer. This is preferred over the emergency repair disk because it can be applied online.

## Restore Permissions

This option has an effect only if the data originated from an NTFS volume and an NTFS volume has been selected as the location to which to restore.

## Verify After Restore

This option will initiate a comparison of the restored files with the data on the backup set to verify that the data has been accurately restored.

# 6.7. Lab

This lab will help in your learning by testing you on the information presented in this chapter, as well as by giving you exercises to hone your skills. You can find answers to the review questions in Appendix B, "Answers to Review Questions."

## 6.7.1. Review Questions

### Question 1

Which of the following levels of RAID are supported by NT Server 4.0 when running as a member server?

A. RAID0

B. RAID1

C. RAID5

### Question 2

What equipment is required to implement disk duplexing on NT Server 4.0?

A. One hard disk

B. Two hard disks

C. One controller

D. Two controllers

### Question 3

Which method of NT backup requires the most tapes during a restoration?

A. Full

B. Differential

C. Incremental

D. Copy

### Question 4

Which of the following disk configurations would provide both increased read performance and fault tolerance?

A. Disk mirroring

B. Disk duplexing

6

C. Stripe sets

D. Stripe sets with parity

## Question 5

Which of the following disk configurations provides the highest level of performance?

A. Disk mirroring

B. Disk duplexing

C. Stripe sets

D. Stripe sets with parity

## Question 6

Which of the following files must be located on a fault-tolerant boot disk in order to access an IDE drive?

A. NTLDR

B. NTDETECT.COM

C. BOOT.INI

D. NTOSKRNL.EXE

E. NTBOOTDD.SYS

## Question 7

Which of the following is true regarding restoring data backed up from an NTFS volume to a FAT volume?

A. The FAT volume will be automatically converted to NTFS.

B. The permissions on the files will be set to EVERYONE (RX).

C. The permissions on the files will be lost.

D. Data backed up from an NTFS volume cannot be restored to a FAT volume.

## Question 8

How many members of a RAID5 stripe set with parity can fail before the data must be restored from a backup?

A. One

B. Two

C. Three

## Question 9

Which of the following backup options gives a higher degree of security to the backup tape?

    A.  Restrict access to owner or administrator.

    B.  Restore to this drive only.

    C.  Verify after restore.

    D.  Restore local registry.

## Question 10

Which tape in a family set holds the tape catalog?

    A.  The first tape

    B.  The last tape

    C.  Each tape contains a separate catalog.

# 6.7.2. Exercises

## Exercise 6.1

You have a new server to install and must design the disks for maximum fault tolerance. The server contains six 1GB drives. How would you configure it?

## Exercise 6.2

You are given the job to design a backup procedure to ensure that the data on your four servers is backed up on a regular basis. You also want to design this plan to allow for the quickest restore. How would you do it?

6

# Day 7

# Managing Users and Groups

*by David Schaer and Theresa Hadden*

## 7.1. Overview

This chapter provides you with the necessary knowledge to meet the MCSE exam objective of managing groups and users.

### 7.1.1. Objectives

The objective of this chapter is to ensure that you have a thorough understanding of NT user and group management. You will understand the following:

- The function and features of User Manager for Domains
- How to manage user and group accounts
- The relationship of user and group accounts to permissions
- How to manage user account policies and profiles
- How to troubleshoot user access problems

### 7.1.2. Fast Facts

The following list of facts is a concise picture of the information presented in this chapter. It acts as both an overview for the chapter and as a study aid to help you do any last-minute cramming.

- User Manager for Domains uses RPC calls to communicate with the PDC.
- Each domain contains only one SAM database, which resides on the PDC; read-only copies are placed on all BDCs.

- Every user and group account is associated with a unique security identifier, or SID.
- The administrator account can be renamed but not disabled or deleted.
- The guest account cannot be deleted but can be renamed or disabled.
- Neither local nor global groups can be renamed.
- A local group is local to the systems that share the SAM database information where it was created.
- Changes made to the SAM database are replicated to all BDCs via the NetLogon service.
- A local group cannot contain other local groups.
- Global groups and users from a trusted domain can be placed into a local group in a trusting domain in order to gain access to resources in the trusting domain.
- Global groups can contain only global users from the same domain.
- You are either a member of the Network or Interactive group, depending on whether you are logging on to the resource locally or not.
- All users by virtue of existence are members of the Everyone group.
- AGLP is the acronym for Accounts go into Global groups which go into Local groups which get Permissions, the proper hierarchy for assigning permissions.
- NTCONFIG.POL should be replicated to all of the domain controllers in a domain.
- The Windows 95 policy file is named CONFIG.POL.
- In the hierarchy of policies, user settings take precedence over group settings.
- Group priorities can be established to resolve conflicting policy settings.
- Never assign the same personal roaming profile to multiple users.
- Mandatory profiles should be replicated to domain controllers using the directory replicator service.

## 7.2. User Manager for Domains

User Manager for Domains is the primary NT application for administering all aspects of user and group management. As the name implies, a user with sufficient privileges can centrally manage accounts in multiple domains from a central point of administration.

### 7.2.1. Features and Functions

User Manager for Domains goes beyond simple user account management. This application is also used for the administration of groups and user rights. In addition, User Manager for Domains provides the ability to apply Account Policies and administer Auditing. This section describes the details of these features and functions.

The first aspect is ensuring that you are administering the proper domain. The name of the domain or computer that is being administered appears in the title bar of the application. Figure 7.1 shows that this is the Knowledge domain.

**Figure 7.1.**
*The active title bar shows that the Knowledge domain is being administered.*

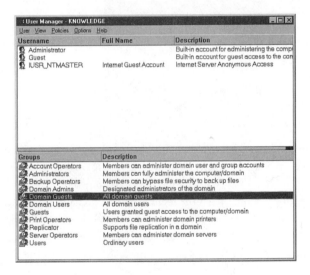

If the focus is not set on the domain you want to administer you may select a different domain from the list of trusting domains or enter a domain or computer name to administer manually.

## 7.2.2. Selecting a Different Domain to Administer

To select a different domain to administer, follow these steps:

1. From the menu bar select User | Select Domain.
2. Choose the name of the trusting domain on which to set the focus from the selection window.
3. If no trust relationship exists, manually enter the name of the domain in the domain box.

7

You can also set the focus of User Manager for Domains to an NT Workstation or stand-alone server by entering \\*computername* in the Domain box.

In Figure 7.2 the focus is being set to the CHICAGO domain.

**Figure 7.2.**
*Selecting the Chicago domain to administer.*

When the focus is set to a domain, User Manager for Domains uses RPC calls to remotely manage the SAM database at the PDC for the selected domain. When the focus is set to an NT Workstation or stand-alone server the RPC calls are directed at the specific station. When the focus is set to a domain, regardless of where the application is run from, the modifications will be made to the SAM database of the PDC in the selected domain. This is true even when you are sitting at a BDC and making changes. The changes are applied to the SAM database at the PDC and then synchronized by the NetLogon service to the BDCs. This chapter demonstrates the features of User Manager for Domains.

# 7.3. Understanding User Accounts

Properly administering NT user and group accounts is greatly simplified by having a proper understanding of the basic structure of accounts and how they relate to other NT objects.

The security features of NT require that when a user or group account is created, a unique security identifier (SID) is created. When a user logs on, the security subsystem creates an access token, similar to an ID card, which specifies the SID of the user and the SID of each of the groups to which the user belongs.

Whenever the user attempts to gain access to any resource on the network the access token is checked against the Access Control List (ACL). The collective rights assigned to the user and groups to which the user has membership will determine the limits of the user's access to the object. This is called *discretionary access control.* Simply because a user has performed the mandatory logon to gain access to the system does not mean that he has all rights to all objects in the system.

## 7.3.1. Automatically Created User Accounts

During the installation, accounts for the administrator and guest are automatically created. If you chose to install IIS during the installation, an account is also created for anonymous Internet access. The accounts created automatically on the KNOWL-EDGE domain are shown in Figure 7.3.

**Figure 7.3.**

*User Manager for Domains showing the user accounts for the Knowledge domain.*

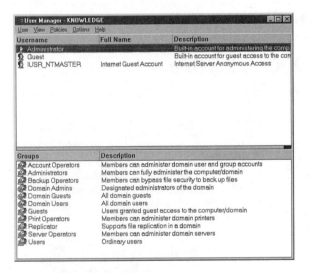

### Built-In User Accounts

Both the administrator and guest accounts are built-in accounts and as such cannot be deleted from the system.

**The Administrator Account**   The administrator account created during the installation is a true superuser. The administrator is automatically granted membership in the Administrators and Domain Admins groups. The built-in administrator account cannot be disabled, deleted, or removed from the administrators group.

7

The administrator account can be renamed. In fact, renaming the administrator account is considered a good practice to enhance security. The administrator account is a frequent target of hacker attacks, and renaming it helps prevent this.

**The Guest Account**   The guest account is used to give access to the system from across the network to users whose names are not in the account database. For example, if the guest account in the KNOWLEDGE domain were enabled, users who tried to access the system from across the network would be aliased as guest. They would receive whatever rights were granted to the guest account.

The guest account is a member of the Domain Guests group. Do not overly empower the guest account by making it a member of a powerful group such as Domain Admins.

Like the administrator account, the guest account is built-in and cannot be deleted. It can, however, be renamed. Renaming the guest account does not prevent it from being used; to prevent it from being used it must be disabled. By default, the guest account is disabled on NT servers.

## 7.3.2. Creating User Accounts

You create user accounts through User Manager for Domains (see Figure 7.4).

**Figure 7.4.**

*Creating a new user account.*

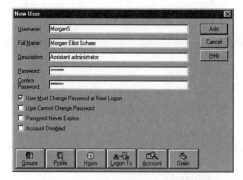

1. From the menu bar select User | New User.
2. Enter the user name: This is the logon ID that will be used by the user. It is not case-sensitive, and can be up to 20 characters in length. The name must be unique to the SAM database where it will be entered; it cannot match another user or group name in the same domain.

The remaining items can be performed optionally during the installation.

- Full Name: This is the descriptive name of the user. This will be helpful later in assigning permissions to the account when the logon ID is not descriptive as to the user name.
- Description: This field is commonly used to describe the function of the user account.
- Password: The password is case-sensitive and may be up to 14 characters in length.

The following option fields can be toggled on or off:

- User Must Change Password at Next Logon: The user will be forced to change her password at the next logon. The user will be directed to the Change Password dialog box.
- User Cannot Change Password: This parameter is often set for service accounts and for accounts shared by multiple people.
- Password Never Expires: The user will not be required to change her password. This will override the option User Must Change Password at Next Logon.
- Account Disabled: The administrator can choose to create an account to use as a template for other accounts. By disabling the template account, no one will be able to log on using the template account.

 Always disable an account instead of deleting it if the account owner might return or the resources of the account will be assigned to a new user.

Clicking the appropriate icons will access details on group memberships, profile, logon hours, station restrictions, account type and expiration, and dial-in authorization. The following list explains the icons:

- Groups: By default, all new users are made members of the Domain Users group (see Figure 7.5). A user receives access to resources based on the collective permissions granted to her account and to the groups to which she belongs.

7

**Figure 7.5.**

*Assigning group memberships*

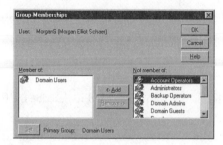

■ Profile: The User Environment Profile dialog box (see Figure 7.6) controls the location the system will look for roaming or mandatory profiles and logon scripts. If an NTFS partition is used, a home directory can also be created. The user will be the only one to receive access rights to the directory.

**Test Tip**

If the account you are creating will be used as a template, substitute the variable %USERNAME% for the account name when setting the profile or home directory. When the user account is copied as a template the new user name will be applied automatically.

**Figure 7.6.**

*Entering the UNC path to the user's profile.*

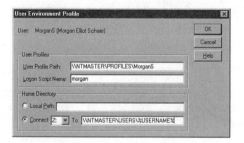

■ Hours: You can assign the hours during which the user is allowed to log on. By default all hours are allowed (see Figure 7.7). If a user stays logged on beyond his approved hours he will be disconnected only if the administrator has specified the option to do so in the global Account Policies. If he stays logged on, he will not be allowed to make any new connections and will receive a warning message every 10 minutes.

**Figure 7.7.**
*Valid logon hours for user MorganS.*

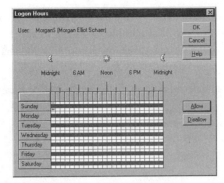

■ Logon to: You can restrict the user to specific workstations by specifying them by computer name. By default, all workstations are allowed (see Figure 7.8).

> By using computer names instead of physical addresses, a conflict does not develop if the network card is replaced.

**Figure 7.8.**
*The Logon Worksta-tions dialog box may be used to designate which workstations may be used to access the network.*

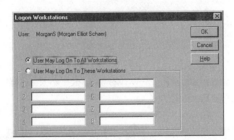

■ Account: A user account can be specified as either a local or a global account (see Figure 7.9). Always accept the default of Global unless the account is being created solely to allow access to a member of an untrusted domain such as LanManager. Local users are identified in User Manager for Domains by an icon of a computer next to a person.

**Figure 7.9.**
*The Account Informa-tion dialog box is used to designate an account as local or global.*

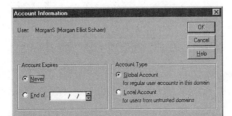

7

You can set an account expiration date. By setting an account to expire when a contract worker's time will be completed you are ensured that he will not be able to gain further access. It he returns, the account can be enabled.

■ Dial-in: Remote users might need access to the network via the remote access service (RAS). The permission to dial in to the network can be set from the Dialin Information dialog box (see Figure 7.10) or from the RAS Administration program. You also can configure here the type of callback security.

**Test Tip**

Although callback security can be used with RAS Multi-link, the return call only initializes a single line.

**Figure 7.10.**

*The Dialin Information dialog box.*

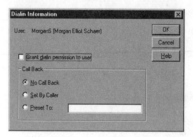

After selecting the Add button the new user is added to the system. The new user account is displayed in Figure 7.11.

**Figure 7.11.**

*User Manager for Domains showing the newly created user.*

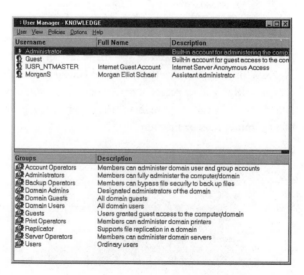

# 7.4. Managing Groups

This section demonstrates the proper methodology for implementing and administering groups within both a single and multiple domain environment.

You implement groups in NT in order to organize user accounts. When you organize accounts into groups, managing permissions and policies becomes easier.

## 7.4.1. Local Versus Global Groups

Two types of groups exist within a Microsoft NT network: local and global. Each of the groups serves a specific purpose. Understanding how each group functions independently is important. After you understand this you can understand how they work together.

Groups cannot be renamed.

Also, you cannot change a group from local to global or global to local.

### Local Groups

A local group is local to the systems that share the SAM database information where it was created. Because each of the listed systems maintains its own unique SAM database, a local group created on an NT Workstation, stand-alone server, or member server can be granted permissions only on the system it was created.

When a local group is created from a controller the group is being added to the SAM database at the PDC. Because the SAM database from the PDC is replicated to all BDCs, the local group will be available to each of the controllers.

Local groups created from a controller will not be available to NT workstations or NT member servers. Although they are members of the domain, they do not receive a replicant copy of the SAM database. Additionally, local groups cannot be made available across trusts to trusting domains.

Permissions are normally granted directly to local groups.

7

Local groups are identified in User Manager for Domains by an icon of a computer and two people.

**Local Group Membership**   A local group can contain the following members:

- Global user accounts from the local groups domain
- Local user accounts from the local groups domain
- Global groups from the local groups domain
- Global groups from trusted domains
- Global users from trusted domains

Note

Local groups cannot contain other local groups.

## Global Groups

Global groups can exist only on controllers. When a global group is created it is placed on the PDC and replicated with the SAM information to each of the BDCs. Although member servers and NT workstation domain members do not receive a copy of the group, they will be able to grant the group permissions to their resources. Permissions can be directly granted to the global group, but it is better to make the global group a member of a local group and assign the local group the resource permissions.

Global groups are available across trusts to members of a trusting domain. Global groups are identified in User Manager for Domains by an icon of a globe and two people.

**Global Group Membership**   A global group can contain only global users from the same domain.

## Creating Local and Global Groups

You use User Manager for Domains to create both local and global groups. Before creating the group you can select the desired group members by highlighting them and holding the Ctrl key while clicking them. After you select the group members, simply choose User from the menu bar and then either New Local Group or New Global Group.

When creating global groups the only potential global group members will be domain users from the same domain (see Figure 7.12). When assigning membership to a global group, all domain users are listed. If there are any local user accounts on that machine, they are not available to membership in this group.

**Figure 7.12.**
*Available user accounts that can be added to the new global group.*

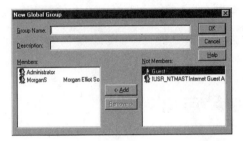

Local group members can include both local and global users and global groups (see Figure 7.13).

**Figure 7.13.**
*Available user and group accounts that can be included in the new local group.*

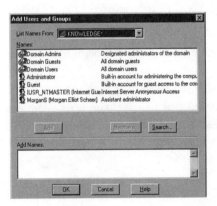

## 7.4.2. Special Groups

You do not directly control the membership of some special groups. The groups are special because membership is based more upon what you do rather than who you are. The name of each group explicitly describes its membership:

- Network: You are a member of the Network group if you are accessing the computer from across the network.
- Interactive: You are a member of the Interactive group if you are accessing the computer locally.

7

■ Everyone: You are a member just by virtue of logging on. The Everyone group includes all logged on users including the guest account.

> **Note**
>
> Because of special group permissions, you might have more or less access to certain resources when you are local to them versus when you are accessing them from the network.

### 7.4.3. Group Strategies

Granting resource privileges to groups rather than to users directly is preferable. The optimum methodology to assign permission is as follows:

1. Create a descriptive global group to organize the user accounts.
2. Make the user accounts members of the global group.
3. Create a descriptive local group at the place of the resource if one does not already exist.
4. Grant the local group the appropriate permissions to the resource.

On the surface, taking all these steps might seem unnecessary. Technically there is nothing wrong with assigning the user account permissions directly to the resource. The benefit in following this order is easier to appreciate when you try to track the permissions of a user from a single point or try to create an additional user with the same privileges of another.

> This is the preferred method of granting permissions. Remember that on the exam you might be asked not only what is the best method, but what is technically possible.

## 7.5. Implementing Policies

By properly implementing user policies, an NT administrator can easily control users' abilities to perform specific system functions. Policies are used to enforce rules on an NT network. These rules may apply to users and groups or even to the system itself.

This section demonstrates how to implement various rights utilizing both User Manager for Domains and the System Policy Editor.

## 7.5.1. Implementing User Rights

The user rights discussed in this section deal with specific abilities to perform actions such as logging on locally to a system. Do not confuse these rights with the rights or permissions assigned to users and groups to shares or NTFS resources.

An NT Server administrator modifies user rights by using User Manager for Domains. Rights allow users and groups to perform certain actions. For example, members of the Backup Operators group are able to both back up and restore local files; this is based on the Backup Operators group being assigned the right to perform these tasks as shown in Figure 7.14.

**Figure 7.14.**

*The Backup Operators group is assigned by default the rights to back up and restore the system.*

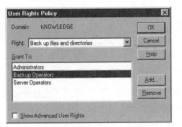

As an administrator, you can control access to the system both locally and from across the network through the use of rights. If a particular server was to be secured so that only members of the Accounting group could gain access from across the network, an administrator could remove the Everyone group from having the right to access this system from across the network. The Accounting group could then be added as the only group with network access to that server.

## 7.5.2. Implementing Account Policies

Account restrictions are another form of policy that an NT administrator can use to secure a system. One of the most common restrictions that an administrator can enforce is how passwords are handled for users of the system or domain. As Figure 7.15 shows, a majority of the account policies deal directly with password-related issues.

7

**Figure 7.15.**

*The majority of account policies deal directly with password issues.*

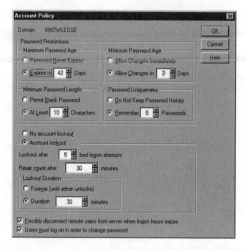

## Password Restrictions

Assigning password restrictions must be done while balancing out the security risks versus user convenience. When in doubt it is always safer to err on the side of caution. In Figure 7.15 the administrator is implementing some relatively strong account policies. The settings in the example vary from the default settings, which are more permissive.

- Users must change their password every 42 days.
- Passwords must be a minimum of 10 characters.
- Users can change their password only once every two days.
- By setting the password uniqueness to 5, it will be a minimum of 10 days before a user could reuse the same password. Multiply password uniqueness (5) by minimum password age (2) to derive the number 10.
- An account will be locked out for 30 minutes if five bad logon attempts occur within a period of 30 minutes.
- Users must log on to change their passwords. If they let a password expire an administrator must reassign a password for them.
- Users will be forcibly disconnected from the system if they remain attached over their allowed time window.

## 7.5.3. Implementing an Audit Policy

Implementing a proper audit policy is part of any good management and security plan. The key is determining which objects will be of value to audit. Never arbitrarily select the objects to audit; auditing the wrong objects will be of no value and auditing all objects will degrade system performance. By default auditing is disabled.

In Figure 7.16 an audit policy that covers the most frequently audited parameters has been implemented.

**Figure 7.16.**

*The audit policy can be configured to track the success and failures for various events.*

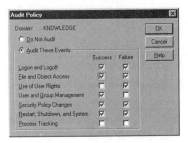

In Figure 7.16 the administrator has implemented an audit policy that will enable her to track basic attempts at security violations.

- **Logon and Logoff:** By tracking both successful and unsuccessful logon attempts, the administrator can verify both valid and invalid logon attempts and their sources.

- **File and Object Access:** Enabling this option as a policy does not in itself create an object audit trail. The administrator is required to identify which NTFS files and directories are to be audited. This option must also be selected for the option to audit the printer to function.

- **User and Group Management:** The administrator has chosen to audit when a successful change has been made to an account, such as a new member being added to a group or a password being changed.

- **Security Policy Changes:** All attempts to modify trust relationships, audit policies, and user rights can be tracked.

- **Restart, Shutdown, and System:** An entry is made to the security log whenever the system is restarted or shut down, or when the security log is truncated or overwritten.

All of the security events that are tracked will be recorded in the security log. The security log can be viewed through the Event Viewer.

7

# 7.6. Implementing System Policies

System policies are restrictions that the administrator can dictate which are effected as changes to the registry. The policies can be established for all computers and users of a domain or for only select users and computers. The primary tool for managing policies is the System Policy Editor. This section details the use and implementation of policies using this application.

## 7.6.1. The System Policy Editor

You can use the System Policy Editor to manage the local registry of a computer or to create a file of registry settings that will be implemented across the domain. The most common methodology is to create files that will be read by the Windows NT and Windows 95 clients at start time in order to ensure that the proper settings have been merged into the local registries of the systems.

### Creating a Domain Policy

Using the System Policy Editor, it is possible to create a single file (NTCONFIG.POL) of settings that will be read by all NT clients in the domain. Windows 95 clients support policies also, but they require a file named CONFIG.POL that is created via the Windows 95 policy editor.

When an NT client is logging on to the network, it will request a copy of NTCONFIG.POL from the NETLOGON share of the validating controller. The settings in the file will be applied to the local registry based upon what the computer name is and which user is logging on. If the network has multiple controllers, it is important to configure the directory replicator service to ensure that the policy files are available throughout the domain.

If the administrator wants to implement the same policies for all NT computers and users in the domain, she can create a single NTCONFIG.POL file that contains settings for the default computer and default user, as shown in Figure 7.17.

By modifying the settings for the default computer, the administrator can control the HKEY_LOCAL_MACHINE settings for all NT computers collectively. Modifying the default user will affect the HKEY_CURRENT_USER setting on all NT computers.

### Selectively Overriding the Domain Policy

It would be a utopian network wherein the same policies should be implemented for all users and computers identically. However, certain settings will need to be modified on an individual basis. The System Policy Editor accounts for this need by allowing overrides based upon username, group membership, and computer name.

**Figure 7.17.**

*The default user and default computer settings can be applied to all NT computers in the domain.*

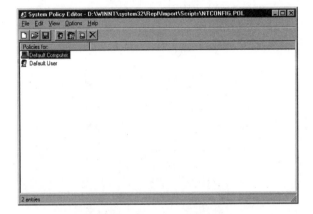

## Overriding Default Computer Settings

An administrator can override the default settings on a particular computer to make them more or less restrictive than the default settings. For example, Figure 7.18 shows how the logon banner could be modified for the computer UpFront.

**Figure 7.18.**

*The settings for UpFront in the NTCONFIG.POL file will override the default computer settings on that computer.*

The individual settings will only affect the computer named UpFront.

## Overriding Default User Settings on an Individual Basis

A different set of policies might need to be implemented when a certain user logs on the network. An administrator might want to restrict a user named Consultant from seeing the entire network. This could be accomplished by adding an entry in the NTCONFIG.POL file for the user as shown in Figure 7.19.

7

**Figure 7.19.**

*The user Consultant is restricted from seeing the Entire Network in Network Neighborhood.*

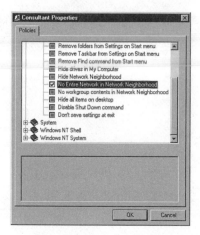

Regardless of which NT machine the user logs on to, the policies can be applied.

## Overriding Default User Settings on the Basis of Group Membership

Another situation might be in a bank. Here the administrator might want to restrict a group of individuals, such as the tellers, to only certain applications. The ability to perform this function also exists in the System Policy Editor, as shown in Figure 7.20.

**Figure 7.20.**

*Members of the Tellers group are restricted to only necessary applications.*

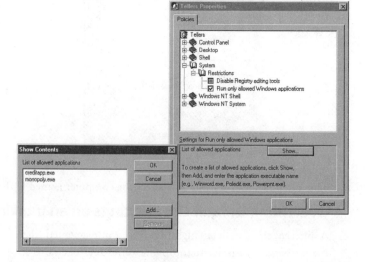

Because it is possible for a user to be a member of many groups, there is a chance that conflicting settings may be assigned in the policy file. In order to accommodate this situation, a group priority can be established as shown in Figure 7.21.

**Figure 7.21.**

*A group priority can be established to resolve conflicting policy settings.*

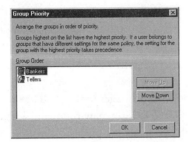

In the example shown in Figure 7.21, the settings in the Bankers group receive precedence over those in the Tellers group. The administrator will have to determine the proper group order in order to ensure that the policies are neither too lenient nor restrictive when a user is a member of multiple groups.

# 7.7. Implementing Profiles

NT 4.0 supports profiles in order to ensure that the proper user environment exists based upon user name. As changes are made to the user's preferences, such as colors, wallpaper, and so on, the changes are stored in the profile and will be available the next time the user logs on.

## 7.7.1. Implementing Local Profiles

A local profile is created automatically when a user logs on for the first time at an NT computer and is subsequently updated as changes to user preferences are made. By default the local profiles are stored in the `\%systemroot%\profiles\%username%` directory. Local profiles provide the most benefit when multiple users share a single computer.

## 7.7.2. Implementing Roaming Profiles

Roaming profiles are an excellent solution when users log on at more than one computer. By implementing roaming profiles held at a network share point, settings can follow users from one computer to another. Within the realm of roaming profiles are two types: personal and mandatory.

A *personal* profile will be modified as the user changes settings regardless of which computer he is working on. If the personal profile cannot be found at logon, the user can use a cached copy of the profile or create a new local.

7

**Test Tip** Never assign multiple users to the same personal profile. He who saves last wins...

A *mandatory* profile does not permit changes to the profile. Sharing a common mandatory profile is a good solution for a secure environment. Because the users cannot modify the profile it is possible to share a single profile with multiple users. If a user's mandatory profile is not available during logon, she will not gain access to the system.

# 7.8. Lab

This lab will help in your learning by testing you on the information presented in this chapter, as well as by giving you exercises to hone your skills. You can find answers to the review questions in Appendix B, "Answers to Review Questions."

## 7.8.1. Review Questions

### Question 1

Which of the following services synchronizes user and group accounts from the PDC to the BDCs?

A. Directory Replicator service

B. Schedule service

C. Alerter service

D. NetLogon service

### Question 2

Which of the following statements are true regarding the administrator account?

A. It cannot be disabled

B. It cannot be deleted

C. It cannot be renamed

D. It cannot be copied

### Question 3

Which of the following statements are true regarding the guest account?

A. It cannot be disabled

B. It cannot be deleted

C. It cannot be renamed

D. It cannot be copied

### Question 4

True or False. When a user account is deleted and then re-created with the same name it will receive a different SID.

7

## Question 5

True or False. An account that has been renamed still maintains the same SID.

## Question 6

Which of the following statements about local groups are true?

   A. Local groups can contain global groups

   B. Local groups can contain local groups

   C. Local groups can be renamed

   D. Local groups can be changed to global groups

## Question 7

Which of the following can be members of a local group?

   A. Global groups from the same domain

   B. Global groups from trusted domains

   C. Global groups from trusting domains

   D. Global users from trusting domains

## Question 8

Which of the following can be members of a global group?

   A. Global groups from the same domain

   B. Global groups from trusted domains

   C. Global groups from trusting domains

   D. Global users from the same domain

## Question 9

Which of the following would need to be enabled to track a print job?

   A. Auditing on the printer

   B. Auditing of file and object access

   C. Auditing of the use of user rights

   D. Auditing of security policy changes

## Question 10

Which of the following registry keys can be controlled through policy settings?

    A. `HKEY_LOCAL_MACHINE`

    B. `HKEY_SECURITY`

    C. `HKEY_HARDWARE`

    D. `HKEY_CURRENT_USER`

## Question 11

What is the best methodology for restricting members of the Accounting group to a specific windows-based application?

    A. Create a personal profile for each member.

    B. Assign a shared mandatory profile to each member of the group.

    C. Set restrictions for the group in `NTCONFIG.POL`.

    D. Set restrictions for the accounting computers in `NTCONFIG.POL`.

# 7.8.2. Exercises

## Exercise 7.1

You are installing a new Windows NT 4.0 network that will support 125 users in three different departments: Sales, HR, and Accounting. Three laser printers (one for each department) and one color printer (for the Sales department to use) are all on the network. Each department wants its managers to have access to all resources in the domain. How are you going to create these users accounts? What groups should you create?

## Exercise 7.2

The company in Exercise 7.1 has bought another company with a similar network. You must continue to support both domains; however, management needs access to resources in both domains. How will this affect your configuration?

7

# Day 8

# Managing Network Resources

*by David Schaer, John Hales, Edgar Torres, and Theresa Hadden*

## 8.1. Overview

This chapter focuses on the requirements necessary to make data available securely to others on the network. The chapter explains the proper methodology for establishing share permissions and demonstrates the interaction between Share and Local permissions.

In addition to managing shares, at the conclusion of this chapter you should be confident that you could determine which print setup is appropriate in a given situation, how to configure the proper print scenario, and how to troubleshoot basic printing errors.

### 8.1.1. Objectives

The following are the objectives for the Windows NT Server and Enterprise exams:

- Adding and configuring a printer
- Implementing a printer pool
- Setting print priorities
- Managing disk resources by creating and sharing resources, as well as implementing permissions and security
- Choosing the appropriate course of action to take to resolve printer problems
- Choosing the appropriate course of action to take to resolve resource access problems and permission problems

## 8.1.2. Fast Facts

The following list of facts is a concise picture of the information presented in this chapter. It acts as both an overview for the chapter and as a study aid to help you do any last-minute cramming.

- Only administrators and server operators can create shares on NT domain controllers.
- Permissions on shares can augment permissions set on files and directories.
- Access rights are collective unless a user or a group they are a member of is granted NO ACCESS.
- Default share permissions are set to Everyone Full Control.
- When Share and NTFS permissions are combined the most restrictive permissions apply.
- You monitor active shares by using Server Manager.
- Pausing the server service before disconnecting users from a share will prevent them from reconnecting.
- Share permissions are the only vehicle in NT for securing FAT partitions.
- A connection limit can control the number of concurrent connections to a share point.
- Older DOS-based clients might not be able to access shares with names longer than 8.3 characters in length.
- When accessing data from across the network you are a member of the network group.
- When accessing data interactively you are a member of the interactive group.
- A printer is a virtual device; it is the software interface between the application and the printer.
- A print device is a physical device; it is the actual physical printing hardware.
- The DLC protocol must be installed as a protocol if you want to print to the Hewlett-Packard Network Port.
- By default, the EVERYONE group is granted print permission when a new printer is created.
- By default, only members of Administrators, Server Operators, and Print Operators can control a new printer.
- Multiple printers can point to a single print device.
- A printer can be serviced by a print device that is either local or remote.

8

- A printer pool is created by pointing a single printer to multiple print devices.
- Print jobs sent to a printer during hours of unavailability will remain in the spooler until the printer is available.
- Print drivers from NT 3.x cannot be used on NT 4.0.
- It is better to install a print driver centrally on the print server rather than at each individual client. This is the case when clients are Windows 95 or NT.
- Changing a printer's priority will change the default priority of print jobs serviced by the printer.
- Although NT can print to a Novell NetWare print server, the driver must be manually installed on the client.
- The right to access specific printers can be granted on a user or group level.
- If applications do not support reprinting of documents, the printer can be set to hold printed documents in the spooler.
- Printing to a TCP/IP-based print device requires Microsoft TCP/IP print services to be installed.
- UNIX-based clients can print to an NT-based printer if the printer is running the Line Printer Daemon.
- The default location for spooling is on the boot partition. This can be changed by modifying the registry.

# 8.2. Sharing Directories

Setting up a server and installing all the hardware, making it fault tolerant, setting permissions on files and folders, setting up users and groups, and creating policies is all for naught without the capability to access the data across the network. If you are familiar with NetWare, this concept might seem foreign to you.

In NetWare, access to folders is automatic if you have the appropriate rights (or in NT parlance, permissions). Windows NT, however, does not operate in this manner. In NT, access to data across the network cannot take place until the data is first shared. Once shared, data can be accessed across the network, subject to NTFS and share permissions.

## 8.2.1. Who Can Share Data?

The question is, who can share data? Average users do not have that authority. The following can share data:

- Administrators
- The Power Users group on NT Workstation or NT Server installed as a Member or stand-alone server
- The Server Operators group

## 8.2.2. What Can Be Shared?

Only folders can be shared, but once shared, they will remain available as long as the computer is running, regardless of who is currently logged on. When a folder is shared, all the information in that folder and all subfolders will also be available. NTFS permissions can be set on folders as well as on files.

The Server service must also be started for the data to be accessed.

## 8.2.3. Implementing Security on Shares

Security is one of the most important aspects of your job as a network administrator. It is important to put the data where users can get to it and do what they need to do, but no more.

The security of the network enables us to have confidence in the data stored on the network. Without it, we can never be sure the data on the network is accurate or that unauthorized individuals have not stolen, changed, deleted, or otherwise accessed or modified the data. So what are the threats to your security?

- Ignorant users: This is probably the biggest source of problems. The term *ignorant users* implies not that they are dumb or stupid, just uninformed about certain issues, including security and what certain files or folders are for.
- Malicious users: Those users who have an ax to grind and are purposely trying to cause problems, for example by deleting files or accessing confidential data such as payroll.
- Industrial spies/competitors: Those who are trying to gather data, such as customer lists, for the competition.

Knowing the source of the threats enables you to deal with them. Because most of the problems that you are likely to encounter are in the form of the accidental mistakes users cause, you must plan a policy that protects the data from, and maybe in spite of, the users. This having been said, the users obviously need the appropriate access to their data to do their jobs, and if you are too restrictive, their productivity will suffer and frustration will mount.

Now take a look at what control you have over the shares you set up. In doing so, please keep in mind that on a FAT partition, share permissions are the only control you have. An NTFS partition has a combination of permissions that will be discussed later in the chapter in section 8.5.

By default, the group Everyone gets full control to all shares you create.

### 8.2.4. The Four Levels of Share Control

The following are the four levels of share control (from most to least restrictive):

- No Access: Disenables all access and overrides and other permission that may be granted from other sources.
- Read: Enables read-only access to all data within the share. Data can be viewed, files can be searched and browsed, but nothing can be changed or deleted. No new files can be written.
- Change: Enables the same access as Read, with the additional capabilities to modify existing files, add new files, and delete existing files.
- Full Control: Enables all the access of Change, with the additional capability to exercise the NTFS permissions of Change Permission and Take Ownership.

As you can see from the preceding list, the default assignment of Everyone to full control will probably need to be modified, unless all permissions will be controlled through NTFS.

## 8.3. Granting Access to Users and Groups

It is better administrative practice to assign permissions based on groups rather than by individual users. This same logic is applied when assigning permissions in an NT environment.

Permissions apply to resources, not to users. They are used to create the access control list (ACL).

### 8.3.1. AGLP

Now that you know the permissions, you must learn to manage them. You can grant access to any user or group (local or global) in your domain and any user or global group in any trusted domains. As was previously discussed, Microsoft's AGLP (Accounts—such as Users—in Global groups in Local groups that are then granted Permissions) policy recommendation dictates that you place your users (from any domain) in the appropriate global groups and then place these global groups in the local groups and then, and only then, grant permissions to the local groups only. This obviously is not a hard and fast rule, but it will make your life easier if you abide by it and forgo assigning permission to users.

## 8.3.2. Combining User and Group Permissions

Knowing that you can assign permission to users and groups, you might wonder what the net, or effective, permissions will be if a user belongs to multiple groups that are granted permissions. The user gets the sum of permissions granted to each group of which she is a member, plus any permissions assigned to her individually. If she or any of the groups to which she belongs is given No Access permission, she will get No Access. For example, If user A is given Read permission and he also belongs to group B, which has Change permission, he will get Read plus Change permission, which equals Change. If you take that example and continue by stating that he also belongs to group C, which has No Access permission, then user A will have No Access.

No Access will always win out over any other permission. Use it sparingly.

# 8.4. How to Implement Shared Directories

Sharing directories is the means by which an administrator must make data accessible on an NT network. This section details how the share is established and how to properly protect the resources with permissions.

### 8.4.1. Setting Up Shares and Assigning Permissions

8

Share permissions are assigned in one of several ways. The most common is to right-click the folder that you want to share, and click Sharing. Figure 8.1 shows the first step in creating a new share.

**Figure 8.1.**

*A shortcut menu is presented when you click a folder with the secondary mouse button.*

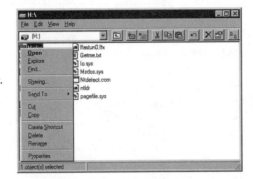

On the Sharing tab of the properties dialog box for the folder Msdos, the administrator then clicks Shared As, instead of Not Shared (the default for all folders) and enters a share name (see Figure 8.2).

**Figure 8.2.**

*Here you can determine the name of your share.*

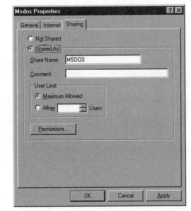

For share names, stick to the familiar DOS 8.3 names unless all of your clients can use long filenames (Windows 95 or NT); otherwise, those clients that don't support long names will not be able to access the share.

> **Test Tip**
>
> To make a share name invisible from across the network, end the name with a $, such as Money$.

While defining a share, the user can also specify a connection limit—for example, to prevent too many users from simultaneously accessing a piece of software. Note that after a folder is shared, a new button, New Share, appears when you return to the Sharing tab. This button enables you to share the same folder with another name and, optionally, apply different permissions. (See Figure 8.3)

**Figure 8.3.**

*You can create more than one share that points to the same folder.*

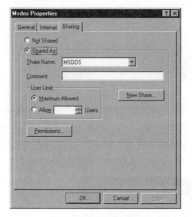

> **Test Tip**
>
> If you want to make your share names descriptive, but you still must support DOS clients, you can share the folder twice, once with a long name for the 95/NT clients and once for the DOS, Windows 3.x, and Windows for Workgroups clients.

The final thing you must do when sharing a file is to set permissions. As mentioned previously, the default is to give everyone full control. As shown in Figure 8.4, click the Permissions button and change the default for Everyone, or add or remove groups and permissions as needed.

To grant permissions to a new user or group, click the Add button as shown in Figure 8.4 and the Add Users and Groups dialog box will appear.

In this box, add groups or click the Show Users button and choose the users you want. You may also pick global groups and users from other trusted domains by clicking the down arrow next to List Names From box (see Figure 8.5).

8

**Figure 8.4.**

*The Permissions button enables you to limit access to the newly created share.*

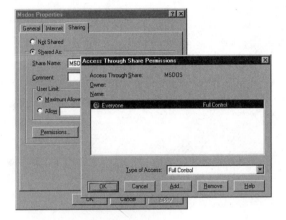

**Figure 8.5.**

*You can add users and groups from trusted domains.*

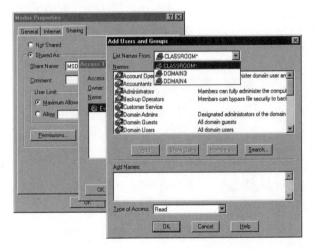

The permission shown in the Type of Access combo box at the bottom of the dialog box applies to all the users and groups you are currently selecting. If one permission will apply to most of the users and groups, set it here now. When you have finished, click OK.

You are presented with the Access Through Share Permissions dialog box shown in Figure 8.6. You can remove unwanted users or groups by clicking the Remove button. You also can change permissions for individual users or groups by first selecting that user or group and then clicking the down arrow next to the permission you want to assign.

**Figure 8.6.**

*Use the Access Through Share Permissions dialog box to remove unwanted users or groups or change permissions.*

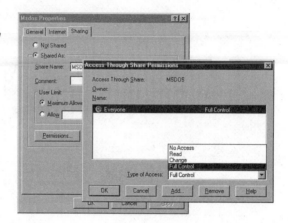

When you have finished, click OK to return to the main sharing dialog box, and then click OK again to finish. When you look at that folder now in Windows Explorer, it is being held by a hand as if it were a platter being served up (see Figure 8.7).

**Figure 8.7.**

*The Msdos share has been created.*

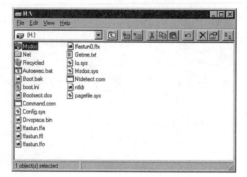

**Test Tip**

You will see the hand only if you have the right to share or stop sharing directories. The average user will not see the hand under any folder.

# 8.5. Calculating Effective Rights

Calculating effective rights is an important aspect in ensuring that the proper permissions have been applied to a resource. Calculating the effective rights takes into account the total set of permissions granted and denied, both individually and as a group member.

8

When a user accesses resources interactively, only the NTFS permissions come into play.

## 8.5.1. Combining NTFS and Share Permissions

Now turn your attention to the issue of how NTFS and share permissions work together. When a user accesses a resource via the network, the combined NTFS and the combined share permissions contained in the ACL (Access Control List) are compared and the most restrictive permission applies. Recall that both NTFS and share permissions are calculated by looking at the user and all group accounts to which the user may belong and taking the sum of permissions, with the exception of No Access, which overrides all other permissions.

The net or effective permissions of NTFS and share permissions is always the most restrictive of the two.

## 8.5.2. Examples of Combined Permissions

Now look at a few examples of combining share and NTFS permissions, beginning with some fairly easy ones and moving on to some more complex ones.

### Example 1

Joe belongs to the group Sales, which has been assigned Read permission to the share and the NTFS permission of Change. What can Joe do across the network? Interactively?

Across the network Joe will have the lesser permission of Read and Change, which is Read. He will have read-only access to any of the data on that share. If he accesses the resource interactively (at the machine with the share), he will have no restrictions from the share, so the local NTFS permissions of Change will be the only restrictions in place.

### Example 2

This scenario is just the opposite of Example 1. This time, Sales has Change permission on the share and the NTFS permission of Read. What can Joe do across the network? Interactively?

The answer is similar to Answer 1. Across the network Joe will have the lesser permission of Read and Change, which is Read. He will have read-only access to any of the data on that share. If he sits at the machine with the share (interactive access), he will also have read-only permission.

### Example 3

Mary belongs to the group Accountants and the group Sales. She needs access to a share with Account Receivable information, called AR. The following share permissions have been assigned: Accountants have Change and Sales has No Access. In addition, the data is stored on an NTFS partition, and the following NTFS permissions have been assigned: Accountants has Full Control and Sales has Read. What can Mary do across the network? Interactively?

Both NTFS and share permissions must be calculated independently. The net result of each of these calculations is compared to get the effective permissions. For the share permissions, Mary will get Change plus No Access, yielding No Access. For NTFS permissions, however, Mary will have Read plus Full Control, netting Full Control. Her effective permissions, however, are No Access across the network but Full Control locally. You might want to use this approach if, for example, you wanted to allow the sales people to access the data in a controlled manner, for example in the accountant's office.

# 8.6. Administering Shares

Now that you know how to set up shares and set permissions on them, next look at how to manage them. How do you see what is shared on a particular computer? How do you see who is accessing those shares? How do you handle management of shares?

## 8.6.1. Monitoring Shares with Server Manager

The tool that you use to manage all these issues is Server Manager. It is located in the Administrative Tools folder under Programs on the Start menu. Figure 8.8 shows the Server Manager.

**Test Tip**

You will see several shares named C$, D$, IPC$, and ADMIN$ from within Server Manager. These shares are hidden administrative shares created by the system.

8

**Figure 8.8.**

*The Server Manager.*

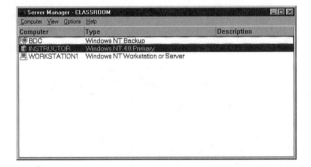

Server Manager enables you to see who is allowed to be a member of your domain by showing you all the computer accounts. Remember that these accounts are required only for NT-based computers. Because most, if not all, of your servers will be NT Server-based, they will all show up here. To see who is using a machine and what they are doing, simply select the computer in question, click the Computer menu, and select Properties to display the dialog box shown in Figure 8.9.

**Figure 8.9.**

*Properties of the selected computer.*

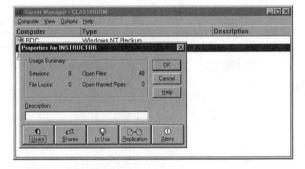

You can also access a computer's properties by double-clicking it in Server Manager.

As Figure 8.9 shows, there are two main ways that you can see who is accessing the server: You can look by Users or by Shares. The Users button lets you see all of the connected users. When you click any given user, any shares they are accessing are displayed on the bottom half of the screen (see Figure 8.10).

**Figure 8.10.**

*The connected users and what shares are being accessed.*

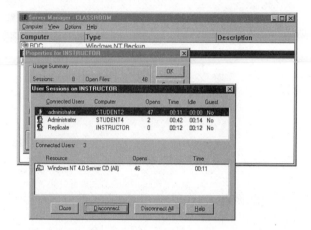

The other method of looking at what is happening is by share. Click the Shares button to see a list of all the shares on that computer. Click the desired share to see a list of who is using that share. This enables you to see the same data as in the user's dialog box, but from the opposite direction as shown in Figure 8.11.

**Figure 8.11.**

*The shared resources.*

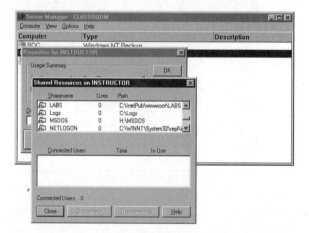

You can disconnect either individual users or all users at once from either dialog box; however, this is not the recommended method because users might have data files open, and this would lose or corrupt data. Use this only as a last resort. Simply disconnecting a user accomplishes very little because the client can reconnect as needed.

8

If you want to prevent the user from reconnecting to the share (as well as all other users connecting to any new share), you should pause the Server service (either by using Control Panel/Services, or Server Manager/Services, selecting the Server service and clicking Pause). (See Figure 8.12.) After you pause the Server service, disconnect the user or all users. Remember, though, this can result in loss or corruption of data.

**Figure 8.12.**
*The service applet.*

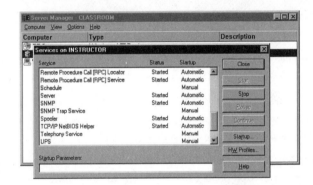

You can also share and stop sharing folders from Server Manager by going to the Computer menu and selecting Shared Directories. In the Shared Directories dialog box (see Figure 8.13) you will see all the shared directories. You can modify existing ones, create new ones, or stop sharing existing ones.

Use this method to remotely manage shares as well as to create them.

**Figure 8.13.**
*All shares.*

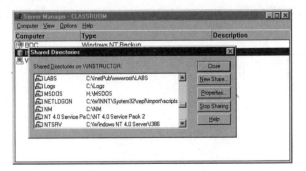

# 8.7. Printing Terminology

Printing has historically been one of the major problem areas for network administrators. With NT Server 4.0, Microsoft has significantly simplified several of the major print operations that must be performed. However, with the simplification of printing comes both more print options and new print terminology.

Before examining this chapter further, be sure you are familiar with a few basic terms. Pay special attention to terminology that is applied differently by other vendors.

A *printer* is defined as the software interface that resides between the application and the physical print device.

A *print device* is commonly called a printer in most other network environments. The print device is the physical device that actually produces the printed page.

A print device is considered a *local print device* when it is directly connected to the computer providing the print services. If the print device is connected to the network directly, it is considered a *remote print device.*

These items certainly are not a complete list of the NT printing terms, but they are enough to start you off as you get into the details of printing.

# 8.8. Creating a Printer

You add a printer both to create a new printer that will control either a local or network print device attached to the local computer, and to connect to a print device managed by a remote print server.

## 8.8.1. Running the Add Printer Wizard

Run the Add Printer Wizard to walk you through the basic installation and configuration of a printer.

The first choice to make when running the wizard is whether the printer being installed will access a print device managed by the local computer or one managed by another system, a print server (see Figure 8.14).

When the selected location of the print device is My Computer you must next specify on which port or ports the print device or devices are located.

**Figure 8.14.**

*The opening screen of the Add Printer Wizard.*

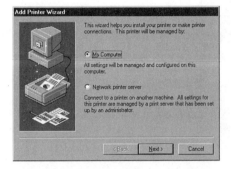

## 8.8.2. Selecting the Printer Ports

To understand printer ports, just remember that the printer is merely the software interface which connects to the print devices. The selected ports are where the printer will send print jobs. The ports can be local ports attached to the computer, as is the case with parallel and serial connections, or they can point to remote network printer devices such as Hewlett-Packard Jet Direct print boxes or even other shared network printers. In Figure 8.15 the printer is configured to print to LPT1.

**Figure 8.15.**

*The printer is configured to print to LPT1.*

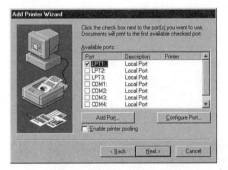

## 8.8.3. Enabling Printer Pooling

Printer pooling enables an administrator to configure a single printer to send print jobs to multiple print devices. The ports selected can be made up of a combination of local and network print devices or exclusively a single type as in Figure 8.16.

The print devices are not required to be identical; however, they must support the same print driver. For example, an administrator could combine both Hewlett-Packard and Epson printers into a printer pool provided that they support the same print driver.

**Figure 8.16.**
*Printer pooling has been enabled. The printer can send to either LPT1 or COM1.*

The printer devices should be located in close physical proximity to one another because the user controls only which printer to print to, not which print device will be used to service the print job.

By establishing a printer pool an administrator can make better use of available resources. An automatic rollover to the next print device in the pool will occur when the first one is busy or unavailable.

## 8.8.4. Installing a Print Driver

The print driver determines the escape code sequence used to initialize the print device and control additional print functions. Each supported printer will come with an NT 4.0 print driver. The example in Figure 8.17 shows the HP LaserJet 5Si selected as the print driver.

**Figure 8.17.**
*The HP LaserJet 5Si is selected as the print driver.*

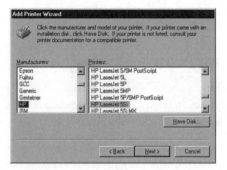

If the print driver is not shown in the default list of print drivers that comes with NT Server 4.0 you can add additional drivers at this time.

**Note**

You cannot use print drivers from NT 3.x with NT 4.0.

8

You can find a list of supported print drivers on the NT 4.0 Server HCL. Remember that when installing a driver for a printer pool it is important to select a driver that can be understood by all the print devices.

If the printer is configured as a shared printer you must then determine which network clients will be accessing the printer. NT provides a slight-of-hand style method of installing print drivers for the clients. In the case of NT and Windows 95 clients the NT print server can pass back the appropriate driver for the client's operating system transparently to the user. On an Intel-based Windows NT 4.0 client the driver will be installed in `\%Winroot%\system32\spool\drivers\w32x86`.

In the example in Figure 8.18 the printer is configured with drivers for both Windows 95 and NT 4.0 DEC Alpha systems. These are, of course, in addition to the driver for Intel-based NT 4.0 machines because that is the operating system of the print server.

**Figure 8.18.**

*Additional drivers for Windows 95 and NT 4.0 for the Alpha platform are selected.*

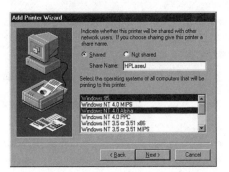

The administrator should install the print drivers only on the print server, not on the client's machines. Multiple clients and platforms are supported.

The installation of multiple drivers is an issue only when the computer will be used as a print server and provide services to other than Intel-based NT 4.0 clients. As can be noted in Figure 8.18, the printer has been shared as HPLaserJ. Sharing the printer is what designates a computer as a print server.

## 8.9. Connecting to a Shared Printer

You can connect to a shared printer in several ways: from the Add Printer Wizard, Network Neighborhood, and from the command prompt. Each of the methods has the same end result: printing is directed from the client computer to the shared printer. The connection can be identified either by a UNC connection, such as \\NTMASTER\HPLaserJ or a redirected logical device name, such as LPT1 or COM1.

### 8.9.1. Printer Security

Access to the printer is controlled by NT security mechanisms. You rarely would attempt to control access to a print device on a user's local system; this is normally reserved for shared network devices. The default permissions assigned on an NT printer are shown in Figure 8.19. Notice that by default everyone can print.

**Figure 8.19.**

*The default permissions assigned to a printer.*

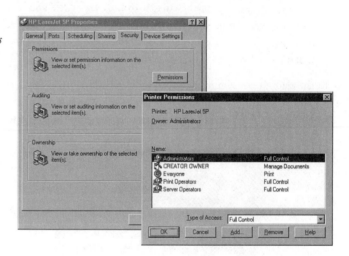

Notice the use of the special group CREATOR OWNER. Although Everyone can print, users become the CREATOR OWNER only of their own print jobs. This enables a user to manage his own print jobs but not those belonging to others unless they have been assigned additional permissions.

Total managerial control of the printer and all print jobs is granted initially only to Administrators, Server Operators, and Print Operators. The administrator can control a user's access individually to the printer by assigning any of the following rights: No Access, Print, Manage Documents, and Full Control. As is the case with security throughout NT, the No Access permission will nullify any other permission to the resource whether received individually or by group membership.

### 8.9.2. Managing Shared Printer Properties

When sharing a printer on a network, the settings applied to the printer properties can have a serious impact on the functionality and availability of the printer.

8

## Scheduling Printer Availability

The hours of the day that a printer services documents can be controlled through scheduling. The range of hours does not control the hours that the user can send jobs to the printer but rather the hours that the printer will service the submitted jobs.

One common implementation of the scheduling feature is to create two printers that point to the same print device. One printer would be scheduled to be serviced 8a.m.–5p.m. and the other from 5p.m.–8a.m. Large jobs such as batch reports could be directed by the user to the printer to be serviced at night (see Figure 8.20).

**Figure 8.20.**

*The printer properties page is used to control printer settings, including scheduling and priority.*

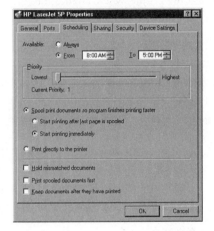

This method provides excellent availability of the printer during the day for more time-critical jobs. Users must make the decision of which printer to direct the jobs to.

## Setting Printer Priority

By setting the printer priority it is possible to adjust the default priority assigned to jobs being serviced by the printer. This setting can be used when several printers point to the same physical print device. Based upon which printer the users submit their jobs to, the level of preference given to those jobs in the print order will be determined.

## Spooling Print Jobs

Spooling is the process of queuing print jobs. By default, print jobs are spooled to the boot partition; however, this can be modified through the registry.

How the NT printer uses the spooler is controlled via printer properties. On the most basic level an administrator can select to either spool print jobs or to print directly to the printer. Printing directly to the printer is faster than spooling; however, the ability to control the print jobs is lost.

When spooling is selected the administrator has the option to modify the following settings:

- Hold Mismatched Documents: The printer will verify that the print job has been submitted in a format understood by the print device before submitting it.
- Print Spooled Documents First: A print job that is fully spooled will be sent to the print device even ahead of higher priority jobs that are still spooling.
- Keep Documents After They Have Printed: Print jobs remain in the spooler even after being submitted to the print device. This is an excellent option to select for users, such as accounting people, whose applications might not enable them to resubmit a print job.

Sometimes a job gets stuck in the spooler, you cannot delete it, and it does not print although the Print Manager indicates that the job is being printed. Stop and then restart the spooler service. This will free up the job so you can remove it.

# 8.10. Printing in a Multi-Vendor Environment

Microsoft will expect an MCSE to be competent in installing NT print services in heterogeneous environments. As an MCSE you will commonly encounter the need to direct printing to non-NT-based systems, including Novell NetWare and UNIX.

## 8.10.1. Printing to a NetWare Server

To print to a NetWare-based print server you must have installed Gateway Services for NetWare. This will allow the NT 4.0 Server to both print to the NetWare print server directly and redirect jobs to the NetWare print server on behalf of its clients.

The NetWare print server is not configured to pass print drivers back to NT clients. It is necessary for the administrator of the NT Server to load a compatible driver manually when connecting to a NetWare-based print server.

8

## 8.10.2. Printing with TCP/IP

Installing the TCP/IP print services provides two functions. The NT server will be able to print to UNIX and other TCP/IP-based print servers, and UNIX clients will be able to direct print jobs to the NT printer.

The configuration of the TCP/IP printing is relatively simple. The first step, as shown in Figure 8.21, is to install the TCP/IP print services.

**Figure 8.21.**

*Installing Microsoft TCP/IP Printing Services.*

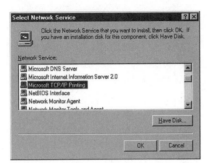

This alone is sufficient to be a client to TCP/IP-based print servers and network printers using the LPR command or to redirect print jobs to the LPR port. However, in order to allow UNIX clients access, the TCP/IP print service must be started on the NT server. This service is essentially a print daemon that will enable the NT server to accept inbound print requests to TCP/IP ports. After the service is started, running the LPQ command will show the status of the printer.

> To print to an LPR port, you must supply the name or IP address of the print server and the name of the printer.

## 8.10.3. Hewlett-Packard Printing Support

Before being able to direct printers to a Hewlett-Packard network print device using a Jet Direct card you must first load the DLC protocol. After the DLC protocol is installed the Hewlett-Packard Network Port is listed as an available port as shown in Figure 8.22.

**Figure 8.22.**

*Loading DLC makes the Hewlett-Packard Network Port available.*

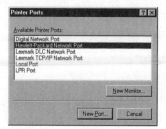

The key is to remember that the only way to enable the Hewlett-Packard Network Port is to load DLC. This will let the NT print server communicate with the print server. As is outlined fully in Chapter 3, "Installing NT Server 4.0," the DLC protocol is not a routable protocol.

# 8.11. Lab

This lab will aid in your learning by testing you on the information presented in this chapter, as well as by giving you exercises to hone your skills. Answers to the review questions can be found in Appendix B, "Answers to Review Questions."

**8**

## 8.11.1. Review Questions

### Question 1

Membership in which of the following groups will let a user share directories on an NT 4.0 Server?

    A.  Domain Users

    B.  Administrators

    C.  Domain Admins

    D.  Server Operators

### Question 2

Which of the following services must be active in order to share data on an NT 4.0 Server?

    A.  Directory Replicator service

    B.  Server service

    C.  Workstation service

    D.  Messenger service

### Question 3

What built-in group are you made a member of when accessing data from a share point on another computer?

    A.  Interactive

    B.  Network

    C.  Domain Users

    D.  Domain Guests

### Question 4

Which of the following administrative tools are used to manage shares?

    A.  Server Manager

    B.  User Manager for Domains

C. System Policy Editor

D. Disk Administrator

## Question 5

A certain user attempts to access a share point on an NTFS partition of a remote computer. The share has been marked Everyone Full Control, yet she is unable to access any files in the directory. What is the probable cause?

A. The user is connecting to the wrong share.

B. The user is running an older version of Windows.

C. The Interactive group has been granted No Access.

D. Her access rights are being blocked by more restrictive NTFS permissions.

## Question 6

What is the safest and most effective way to prevent new users from attaching to a server's share points?

A. Remove the right to Access this Computer from the Network from the Everyone group.

B. Stop the Server service.

C. Pause the Server service.

D. Pause the Netlogon service.

## Question 7

What is designated by a share name ending in a dollar sign ($)?

A. The share is inactive.

B. The share is hidden.

C. The share has reached the maximum concurrent connections.

D. The share is permitted for administrators only.

## Question 8

While logged on the server as an administrator you shared a directory. Now logged on with your standard user account you are unable to see the hand icon designating the directory as shared. What is the most probable reason the directory does not show as having been shared?

A. Only administrators can see shared directories.

B. You assigned the Everyone group No Access to the share.

C. You are not a member of administrators or server operators.

D. The server service has been paused.

## Question 9

When applying the rules of AGLP, which of the following would ideally be permitted at the share point?

A. Local users

B. Global users

C. Local groups

D. Global groups

## Question 10

The members of the accounting department have complained that when the printer jams they cannot resubmit jobs from their application and the print jobs are lost. Which of the following settings will help prevent this?

A. Print Directly to Printer

B. Hold Mismatched Jobs

C. Keep Documents after Printing

D. Set Allow Global Reprint to true

## Question 11

Which of the following statements about printer pools are true?

A. A printer pool requires that every print device be from the same manufacturer.

B. A printer pool requires that every print device support the same print driver.

C. A printer pool can utilize only local print devices.

D. A printer pool is created by directing multiple printers to the same print device.

## Question 12

An administrator has installed a Hewlett-Packard network port print device. However, the option to select the HP port does not appear as an option. What must the administrator do to enable the HP print port as an available option?

A. Start the print server daemon.

B. Install TCP/IP.

C. Install DLC.

D. Load an HP print driver.

## Question 13

The administrator of an NT network has Windows 95, NT, and Windows for Workgroups clients. The NT clients are comprised of both Intel-based and RISC-based machines. Which of the following steps must the administrator perform in order to let all users access a common print device?

A. Load the proper print driver on the RISC-based clients.

B. Load drivers for the Intel-based clients on the print server.

C. Load drivers for the RISC-based clients on the print server.

D. Load the proper print driver on the Windows for Workgroups clients.

## Question 14

The administrator of an NT network wants to restrict printing to a particular print device only to members of the accounting group and those who perform printer support. Which of the following steps will the administrator be required to perform after installing the print device?

A. Create a printer that directs output to the print device.

B. Grant No Access to the Everyone group.

C. Remove the Everyone group.

D. Grant Print to the Accounting group.

## Question 15

Members of which of the following groups would be capable of removing a newly created printer?

A. Administrators

B. Server Operators

C. Print Managers

D. Everyone

## Question 16

A particular printer is scheduled to be available only during certain hours of the day. What will the results be when a user's job is sent to the printer during unavailable hours?

A. The job will be rejected and the user will be notified.

B. The job will be rejected but the user will not be notified.

C. The job will be accepted and printed during available hours.

D. An error will be logged in the security log.

## Question 17

A network contains a printer configured with default settings and a single print device. What is the most effective method for the administrator to ensure that jobs printed by the Accounting group are ordered before all other print jobs?

A. Create a second printer that is permitted only to the Accounting group.

B. Create a second printer that is permitted only to the Accounting group and set the priority to 1.

C. Create a second printer that is permitted only to the Accounting group and set the priority to 99.

D. Install a second print device and configure a printer pool.

## Question 18

Which of the following are the minimal permissions required to delete jobs submitted to a printer by another user?

A. Full control

B. Creator/Owner

C. Manage documents

D. Print

## Question 19

When accessing a Novell NetWare print server via a Microsoft NT Server running Gateway Services for NetWare, which of the following steps must be performed at an NT client?

A. Install NWLink, the IPX/SPX-compatible transport.

B. Load Client Services for NetWare.

C. Install the print driver.

D. None of the above.

## 8.11.2. Exercises

### Exercise 8.1

Plan a file structure that would allow access to all files and directories under the SALES directory to the Manager group. However, you want to limit access to read only to the User group and deny all access to Myria.

### Exercise 8.2

Describe how you would install a single print device with two bins; one contains forms for printing checks and one contains forms for printing orders. You want the Accountants group to only be able to print checks on this print device and the Sales group to only be able to print orders from their customers.

# Day 9

# NT Server 4.0 Network Clients

*by David Schaer, Keith McCabe, and Theresa Hadden*

## 9.1. Overview

This chapter provides you with the necessary knowledge to meet the MCSE exam requirement of determining which client should be used in a given situation.

### 9.1.1. Objectives

This section reviews the clients that are included as part of the Windows NT Server 4.0 software library. It covers which clients work with which protocols. In addition, it discusses added tools and their benefits in the software library to give the clients improved functionality. The following are the Microsoft objectives covered in this chapter:

- Configure a Windows NT Server computer for various types of client computers including Windows NT Workstation, Microsoft Windows 95, and Microsoft MS-DOS–based clients.
- Administer remote servers from Windows 95 and Windows NT Workstation client computers.

### 9.1.2. Fast Facts

The following list of facts is a concise picture of the information presented in this chapter. It acts as both an overview for the chapter and as a study aid to help you do any last-minute cramming.

- Windows NT Workstation 4.0 supports TCP/IP, IPX/SPX, NetBEUI, and DLC.
- Windows 95 supports TCP/IP, IPX/SPX, NetBEUI, and DLC.
- Microsoft Client for MS-DOS and Windows does not support SPX compatibility, but does support IPX compatibility.
- Microsoft Client for MS-DOS and Windows has a full redirector enabling it to log on, access network file and print sharing, and access RAS services as well as IPCs.
- Windows 95 and NT Workstation use 32-bit protected-mode network drivers to give greater speed with fewer problems.
- Network client-based administrator software is specific to Windows NT Workstation and Windows 95 machines, and each has its own client-based administrative software.
- Windows NT Workstation Administrator Tools require 2.5MB of free hard disk space on the System partition in addition to the minimal requirements for NT Workstation.
- Administrative tools that can be added to NT Workstation are DHCP Manager, Remote Access Administrator, Remoteboot Manager, Server Manager, System Policy Editor, User Manager for Domains, and WINS Manager.
- Windows 95 requires a 486/33 CPU or better, at least 8MB of RAM and 3MB of free disk space on the system partition to use the administrative tools.
- Windows 95 Server tools include Event Viewer, File Security, Print Security, Server Manager, User Manager for Domains, User Manager Extensions for Services for NetWare, and File and Print Services for NetWare.
- To use Administrator Tools Windows NT Workstation needs both Workstation and Server services running. Windows 95 must be running Client for Microsoft Networks.
- In order for Windows 95 User Manager Extensions for Services for NetWare to run, either FPNW or DSMN must be loaded on the NT Server. Windows 95 File and Print Services for NetWare requires File and Print Services for NetWare to be loaded on the Windows NT Server 4.0.
- Services for Macintosh require NTFS partitions.
- The partitions used by Services for Macintosh should be less than 2GB.
- Macintosh client computers must use Macintosh operating system version 6.0.7 or later.

■ Macintosh client computers must use AppleShare Network Software.

■ NT Server 4.0 using Services for Macintosh can become a AppleTalk router.

■ Services for Macintosh run transparently from the client's perspective.

## 9.2. Windows NT Server 4.0 Clients

9

There are many ways to access the Windows NT server. Four principal pieces of client software included with Windows NT Server are Windows 95, LAN Manager 2.2 Client software, Microsoft Network Client for MS-DOS, and Windows. Although both NT Workstation 4.0 and Windows for Workgroups can be a client of NT Server 4.0, the client software is not included as part of NT Server. It does, however, include TCP/IP32 for Windows for Workgroups to allow greater connectivity.

Table 9.1 lists which protocols and services can be supported by which clients.

**Table 9.1. NT Server 4.0 clients and the protocols and services that the clients are compatible with.**

| Network Protocol | IPX compatible | IPX/SPX compatible (DLC) | NetBEUI | Data Link Control | TCP/IP | DHCP | WINS | DNS |
|---|---|---|---|---|---|---|---|---|
| Windows 95 | | X | X | X | X | X | X | X |
| LAN Manager 2.2C for MS-DOS | | X | X | X | X | X (Default) | X | |
| LAN Manager 2.2C for OS/2 (1.x and 2.x) | | X | X | | X | | | |
| MS Network Client for MS-DOS and Windows | X | | X | X | X | X | X | |
| NT Work-station 4.0 | | X | X | X | X | X | X | X |

With each of these included pieces of client software, certain accessories are included to make the software better for user applications. For example, Microsoft Network Client 3.0 for MS-DOS and Windows includes a full redirector as part of the package. This allows the client to log on and run the user logon scripts as well as remote access services (RAS), messaging and interprocess communications (IPC) calls such as Named Pipes, remote procedure calls (RPC), and Winsock. However, this client service does not give the MS-DOS or Windows client the capability to browse unless a Windows NT or Windows for Workgroups computer is sharing the network with them and is enabled as a browse master.

LAN Manager for MS-DOS also includes Novell NetWare connection software as well as a remote boot service that enables computers running MS-DOS or Windows to be initialized remotely by the Remoteboot service.

Windows 95 and NT Workstation have the advantage of using 32-bit protected-mode drivers, redirectors, and application programming interfaces (APIs). These are faster and less troublesome than the 16-bit APIs and drivers.

## 9.2.1. Network Client Administrator

The Network Client Administrator program is located in the Administrative Tools group off the Programs icon from the Start menu. You use it to install or upgrade client operating systems, copy the Network Administration Tools to supported clients, and examine information on remote boot clients (see Figure 9.1).

The Network Client Administrator enables the administrator to create the client disks for LAN Manager and Microsoft Network Client 3.0 as well as to create a network startup disk that attaches the client to a network share enabling installation of an operation system such as Windows for Workgroups, MS Network Client for MS DOS, Windows 95, Windows NT Workstation, and Windows NT Server.

**Figure 9.1.**

*The Network Client Administrator.*

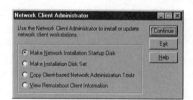

Network Client Administrator also enables you to remotely administer certain domain functions from a workstation or client. To do this, use the Copy Client-based Network Administration Tools command from the Network Client Administrator dialog box (see sections 9.2.3, "Windows NT Workstation Client-Based Network Administrator

Tools," and 9.2.4, "Windows 95 Client-Based Server Tools," for a further explanation of these functions). View Remoteboot Client Information enables you to see which MS-DOS, Windows 3.1x, or Windows 95 stations have the Remoteboot option enabled and reboot any of these stations from the NT Server console.

Selecting Make Network Installation Startup Disk and then clicking on the Continue button brings up the Share Network Client Installation Files dialog box shown in Figure 9.2.

**9**

**Figure 9.2.**

*Selecting the source for the installation files.*

The Share Network Client Installation Files dialog box allows the administrator to select the path to the client installation files. The administrator may select one of three options: use an existing share, create a share for this directory (from the CD-ROM), or copy the files to a directory and then share the new directory. When you click OK you see the Target Workstation Configuration dialog box, shown in Figure 9.3.

**Figure 9.3.**

*Target Workstation Configuration.*

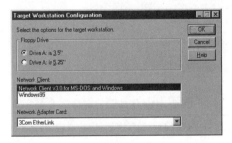

You must fill out three items on this screen:

- On which floppy drive the startup disk is being written.
- What client software is being placed on the disk.
- Which network card is on the client's machine.

Next, you must provide a unique computer name for the client, the domain name, the network protocol, and an administrative logon name as shown in Figure 9.4.

**Figure 9.4.**

*Configuring the network startup disks.*

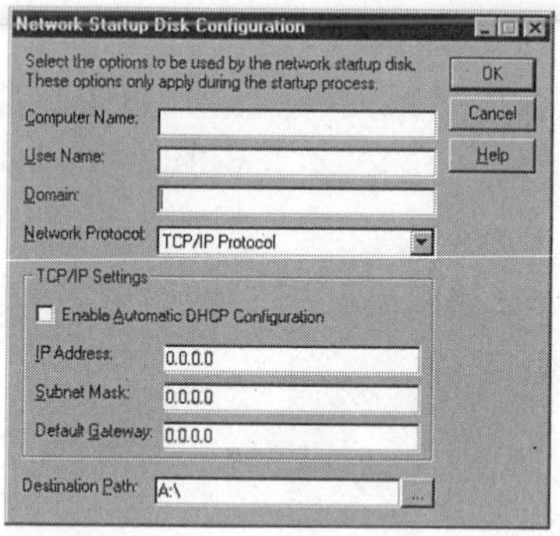

## 9.2.2. Making a Disk Installation Set

As previously discussed, the Make Installation Disk Set option allows Windows NT server to create installation floppy disks for the Microsoft Network Client for MS-DOS and Windows as well as the TCP/IP32 disks for Windows for Workgroups as shown in Figure 9.5. In creating these disks, the administrator has three decisions to make:

- Which disks to create
- Whether to format the disks before creating the software on them
- Which floppy drive to use

**Figure 9.5.**

*Selecting which installation set to create.*

## 9.2.3. Windows NT Workstation Client-Based Network Administrator Tools

Which client-based administration tools can be installed is dependent on which operating system is being used. Because the different tools can be used by a Windows 95 machine or a Windows NT Workstation each of these systems should be considered separately as to which tools may be used and the requirements to run these.

The following are the requirements for running the administrative tool on Windows NT Workstation:

- 486/33 or higher CPU.
- 12MB of RAM.
- 2.5MB of free disk space on the system partition. (The administration tools are installed to the SRVTOOLS folder of the system partition.)
- Both Workstation and Server Services must be already installed.

Installing the administration tools on an NT Workstation is a relatively easy affair. First, insert the NT Server 4.0 compact disk into the CD-ROM drive of the NT Workstation (or a shared CD-ROM if one is not available). Then, from the Start/Run menu open the following file: (CD-ROM drive letter):\Clients\Srvtools\Winnt\ Setup.exe. This copies the administrative tool files to the (system root):\System32 folder of the NT Workstation.

Press Enter and remove the CD-ROM to complete the setup of the administrative tools.

The setup results in eight tools that let an administrator perform a series of services that would normally be performed from the NT Server 4.0 hosting the service. They are shown in the following table:

| Tool | Filename | Description |
| --- | --- | --- |
| DHCP Manager | dhcpadmin.exe | Enables the user at the NT Workstation to administrate the DHCP service running on the NT Server 4.0. This lets the user configure default, global, and scope settings. |
| Remote Access Administrator | rasadmin.exe | Allows the NT workstation to administer the RAS server on a computer running Windows NT. |
| Remote Boot | rplmgr.exe | Allows the NT workstation to Manager configure the Remoteboot service on NT Server 4.0. |
| Server Manager | srvmgr.exe | Allows the NT Workstation machine to administer not only the NT domain but also NT computers inside that domain. |

*continues*

| Tool | Filename | Description |
|---|---|---|
| System Policy Editor | poledit.exe | Allows the NT Workstation user to edit policies and thus to be able to edit registry settings on any computer in the domain. |
| User Manager for Domains | usrmgr.exe | Allows the NT Workstation to change user properties—passwords, access times, share rights, right to change password, domain logon scripts—as well as group rights—memberships, logon scripts, and so forth—for NT-based systems on the domain, or a multiple of domains to which the NT Workstation user has rights. In addition, trusts to other domains can be configured from this software. |
| WINS Manager | winsadmin.exe | Configures the NT Workstation to administer the WINS (Windows Internet Name Service) that is operating on the Windows NT 4.0 Server. |

These pieces of software help the administrator by not tying him down to just operating from the Windows NT Server. Now, any workstation that has these installed will allow him to change user rights, add users, change the desktop and Control Panel settings, and add security logon scripts to the entire domain, all from within the access of one workstation and without having to go to the Windows NT Server each time these processes are needed in an office environment.

## 9.2.4. Windows 95 Client-Based Server Tools

The Windows 95 configuration is different from the minimal Windows 95 configuration. This is because where Windows 95 normally can be set up with a 386 CPU and 4MB of RAM, the minimum for running the NT Server 4.0 Administration Tools is a 486/33 with at least 8MB of RAM. Thus, the requirements for a Windows 95 computer to run Administration Tools for NT Server 4.0 are

- Client for 486/33 or better CPU
- 8MB of RAM
- 3MB of free hard disk space on the system partition
- Microsoft Networks installed on the Windows 95 machine

The installation of these tools is also different from that of the NT Workstation. From Control Panel on the Windows 95 machine, double-click the Add/Remove Programs icon to bring up the dialog box in Figure 9.6. The Control Panel can be found by several ways, such as Explorer, opening the My Computer Desktop icon, or from Settings on the Start Menu options.

**Figure 9.6.**

*Using the Windows setup option from the Add/Remove Programs applet in Control Panel.*

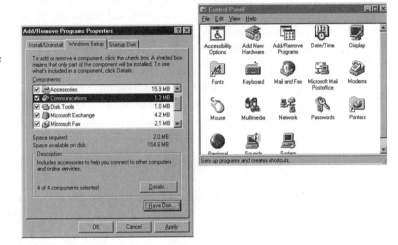

Clicking the Have Disk button in the Add/Remove Programs Properties dialog box brings up the Install From Disk dialog box, shown in Figure 9.7.

Place the Windows NT Server 4.0 CD-ROM in your computer's CD-ROM drive (or a shared CD-ROM drive). Under Copy Manufacturer's Files From in the Install From Disk dialog box, type (*CD-ROM drive Letter*): \Clients\Srvtools\Win95 and then click OK. Click Windows NT Server Tools and Install to install the Server tools to the C:\Srvtools directory, which you can add to your Path statement in Autoexec.bat. Restart the Windows 95 computer to complete the installation of the Server Tools for Windows 95.

Just as the installation method differed from the Windows NT, so too do the tools involved. Seven tools compose Server tools for Windows 95:

- Event Viewer (Eventvwr.exe): Enables the Windows 95 machine to view and manage application event logs, system event logs, and security event logs produced by the Windows NT server.

- File Security: A File Security tab is added to both Windows NT Explorer and to My Computer, enabling the user to view or change file security on the Windows NT Server. As the administrator, you can use this to maintain security on the file shares on the Windows NT Server 4.0 machine.

■ Print Security: A Print Security tab is added to the Windows NT Explorer and My Computer screens. This enables the user to manage print permissions on the domain from the Windows 95 Workstation. It is controlled through the Properties tab in the Printers dialog box found in either the Start Menu settings area or My Computer or Windows NT Explorer categories.

■ Server Manager (Srvmgr.exe): Manages the computer resources for the domain computers, including shared folders, printers, and permissions on the shared folders. In addition, you can view users on any resource and, if necessary, disconnect users from a given resource.

■ User Manager for Domains (Usrmgr.exe): Lets the NT Workstation change user properties—passwords, access times, share rights, rights to change passwords, domain logon scripts—as well as group rights—memberships, logon scripts, and so on—and trusts for NT-based systems on the domain, or a multiple of domains to which the NT Workstation user has rights.

■ User Manager Extensions for Services for NetWare: If FPNW or DSMN is installed this allows the Windows 95 Workstation to create a NetWare user account, enable it, and configure its properties as well as create a home directory on the NetWare server and set rights and inherited rights filters for the user account.

■ File and Print Services for NetWare: If FPNW is installed, enables the Windows 95 Workstation to create and manage volume and print objects—user accounts, rights, volume directory structure, printers, print queues, and send messages.

**Figure 9.7.**

*Using the Have Disk option on Windows 95 setup to enter the path to the Server Tools.*

These Server tools allow the administrator to control from a Windows 95 computer a variety of settings on the domain—user groups, user accounts, shares, properties of printers, and so on—but can also help in the administration of Novell NetWare products.

The functions of both Windows Administration Tools for Windows Workstations and Windows Server Tools for Windows 95 is that they free up the administrator, helping him or her to administer the domain from nearly any location. These tools save time without adding to administrative burdens.

## 9.2.5. Services for Macintosh

9

You can install Services for Macintosh on a Windows NT Server 4.0, which provides the capability to manage networks in which Macintosh computers are included. It can also permit a Macintosh user to log on to an NT Server in order to provide file and print sharing for the Macintosh. This greatly simplifies administrative duties. The Windows NT Server can also act as an AppleTalk router.

The following are the requirements to access Services for Macintosh:

- 2MB of free hard disk space.
- The NTFS partition cannot exceed 2GB due to Macintosh's 2GB partition size limit. If it is greater than 2GB a message might appear on the Macintosh systems saying 0 bytes are available.

Even more requirements exist for the Macintosh client computers:

- Macintosh clients must be using Macintosh operating system version 6.0.7 or later.
- Macintosh clients must be using AppleShare Network software. This excludes using either the Macintosh XL or Macintosh 128K computers.
- If LaserWriter printers are being used, only version 6.x or later drivers can be used.
- AppleTalk Filing Protocol versions 2.0 or 2.1 for file and application sharing.

To install Services for Macintosh on a Windows NT Server, go into Control Panel, double-click the Network icon, and select the Services tab. Click Add, select Services for Macintosh, and then click OK. This loads the Services for Macintosh and brings up the configuration screen. This screen lets you choose which Windows NT-supported NIC card is being used to communicate with the Macintosh Zones being used. The Routing tab allows you to enable AppleTalk routing as shown in Figure 9.8.

**Figure 9.8.**

*Routing is enabled by the Services for Macintosh setup Routing tab.*

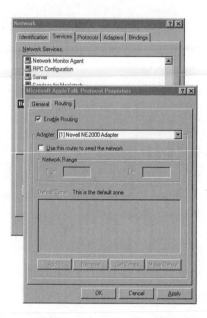

After you install Services for Macintosh, a MacFile menu is added to the Server Manager under common administrative tools on the Windows NT Server Start menu options. You can use the MacFile menu to create Macintosh accessible volumes that can also be shared to allow MS-DOS or Windows clients to access files as demonstrated in Figure 9.9.

**Figure 9.9.**

*MacFile options in the Server Manager.*

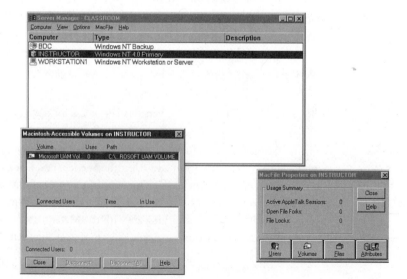

Services for Macintosh automatically sets up several fine features:

- AppleTalk protocol, which is configured via the Network applet in the Control Panel.
- File Services for Macintosh (MacFile), used to manage folders, files, and volumes for Macintosh.
- Print Services for Macintosh that enables Windows, MS-DOS, or Macintosh clients to send print jobs to either AppleTalk- or non-AppleTalk–based printers.
- Supports Ethernet, LocalTalk, Token-Ring and Fiber Distributed Data Interface (FDDI).

9

# 9.3. Lab

This lab aids your learning by testing you on the information presented in this chapter as well as by giving you exercises to hone your skills. Answers to the review questions can be found in Appendix B, "Answers to Review Questions."

## 9.3.1. Review Questions

### Question 1

You are the SA of a network consisting of a PDC, BDC, Novell NetWare 3.12 server, and 25 workstations with no client software installed. Your boss wants the workstations to access the Internet as well as the file and printing services of each server. Which client software could you install to accomplish this?

A. Windows 95

B. Windows NT Workstation 4.0

C. Microsoft Client for MS-DOS and Windows

D. Microsoft LAN Manager 2.2c client for MS-DOS

### Question 2

The PDC named Blue has 20 workstations located in different areas of a three-story building. They are all using TCP/IP with a member server named Red providing DHCP, DNS, and WINS Services. These servers are locked in a room on the first floor. Your boss has just bought a new Pentium 133 MHz computer with a 1.2GB hard disk and 12MB of RAM as a workstation for his own use. He wants to manage the DHCP server from this workstation to cut down on building traffic to the server room.

As the system administrator you must configure his computer. What do you do?

A. Install Windows 95 with Server Tools.

B. Install LAN Manager 2.2c for MS-DOS with DHCP.

C. Install Windows NT Workstation 4.0 and Administration Tools.

D. Nothing. Your boss will just have to go in the server room and edit the DNS from the server.

## Question 3

Which of the files system is required to support Services for Macintosh?

A. FAT

B. FAT32

C. HPFS

D. NTFS

9

## Question 4

Which of the following is used on a Windows 95 computer with Server Tools installed to change users ability to access shares on NT Server 4.0?

A. Windows Explorer

B. Server Manager

C. User Manager

D. Remote Access Administrator

## Question 5

To install Windows 95 from an NT Server 4.0, which of the following must be done?

A. Share the `<winnt_root>\clients\Win95` directory.

B. Create a Network Installation Startup disk from Administrative Tools.

C. Boot the computer onto which you want to install Windows 95 from the Network Installation Startup disk.

D. Check Create Windows 95 Setup Disks on the Disk Administration Tools.

## Question 6

Which of the following is used to create a Network Installation Startup disk?

A. Disk Administration Tools

B. Server Manager

C. User Manager for Domains

D. Network Client Administrator

## 9.3.2. Exercises

### Exercise 9.1

You are the system administrator for a network consisting of four servers and 250 client machines. The servers consist of a PDC, a BDC, a SQL server, and an Exchange server. Your servers are in the locked server room and you use NT Workstation 4.0 as your personal workstation in your office, which is on a different floor than the server room.

How would you set up your workstation to simplify your administrative duties?

### Exercise 9.2

You now must add 10 workstations to the network in Exercise 9.1. They have been delivered with network cards installed but no operating systems, and you must install Windows 95 on all 10 machines.

How would you set up your network share to allow over-the-network installation of Windows 95? How would you use this share to install each client machine?

# Day 10

# Optimizing Your Server

*by Theresa Hadden and David Schaer*

## 10.1. Overview

An MCSE should understand how to properly monitor systems for two reasons. The MCSE must perform proactive system maintenance by identifying potential system bottlenecks. Also, when faced with a problem the MCSE must be able to identify the problem's symptoms, evaluate their cause, and then develop a solution that removes that cause. This chapter will address these issues and present appropriate solutions.

### 10.1.1. Objectives

This chapter instructs you in how to use the Performance Monitor to evaluate the performance of system objects. Additionally, the chapter shows you how to identify the most common physical objects and then evaluate them under a given set of circumstances. This chapter shows how to

- Use the Performance Monitor to assess the performance of various functions.
- Use Network Monitor to watch network traffic.
- Identify performance bottlenecks.
- Choose the appropriate course of action to resolve performance issues.

Remember that your objective will be to identify a *bottleneck*, which is the physical object responsible for degraded performance, and then evaluate how to decrease its negative effect on performance.

## 10.1.2. Fast Facts

The following list of facts is a concise picture of the information presented in this chapter. It acts both as an overview for the chapter and as a study aid to help you do any last-minute cramming.

- The Performance Monitor is the primary tool for monitoring system performance.
- Use thresholds, which you set in the Alert view, to generate a response message or log an error to the event log.
- You commonly would use the Log view to establish a baseline.
- Processor utilization is high if it constantly exceeds 80 percent.
- Track multiple processors collectively by selecting the System object and the counter %Total Processor Time.
- The addition of memory is the generic fix-all solution in NT; high pages/second can indicate the need for more RAM.
- To track Physical Disk utilization, you first must enter DISKPERF -Y (-YE if you are tracking a stripe set) and then reboot the system.
- Multithreaded applications benefit most from multiple processors.
- Track the traffic on the physical segment in the Performance Monitor by selecting the Network Segment object and the %Network Utilization counter.
- Track individual process statistics in the Performance Monitor by selecting the Process object.
- Collectively monitor services that are not listed individually.
- Use the object Network Interface to track the statistics of an individual network interface card.
- The Process Viewer from the NT 4.0 Resource Kit provides you with full details of each active process.
- Use the Network Monitor tool, which is a protocol, or packet, analyzer, to capture and analyze network traffic.
- Use the Network Monitor Application component to display and save captured data.
- You must install the Network Monitor Agent, which allows for the capture of data on a remote subnet, on the computer that will capture data.
- There are four sections to Network Monitor's display: Graph Pane, Session Statistics, Total Statistics, and Station Statistics.

- You can apply filters in Network Monitor either to the data as it is captured or to limit the amount of data displayed from a captured file.
- There are two ways to display the Task Manager. Either press Crtl+Alt+Del and then select Task Manager, or simply click the taskbar with the right mouse button.
- The Task Manager can report the Process ID (PID), CPU utilization, and memory utilization for each individual process.
- The Process Viewer can retrieve detailed information on the memory allocation of any active process.

## 10.2. The Performance Monitor

**10**

The NT Performance Monitor is the administrator's primary tool for evaluating the performance of a system running NT Workstation or Server. The Performance Monitor primarily is for the measurement of a given system's performance, but it also provides some rudimentary information on network performance.

The Performance Monitor has four major views that you can use to analyze system objects: Chart, Alert, Log, and Report. Each view simply presents data in a different way. This data can be either from the local computer or from remote computers. In addition to selecting which objects and counters to monitor, you can set how frequently you update your counters.

After you have configured the Performance Monitor's attributes, save the settings to use again later.

### 10.2.1. The Chart View

When monitoring current activity, you most commonly would use the Chart view, as shown in Figure 10.1, to get a quick overview of system performance in real time. Two types of charts are available: graph and histogram. This view is most helpful when you need a quick look to determine where a problem might be.

When using the graph mode, you can customize line color, width, and style to optimize viewing and printing. You also can edit histogram bars.

**Figure 10.1.**

*You can use the Chart view in the Performance Monitor to show %Processor Time.*

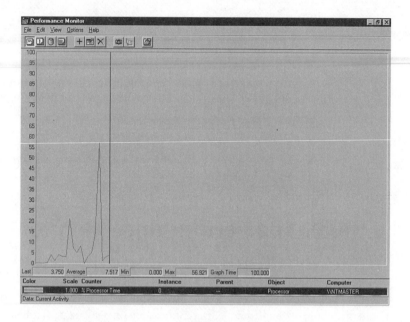

Select a legend and press the backspace key to highlight that line.

## 10.2.2. The Log View

The Log view, as shown in Figure 10.2, shows the log file's name and status. A system administrator can use the Log view to select a series of objects and track them over an extended period of time. The administrator can change the time interval without closing the log file. After the log has captured the requisite amount of data, the administrator then can view the data in chart, report, or alert format by changing the view and setting the Data From option.

Because the log file can accumulate over a period of hours or even days, it is the best method to use both when you are establishing a baseline and for routine monitoring. You also can export data from log files either to a spreadsheet or database program for further evaluation.

You can insert bookmarks into the log to identify major events. Using bookmarks and alerts enables you to analyze a large log file with considerable speed.

**Figure 10.2.**

*In the Log view, the Performance Monitor displays the log filename, log interval, and log file status.*

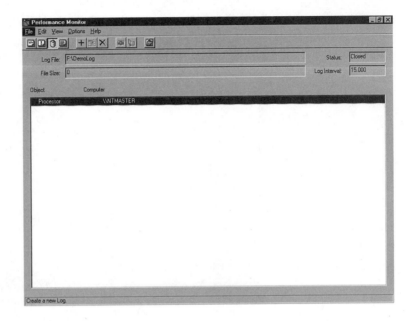

### 10.2.3. The Alert View

The Alert view enables you to monitor multiple counters or computers with minimal overhead. You must set a threshold value for each counter, as shown in Figure 10.3. For example, if the amount of used pagefile space was to exceed a certain threshold, the system could log the event automatically, notify an administrator, or execute an application. You can configure more than one alert at one time; however, this is processor-intensive, and you should do this only when necessary.

### 10.2.4. The Report View

As the name implies, the Report view, as shown in Figure 10.4, presents the selected data in a report format. Objects display in the order you select them. The Report view gives you a quick picture of the available data to assist you in selecting the objects you want to monitor. There is not an option in Performance Monitor to print the report, although you can export the data into another application, such as Excel or Access, to generate and print reports and graphs.

**Test Tip**

To reduce the amount of real estate Performance Monitor occupies, remove the title bar, menu bar, and status bar.

**Figure 10.3.**

*An Alert set with a threshold > 80 %Processor Time.*

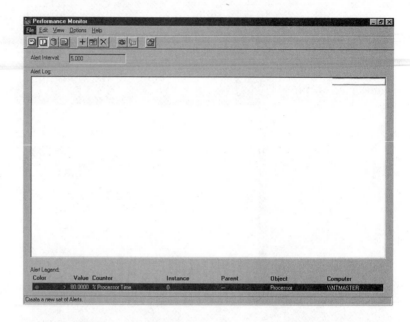

**Figure 10.4.**

*A Report view displays %Processor Time.*

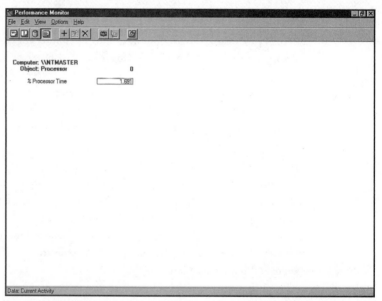

# 10.3. Selecting the Key Elements to Monitor

Knowing which are the key elements to select and monitor is essential to the proper evaluation of system performance. It is necessary for you to understand that although you can track individual objects, the first object you identify as performing poorly is not always at fault.

As you examine each of the following objects, you must consider how each object affects the performance of the others. For example, an abnormally high processor utilization average is often the result of insufficient memory.

> When you select which counter to monitor, remember that the default counter usually provides the most significant information about that object.

Each object you track is matched by a list of corresponding counters and instances. For example, in Figure 10.5 the selected object is the Processor; because this is a single-processor system, there is only one instance, 0. The counters are the specific areas of the object you might track; in this case, the counter is %Processor Time.

**Figure 10.5.**
*Select counters in the Add to Chart dialog box.*

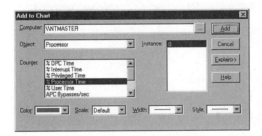

> When selecting objects, use the Explain button in the Add to Chart dialog box to display a short description of the purpose of each counter.

## 10.3.1. The Processor Object

The Processor object, as shown in Figure 10.5, displays the percentage of time in which the processor executes the active threads from both user and system processes. Before you decide that a processor upgrade is required, look for a lack of memory in the system. Excessive paging can increase significantly the work that both the processor and disk subsystem require. If you are monitoring a multiple-processor system, be sure to monitor each processor.

Don't concern yourself overtly with sporadically high readings, or *spikes*. The key to watch for here is whether the percentage processor utilization remains consistently above 80%.

### 10.3.2. The System Object

The System object and its related counters reflect the collective performance of objects. Two common counters are set with the System object.

%Total Processor Time is useful in a multiprocessor system, where there would be a separate instance for each processor in the system tracked by the Processor object. In such a system, you can determine an average percentage of processor utilization across all processors by tracking the System object and the %Total Processor Time counter, as shown in Figure 10.6.

**Figure 10.6.**

*Notice that no instances are listed because this counter is reported as a total amount.*

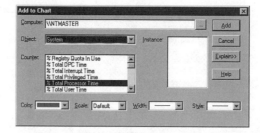

As shown in Figure 10.7, you can track the total interrupts per second over a period of time in the Log view to create a baseline. An abnormal increase in the Total Interrupts/ second could indicate a potential component failure.

**Figure 10.7.**

*Again notice that no instances are listed because this counter is reported as a total.*

### 10.3.3. The Memory Object

The Memory object includes a series of counters that provides an insight into how the system is utilizing its memory.

**Test Tip** The Pages/second counter of the Memory object is the most critical counter to track.

Pages/second, as shown in Figure 10.8, is the most critical memory counter. This number will be high when a significant amount of the data you request cannot be located in physical RAM.

**Figure 10.8.**
*The Add to Chart dialog box shows the Pages/sec object selected.*

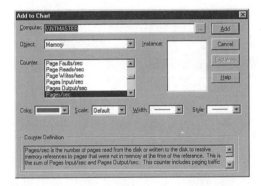

**Test Tip** A lack of memory causes a multitude of inadequacies. Given a choice between a faster processor and more RAM, choose additional RAM.

The following are additional memory counters of which you should be aware:

- Available Bytes. The amount of virtual memory that can be called on by the system. Add memory if the available bytes continually remain below 4MB.
- Committed Bytes. The amount of virtual memory that has been assigned to processes. Add memory if the committed bytes are approaching the amount of physical RAM in the system.

## 10.3.4. The Physical Disk

Physical disk counters show the statistics for all access to a specific physical disk. For performance reasons on older systems, physical disk tracking is disabled by default. Before tracking physical disk performance, you must execute the command DISKPERF -Y and then reboot the system. When tracking the physical disk performance on a stripe set, first execute DISKPERF -YE.

When logging disk performance, write the log file to another disk to avoid additional load on the disk, which will skew your results.

%Disk Time, as shown in Figure 10.9, tracks both read and write operations to the physical disk. Remember that a single physical disk might contain multiple logical drives.

**Figure 10.9.**

*Note that this counter can be reported as a total or as a separate instance for each physical disk.*

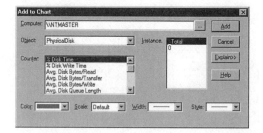

If the %Disk Time is constantly over 90%, it might be beneficial for you to consider moving the pagefile to a different disk, purchasing a faster disk controller, or implementing a stripe set.

Before making radical physical changes based on high physical disk readings, check the Pages/second. Remember that simply by adding more RAM you often can reduce the activity level of disk counters.

Another helpful counter is Avg. Disk Queue Length. This counter reports the average amount of disk read and write requests that are waiting during the sampling period.

## 10.3.5. Logical Disk

Tracking the logical disk counters shown in Figure 10.10 can be helpful when you want to determine where to place specific applications or data files. Notice that in Figure 10.10 there is a separate instance for each logical disk.

It is best to use the Free Space counter with the Alert view so that the system reports when free disk space falls below a preset level. In Figure 10.11, an alert is configured to send to NTMASTER if the free disk space on disk C falls below 100MB. If you want, an application could launch based on the alert.

**Figure 10.10.**

*This counter can be reported as a total or per each logical disk.*

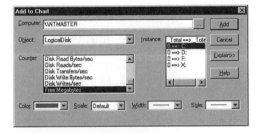

**Figure 10.11.**

*Other options include logging the event or switching to the Alert view. The counter is configured to be updated manually.*

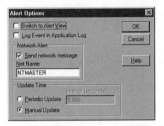

10

When the alert threshold is reached, an alert is generated and sent via the messenger service to NTMASTER, as shown in Figure 10.12.

**Figure 10.12.**

*A message goes to NTMASTER in response to a previously set threshold having been exceeded.*

## 10.3.6. The Network Segment

The Network Segment object provides information on how the system is utilizing its network media.

The %Network Utilization counter shown in Figure 10.13 represents the percentage of the media capacity in use. Although people commonly think about network implementations, such as 10BaseT, supporting 10mbps, a 10BaseT network that is performing well should run at no more than 40 percent of the segment capacity.

Although the instance enables you to select a specific network interface, this is only so that you might identify the path to the segment. The Network Segment object tracks the collective frames from all systems placed on the segment.

**Figure 10.13.**

*The adapter is listed as an instance. If more than one adapter were present, each would be listed.*

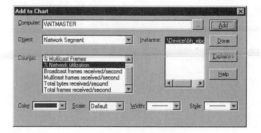

## 10.3.7. The Network Interface

The Network Interface object, shown in Figure 10.14, tracks information on how a specific network interface card is utilized. Although the network segment might be capable of handling additional traffic, the network interface card might be working at capacity.

**Figure 10.14.**

*Notice that two instances are available.*

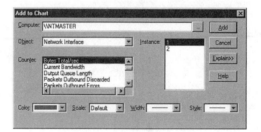

By tracking the counter Bytes Total/sec you can determine whether the capacity of the network interface card is nearly full. The use of a 32-bit network interface card in the server would improve the server's capability to handle multiple clients on the segment.

## 10.3.8. The Paging File

Use the Paging File object to track the utilization of the pagefiles, as shown in Figure 10.15. Because NT supports multiple pagefiles, you can specify the instance of the pagefile you want to track, or you can track the pagefiles collectively.

**Figure 10.15.**

*Notice that the instance defaults to the individual pagefile rather than the total.*

You can track either the %Usage or %Usage Peak. The first gives you a reading at the sample point, whereas the second shows the highest percentage obtained.

### 10.3.9.  The Process Object

You should not confuse the Process object with the Processor object. The Process object lets you track the statistics of a specific process. Some services, such as the Alerter and Messenger services, do not report themselves individually but are tracked as a collective pool, as shown in Figure 10.16.

**Figure 10.16.**
*Here you have chosen to monitor the services instance.*

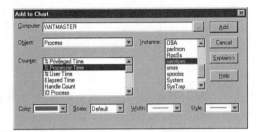

**10**

### 10.3.10.  Monitoring Remote Computers

Performance Monitor enables you to monitor as many computers from your workstation as you want. The overhead of remote measurement is relatively small, but it grows with the number of computers from which you are collecting data. You can do several things to reduce this overhead.

First, lengthen the time interval between measurements. Overhead and time interval are inversely related. Next, reduce the number of objects you are monitoring. The two objects that are the most costly to monitor are the Thread and the Process objects.

Because graphic displays are resource-intensive, use alerts to monitor objects when possible. You also may run numerous instances of Performance Monitor where each one is dedicated to monitoring one object. This lets you individualize sampling parameters per object.

Finally, consider monitoring each computer locally. This removes the cost of the increase in network traffic.

When optimizing your parameters for Performance Monitor, make only one change at a time, and evaluate its effect before making more changes.

# 10.4. Network Monitor

A protocol, or packet, analyzer is a tool you would use to capture and analyze network traffic. One such tool is Microsoft's Network Monitor, which is available in two versions.

The simple version, which is included with Windows NT Server 4.0, is capable of capturing either the addresses of packets moving to and from the computer running Network Monitor or broadcast packets.

The full version, which comes with Microsoft Systems Management Server, can capture all data on the local subnet. The full version has additional capabilities, such as the capability to capture and edit data remotely and to resend captured data.

The full version of Network Monitor no longer requires that the network adapter card run in promiscuous mode under Windows NT 4.0. This is a feature of NDIS 4.0.

## 10.4.1. Installation of Network Monitor

There are two components of Network Monitor, the Network Monitor Application and the Network Monitor Agent. The Network Monitor Application displays and saves captured data.

You must install the Network Monitor Agent, which allows for the capture of data on remote subnets, on the computer that will capture data. It also provides the Network Segment object in Performance Monitor.

You install both of these components via the Network Applet under Services.

### Capturing Data

When you start Network Monitor, you see the Capture window shown in Figure 10.17.

This display has four sections:

- Graph pane. In the upper-left is a window that shows a horizontal bar graph of current activity.
- Session Statistics. Under the Graph pane is a summary of the conversations that have occurred during this session.

- Total Statistics. On the right is a summary of network traffic as a whole.
- Station Statistics. On the bottom is a summary of network traffic, including multicast and broadcast traffic, that the host either initiated or received.

**Figure 10.17.**

*The Network Monitor Capture window is divided into four sections.*

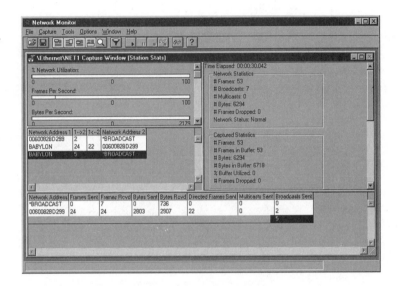

Before starting the capture, you might want to limit the amount of data that is captured by applying a filter, as shown in Figure 10.18. You can filter data by protocol or by address.

**Figure 10.18.**

*You can set a filter's configuration in Network Monitor. Set the filter to ANY to capture all data.*

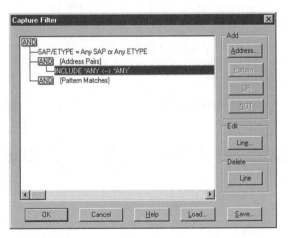

## Displaying Data

You can display data immediately after you have captured it or display data that you previously saved. You can apply a display filter to view only the data you consider pertinent. Figure 10.19 shows a captured file.

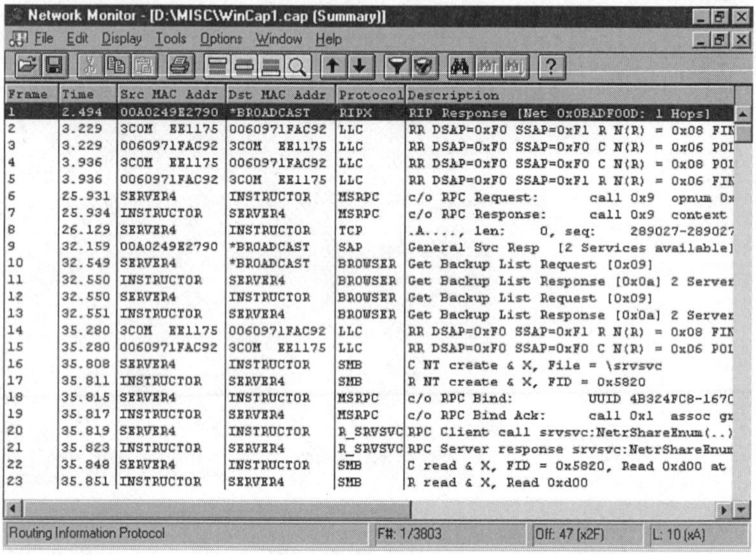

**Figure 10.19.**

*You can view captured data in Network Monitor. The frames display in the order in which you captured them.*

The display comprises three frames:

- The Summary pane is located on the top and lists all frames for the current view. Select a frame here to display the details in the other two frames.

- The Detail pane shows the protocol information for the frame you have selected. If the frame contains more than one protocol, the Detail pane shows the outermost one first.

- The Hexadecimal pane on the bottom shows the contents of the frame.

# 10.5. Additional System Monitoring Utilities

The Performance Monitor requires at least a minimal amount of configuration in order to provide statistics. Microsoft provides additional utilities, such as Task Manager and Process Viewer, to present the most commonly requested statistics without configuration requirements.

## 10.5.1. Task Manager

Activate Task Manager by pressing Crtl+Alt+Del and then selecting Task Manager, or simply click the task bar with the right mouse button. From within Task Manager, you can track applications, processes, and system performance.

### Applications

Applications are synonymous with tasks. You can use the Task Manager to view the active applications, as shown in Figure 10.20.

**Figure 10.20.**

*The Task Manager shows four active applications.*

**10**

You can use the Task Manager to switch between tasks, end a non-responsive task, or launch a new task.

### Processes

The Task Manager also can report the Process ID (PID), CPU utilization, and memory utilization for each individual process, as shown in Figure 10.21.

A high number reported for the System Idle Process is an indication that the system has processor time available.

### Performance

Select the performance tab in the Task Manager to view, in both text and graphics, several of the most common counters, including CPU and memory utilization, as shown in Figure 10.22.

**Figure 10.21.**

*You may stop individual processes from the Task Manager.*

**Figure 10.22.**

*The Task Manager presents much valuable information in that it provides you with a quick snapshot of how your system is functioning.*

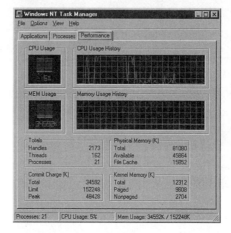

## 10.5.2. The Process Viewer

The Process Viewer is included with the NT 4.0 Resource kit. It goes beyond simply allowing a user to kill a process, such as Task Manager would allow. Through the Process Viewer an administrator also can retrieve detailed information on the memory allocation of any active process, as shown in Figure 10.23.

**Figure 10.23.**

*The Process Viewer shows memory allocation on a per-process basis.*

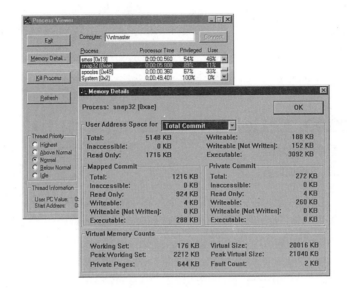

**10**

# 10.6. Lab

This lab will aid you in your learning by testing you on the information presented in this chapter, as well as by giving you exercises to hone your skills. You will find answers to the review questions in Appendix B, "Answers to Review Questions."

## 10.6.1. Review Questions

### Question 1

How should you go about establishing a baseline of server and network performance?

A. Use Network Monitor to capture network traffic periodically over several days.

B. Use Performance Monitor to capture performance data on each of your servers during peak usage times during the day.

C. Use Performance Monitor to capture performance data on each of your servers during nonpeak usage times during the day.

D. Use Network Monitor to capture network traffic originating from your PDC every hour for several days and then average the numbers.

### Question 2

You use the Chart view in Performance Monitor best to

A. Obtain data to use as baseline information.

B. Notify the System Administrator of resource limitations, such as available free disk space.

C. View data in real time.

D. Identify objects to monitor in greater detail.

### Question 3

After configuring Performance Monitor to log physical disk utilization, you notice that the counters have remained at zero. What is the probable cause?

A. The DISKPERF service was not loaded.

B. There was no activity to monitor.

C. There is no object called Physical Disk.

D. You cannot monitor physical disk activity unless you also monitor page faults.

## Question 4

True/False. To obtain information on the purpose of each counter, you should use the Explain button while selecting objects.

## Question 5

You want to use the Chart view to monitor processor utilization on your multiprocessor system. How should you do this?

A. Select the Processor object. All counters will be added automatically.

B. Select the Processor object and the %Processor Time counter. A line will be placed on the chart for each processor.

C. Select the Processor object and the %Processor Time counter. You also must select an instance for each processor.

D. Select the Processor object and the %Processor Time counter for each processor.

**10**

## Question 6

You notice that your system exhibits an excessive amount of hard disk activity and your %Processor Time is staying over 80%. What is the most likely cause?

A. Excessive paging

B. Heavy network usage

C. Increased utilization of your SQL Server

D. A lack of free disk space

## Question 7

You want to gather information on the amount of traffic generated by your WINS server, and you do not want to capture any other frames. You should

A. Capture all the frames, export them to Access, delete the frames in which you are not interested, and then import this information into Network Monitor for analysis.

B. Capture all the frames and set a display filter to display only the information applicable to the WINS server.

C. Capture all the frames and scroll through the data to find the frames in which you are interested.

D. Set a capture filter to capture only the information from the WINS server.

## Question 8

You want to set alerts on each of your four servers to notify you when free disk space falls below a certain threshold. You should

A. Run Performance Monitor on each of the servers for an alert. Check each server periodically to see whether an alert has been generated.

B. Configure an alert for each server through Performance Monitor running on your workstation.

C. Run four instances of Performance Monitor on your workstation and tile them so you can see if any alerts are generated.

D. Configure an alert for each server through Performance Monitor running on your workstation and enter your user name as a destination for the alert.

## Question 9

The Task Manager can provide you with information on

A. CPU utilization

B. The amount of free disk space

C. Memory utilization

D. Which applications are running

## Question 10

In order to determine how memory is allocated to processes, you should use

A. Task Manager

B. Process Viewer

C. Network Monitor

D. User Manager

# 10.6.2. Exercises

## Exercise 10.1

Use Performance Monitor to configure an Alert on a remote computer monitoring free disk space. Have the Alert message sent to you on your workstation.

## Exercise 10.2

Use Network Monitor to capture data on your network. Apply a display filter to show all broadcast traffic.

## Exercise 10.3

Track your CPU utilization using the Task Manager while you work on several different applications.

**10**

# Day 11

# Configuring and Optimizing NT 4.0 Services

*by Walter Glenn and Theresa Hadden*

## 11.1. Overview

This chapter will help you understand the implementation, configuration, and optimization of the major NT 4.0 services. These services include Dynamic Host Resolution Protocol (DHCP), Windows Internet Naming Service (WINS), Domain Naming System (DNS), Internet Information Server (IIS), and Directory Replication. A solid understanding of these services is essential to the success of any NT-based network and represents a major portion of both the Implementing and Supporting NT Server and Implementing and Supporting NT Server in the Enterprise exams.

In addition to configuration guidelines, this chapter helps you evaluate the effects of various services on system and network performance. This information can then be used to tune your system for maximum performance.

### 11.1.1. Objectives

Microsoft presents the following guidelines regarding these Windows NT services. The guidelines for the Windows NT Server exam include

- Configuring Windows NT Directory Replicator Service
- Installing and configuring the Internet Information Server for the WWW
- Installing the major services of Windows NT, including DNS, WINS, and DHCP

The following are the guidelines for the Windows NT Server Enterprise exam:

- Implementing TCP/IP (with WINS and DNS) for various situations
- Installing and configuring multi-protocol routing to serve various functions, including DHCP/BOOTP relay agent
- Installing and configuring Internet services, including WWW, DNS, and intranet

## 11.1.2. Fast Facts

The following list of facts is a concise picture of the information presented in this chapter. It acts as both an overview for the chapter and as a study aid to help you do any last-minute cramming.

- DHCP, or Dynamic Host Configuration Protocol, is used to assign IP addresses (and sometimes other parameters) automatically to clients on a TCP/IP network.
- DHCP information always includes an IP address and a subnet mask.
- DHCP is an extension of the BOOTP protocol, and only routers that can act as BOOTP relay agents can pass DHCP broadcasts.
- Using the IPCONFIG utility in Windows NT is the quickest way to determine IP lease information.
- In order to be a DHCP server, a computer must be running Windows NT Server and must be assigned a static IP address.
- To install the Microsoft DHCP Server service, use the Network applet in the Control Panel.
- The pool of IP addresses from which DHCP assigns client addresses is known as a *scope*. IP addresses within a scope can be excluded from the available pool.
- An IP address is assigned for a period of time that is referred to as a lease, the duration of which is configurable.
- If you are configuring multiple DHCP servers on a network, Microsoft recommends that each DHCP server should contain a scope consisting of 75 percent of all the IP addresses available on the local subnet. Backup servers should also have a scope containing the remaining 25 percent of available IP addresses for one other subnet.
- You can reserve an IP address for a specific client that must maintain a consistent IP address.

■ Options that DHCP can pass along to a Microsoft-based DHCP client include the addresses of routers, DNS servers, and WINS servers. Additionally, client node type and NetBIOS scope IDs can also be assigned.

■ Global options are passed along to every DHCP client that obtains an address from that DHCP server. Scope options are passed to every client receiving an IP address from that scope, and override global options. Client options are entered directly at the client and override scope and global options.

■ WINS, or Windows Internet Naming Service, resolves NetBIOS names to IP addresses.

■ WINS needs little configuration after setup and should run automatically.

■ Replication of a WINS database may be accomplished by defining a push partner or a pull partner. The push partner notifies its partner when a set number of changes have occurred. The pull partner asks for changes at preset intervals.

■ You can add static mappings to WINS to enable name resolution of non-WINS clients. You can also import an LMHOSTS file into the static mappings database.

■ LMHOSTS files are text files containing a list of NetBIOS names and IP addresses.

■ HOSTS files resolve host names or fully qualified domain names (FQDN) to IP addresses. HOSTS files are text files listing host names or FQDN and IP addresses.

■ DNS, or Domain Naming System, is a distributed database of IP addresses to host name mappings using a hierarchical name structure.

■ Each DNS server maintains its own zone of authority, under which are domains, in which are records.

■ There are four primary types of domain name servers: Primary Name Servers, which maintain a zone of authority; Secondary Name Servers, which provide backup and redundancy; Master Name Servers, from which Secondary Name Servers download their information; and Caching-Only Name Servers, which only perform and cache queries.

■ Important types of resource records are A records, which are mappings of host names to IP addresses; CNAME records, which are aliases pointing to an existing host; NS records, which point to other name servers; and MX records, which point to mail servers.

■ DNS can be configured to use WINS to resolve NetBIOS names, thereby allowing the use of DHCP assigned IP addresses rather than static IP addresses.

**11**

- Internet Information Server (IIS) is a networking service that runs under Windows NT Server and provides publishing capability for use on the Internet or an intranet.

- IIS can publish by using WWW, FTP, and Gopher technologies. You can even set up multiple virtual servers on a single computer.

- Directory Replication is a feature of Windows NT Server that enables you to replicate logon scripts, policy files, and other important files to other computers on your network.

## 11.2. Dynamic Host Configuration Protocol

In a network based on the TCP/IP protocol, every node on the network must be assigned a unique IP address. In a large networked environment, assigning and managing these addresses manually can become quite a time-consuming project. You run into problems such as the following:

- Determining the addressing scheme for assigning IP addresses

- Correcting problems caused by users who do not have the knowledge to correctly configure a network client computer

- Managing the pool of addresses when computers are removed or retired

The Dynamic Host Configuration Protocol (DHCP) is a method of lessening this administrative burden. A DHCP server is used to dynamically assign IP addresses while offering centralized management of IP addresses on a TCP/IP-based network. DHCP also offers the capability to assign other parameters along with the IP assignment, such as the location of WINS servers, DNS servers, default gateways, and node type.

Although optional parameters may be provided by the DHCP server, the IP address and subnet mask are always included. Any settings that might already be manually configured on the client will override parameters assigned by the DHCP server, including the IP address and subnet mask.

Before a client on an IP network can communicate, the host must initialize TCP/IP, which requires a unique IP address and a subnet mask as a minimum. These can be entered manually on each host machine or assigned dynamically by a DHCP server.

Although the acquisition of an IP address from a DHCP server results in increased network traffic, the amount of traffic generated is not significant. The two types of DHCP traffic are address acquisition and address renewal.

## 11.2.1. DHCP Address Acquisition

Upon booting, the host machine broadcasts a request for an IP address. Because TCP/IP has not initialized, packets requesting this IP address must be broadcast. However, each of these four frames are 342 bytes in size, for a total size of about 1,368 bytes, and take about 1/3 of a second to transmit. Figure 11.1 shows these four packets using Network Monitor.

**Figure 11.1.**

*Network Monitor showing the four packets of address acquisition. Notice frames 1874, 1875, 1876, and 1877.*

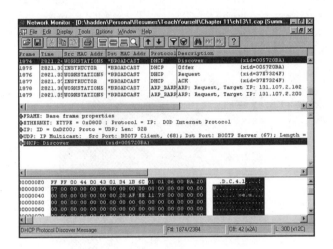

**11**

These four packets are

- DHCPDISCOVER packet. This packet is broadcast by the client to locate a DHCP server from which the client can acquire an IP address.

- DHCPOFFER packet. All available DHCP servers receive the request. Each one determines whether it can fulfill the request and then sends a packet containing an available IP address.

- DHCPREQUEST packet. The client selects one of the offers, if multiple ones are received, and sends a packet back informing the DHCP server of its acceptance.

- DHCPACK packet. This packet is sent from the server to the client and contains the length of the lease and any optional TCP/IP parameters.

DHCP is an extension of the BOOTP protocol, which enables diskless clients to boot up and configure TCP/IP parameters. As such, DHCP can only pass over routers on your network that support RFC 1542 and can act as BOOTP relay agents.

## 11.2.2. Configuring the DHCP Client

All Microsoft clients, with the exception of LAN Manager for OS/2, can be configured to use DHCP. Setting up a client to use DHCP is simply a matter of setting its TCP/IP properties to use a DHCP server. The rest is automatic. Go to Control Panel/Network/Protocols. Select the TCP/IP component and choose Properties, which will bring up the property sheet shown in Figure 11.2.

**Figure 11.2.**

*A client is configured to use DHCP.*

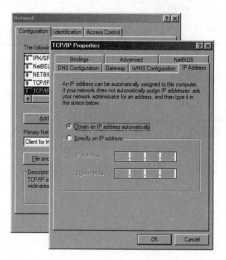

Simply choose the radio button Obtain an IP Address Automatically and the client computer is configured. Restart the computer when Windows asks you to.

You can confirm the new IP lease at the client by typing `ipconfig /all` at a command prompt (see Figure 11.3).

**Figure 11.3.**

ipconfig /all
*provides full IP lease
details on an NT client.*

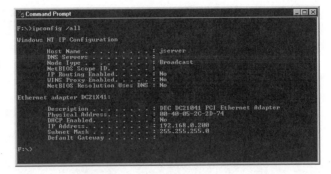

You can use ipconfig for more than just verifying your IP configuration. Use ipconfig /release to cause the client to give up its lease and notify the DHCP server. Use ipconfig /renew to update a current lease or obtain a new one after releasing the old one.

## 11.2.3. DHCP Address Renewal

**11**

The client attempts to renew its IP address lease every time it reboots. In addition, if the client is left up long enough, it will attempt to renew after 50 percent, 87.5 percent, and 100 percent of its lease period has elapsed. Because TCP/IP is already initialized and the client and server know about each other, this renewal is sent via directed packets and consists of only two packets:

■ DHCPREQUEST. The client sends a request to renew its lease.

■ DHCPAck. If the renewal is successful, the DHCP server sends an acknowledgment to the client, which resets the lease period.

These packets are the same size as those used for acquisition (342 bytes each), for a total of 684 bytes, and take 200 milliseconds to complete. Figure 11.4 shows these packets using Network Monitor.

**Figure 11.4.**

*Network Monitor showing address acquisition. Notice frames 322 and 323.*

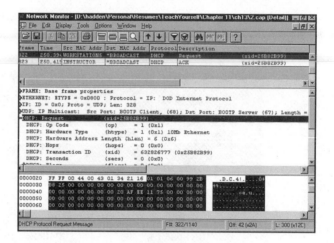

## 11.2.4. Configuring the DHCP Server

Configuring the DHCP server requires a little more effort, including the following:

- If you are configuring DHCP on a single subnet or if your routers can act as BOOTP relay agents, you must configure only one DHCP server to handle your network.

- If your routers cannot act as BOOTP relay agents, you need a DHCP server for each subnet or a DHCP relay agent.

- A DHCP relay agent may be located on your router or on the subnet segment that is without a DHCP server.

- The DHCP server must be configured with a static IP address. The DHCP server cannot also be a DHCP client.

- A pool of IP addresses must be assigned to the DHCP server, which it can assign to clients.

- The DHCP server must be running Windows NT Server (it does not have to be a domain controller), and the DHCP service must be installed.

### Installing the DHCP Server Service

To install the DHCP Server service on a Windows NT Server, do the following:

1. Open the Control Panel/Network and select the Services tab.

2. Choose the Add button.

3. On the list presented, select Microsoft DHCP Server and choose OK.

4. You will be asked for the path of the Windows NT Server 4.0 installation CD-ROM. Enter the drive letter of your CD-ROM drive or choose Browse to find the appropriate drive and the installation will then take place.

5. Choose Close on the Network Control Panel.

6. Verify that a static IP address, subnet mask, and default gateway have been assigned for each network adapter interface installed on the computer. After you have done this, choose OK and restart the computer.

After this is finished, the DHCP service should be running and will run automatically whenever the computer is started.

## Creating a DHCP Scope

Before the DHCP server can assign IP addresses to client computers on the network, you must define a range of addresses it is allowed to assign. When you installed the DHCP server, the DHCP Manager software was also installed and is available from the Administrative Tools group within the Start menu. Use the following procedure to create a DHCP scope:

1. Open the DHCP Manager and you should see a window similar to the one shown in Figure 11.5. The left pane of this window shows the server you are currently administering and the scopes that have been created on it (there should be none now). The right pane shows any options that have been defined for the current scope.

**11**

**Figure 11.5.**
*The DHCP Manager main window.*

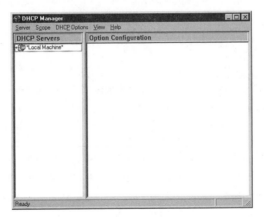

2. From the Scope menu, choose Create. The Create Scope dialog box shown in Figure 11.6 appears.

**Figure 11.6.**

*Creating a scope with DHCP Manager.*

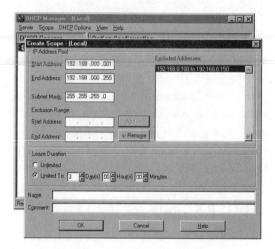

3. The Start Address and End Address fields define the range of the scope you are now creating. Enter valid IP addresses in these fields now.

4. Enter a valid subnet mask in the Subnet Mask field.

5. The Exclusion Range section of this window enables you to define one or more ranges of IP addresses within the current scope that you do not want the DHCP server to assign. You can define a range by entering the Start Address and End Address and choosing Add. You can exclude a single address by entering just the Start Address and choosing Add. You may remove excluded ranges by selecting the range and choosing Remove.

6. You may also define the duration of the lease to be Unlimited or Limited To a specified amount of time.

If the number of available IP addresses and the number of DHCP clients are nearly equal, keep the duration of the lease short.

7. You can add a name for your new scope and any comments you want to include. These are optional components and do not affect the scope in any way.

8. When you are finished, choose OK and the Activate Scope Now dialog box appears, asking if you want to activate the scope. Choose Yes and you are returned to the DHCP Manager main window. Note that there will now be a scope defined for your server, denoted with a yellow light bulb icon, as shown in Figure 11.7.

**Figure 11.7.**
*You have created your first scope.*

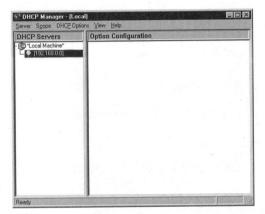

If you want to modify the properties of this scope, you can do so by choosing Properties from the Scope menu of DHCP Manager. You can also activate, deactivate, and delete scopes using the appropriate choice under the Scope menu.

When you deactivate a scope, DHCP no longer can assign new leases to clients. It does not, however, cancel any leases that are currently active.

**11**

If you are configuring multiple DHCP servers on your network, Microsoft recommends that you split your pools of IP addresses. Each DHCP server should contain a scope with 75 percent of the IP addresses available on the local subnet. Each server should also have a scope containing the remaining 25 percent of available IP addresses for one other subnet.

## Managing IP Address Leases

You can view and manage leases that have been assigned by DHCP by using the DHCP Manager. Under the Scope menu, select Leases and a window similar to the one in Figure 11.8 appears.

The information near the top of this window lets you determine the total number of leases available, how many are active or excluded, and how many are currently available. From this window you also can view the properties of or delete any individual active lease.

**Figure 11.8.**

*Managing IP address leases using DHCP Manager.*

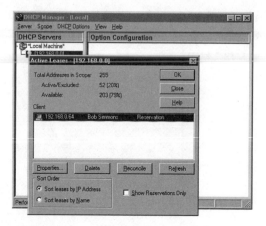

## Reserving IP Addresses Within a Scope

Although having DHCP assign IP addresses automatically is great, there are times when you must reserve IP addresses for specific DHCP clients. This enables that client to always be assigned the same address whenever it is initialized.

By reserving IP addresses on the DHCP server instead of simply configuring the client with a static IP address, the optional information that is passed along from a DHCP server to a client during initialization is preserved. This also allows more centralized management of addresses. To reserve a lease using DHCP Manager, use the following procedure:

1. Select a scope for which you want to reserve a lease and choose Add Reservation under the Scope menu. This brings up the Add Reserved Clients window shown in Figure 11.9.

**Figure 11.9.**

*Reserving a lease using DHCP Manager.*

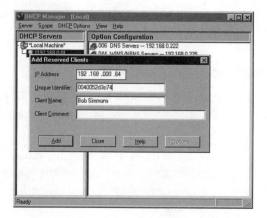

2. In the IP Address field, enter the address you want that client to be assigned.

3. In the Unique Identifier field, enter the MAC hardware address of that client. This can be determined by issuing the IPCONFIG /ALL command at a command prompt on a Windows NT client (refer to Figure 11.3). When you enter the MAC address, do not enter the dashes or any spaces.

4. In the Client Name field, enter the name of the client computer.

> This field is used to refer to the client only within DHCP Manager and does not have to match the computer's actual NetBIOS name. However, using the NetBIOS name simplifies administration.

5. You also may add any comments about the client in the Client Comment field.

After you have added a reservation, you can view and manage it as described in the previous section.

## Configuring Other DHCP Options

Previously, it was mentioned that additional information could be included with the DHCP information during client initialization. The following are some of the more commonly used parameters that can also be passed to the client:

- 003 Router: This is the IP address of a router or default gateway that can be passed along to the client. If a default gateway is already defined on the client, however, it takes precedence over the DHCP information.

- 006 DNS Servers: This is the IP address of any DNS server on the network. Multiple entries are allowed. Remember to enter the address of your primary DNS first.

- 044 WINS/NBNS Servers: Enter here the IP address of any WINS server on the network. You can enter multiple addresses. If any are configured manually on the client, they override the DHCP information.

- 046 WINS/NBT Node Type: This option sets the type of NetBIOS over TCP/IP naming resolution to be used by the client. Valid types are 0x01(b-node or broadcast), 0x02(p-node or peer), 0x04(m-node or mixed), and 0x08(h-node or hybrid).

- 047 NetBIOS Scope ID: Use this option to assign the local NetBIOS scope ID.

11

**Note**   Many other options can be configured for a DHCP server to pass along to clients, but the preceding list represents the most commonly assigned ones. These are the only ones that you are likely to use or be tested on.

You can assign to a scope the DHCP scope options just presented in one of three ways:

- Global Options: These options are passed along to every DHCP client that gets its information from this DHCP server.

- Scope Options: These options are passed along to every client that leases an address from the particular scope. Scope options override global options.

- Client Options: These options are those entered manually on the client. Client options override scope options and global options.

To configure scope options, use the following procedure:

1. From DHCP Manager, choose the scope for which you want to assign scope options.

2. From the Options menu, select Global or Scope, depending on the level of options you want to assign.

3. In the Unused Options section, select the option you want to assign. In this case, use 006 DNS Servers, but the procedure is similar for each option. After you select the option, choose Add.

4. In the Active Options sections, select the option you just added and choose Value to extend the window to edit the values for the options selected. Your window should now look like the one in Figure 11.10.

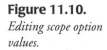
**Figure 11.10.**
*Editing scope option values.*

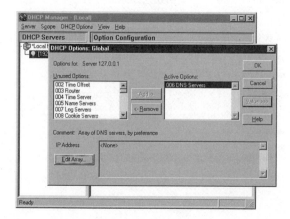

5. Choose the Edit Array button and the IP Address Array Editor dialog box in Figure 11.11 should appear.

**Figure 11.11.**
*Editing the IP addresses for a scope option.*

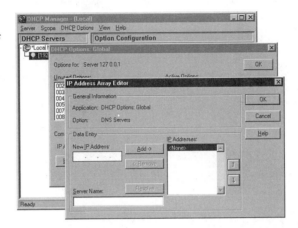

6. Enter the IP address for the DNS server in the New IP Address field and choose Add. You may define multiple DNS servers.

## 11.2.5. Configuring a BOOTP/DHCP Relay Agent

Any computer running Windows NT 4.0 can be used as an RFC-1542-compliant relay agent. The Microsoft DHCP Relay Agent is an NT networking service and, like other services, can be added by using the Control Panel/Network.

After it is configured, this server can relay DHCP messages, allowing them to be passed to and from computers on different subnets. The server is configured with the IP addresses of known DHCP servers. When a client on the relay agent's local subnet issues a DHCP Lease Request broadcast, the relay agent intercepts it and forwards it to its list of DHCP servers.

You configure the DHCP relay agent by using the DHCP Relay tab of the TCP/IP Protocol property sheet available from the Control Panel/Network. The configuration is detailed in Figure 11.12.

Under DHCP Servers in the Microsoft TCP/IP Properties dialog box, type the IP address of the server that provides IP addresses to your local subnet and choose Add. You can define multiple servers if necessary. You are now set up as a DHCP relay agent.

11

**Figure 11.12.**

*Configuring a DHCP relay agent.*

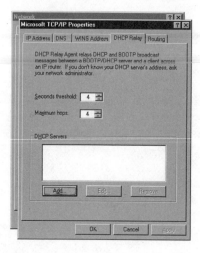

## 11.2.6. DHCP Optimization

Although DHCP does not significantly increase network traffic, you might want to optimize this traffic if network utilization is routinely high. DHCP traffic occurs as the result of one of four events:

- When a DHCP client initializes for the first time, four broadcast frames occur.

- When a DHCP client renews its lease, two directed frames are sent. This occurs when the client reboots as well as periodically during the lease period. These renewals occur at 50 percent, 87.5 percent, and 100 percent of the lease period.

- If a DHCP client replaces its network adapter card, a new request for a new IP address occurs. This involves four broadcast frames.

- Whenever a DHCP client uses IPCONFIG to renew or refresh its lease, two directed frames are sent. If IPCONFIG is used to release its IP address, then the IPCONFIG renew will result in four broadcast packets.

By lengthening the lease duration, you reduce the frequency of renewal requests, providing the clients do not reboot. The major disadvantage of doing this is that a larger percentage of your available leases will not be available at any given time. If the number of available leases is close to the number of hosts requiring IP addresses, this might result in a lack of availability of needed leases.

The other aspect of DHCP traffic to consider is forwarding of the DHCPDISCOVER messages across BOOTP capable routers. If the router supports configuration of retries before forwarding, increase this number to lengthen the amount of time the host waits for a response before the request is forwarded by the router. This gives the local DHCP server time to respond to the request and keeps this traffic local.

## 11.3. Computer Browsing

The browser service enables users to access resources on other computers. However, this traffic is broadcast-based. These broadcasts are not forwarded by routers, so it remains on the local subnet. Accessing resources on other subnets can be accomplished via the WINS server.

A computer will announce itself to the network every 12 minutes whether it has something to share or not. When a client wants to access a remote resource it first requests a list of backup browsers. If this request is not answered, an election packet is then sent, forcing an election.

After the browse list is acquired, the client then selects the server that has the desired resource. As a result, a list of shared resources controlled by that computer is sent to the client. The amount of traffic generated by this process depends on the number of servers and how many resources the selected server has to offer.

The best method for reducing browser traffic is to disable the server service on computers that do not share resources. Not only does this reduce the size of the browse list, but it also reduces the number of announcements sent over the network.

Because all browser announcements are sent over all utilized protocols, reducing the number of protocols also reduces the amount of browser traffic. Configuring your computers by whether they should participate as browsers is a good idea. You can disable the capability to be a browser by setting the `HKEY_LOCAL_MACHINE\SYSTEM\CurrentControlSet\Services\Browser\Parameters\MaintainServerList` value to No.

## 11.4. Windows Internet Name Server (WINS)

You use your network primarily so that users can access and share resources located elsewhere on the network. For that to work, one computer must be able to find another computer on a network. At the lowest level, this is done using media access control

(MAC) hardware addresses. Every network interface device in the world is given a unique MAC address by its manufacturing company; this address looks something like *04-00-34-2d-3d-74*.

When you use the TCP/IP protocol on your network, all network interface devices are also assigned unique IP addresses. When TCP/IP must transmit a message from one computer to another, it uses IP addresses. A part of the TCP/IP protocol stack known as ARP, or Address Resolution Protocol, resolves the IP address to a MAC hardware address on the transmitting end and from a MAC hardware address back to an IP address on the receiving end.

This is all great for computers that can remember infinite combinations of obscure numbers, but we humans like to call things by name. This solves two problems for us. First, IP addresses are hard to remember. Remembering common names is a much easier task. Second, when a computer moves to a different location on a network, its IP address often changes but its name does not.

Windows Internet Naming Service (WINS) solves this problem by allowing users to refer to computers by their familiar NetBIOS computer names over a TCP/IP network. WINS maintains an up-to-date list of NetBIOS computer names and their respective IP addresses.

**Note**  WINS can provide naming services only for WINS-enabled clients. Users on or outside of your network who are using different systems will not be able to use WINS to resolve NetBIOS names. For this, DNS may be used. Fortunately, DNS and WINS can be used together.

## 11.4.1. NetBIOS Over TCP/IP

NetBIOS was originally designed for use on small LANs and relies heavily upon broadcasts. On a small network, when a computer must find another computer by using a NetBIOS name, it broadcasts its request and each computer on the network reads the message to see if they are its intended target. Also, whenever a computer initializes, it sends a broadcast to see if its NetBIOS name is already registered on the network.

The problem with all of this is that broadcasts generally will not pass through routers. Thus, NetBIOS does not perform well on large, segmented networks.

This is where WINS comes in. The WINS server maintains an up-to-date list of each computer on the network containing its NetBIOS name and corresponding IP address. WINS solves the broadcast problem by using directed communications.

Client computers are preconfigured with the IP address of their WINS server. Thus, when the client initializes, it sends its registration message directly to the WINS server, which then checks to see whether the name is already registered. If it is not, the WINS server updates its database.

When a client must locate another computer on the network by its NetBIOS name, the request is sent directly to the WINS server, which in turn sends the IP address of the computer back to the client.

**Note**

Actually, when an h-node client must resolve a NetBIOS name, it first checks its local cache of names previously resolved. If the name is not found there, it then tries to resolve it from the WINS server. If the WINS server cannot resolve the name, the client tries a broadcast. If that fails, the client then tries the local LMHOSTS file, if any, then the local HOSTS file, if any. If these fail, and if one is available, it finally tries to resolve the name using a DNS server.

**11**

## 11.4.2. Configuring WINS Server

Minimal configuration is required when you set up a WINS server. This configuration consists of setting up replication and entering any needed static entries in the WINS database.

### Installing the WINS Server Service

To install the WINS Server service on a Windows NT server, do the following:

1. Open the Control Panel/Network and select the Services property sheet.
2. Choose the Add button.
3. On the list presented, select Microsoft WINS Server and choose OK.
4. You are asked for the path of the Windows NT Server 4.0 installation CD-ROM. Enter the drive letter of your CD-ROM or choose Browse to select an appropriate location. The installation then takes place.
5. Choose Close on the Network Control Panel.

6. If TCP/IP had not already been configured on your computer, the TCP/IP property sheet is displayed, asking you to choose a static IP address, subnet mask, and default gateway for each network adapter interface installed on the computer. After you have done this, choose OK.

After this is finished, the WINS service should be running and will run automatically whenever the computer is started. After installing the WINS server, it is ready to begin its job and little other configuration is required. All you must do is configure the client computers you want to use WINS with the IP address of the WINS server.

## 11.4.3. Managing WINS Server

The primary tool you use to administer the WINS server is WINS Manager (see Figure 11.13). It is available in the Administrative Tools group under the Start menu.

**Figure 11.13.**

*WINS Manager.*

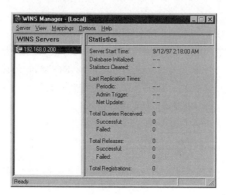

The options for configuring your WINS server are available by selecting Configuration under the Server menu. This brings up the WINS Server Configuration dialog box shown in Figure 11.14.

The WINS Server Configuration section enables you to modify the following parameters:

| Parameter | Description |
| --- | --- |
| *Renewal Interval* | Enables you to set how frequently clients must renew their NetBIOS name with the WINS server and defaults to six days. When a name is not renewed, the WINS server marks it as released. |
| *Extinction Interval* | Lets you define the time between when the WINS server marks a name as released and when it marks it as extinct. |

| Parameter | Description |
|-----------|-------------|
| | The default for this parameter is six days. An extinct name may be purged from the WINS database. |
| Extinction Timeout | Defines the time between when a name is marked as extinct and when it is actually purged from the WINS database. It defaults to the renewal interval. |
| Verify Interval | Specifies the time at which the WINS server must verify that names in its database replicated from other WINS servers are still active. The default is 24 days. |

**Figure 11.14.**

*Configuring a WINS server.*

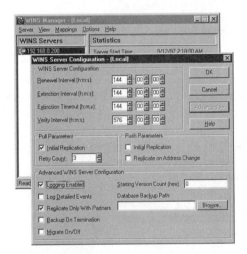

## Push and Pull WINS Replication

Although it is possible to run only one WINS server on a network, it is advisable to use two or more servers. Doing so not only provides for backup of the WINS database, but it also reduces the load on a single WINS server if your network is large.

WINS servers can be set up to replicate their databases to other WINS servers. Each replication relationship between two servers may consist of a push, a pull, or a push/pull relationship. The *push* partner notifies its partner that changes were made and the *pull* partner queries its partner if changes have been made. You configure replication using the WINS Manager shown in Figure 11.13. Choosing the Replication Partners command under the Server menu brings up the Replication Partners dialog box in Figure 11.15.

**Figure 11.15.**

*Configuring WINS replication partners.*

Initially, this window lists only the WINS server you are currently managing. To add a replication partner, choose the Add button and then enter the IP address of the WINS server with which you want to partner. The replication partner is now listed in the WINS Server menu (see Figure 11.16).

**Figure 11.16.**

*Adding a new replication partner with WINS Manager.*

Note that the default is to configure a new replication partner as both a push and a pull partner. To configure a partner as only one or the other type, uncheck the appropriate box in the Replication Options section.

A push partner is a WINS server that sends a message to its partners when its database has changed. The partner then downloads the database from the push partner. To configure a push partner, select it in the list of servers, and choose the Configure button next to Push Partner in the Replication Options section. This brings up the Push Partner Properties dialog box shown in Figure 11.17.

**Figure 11.17.**

*Configuring a push partner for WINS replication.*

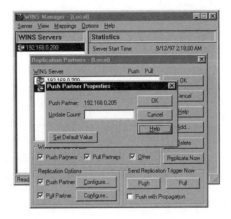

The only thing you can configure here is the Update Count. This value represents the number of changes that can be made to the WINS database before the push partner notifies its partners of the changes.

A pull partner is a WINS server that requests new database entries from its partners. To configure a pull partner, choose the Configure button next to Pull Partner in the Replication Options section. This brings up the Pull Partner Properties dialog box shown in Figure 11.18.

**11**

**Figure 11.18.**

*Configuring a pull partner for WINS replication.*

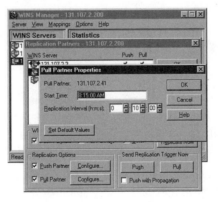

You may modify two parameters here. The first is the Start Time, which is the hour of the day that replication should begin. The second is the Replication Interval, which specifies the intervals at which replication should occur.

You also can manually force a replication to occur. There are two methods of doing this. The first is to force an immediate replication. You can do this by selecting the Replicate Now button on the Replication Partners dialog box (refer to Figure 11.15).

The other method is to send a replication trigger. You can send a replication trigger by the following method:

1. Select the destination server in the WINS Server window of the Replication Partners dialog box.

2. Select Push with Propagation if you want the trigger to be sent to all pull partners of the destination server.

3. Choose Pull in the Send Replication Trigger Now section of the dialog box.

You can also send a push replication trigger by using this method:

1. Select the destination server in the WINS Server window of the Replication Partners dialog box.

2. If you want the partner to, in turn, send push replication triggers to its pull partners, select the Push with Propagation box.

3. Choose Push in the Send Replication Trigger Now section of the dialog box.

It is generally better to configure a pull partner if the link between the WINS servers is a slow one. In this way, replication can be timed to occur at specified intervals when other network traffic is low. Across a fast link, choose a push partner because replication occurs when the database is updated. This maintains a more current replication.

When configuring your WINS servers for replication, you want to take into account the size of the database and available bandwidth when planning for network traffic. Each entry in the WINS database varies from 40 to 280 bytes. Therefore, each host that registers adds a minimum of 40 bytes to the database for every name registered.

If more than one IP address is configured for the host, then the amount of space increases proportionately to the number of IP addresses. In addition, if the registered name is a group name such as domain name (1C), the record can be up to 480 bytes if it contains the maximum number of registered hosts.

During replication, the amount of network traffic depends on the number of records to be transferred, which will vary for each session. In addition, the number of records to be transferred may be different for each session.

Each entry is about 50 bytes. When replication occurs, these entries are combined to create the smallest number of packets. The replication traffic consists of session establishment and WINS control frames as well as the frames containing the data.

## Name Registration

After initialization of TCP/IP, the host then registers its NetBIOS names. This can be done either through b-node broadcasts or by sending the registration to a NetBIOS name server such as WINS.

All services and applications that use NetBIOS must be registered. The number of names a host registers is variable and reflects network services and applications that the host initializes. These include the computer's role—PDC, the Workstation and Server services, or NetBIOS applications such as Network Monitor. Each host registers an average of three or four names.

Each NetBIOS name is 16 characters long with the 16th character reserved as a designator of the service or application that owns the name. The configurable portion of the NetBIOS name can be up to 15 characters long, and can be something like the computer's name. If this portion of the name is less than 15 characters, then the name will be padded to a length of 15 characters.

The registration of each name generates a packet 214 bytes long and takes less than 100 milliseconds to complete the registration process. Figure 11.19 shows the registration process using Network Monitor.

**11**

**Figure 11.19.**

*Network Monitor showing WINS registration.*

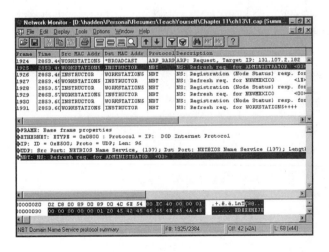

## WINS Name Renewal

After a name is registered, the WINS server sends a success message that assigns a Time to Live (TTL) to that name. The TTL is used to determine when the host must renew that name. The default TTL is 144 hours, or 518,400 seconds.

Each host renews its names when half of its TTL has elapsed, or every three days with the default configuration. After a successful renewal, the TTL for the host's names is reset to the original length. The length of the TTL determines how much traffic will be generated for name renewals.

## Name Resolution

NetBIOS names enable us to use friendly names to access various resources on the network. To find the resource we need, however, a method must be in place to ensure that no two resources use identical names.

WINS resolves NetBIOS names to IP addresses to provide a way to locate these resources. When a host wants to locate a resource it sends a name query request to the WINS server containing the name to be resolved and a query flag. The WINS server responds with a name query response packet if that name is registered. This packet contains the IP address of the registered owner of the resource.

Name resolution involves only two packets. The host sends a name query request and the WINS responds with a name query response containing either the IP address of the name's owner or a "Requested name does not exist" message. These two frames are less than 200 bytes in size and can take only a couple of milliseconds if network traffic is light.

If the name is not registered with WINS, the client assumes that the name's owner is not a WINS client and resorts to broadcasting to resolve the name if configured to do so.

Note in Figure 11.20 the two frame conversation resulting in a `Requested name doesn't exist` message (frames 1378 and 1379). The host then sends a broadcast message to locate the name's owner.

## Name Release

When a host shuts down or stops a service, it sends a release request to the WINS server. This release is the same size as a registration (110 bytes) and the WINS responds with a success message (104 bytes) which sets the TTL to zero. After a name is released, another host can register it. When a computer shuts down, two frames are sent for each registered name.

**Figure 11.20.**
*Network Monitor showing failure of WINS name resolution.*

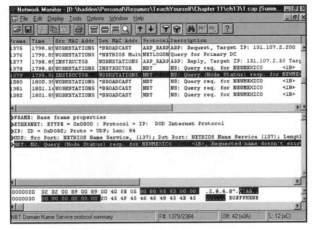

## Managing Static Mappings in WINS

One of the strongest features of WINS is that it dynamically keeps up with NetBIOS names and IP addresses, and little manual configuration is required. Non-WINS clients, however, cannot participate in this in the normal way.

When a client that cannot use WINS initializes itself, it does not register its NetBIOS name with the WINS server. For WINS clients to be able to locate non-WINS clients, you must configure static mappings. This entails manually entering the NetBIOS name and IP address for a computer into the WINS database. You do this in the following manner:

1. In WINS Manager, choose Static Mappings from the Mappings menu. This brings up the Static Mappings dialog box shown in Figure 11.21.

**Figure 11.21.**
*Editing static mappings using WINS Manager.*

2. Choose the Add Mappings button to bring up the Add Static Mappings dialog box (see Figure 11.22).

**Figure 11.22.**

*Adding a static mapping to the WINS database.*

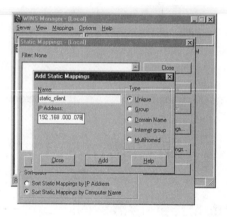

3. Enter the NetBIOS name and IP address of the client computer. You also can choose the type of client you are mapping. These types are described in Table 11.1.

**Table 11.1. Types of static mappings in a WINS database.**

| Type | Description |
| --- | --- |
| Unique | This type is the most common and maps a single name to a single IP address. |
| Group | If a destination NetBIOS name is a group, multicast packets are sent to that group. |
| Domain Name | A NetBIOS name-to-address mapping that stores up to a maximum of 25 addresses for members. |
| Internet Group | A user-defined group that enables you to group resources for easy accessibility. |
| Multihomed | A unique name that can have more than one IP address, used for multihomed computers. |

4. Choose OK. This brings you back to the Static Mappings window, but you should now see your new entry in the mappings window (see Figure 11.23).

**Figure 11.23.**

*Static mappings have been added to the WINS database.*

Note that although you added only one static mapping, three now show up in the window. In actuality, each service running on a WINS client requires a NetBIOS name of its own. NetBIOS names are actually 16 characters. The first 15 characters are the familiar name of the computer and the 16th, a hexadecimal number, represents the service. In this example, the Workstation [00h], Messenger [03h], and Server [20h] services each have their own NetBIOS name.

By using the Static Mappings window in Figure 11.23, you may also select Import Mappings to import an existing LMHOSTS file into the WINS database.

## Viewing and Backing Up the WINS Database

You can view the WINS database at any time from the WINS Manager. Select Show Database from the Mappings menu to bring up the Show Database window, shown in Figure 11.24.

This dialog box enables you to view all mappings in the WINS database or only the mapping owned by a particular server based on various sort options. You also can delete a server from the database by selecting the server and then choosing Delete Owner.

To back up the WINS database, you must first choose a backup directory. To do this, in WINS Manager select Back Up Database from the Mappings menu. After you have done this, the database will be backed up automatically every 24 hours. You can restore the database by using one of two methods. The first is to simply stop and restart the WINS Server service. This automatically restores a corrupted database. The second method is to choose Restore Database from the Mappings menu in WINS Manager.

11

**Figure 11.24.**

*Viewing a WINS database using WINS Manager.*

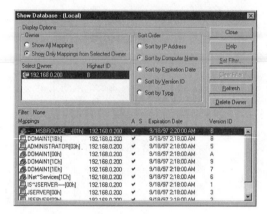

## 11.4.4. WINS Optimization

The traffic that occurs between the WINS server and its clients consists of name registrations, renewals, and releases as well as name resolution. The two areas that can be optimized are the frequency of name renewals and the number of names per host that are registered.

When a name is registered with a WINS server, a time to live (TTL) is assigned to it. Although the size of the renewal frames and the resulting network traffic is fairly small, this traffic can be further reduced by lengthening the TTL. Name renewal then occurs at one-half of the new TTL. This helps reduce network traffic only if the host does not shut down during this period.

The other main area of optimization is to reduce the number of names a host registers and must periodically renew. You can do so by stopping any unnecessary services. For example, if the host does not share resources over the network, stopping the server service prevents the host from having to register or renew this service. Stopping any unnecessary services is also wise from a security aspect.

After a NetBIOS name as been resolved, it is placed in the NetBIOS name cache. This cache is checked before sending a request to the WINS server. The default length of time that names remain in the cache is 10 minutes and is configured in the registry. By lengthening the
`HKEY_LOCAL_MACHINE\SYSTEM\CurrentControlSet\Services\NetBT\Parameters\CacheTimeout`
to a higher value, those most frequently accessed names are resolved from the cache rather than by requesting the resolution from the WINS server, thereby reducing network traffic.

The other method of reducing NetBIOS name resolution from the WINS server is by using an LMHOSTS file. By preloading the names of domain controllers or other frequently accessed servers, the amount of network traffic for name resolution is also reduced.

When optimizing push/pull partners for WINS, you should take into consideration the type of link between the two servers. If your WINS servers are local to each other, configure pull requests for every 30 minutes but extend this to every six hours if the replication is occurring over a slow WAN link.

Push notifications default to 20 changes in the database. If this replication occurs across a WAN link, increasing this number results in a decrease in network traffic. Although this decreases network load, it may lead to using an out-of-date database for name resolution.

## 11.4.5. LMHOSTS Files

Before WINS, NetBIOS name resolution relied on a file called the LMHOSTS file. This file is very simple and looks something like the following:

```
192.168.0.1      Server1        #PRE    #DOM:Domain1
192.168.0.2      Server2        #PRE    #DOM:Domain2
192.168.0.100    Workstation1   #PRE
192.168.0.101    Workstation2
```

11

Each entry in this file lists an IP address and its corresponding NetBIOS name. Each entry can also include one or more keywords. The keywords that may be used are summarized in Table 11.2.

**Table 11.2. Keywords in an LMHOSTS file.**

| Keyword | Description |
| --- | --- |
| #PRE | Indicates that the entry should be preloaded into the computer's NetBIOS name cache. |
| #DOM: | Indicates a domain to be associated with the entry; particularly useful on a routed network. |
| #INCLUDE | Allows the LMHOSTS file to automatically include the entries in a remote LMHOSTS file, centralizing the management of NetBIOS name mappings. |

The LMHOSTS file requires that all mappings be entered manually. Obviously, the capability of WINS to dynamically associate mappings is a great improvement over the

LMHOSTS file, but LMHOSTS can still be useful on clients that do not support WINS.

### 11.4.6. HOSTS Files

One flaw in the WINS and LMHOSTS scheme is that non-WINS enabled clients cannot use WINS to resolve NetBIOS name to IP address. The HOSTS file is used for just that purpose. It is structured similarly to the LMHOSTS file:

```
127.0.0.1          localhost
192.168.0.1        server1
192.168.0.1        server1.domain1.com
192.168.0.2        server2
192.168.0.2        server2.domain1.com
192.168.0.100      workstation1
192.168.0.101      workstation2
```

In each entry is the IP address and corresponding host name of a computer. Note the difference between this and the LMHOSTS file, however. In the LMHOSTS file, one IP address can be associated with exactly one NetBIOS name. In the HOSTS file, however, the same IP address can be associated with multiple host names. Thus, you can get to 192.168.0.1 by using either server1 or server1.domain1.com.

> **Note**
>
> The first entry of localhost refers to the local client by the loopback address 127.0.0.1, which is typically used for diagnostics.

# 11.5. Domain Name System (DNS)

During the Internet's early years, when it was known as ARPANET, it consisted of only a few hundred computers networked together. With these few computers, keeping track of the host names and IP addresses of these computers was a fairly simple task. These mappings were located in a central file called Hosts.txt, which was located on a host computer at the Stanford Research Institute. As the ARPANET grew, however, this file became more difficult to manage for a few reasons:

- The file was growing too large to manage efficiently.
- All of the traffic on ARPANET had to be routed through the Stanford computer to resolve computer host names.

■ The file had a flat name structure, meaning that every computer connected to ARPANET had to have its own unique host name.

The domain name system (DNS) is a distributed database that uses a hierarchical name structure. The function of this database is to resolve host names or fully qualified domain names (FQDN) to IP addresses. The database is distributed across many computers on the Internet, which means that name resolution no longer requires going through a central point, as it did with the Hosts.txt file. Its name space is also hierarchical, which means that it is like a tree structure (see Figure 11.25).

**Figure 11.25.**
*The domain name space.*

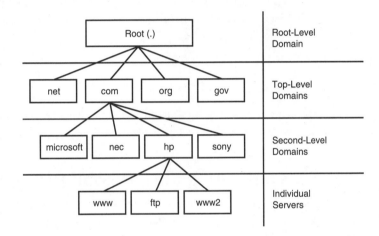

Each node in this structure is called a *domain*. The domain name space is typically divided into three domain levels: root level, top level, and second level. Domains represent different levels of authority in this hierarchical structure. The highest level of authority is called the *root domain*. The *top-level domains* are organizationally defined, as shown in Table 11.3.

**Table 11.3. Top-level domains in the domain name space.**

| Domain | Description |
| --- | --- |
| com | Commercial organization |
| net | Networks and Internet service providers |
| gov | Government organizations |
| mil | Military organizations |

*continues*

**Table 11.3. continued**

| Domain | Description |
|--------|-------------|
| org | Non-commercial or non-profit organizations |
| int | International organizations |
| edu | Educational institutions |
| xx | Two-letter country code (such as uk for Great Britain) |

The second-level domain is defined by the organization that registers under a top-level domain. Further second-level domains can also be defined under this second-level domain. For example, Hewlett-Packard owns the second-level domain hp. This domain falls under the com top-level domain. This gives Hewlett-Packard the domain name hp.com. Hewlett-Packard also maintains a Web site on a server called www. This server falls under the second-level domain hp. Thus, the domain name for that server is http://www.hp.com.

As you can see, the hierarchical nature of DNS provides much more flexibility than a simple flat name space. With a flat name space, only one host name in the database could ever be called www.

## 11.5.1. Configuring the Microsoft DNS Server

The following sections take you through the setup and configuration of the Microsoft DNS Server. They cover the installation of DNS, the configuration and optimization of zones and host records, and the methods of name resolution that DNS uses.

### Installing the DNS Server Service

To install the DNS Server service on a Windows NT server, do the following:

1. Open the Control Panel/Network and select the Services property sheet.
2. Choose the Add button.
3. On the list presented, select Microsoft DNS Server and choose OK.
4. You are asked for the path of the Windows NT Server 4.0 installation CD-ROM. Enter the drive letter for your CD-ROM or choose Browse to select an appropriate location. The installation will then take place.
5. Choose Close on the Network Control Panel.

After this is finished, the DNS service should be running and will run automatically whenever the computer is started. After installing the DNS server, it automatically performs as a caching-only name server for the Internet.

## Zone of Authority

A *zone of authority* is simply a portion of the domain name space for which a name server is responsible. The name server maintains a database of host names and IP addresses for the computers that fall into its authority and is responsible for resolving queries of those names. An *authority* can really be thought of as all of the host names and IP address mappings that a particular name server is responsible for keeping up with and being the ultimate authority on.

A *zone* is defined as the part of the name space that is documented in the zone file. A name server can contain more than one zone. A zone of authority must contain at least one domain, known as the root domain. From the preceding example, a zone might be defined for Hewlett-Packard. The root domain would be hp.

## Name Server Roles in DNS

A DNS server can play four roles:

- Primary Name Server: The primary name server hosts the local zone files, and all changes made to the file are made on this server.

- Secondary Name Server: The secondary name server is a backup to another name server. It downloads the database information from a master name server. The secondary name server provides redundancy of data and helps reduce the query load on the primary name server.

- Master Name Server: A name server from which a secondary name server downloads its database information. The master name server can be either a primary or a secondary name server.

- Caching-Only Name Server: All name servers cache the queries that they have resolved locally in addition to their other services. The caching-only name server, however, only performs and caches queries. It is not an authority over any zone data.

## Setting Up Zones, Domains, and Resource Records

Before your DNS server can act as anything other than a caching-only server, you must provide it with information about your network. This includes adding zones of authority, domains, and resource records. The tool you use to administer your DNS server is called Domain Name Service Manager, and it is available in the Administrative Tools group under the Start menu. Domain Name Service Manager is pictured in Figure 11.26.

**Figure 11.26.**
*Domain Name Service Manager.*

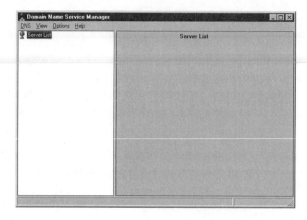

To create a new zone, highlight the server for which you want to configure the zone and select New Zone under the DNS menu. This brings up the dialog box shown in Figure 11.27.

**Figure 11.27.**
*Creating a new zone with DNS Manager.*

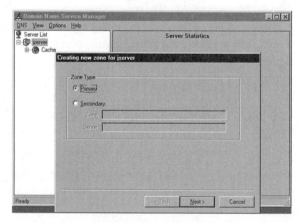

Note

You might need to add a server before creating a zone. If you do, choose New Server under the DNS menu and enter the name or IP address of the server.

Select whether you want to create a primary or secondary zone. If you are creating a secondary zone, you must also fill in the master zone and master server name. After you have done this, click Next and you see the dialog box shown in Figure 11.28.

**Figure 11.28.**

*Filling in new zone information.*

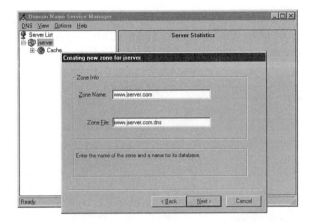

The zone name is the name by which your zone is referenced and is usually something like servername.com. The zone file can be anything, but must end with the extension .dns. After you have entered the zone name, press Tab to have Windows NT name the file for you. After you have finished creating your zone, the DNS Manager window should look like Figure 11.29.

**Figure 11.29.**

*A new zone in DNS Manager.*

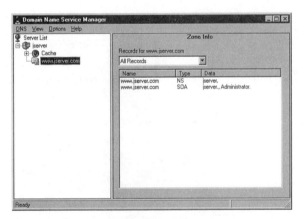

In the left pane, you should see the new zone you just added under the corresponding server. If you highlight this, you see current zone information in the right pane. You now are ready to add any subdomains you need. To add a subdomain, highlight the domain and then select New Domain under the DNS menu. Add any more subdomains you want in this manner. You also can add subdomains under other subdomains.

Now that you have created your zone and any subdomains, you are ready to start adding resource records to your domains. Resource records are the meat of your DNS database; the common types of resource records are summarized in Table 11.4.

**Table 11.4. Resource records in a DNS database.**

| Record Type | Description |
| --- | --- |
| SOA | The name server that is the best source for finding name resolution. |
| A | Also known as a host, this is the basic record of the database and maps a single host name to an IP address. |
| CNAME | A canonical name record, this is essentially an alias pointing to an existing host. |
| MX | Identifies the host that processes mail for this domain. |
| NS | Name server record. This points to additional domain name servers. |

You can add a record simply by selecting the domain to which you want to add it and selecting New Record from the DNS menu. This brings up the window shown in Figure 11.30.

**Figure 11.30.**

*Adding a record to the DNS database.*

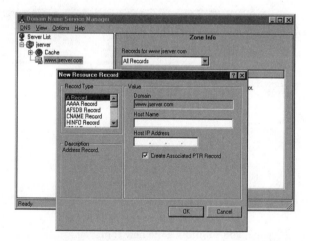

Select the type of record you want to add in the Record Type section and enter the parameters in the Value section. For example, if you need the name ftp to point to IP address 192.168.0.141, simply add an A Record. Select A Record in the Record Type section. In the Value section, enter ftp in the Host Name field and enter the IP address in the Host IP Address field. Clicking OK should return you to the DNS Manager, where your new record should show up in the right pane (see Figure 11.31).

**Figure 11.31.**

*Viewing a new record in the DNS database.*

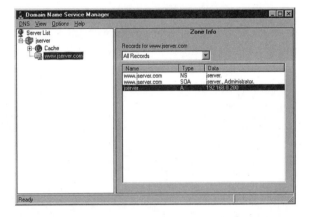

Note

You also can administer Microsoft DNS Service the same way you would a traditional DNS by working with the files in the default installation path `\systemroot\system32\dns`.

**11**

## 11.5.2. Name Resolution with DNS

A client can make three types of queries to a DNS server:

- Recursive queries: In a recursive query, a client requests information of a DNS server. The DNS server can reply with the IP address of the domain name requested or a message stating that the information could not be found. The DNS server cannot pass information along to another server.

- Iterative query: In an iterative query, the DNS server can return the resolved IP address of a domain name or a referral to another DNS server with more information.

- Inverse query: In an inverse query, the client requests that a computer name be found given a known IP address.

In Figure 11.32, a client computer in Chicago requests the IP address for the domain name http://www.hp.com. It does this using a recursive query, meaning that the information the client computer gets back will be either the IP address or an error message. The DNS server makes an iterative query to the DNS server whose zone of authority is the root-level domain names. The root DNS server refers the Chicago DNS server to the DNS server whose zone of authority is the top-level domain name com.

This server then refers the Chicago server to another DNS server, whose zone of authority is hp. This server has the correct mapping in its database and returns the information to the Chicago DNS server, which in turn passes it back to the client.

**Figure 11.32.**

*Querying a DNS server for domain name resolution.*

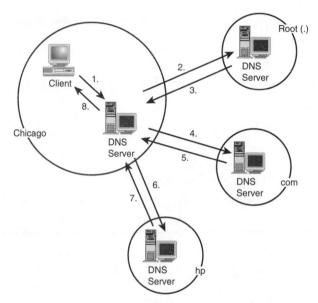

## 11.5.3. Using WINS with DNS

DNS is a static database, which means that all information must be manually entered into it. WINS allows client computers to automatically register themselves with the WINS server so that their computer names can be resolved to their IP addresses. You can configure DNS and WINS to work together to provide quite a flexible name resolution scheme.

To do this, you simply must configure DNS to enable WINS lookup. This allows DNS to forward NetBIOS names to a WINS server for resolution. In DNS Manager, select the zone for which you want to enable WINS lookup and select Properties from the DNS menu. This brings up the property sheet shown in Figure 11.33.

Select the WINS Lookup tab and check the box next to Use WINS Resolution. In the WINS Servers section, enter the IP addresses of any WINS servers you want to use. You can also order them by priority.

**Figure 11.33.**
*Enabling WINS lookup for a zone in DNS Manager.*

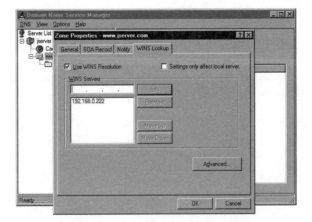

## 11.5.4.  Optimizing Domain Name Server

The amount of network traffic involved in using a domain name server (DNS) for name resolution consists of a client request and a DNS response, so it is of small impact on overall network traffic. However, traffic can be increased by the need for the DNS to do recursive lookups whether to another DNS or a WINS server.

Preventing recursive lookups altogether reduces network traffic but also decreases the effectiveness of the DNS for name resolution. Optimizing DNS traffic, therefore, should be aimed toward decreasing the number of recursive lookups while maintaining the effectiveness of DNS to provide for name resolution. This can be enhanced by pointing clients to the DNS that is most likely to have the requested address.

When a DNS does a recursive lookup, this information remains in the cache for 10 minutes. By increasing the time to live (TTL) of these cached entries, the results of recursive lookups remain in the cache longer, thereby preventing further lookups for those destinations that are accessed most frequently.

# 11.6.  Directory Replication

Directory services traffic include both synchronization of the Security Accounts Manager (SAM) database from the PDC to each BDC as well as directory replication. A Windows 95 client logging on generates 39 frames and 6,538 bytes of data. Synchronization of only two user accounts generates approximately 28 frames and 5,654 bytes of traffic. This does not include any additional logon processes that might take place, such as login scripts and user profile validations.

**11**

## 11.6.1. SAM Synchronization

The NetLogon service handles the job of keeping the SAM synchronized on all BDCs with the PDC. If an organization has multiple sites at various geographical locations, then optimization includes evaluating the amount of traffic generated across the WAN link by user logons as well as the amount of synchronization traffic.

Having a BDC at the remote site ensures that users are able to log on to the domain even if the WAN link is down. However, synchronizing the entire user database may make the WAN link unavailable for other purposes during synchronization.

Synchronizing the user database takes an average of 1KB per change, so fully synchronizing a SAM containing 30,000 users across a slow link can take up to 24 hours.

Both synchronization events and changes to the SAM are recorded by the PDC in a file called the *change log*. If this file becomes full, the older events are overwritten. If too many changes occur between synchronizations, a full copy of the SAM from the PDC to the BDC is made to ensure that the SAM on the BDC is accurate. If the WAN link is unstable, the BDC might also force a full synchronization—increasing network traffic even more.

The parameters you can change to affect how synchronization occurs include `ReplicationGovernor`, `PulseConcurrency`, `Pulse`, and `Randomize`.

### ReplicationGovernor

The `ReplicationGovernor` parameter controls the percentage of bandwidth that the NetLogon service can use during synchronization and is found at `HKEY_LOCAL_MACHINE\SYSTEM\CurrentControlSet\Services\Netlogon\Parameters\ReplicationGovernor`. The default value is 100 percent. Changing to 50 percent allows other traffic access to the link while synchronization occurs.

### PulseConcurrency

NetLogon sends pulses to individual BDCs, which then respond by requesting any changes. The `PulseConcurrency` determines how many simultaneous replications the PDC can handle. The default value is 20 and can be set between 1 and 500. Lowering this number results in a lower utilization of bandwidth but lengthens the amount of time before complete synchronization occurs, especially if there is a large number of BDCs.

### Pulse

The `Pulse` parameter controls how often the primary domain controller sends messages to backup domain controllers that need updating. The default value is five minutes to a maximum of 60 minutes. If changes in the SAM occur infrequently, a setting of 60 minutes results in less traffic across the WAN link while maintaining accuracy of the BDC's copy of the SAM.

### Randomize

The `Randomize` number determines how long the BDC waits after receiving a pulse before contacting the PDC. The default is 1 second with an allowable range of 0 to 120 seconds.

### PulseMaximum

The `PulseMaximum` parameter determines how often the PDC sends a pulse message to the BDCs even when no changes have occurred. The default value is 2 hours and can be increased to 24 hours. Extending this value also reduces WAN traffic.

### ChangeLogSizeControls

The `ChangeLogSizeControls` parameter determines the number of changes that must occur to the SAM before a full synchronization occurs. The default is 64KB or about 2,000 changes. If changes occur frequently, such as users changing passwords, this amount can be quickly exceeded, resulting in a need to perform a full synchronization—causing excessive WAN traffic.

## Logon Optimization

When planning how to set up various NETLOGON parameters, you must consider how frequently changes occur as well as the location of each of the BDCs in relation to the PDC. Don't forget to take into consideration the total number of servers in your network because each server changes its internal password every seven days.

## 11.6.2.  Directory Replication

Directory replication is a feature of Windows NT Server that enables you to replicate logon scripts, policy files, and other important files to other computers on your network. By using this feature, you can set up identical directories on many computers on your network. One Windows NT Server computer will maintain the master copy of this directory, and replication is set up to occur automatically.

The Windows NT Server computer that maintains this master copy of the replicated directory is known as the *export computer*. Computers that are set up to receive copies of this directory are known as *import computers*. The following types of computers can be import computers:

**11**

- Windows NT servers
- Windows NT workstations
- Microsoft LAN Manager OS/2 servers

The export server keeps the directories which will be replicated in an export directory that, by default, is \winnt\System32\Repl\Export. Any subdirectories under this directory automatically are replicated. Each import computer has a corresponding import directory that, by default, is \winnt\System32\Repl\Import.

You set up directory replication by using Server Manager, which can be found in the Administrative Tools group under the Start menu. Highlight the server for which you want to set up replication, and select Properties under the Computer menu. This brings up the properties dialog box for that server (see Figure 11.34).

**Figure 11.34.**

*Viewing the properties for a server in Server Manager.*

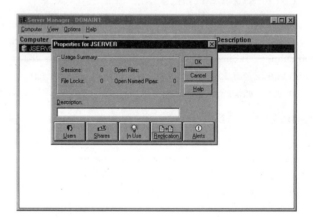

Click the Replication button and you see the Directory Replication dialog box for the server (see Figure 11.35).

A Windows NT server can be set up as an export server, an import server for another Windows NT server, or both. To set up an export server, choose the Export Directories radio button from the Directory Replication dialog box. The path to the default export directory is automatically entered in the From Path field. To add a computer to export to, click the Add button and enter the name of the domain or the computer to which you want to export.

**Figure 11.35.**

*Setting up replication in Server Manager.*

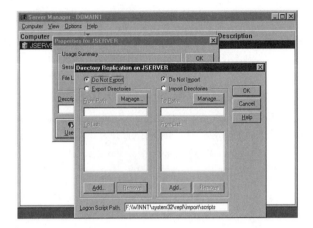

Replication is a two-way relationship. For replication to take place, the import computers must also be set up with the name of the export computer. You do this by following the same process just described, except that you select the Import Directories radio button and click the Add button in that section. Again, you must enter the domain or computer name of the export computer.

The amount of network traffic generated depends on the amount of data to be replicated from the source computer to the destination computers.

By default, the export computer checks every five minutes for changes. Because the Directory Replicator service copies the entire structure if one file changes, using a shallow directory structure rather than a deep one is more efficient. In this manner, those directories with files that have not changed are not replicated, thereby reducing network traffic.

## Server Manager

If you want to limit replication to off hours when traffic is at its lowest, you can use Server Manager to lock a directory. While the lock is in place, the directory is not replicated.

The Wait Until Stabilized option in Server Manager causes the server to recopy the entire subtree whenever any file is changed. By deselecting this option, the import server checks the date, time, name, attributes, and size of each individual file and copies only those files that have changed.

### Registry Parameters

You also can alter directory replication by editing the registry. These entries are found in `HKEY_LOCAL_MACHINE\SYSTEM\CurrentControlSet\Services\Replicator\Parameters`. The `Interval` and `Pulse` parameters are the most useful.

The `Interval` parameter determines how often the export server checks for updates to the directories to be exported. If changes have occurred, the import server is notified to retrieve the changed files. The default value is five minutes but can be extended. The greater this value, the longer it takes for changes to be reflected on the import servers. However, lengthening this parameter also results in less network traffic.

The `Pulse` parameter determines how often the import server contacts the export server asking for an update. The default is 2. If the `Interval` parameter is left at the default of five minutes, the import computer will contact the export computer if it has not heard anything after 10 minutes—a `Pulse` of 2 times an `Interval` of 5 minutes. Increasing the pulse lengthens the time interval before the import computer contacts the export computer for updates.

# 11.7. Internet Information Server (IIS)

Internet Information Server (IIS) is a networking service that runs under Windows NT Server and provides publishing capability for use on the Internet or an intranet. It combines the features of a Web server, an FTP server, and a gopher server into one, integrated network service.

IIS ships with Windows NT Server and can be installed via Control Panel/Network/Services/Add. Follow the steps in the installation wizard and choose which of the services you want to install. Setup is mostly automatic.

After IIS is set up, you can administer it with the Internet Service Manager, located in the Microsoft Internet Server group under the Start menu. The main window of the Internet Service Manager (shown in Figure 11.36) shows simply which services are installed on your system and whether they are running, paused, or stopped.

It is also possible to manage multiple servers from one machine by using the Internet Service Manager. To add a server to the list, simply select Connect to a Server under the Properties menu and enter the server's name.

**Figure 11.36.**

*Managing Internet services in IIS.*

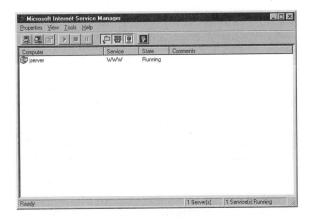

You also can have Internet Service Manager find all servers on the network that are running IIS by selecting Find all Servers under the Properties menu.

## 11.7.1. Setting General Properties for the WWW Service

11

The rest of this section presents some of the procedures for managing the WWW publishing service. Select a WWW service and choose Service Properties under the Properties menu. A property sheet like the one in Figure 11.37 is displayed.

**Figure 11.37.**

*Managing the WWW service.*

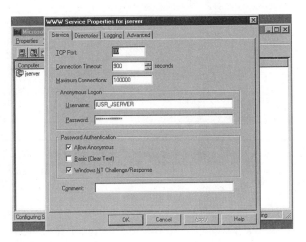

This property sheet enables you to configure general items such as the port information for the WWW service and the logon parameters. You can choose here whether to allow anonymous access to your Web site and what the anonymous guest account should be called.

When IIS is installed, it creates a user account on your system called IUSR_computername. Configure permissions for this account the same as with any other user account.

## Virtual Directories in IIS

The Directories property sheet enables you to configure directories and directory behavior for each service (see Figure 11.38). Each service must have a home directory for its content, and that directory is the root directory for the service. In this example, the picture of a house represents the home directory for the WWW service. Any files that you place into this directory will be available to browsers coming to your site.

**Figure 11.38.**
*Managing directories with the WWW service.*

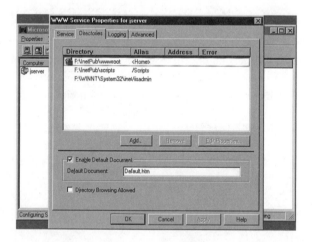

You also can add directories that do not physically exist under the real root directory. These are known as virtual directories. In this example, the scripts directory does not really exist inside the wwwroot directory on the hard drive. People browsing your Web site, however, see it as if it did.

To add a virtual directory, click the Add button on the Directories property sheet (refer to Figure 11.38). This brings up the Directory Properties dialog box shown in Figure 11.39.

**Figure 11.39.**
*Adding a virtual
directory to IIS.*

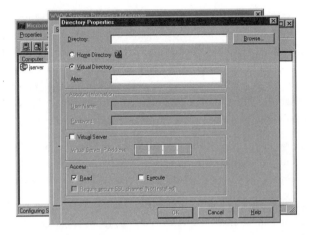

Type the path of the actual directory you want to publish (or click the Browse button) and enter the alias by which you want this directory known. Choose whether you want Read access, Execute access, or both, and click OK. Your new virtual directory is now set up.

### Virtual Servers in IIS

IIS also gives you the ability to host more than one Web site on the same computer. Additional Web sites are hosted on what are known as *virtual servers*. Each virtual server must have its own IP address and have that address registered with InterNIC. Next, you must bind that IP address to your network adapter card.

To set up a virtual server, click the Add button from the Directories property sheet (refer to Figure 11.38). This brings up the window you saw in Figure 11.39. Simply enter the IP address associated with this server and the directory that contains the information you want to publish, and click OK.

## 11.7.2. Optimizing Internet Information Server (IIS)

The inclusion of Internet Information Server with Windows NT Server makes establishing an intranet or an Internet presence easy. The introduction of this technology makes communication with all the employees of your organization easy and fun. With this additional capability comes the overhead and administrative responsibilities of managing an additional resource.

Optimizing your network traffic when a Web server is present can be viewed from two perspectives. The first is the efficiency of your Web server—how quickly does it respond to user requests? The second is what impact this additional server has on your overall network health.

**11**

The best way to maximize IIS performance is to have IIS fulfill requests from its cache rather than read from the physical drive. IIS maintains its own cache separately from that maintained by the Windows NT operating system. The cache can be configured by editing the registry key HKEY_LOCAL_MACHINE\SYSTEM\CurrentControlSet\ Services\InetInfo\Parameters\MemoryCacheSize. The range is 0 to 4GB. A setting of 0 disables caching. If the cache size is adjusted to a size greater than the amount of available physical memory, other processes on the server will be adversely affected.

When evaluating the effect of your IIS server on network traffic, you must determine the amount of bandwidth utilization. Bandwidth can be assessed both from the user's standpoint (can your site be accessed?) and its effect on other network traffic.

If users complain of having difficulty accessing your server, then demand might be exceeding your available capacity. You can increase capacity by increasing the number of allowable connections using the Internet Information Server Manager. If this change does not solve the problem, then consider adding extra high-speed network adapters or mirror your server. The later option is helpful when you must deal with a low-speed WAN connection.

If your problem is one of other network processes being adversely affected by the traffic generated by IIS, you can decrease the percentage of bandwidth that is utilized using the Internet Information Server Manager. Changes made here affect all Internet services, not just the Web server. Decreasing the amount of allowable bandwidth, however, decreases the number of connections that can be made to your server. Another option is to place your IIS server on its own network segment.

To guarantee that your IIS gets its share of the processor, run only the processes necessary for the Web server to function. Do not expect your IIS server to fill other roles such as a file and print server or an application server.

# 11.8. Lab

This lab aids your learning by testing you on the information presented in this chapter as well as giving you exercises to hone your skills. Answers to the review questions can be found in Appendix B, "Answers to Review Questions."

## 11.8.1. Review Questions

### Question 1

DHCP requires that which protocol be enabled on your network?

    A. NWLink

    B. TCP/IP

    C. NetBEUI

    D. None of the above

### Question 2

If your network is routed and you want to use DHCP to assign IP addresses to computers on all of your subnets, what must your routers support?

    A. They must be able to act as a DHCP relay agent.

    B. They must be able to route BOOTP packets.

    C. They must support IP Address Automatic Configuration.

    D. Nothing. This can be done with all routers.

### Question 3

What utility would you use in Windows NT if you needed to know the current IP address of your computer?

    A. IPCONFIG

    B. ARP

    C. Network Control Panel

    D. NBTSTAT

### Question 4

You are configuring multiple DHCP servers on a network and want to provide some level of redundancy. On each DHCP server, how many local IP addresses should be included in the scope?

**11**

A. All the local addresses

B. 50 percent of the local available addresses

C. 75 percent of the local available addresses

D. 80 percent of the local available addresses

## Question 5

You are setting up WINS replication across a slow WAN link. How should you configure the replication partners?

A. As push partners

B. To replicate only at certain times of the day

C. As pull partners

D. To replicate manually only

## Question 6

Your company has been using an LMHOSTS file for NetBIOS name resolution, but wants to switch over to WINS. However, it wants to import the information from the LMHOSTS file into WINS. How would you do this?

A. Import it as static mappings using WINS Manager.

B. Manually enter the information into WINS.

C. Convert the LMHOSTS file to a HOSTS file and set WINS to use DNS Lookup.

D. Configure the WINS Server to use the LMHOSTS file for lookup after checking its own database.

## Question 7

Your network also consists of non-WINS-enabled clients and you need them to resolve computer names to IP addresses. What two methods could you implement to accomplish this?

A. Use a HOSTS file on each of the non-WINS enabled clients.

B. Use an LMHOSTS file on each of the non-WINS enabled clients.

C. Use DNS.

D. Use a WINS proxy agent.

## Question 8

What advantage does the hierarchical name structure implemented in DNS have over the flat name space used previously? (Choose two)

A. More than one computer on the network can have the same host name.

B. Each domain level is responsible for its own naming scheme.

C. It is a much smaller and easier to handle database.

D. The hierarchical name space provides some level of redundancy.

## Question 9

From where does a secondary DNS name server download its database information?

A. From a primary name server

B. From a master name server

C. From a backup name server

D. From a proxy name server

## Question 10

To use the Virtual Server feature of Internet Information Server, how must the computer first be configured?

A. As a DNS server

B. With a dedicated connection to the Internet

C. With multiple network adapters, each with a unique IP address bound to a single virtual server

D. With a single network adapter having multiple unique IP addresses, each bound to a single virtual server

## Question 11

For what is the Windows NT Server Directory Replication feature primarily used?

A. For the replication of logon scripts, system policy files, and other commonly used information

B. To manage WINS replication

C. To manage DNS replication

D. As a primary backup system

11

## Question 12

What would you use to configure directory replication?

A. User Manager for Domains

B. Replication Governor

C. Server Manager

D. WINS Manager

## Question 13

You have noticed a marked increase in network traffic and suspect it is the result of either Pulse or PulseConcurrency being incorrectly configured. What registry hive contains these settings on each domain controller?

A. HKEY_CLASSES_ROOT

B. HKEY_LOCAL_MACHINE

C. HKEY_CURRENT_CONFIG

D. HKEY_DYN_DATA

## Question 14

You think that the amount of network traffic has increased over the past six months. In an effort to decrease this traffic you should

A. Place a backup domain controller on each subnet of your network.

B. Eliminate traffic generated by DHCP by manually entering IP addresses on all clients.

C. Configure each client to use broadcasts for all name resolution.

D. Use Network Monitor to capture and analyze network traffic and compare it to baseline data.

## Question 15

To optimize the efficiency of your domain name server, you should

A. Install a domain name server on each segment of your network and make each one a secondary server to its closest neighbor.

B. Locate all domain servers on the same segment as your primary domain controller. Lengthen the TTL of the cache.

C. Configure each client to use the domain name server that is most likely to be able to resolve its name requests.

D. Configure your domain controller to use WINS to resolve NetBIOS names.

## Question 16

After installing an intranet hosted by an Internet Information Server, users complain that it takes longer to log on or to access network resources. Information obtained by using Network Monitor indicates that the use of the intranet has doubled your network traffic. You should

A. Instruct your users to stop using the intranet during peak usage time.

B. Configure the IIS server to limit bandwidth utilization to 50 percent of available bandwidth.

C. Move your IIS server to the same computer that hosts your users' home directories.

D. Decrease the amount of information available to your users via the intranet.

## Question 17

After installing a WINS server at a remote office, the users start complaining that network access is periodically slow. After analyzing it, you feel that this periodic slowdown is the result of WINS replication. In order to reduce this problem you should

A. Remove the WINS server and return to using broadcasts for name resolution at the remote office.

B. Remove the push/pull relationship between the WINS server at the remote location and the WINS server at the home office.

C. Set the pull interval on the remote WINS server to occur every six hours. Do not configure the WINS server at the home office as a push partner.

D. Increase the NetBIOS cache timeout at the remote office.

## Question 18

Users at a remote office must access a directory containing forms located on a server at the home office frequently throughout the day. You set up directory replication between the server containing the forms and an NT workstation located at the remote office. In order to optimize traffic across the WAN link, you should

A. Configure directory replication to occur once a day using the Windows Explorer.

B. Lengthen both the `Interval` and `Pulse` parameters in the registry of the export server.

C. Lengthen the `Interval` parameter on the export server and the `Pulse` parameter on the import workstation.

D. Lengthen the `Interval` parameter on the import workstation and the `Pulse` parameter on the export server.

## Question 19

Users at a remote site complain about slow logons every morning. To correct this problem you install a backup domain controller at the remote office. Users then begin complaining of slow access across the WAN link to the home office throughout the day. To alleviate this problem you should

A. Increase both the `ReplicationGovernor` and the `PulseConcurrency` parameters.

B. Increase the `ReplicationGovernor` parameter and decrease the `PulseConcurrency` parameter.

C. Decrease both the `ReplicationGovernor` and the `PulseConcurrency` parameters.

D. Decrease the `ReplicationGovernor` parameter and increase the `PulseConcurrency` parameter.

## Question 20

During your periodic monitoring of network traffic you notice that one of your Windows 95 clients is forcing a browser election every time it boots. To correct this you should

A. Tell the user of that client not to reboot his machine.

B. Configure the Windows 95 client to never be a browser.

C. Configure the Windows 95 client to be a backup browser.

D. Do nothing. This is normal behavior for a Windows 95 computer.

## Question 21

When looking at your WINS database, you notice that each of your clients has registered both a workstation and server service. To decrease traffic related to your WINS server, you should

A. Do nothing. Both services are necessary for clients to be able to access network resources.

B. Stop the workstation service on those clients that do not share resources.

C. Stop the server service on those clients that do not share resources.

D. Stop both the server and workstation services on all NT workstation clients.

## 11.8.2. Exercises
### Exercise 11.1

Now that your head is full of figures, how can you use this new-found knowledge? Suppose you work for a company with an office in Baton Rouge and another in Lafayette.

As the MIS manager it is your responsibility to implement a way for the two offices to communicate and share data. You also must provide for centralized administration of users and resources. Your home office has 800 users and the remote office contains only six users. The two offices are connected by a 28.8Kbps dial-on-demand RAS connection.

What domain model would you use?

How would you provide services such as domain controllers, WINS, DHCP, and DNS servers?

### Exercise 11.2

As time goes by, your company grows, especially the branch office in Lafayette. You now must support 95 users at the branch office as well as 1,100 users at the home office in Baton Rouge. Your users in Lafayette are beginning to complain about slow logons on almost a daily basis.

Although you have recommended to management that the WAN link must be upgraded, the decision is still pending. What can you do to optimize the functioning of your network so that users can more efficiently do their work while waiting for the faster link to be approved and then installed?

11

# Day 12

# Managing a Heterogeneous Environment

*by Theresa Hadden, Marcus Barton, and Russell Mickler*

## 12.1. Overview

As of this writing, Novell NetWare is installed on a majority of PC-based networks in corporate America. With that in mind, Microsoft designed Windows NT knowing that it would probably have to survive in heterogeneous environments. Several capabilities were built into Windows NT with NetWare in mind:

- NWLink, Microsoft's IPX/SPX-compatible protocol, was designed to connect with NetWare servers.
- Windows NT possesses a gateway service to allow NetWare resources to be accessible from clients that are configured only to connect to Windows NT.

### 12.1.1. Objectives

The information in this chapter is provided mainly as a basis for understanding how to properly configure services and the use of the registry. This chapter addresses how you

- Configure Windows NT server for interoperability with NetWare servers by using the Gateway Service for NetWare
- Configure protocols and protocol bindings for NWLink
- Configure NT Server to migrate a NetWare server

### 12.1.2. Fast Facts

The following list of facts is a concise picture of the information presented in this chapter. It acts both as an overview for the chapter and as a study aid to help you do any last-minute cramming.

■ Using NWLink alone enables you to connect NetWare clients to Windows NT and vice versa for client/server applications only.

■ The Gateway Service for NetWare is used to allow Windows NT clients to access the file and print services of NetWare without installing any additional software on the client computers.

■ If NWLink is not installed when the Gateway Service for NetWare is installed, NWLink is installed automatically.

■ The Gateway Service for NetWare is not available on Windows NT Workstation.

■ The Gateway Service for NetWare translates Server Message Blocks (SMB) to NetWare Core Protocol (NCP).

■ When NWLink is configured for automatic frame-type detection, it defaults to 802.2 if the frame type is not detected.

■ The NetWare Migration Tool allows for the expedient transfer of user and group objects to an NT domain controller; NWCONV is not intended for use with member servers.

■ NWCONV enables you to transfer file and directory objects from NetWare volumes to NTFS partitions while retaining permission equivalence.

■ Neither passwords nor NetWare login scripts are migrated using NWCONV.

■ You must have supervisor rights on the NetWare server to execute NWCONV successfully.

■ Logs are maintained during the process to assist in troubleshooting migration problems.

# 12.2. Gateway Service for NetWare (GSNW)

Gateway Service for NetWare has two functions. It provides client services that allow an NT server to access a NetWare server. The Gateway Service for NetWare also allows a Windows NT server to act as a gateway to a NetWare server. Once installed, clients that are configured to connect to the Windows NT server can access file and print services of the NetWare server through the Windows NT server. There is no need for additional configuration of the clients.

When using Gateway Services, you can use whatever protocols you want on the client because the Windows NT server establishes the connection to the NetWare server. As long as the client can connect to the Windows NT server (using NetBEUI or TCP/IP, for example), it can use resources on the NetWare server.

If you have Remote Access Service (RAS) installed on your Windows NT network, GSNW gives you the capability to connect to the NetWare server while connecting to your network remotely. Without GSNW, you must install a similar remote service on the NetWare server, complicating administration and the access of resources.

There is another advantage to using the GSNW. If you have a small amount of NetWare servers, and users need only occasional access to them, you can use the GSNW to cut down on your administrative tasks. Create all the user accounts on your Windows NT server and not on the NetWare server. The authentication of the users accessing the NetWare server is accomplished through the GSNW. This prevents you from having to manage accounts on both servers. Without the GSNW, you must create accounts on both servers for users to have access to both servers.

Note

The Gateway Service NetWare is available only on Windows NT servers. It is not available on Windows NT Workstation. To connect to a NetWare server using Windows NT Workstation, Microsoft includes the Client Service for NetWare with Windows NT Workstation.

**12**

Windows NT clients access the Windows NT server. The GSNW shares out NetWare resources as though they are Windows NT server resources. This means that there is no need for additional setup on the client computers if they are already configured to access the Windows NT server. The only computers on which you must make changes are the NetWare server and the Windows NT server.

## 12.2.1. NetWare Core Protocol

For the Windows NT server and the NetWare server to be able to communicate, they must speak the same language or protocol. The main protocol that NetWare uses is IPX/SPX, so Microsoft created its IPX/SPX-compatible protocol, NWLink.

The second battle was how the two operating systems communicate with other computers on the network. Traditionally, Microsoft networks use Server Message

Blocks to communicate. NetWare networks use NetWare Core Protocols to communicate (see Figure 12.1). The GSNW translates Server Message Blocks (SMB) to NetWare Core Protocol (NCP).

**Figure 12.1.**

*The GSNW translates SMB to NCP.*

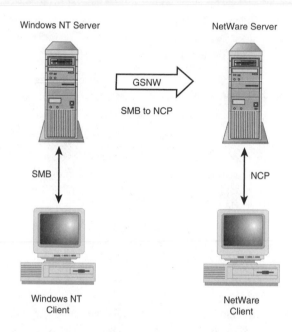

The commands in NetWare Core Protocol do not directly translate to SMB commands. The GSNW acts as a translator between the SMBs used by Microsoft networks and the NCPs used on NetWare networks so that clients using SMB (Windows NT clients) can communicate with NetWare servers that use NCP. For the exam, just remember that the GSNW translates SMB to NCP.

One use for GSNW is in situations in which you migrate a NetWare server to a Windows NT server but want a slower transition to the Windows NT server. It also works well for occasional access to NetWare servers or in situations in which people need the same type of access to the NetWare server (for printing, as an example).

If numerous people need access to the NetWare server, or if different levels of security are needed, install the proper client services on the client computer to access the NetWare server.

In previously published writings, you might have read that GSNW does not support NetWare's Directory Services. This is not true. Now the GSNW supports the NDS and enables users to navigate NDS trees, print from NDS, and authenticate with an NDS-aware server and also permits the use of NetWare 4.x login scripts.

## 12.2.2. Installing the Gateway Service for NetWare

Installing the Gateway Service for NetWare is a relatively easy task. The GSNW provides client services as well as the Gateway Service for NetWare. The client side is what makes the connectivity happen from the Windows NT server. The Gateway Service for NetWare is what allows other Windows NT clients to access the NetWare server.

The NetWare server must have a user that matches a user on the Windows NT server. This user is the account used to establish the connection for the gateway and must be a member of the NTGATEWAY group. To make administration of the NetWare easier, set up a separate account on the NetWare server that matches an administrator account on the Windows NT server.

If you specify an account that is a supervisor equivalent on the NetWare server as the account to use for the gateway, then anyone connecting could have administrative rights to the NetWare server.

**12**

Here is what you must have on the NetWare server for GSNW to work properly and smoothly:

- A gateway user account.
- A group for all gateway accounts. If you must set up more than one gateway for access to the NetWare server, you can use more than one user account. Give the user accounts the appropriate access by placing them all in this group.
- An administrative user account that you will use to access the NetWare server from the Windows NT server to administrate the gateway is not necessary but is helpful.

After you have those three items in place, you're ready to set up the GSNW on the Windows NT server. To install the GSNW, follow these steps:

1. Access the Control Panel and double-click the Network icon.

2. Under the Services tab, click Add.

3. You should be able to locate the Gateway (and Client) Services for NetWare (see Figure 12.2). When you do, select it and click OK.

4. Enter the path to the CD-ROM.

5. Restart the computer when prompted.

**Figure 12.2.**

*You add the GSNW through the Network applet of the Control Panel.*

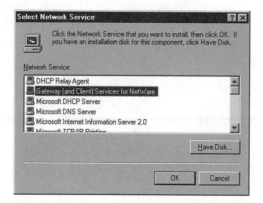

Note

If you do not already have the NWLink IPX/SPX protocol installed when you install the GSNW, it is installed automatically for you.

When the server restarts and you log on, you are prompted for the NetWare account information to establish a connection to the NetWare server, as shown in Figure 12.3. You should use the administrator account that you set up on the NetWare server. This does not establish the gateway; it only establishes local connectivity to the server.

If you are logging onto a 3.x server or a 4.x server running bindery emulation, you should use the preferred server option (see Figure 12.4). Enter the name of the NetWare server.

If you are logging onto a NetWare 4.x server that is not running bindery emulation, you must specify the tree and context information (see Figure 12.5). Writing the parameters such as cn= or o= in the tree and context blocks is not necessary.

**Figure 12.3.**

*Logging onto a
NetWare server from
Windows NT server.*

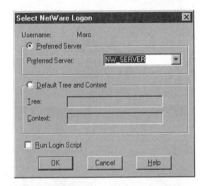

**Figure 12.4.**

*Logging onto a bindery-
based NetWare server
from Windows NT
server.*

**Figure 12.5.**

*Logging onto a
NetWare Directory
Service tree from
Windows NT server.*

**12**

Verify that the client service portion of the gateway is working before
proceeding to the next step of setting up the gateway.

*continues*

After you log on to the Windows NT server, you can browse the Network Neighborhood or the Explorer to verify that you can access the NetWare server. Just look under the Entire Network option and you should find NetWare Compatible Network. Double-clicking it should reveal your NetWare server or NDS tree.

You now have a new icon in the Control Panel titled GSNW. When you open the GSNW applet in the Control Panel, you see a dialog box similar to that in Figure 12.5. Here you find the same type of information that you specified at logon along with some printing options and an option to run the NetWare logon scripts.

In the GSNW dialog box, click the Gateware button to reach the Configure Gateway dialog box in Figure 12.6. Here is where you set up the gateway using the user account that you set up previously on the NetWare server.

**Figure 12.6.**

*Specifying the gateway user account.*

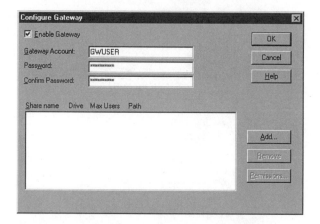

After you enter the username and password, click the Add button to create the gateway. A New Share dialog box appears (see Figure 12.7). This dialog box is where you specify the necessary information to create a gateway.

The following information defines what you should place in the New Share dialog box:

- Share Name: The name as it will appear to the client.
- Network Path: The UNC name to the resource on the NetWare server.
- Comment: A description that will appear when browsing for the resource.

- Use Drive: The drive letter to which the resource will be mapped on the Windows NT server.

- User Limit: Where you can specify a maximum amount of users who can connect to the resource simultaneously.

**Figure 12.7.**

*Specifying the server share name for a NetWare gateway.*

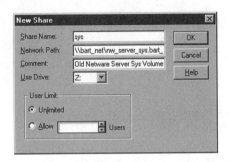

The network path is the location of the resource on the network. The UNC name that is most commonly used with Windows NT and bindery-based servers such as with NetWare 3.12 and earlier versions is

```
\\servername\volume\directory
```

However, when using NDS resources, separate each level of the tree with a period. The proper syntax is

```
\\ndstree\volumename.orgunit.org
```

**12**

After you enter all the appropriate information, click OK and the gateway is added. Notice that you can add more than one gateway by clicking the Gateway button again.

After the gateway is established, it appears in a Configure Gateway dialog box similar to Figure 12.8. You handle permissions by clicking the Permissions button. Configuring permissions on the gateway is identical to configuring permissions on a directory that is local to the server. The drive shows up as a network drive in the My Computer and Explorer interfaces. On the client machine, it appears as a share on the Windows NT computer that is configured with the GSNW.

The only available type of security for the gateway is share security. You do not have the capabilities of NTFS security.

**Figure 12.8.**

*Viewing the NetWare gateways.*

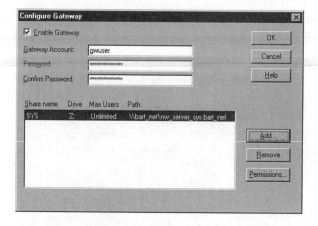

You can share NetWare print queues through the gateway by clicking the Add Printer icon in the Printers folder. Using the Add a Printer Wizard, you should select that you will connect to a network print server. After you have done so, you can browse for the printer or enter the UNC path (see Figure 12.9).

**Figure 12.9.**

*Selecting the NetWare print queue to connect to using the Add a Printer Wizard.*

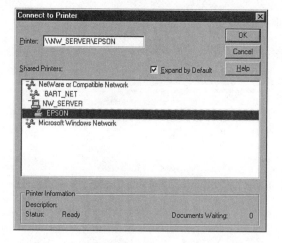

During normal connections to network print servers, Windows NT automatically downloads the driver from the remote server. However, because NetWare servers do not use Windows-based drivers, Windows NT prompts you to select which printer you want to install. This lets you load the driver using the Windows NT CD-ROM or using driver disks from the manufacturer of the printer.

After the printer is installed properly, you can use the printer locally on the Windows NT server. Click the printer icon with your secondary mouse button and select Properties. In the property sheet for the printer, select the Sharing tab. Now simply share it to the network. When you share it, clients can access it by connecting to the

Windows NT server. Any print jobs are rerouted to the NetWare print queue via the GSNW.

# 12.3. NWLink, the IPX/SPX Compatible

Connectivity to NetWare requires the use of NWLink (short for NetWare Link), Microsoft's protocol that is compatible with Novell's IPX/SPX (Internetwork Packet Exchange/Sequenced Packet Exchange) protocol.

NWLink is required in situations in which you must make connections to NetWare servers or where NetWare clients must access Microsoft resources. NWLink supports Novell NetBIOS, Windows Sockets, Remote Procedure Calls, and named pipes.

## 12.3.1. Integrating Application Servers

Because NWLink supports Windows Sockets (WinSock), you can use NWLink with applications that are specifically written for NetWare's IPX/SPX Sockets interface, allowing the Microsoft clients to access NetWare servers for client/server applications. Additionally, NWLink also allows NetWare clients to access client/server applications on Windows NT servers. Examples of client/server applications include Microsoft SQL Server and Microsoft SNA Server host connectivity.

Installing NWLink alone does not give you full connectivity to NetWare due to the fact that NWLink does not include a NetWare-compatible redirector. To use the file and print services of NetWare, you must install the Gateway Service for NetWare.

12

Note

The Client Service for NetWare and Gateway Service for NetWare included with Windows NT gives you connectivity to Novell NetWare servers. However, they do not give NetWare clients access to Windows NT servers.

Available as an add-on, the File and Print Services for NetWare (FPNW) utility gives NetWare clients access to shares and printers on a Windows NT server.

Directory Service Manager for NetWare (DSMN) allows integration of user and group accounts between NetWare and Windows NT servers. This utility lets you manage all user accounts on the network through the User Manager for Domains.

Because FPNW and DSMN are add-on utilities, knowing extended information about them on the exam is not necessary.

## 12.3.2. Installing NWLink

You can add NWLink as a protocol through the Network applet of the Control Panel. Figure 12.10 shows the Protocols tab of the Network applet. Clicking the Add button produces a list of available protocols to be installed (see Figure 12.11).

**Figure 12.10.**
*The Protocols tab of the Network properties dialog box is where you can add, remove, and update network protocols.*

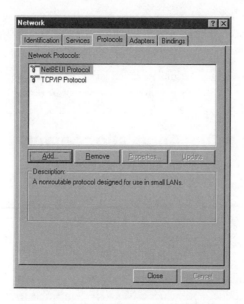

**Figure 12.11.**
*Adding NWLink from the list of network protocols.*

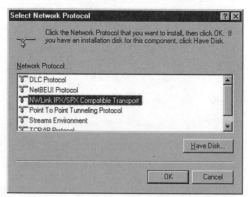

After you add NWLink, you can configure it by clicking the Properties button or by double-clicking NWLink in the list of protocols. When you open the NWLink Properties dialog box (see Figure 12.12), you notice two tabs, General and Routing.

**Figure 12.12.**
*Viewing the NWLink
properties dialog box.*

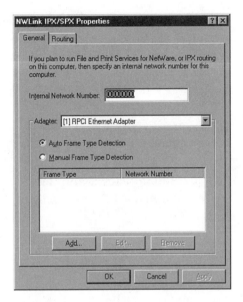

Under the General tab, you can configure different items including the network
number, which adapter will use NWLink, and the frame type. The network number is
an eight-digit hexadecimal identification number, which assigns a logical network for
NetWare servers. It allows identification of NetWare servers running on a multinet
host.

## 12.3.3. Frame Type

The frame type is probably the most significant setting for NWLink. If the frame type
is incorrect, NWLink fails to make a connection. The frame type is how the network
card sends information across the network using NWLink. NWLink is the language
that is spoken, but the frame type is the dialect. You can use NWLink on several
different type of topologies. Table 12.1 shows the different frame types you can have on
the different topologies.

**Table 12.1. NWLink topologies and frame types.**

| Topology | Frame Type |
| --- | --- |
| Ethernet | 802.2, 802.3, Ethernet II, and SNAP |
| Token Ring | 802.5 and SNAP |
| FDDI (Fiber) | 802.2 and SNAP |

You can specify any of these frame types that might be in use on your network. NetWare uses 802.2 or 802.3. The type that you use depends on which version of NetWare you must access. If you are using NetWare version 3.11 or earlier, the standard frame type is 802.3. If you are using NetWare version 3.12 or later, then select 802.2.

> Don't let the number confuse you. It is not like software versions where the bigger the number, the newer the version. 802.2 and 802.3 are just two different standards. 802.3 uses a Carrier-Sense Multiple Access with Collision Detection (CSMA/CD) format on the network. 802.2 uses a Logical Link Control (LLC) format.

You can configure Windows NT to automatically detect the frame type on the network and to use the type that it detects when Windows NT starts. If it does not get a response, or if it gets multiple responses, then it defaults to 802.2.

If NWLink does not receive a response on 802.2 but does get a response on other frame types, it picks a frame type from one of the types from which it received responses. NWLink picks a frame type in the following order:

- Ethernet 802.2
- Ethernet 802.3
- Ethernet II
- SNAP

For example, if NWLink did not receive a response for Ethernet 802.2 and did receive a response for Ethernet 802.3 and SNAP, it uses a frame type of Ethernet 802.3. After NWLink sets a frame type, it becomes the default frame type so that the next time the system boots, the process of picking the frame type happens faster.

## 12.3.4. Server Advertising Protocol

Servers on an IPX network need some way of letting the other computers on the network know of the resources that they have available. To do this, the server issues a broadcast every 60 seconds. This broadcasting is called Service Advertising Protocol (SAP). Clients on the network then use SAP to locate resources on the network. SAP is installed automatically with Windows NT server and needs no configuration.

# 12.4. Using the Windows NT NetWare Migration Tool (NWCONV.EXE)

You can find NWCONV.EXE in the %sysroot%\system32 subdirectory or as a program shortcut located on the Administration menu after GSNW is installed. As a utility, the primary function of the migration tool is to extract user and group account information from NDS (or a NetWare 3.1x server's bindery) for import into a domain controller's SAM. If re-creating all your NetWare accounts under User Manager for Domains seems a chore to you, the NWCONV program is your ticket to getting NT server up and running quickly.

**Note**

You will not be tested on the use of any NetWare console or command-line utility. The server exam expects you only to know the proper use of the NetWare Migration Tool. Keep that in mind when preparing for your exam.

Second, the NWCONV utility is used to migrate NetWare files and directories to NT while maintaining equivalent rights and permissions. NWCONV allows for something entirely different than moving or copying files where they normally acquire the permissions of their parent containers. Instead, it automatically converts them to equivalent NT permissions and drops non-applicable permissions.

The following conditions must be met before the administrator can use the NetWare Migration Tool:

1. The target NT server must be a domain controller if you are migrating users.
2. If you will be using NWCONV to migrate files to NT and want to retain permissions, the destination partition on the NT server must be formatted using NTFS.
3. NWLink must be appropriately configured and the Gateway Service for NetWare (GSNW) must be installed on the NT server as an active service.
4. The NT administrator must know the name and password to the NetWare supervisor account (or supervisor equivalent account) to perform the migration.

**12**

**Preparing the NetWare Server**

When preparing the NetWare server for migration, remember the old adage "Garbage in, garbage out." Make certain the source data reflects the way you want it in the NT environment. Although not entirely necessary, exercising a little cautious optimism goes a long way in ensuring data integrity.

1. **Perform routine file system maintenance.** Weed unnecessary files on any volume that is to be migrated. Purge the volume and back it up.

2. **Perform user/group object maintenance.** Crank up NWADMIN or SYSCON and remove inactive user accounts and groups. Be wary of duplicate user or group objects on 3.1x servers if you plan to migrate multiple 3.1x servers; such duplication will cause errors in the NT migration process. Perform any group assignments or security modifications you've been putting off before running a live migration.

3. **Repair the NDS/bindery.** In a NetWare 4.1x environment, run DSREPAIR to fix any invisible problems in the NDS and synchronize all servers in all replicas (if applicable). On your NetWare 3.1x server, run BINDFIX to verify the integrity of the NetWare bindery.

4. **Perform an NLM audit.** NetWare Loadable Modules are server-side programs launched from the NetWare system console and are not migrated to Windows NT, but they may be critical to some level of user functionality. Review the NLMs loaded on your server and secure the NT equivalents if necessary.

5. **Perform a client-side audit of file and print services.** Remember that UNC locations on your clients change after the migration. NPRINTERS and PSERVERS are inactive after the Novell box is shut down, and device mappings not handled through logon scripts may be adversely affected after the migration. Perform the audit before your migration to guarantee that user functions aren't disabled after moving to Windows NT.

# 12.5. Starting the NetWare Migration Tool

From the Windows NT desktop, access the NWCONV.EXE shortcut from the Administrative Tools folder found under the program group as shown in Figure 12.13.

**Figure 12.13.**

*Selecting the Migration Tool for NetWare.*

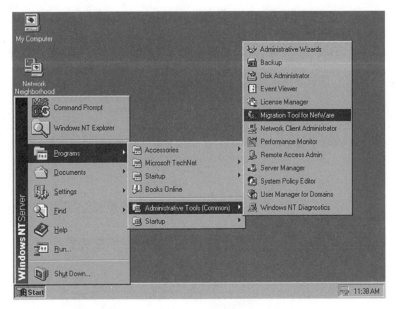

When the migration tool is launched, you see the Select Servers For Migration dialog box, where you identify the source NetWare server and target NT server involved in the migration (see Figure 12.14).

**Figure 12.14.**

*Designate the NetWare Server (source) and Windows NT Server (target).*

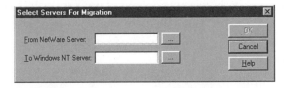

**12**

Either manually enter the UNC to the desired NetWare server or select the ellipses button to browse to the server as shown in Figure 12.15.

Using the interface, highlight the desired NetWare server and click the OK button. You return to the Select Servers For Migration dialog box.

Next, identify the target NT server. After selecting the target NT server, you return to the Select Servers For Migration dialog box. Both the NetWare server and NT server should be identified. Click OK to continue.

At this time, NWCONV verifies your current access restrictions to the NetWare server. If your current account is not a supervisor equivalent on the specified NetWare server, you see the Enter Network Credentials dialog box (see Figure 12.16). You must provide a NetWare supervisor account and password or you return to the Select Servers For Migration dialog box. Click OK to continue.

**Figure 12.15.**

*Select your server from the browse list.*

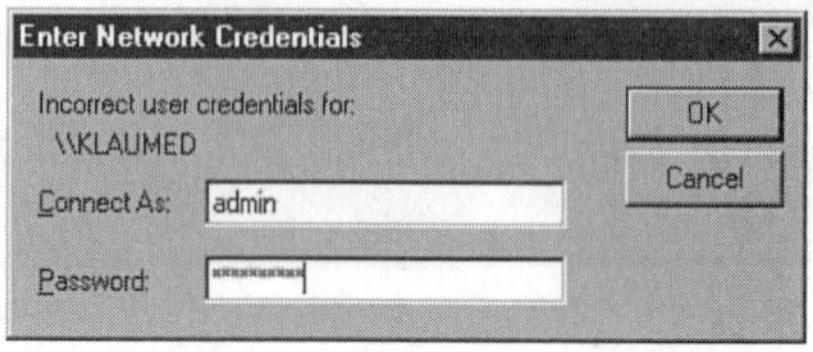

**Figure 12.16.**

*Enter NetWare credentials for access to the NetWare server.*

After the credentials verification, you see the main Migration Tool for NetWare dialog box (see Figure 12.17). The servers you specified are listed in the left columns as the first set involved in the migration process. If you want, you can add more servers using the selection process just described or you can delete additional servers before continuing.

**Figure 12.17.**

*Both the source (NetWare) and target (Windows NT) servers have been selected.*

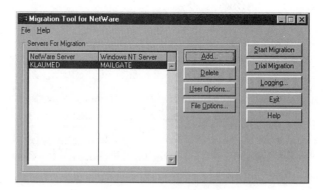

Adding additional servers is practical only in a NetWare 3.1*x* environment where multiple servers contain different bindery objects. In a NetWare 4.1*x* environment, you need only specify an NDS server to capture all the user objects in your environment.

On the Migration Tool for Netware dialog box, you see two option buttons for customizing the migration process for files and users. When you select the User Options button, the User and Group Options dialog box displays.

# 12.6. Selecting User and Group Migration Options

The User and Group options enable you to control how user and group objects are imported into the domain controller. You can specify how the migration tool handles password assignments, duplications in user or group names, whether NetWare account restrictions should be migrated, and whether NetWare supervisors should be added to the Administrator group on the NT server. You choose options by clicking radio buttons, completing entry fields, or toggling checkmarks under four tabs in the User and Group Options dialog box.

## 12.6.1. User and Group Migration Options: Passwords

You cannot migrate NetWare passwords to Windows NT using NWCONV. The Passwords tab of the User and Group Options dialog box presents three options (see Figure 12.18):

- No Password: No password assignment.
- Password is Username: The account username is appended as a password.
- Password is [password]: The administrator can specify one password to be assigned to all migrated user accounts.

The checkbox at the bottom of the dialog box enables you to flag password assignments as temporary on the NT server, forcing the user to change the password at the next logon.

**12**

**Figure 12.18.**

*Selecting User and Group options for passwords.*

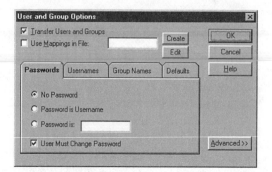

## 12.6.2. User and Group Migration Options: Usernames

Options specified under the Usernames tab in the User and Group Options dialog box instruct NWCONV on how to handle duplications in migrated usernames (see Figure 12.19). The four options are

- Log Error: When you select this option, username duplication conflicts are recorded in an error log maintained by NWCONV.

- Ignore: NWCONV does not migrate duplicated user accounts to NT or log the error to the log file if a duplicate is encountered on the NetWare server.

- Overwrite with New Info: Duplicate users on the NT domain controller are overwritten with NetWare user information.

- Add Prefix: Here you specify a prefix to be appended to the username (such as nw) to easily identify it as a duplicate.

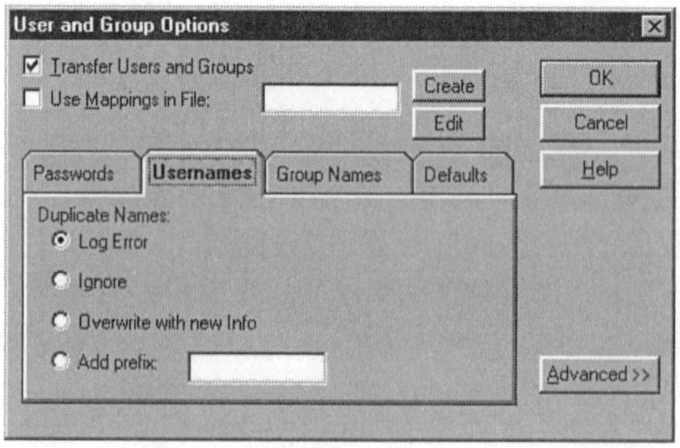

**Figure 12.19.**

*Selecting User and Group options for usernames.*

### 12.6.3. User and Group Migration Options: Group Names

Options specified under the Group Names tab instruct NWCONV on how to handle duplications in group names (see Figure 12.20). The three options have the same functions that are applied to usernames except that groups on the NT server cannot be overwritten by migrated NetWare groups.

**Figure 12.20.**

*Selecting the manner in which to handle duplicate group names.*

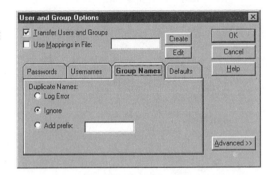

### 12.6.4. User and Group Migration Options: Defaults

Two options concerning supervisor rights are handled under the Defaults tab (see Figure 12.21):

- Use Supervisor Defaults: Account restrictions are migrated to the NT server if this option is checked. Otherwise, users default to Windows NT account policy settings.

- Add Supervisors to the Administrators Group: Selecting this option automatically assigns imported supervisors to the Administrators group on the Windows NT domain controller.

**12**

**Figure 12.21.**

*Indicating what to do with the NetWare account restrictions and supervisor accounts.*

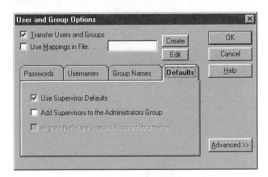

## 12.6.5. Selecting User and Group Options: Mapping File

An alternative approach to migrating user and group objects is available to you through a mapping file. You use a mapping file to assert extra control over destination user and group names and passwords. You may either create a mapping file or edit an existing one by selecting the appropriate button on the User and Group Options dialog box. Figure 12.22 shows the Create Mapping File dialog box.

**Figure 12.22.**

*Creating a mappings file.*

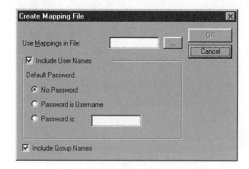

NWCONV creates the mapping file for you when you choose the Create button from the User and Group Options dialog box. The utility creates the mapping file based on your responses to similar options for passwords and groups.

The mapping file, which is simply a comma-delineated text file, contains two headers denoted by brackets ([Users] and [Groups]), where NetWare usernames and group names are specified. The NT username is listed in the field beside the NetWare username, and then the destination password is listed (see Figure 12.23). You can save and edit the file at any time.

**Figure 12.23.**

*An example of a mapping file showing usernames.*

```
 nwmap.map - Notepad                        _ □ ×
File  Edit  Search  Help
;+---------------------------------------
;| NWConv Mapping For: KLAUMED
;| Version: 1.1
;|
;| Format Is:
;|     OldName, NewName, Password
;|
;+---------------------------------------
[USERS]
ABAUMAN, ABAUMAN,
ASCHAFER, ASCHAFER,
ATIEDEMA, ATIEDEMA,
AWRIGHT, AWRIGHT,
BMCINTYR, BMCINTYR,
BOLSON, BOLSON,
BVANGORD, BVANGORD,
DBERGQUI, DBERGQUI,
DHICKMAN, DHICKMAN,
```

The usefulness of the mapping file is evident when NetWare usernames or groups already exist in the target NT domain. You could manually exclude those users or groups from the migration by commenting out their entries in the mapping file or rename accounts individually to meet your Windows NT naming convention. You can also use the mapping file to define individual passwords.

After you select a mapping file in the User and Group Options dialog box, the options previously discussed under the Passwords, Usernames, and Group Names tabs are grayed out (see Figure 12.24). The mapping file is then used exclusively for user and group migration.

**Figure 12.24.**
*Password options are grayed out after selecting a mapping file.*

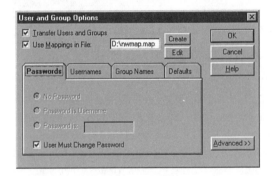

## 12.7. Selecting File Options

The File Options dialog box allows the administrator to identify directories and files on NetWare volumes for migration to an NTFS partition (see Figure 12.25). The columns on the left list all mounted volumes on the specified NetWare server, including CD-ROM volumes.

**12**

**Figure 12.25.**
*NetWare volumes and their destinations have been selected.*

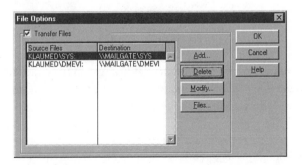

From the File Options dialog box, you have the option to delete volumes from migration, modify their destination path and share name on the NT server, and identify only specific files and directories for migration. The Add button becomes active only after you delete a volume from the list.

### 12.7.1. File Migration Options: Modifying Destination Directory Paths and Share Names

You might want to modify the destination paths for your files on the NT server. By default, NetWare volume names are retained as both directory and share names on the NTFS partition (see Figure 12.26).

**Figure 12.26.**

*Shares may be created as part of the migration process.*

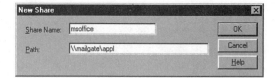

To change the destination path or share name, click the New Share button on the Add Volume to Copy dialog box. A second dialog box is displayed as shown in Figure 12.26. Here, you can provide an alternative share name and the desired path on an NTFS partition. The example I provided points to my NTFS-formatted partition on the MAILGATE server. Click OK to continue. When you return to the File Options dialog box, changes are reflected in the columns on the left as seen in Figure 12.25.

### 12.7.2. File Migration Options: Selecting Files and Directories for Migration

You might want to deselect some files and directories that are migrated to NT. Migrating nearly all of the SYS: volume, for example, is impractical; you can usually ignore the contents of ETC, PUBLIC, SYSTEM, and LOGIN. However, you might want to migrate user home directories. NWCONV allows for migration down to the individual file level.

In the example in Figure 12.27, the NetWare volume is identified as DMEVI: and the directories that aren't to be transferred (because all the directories and files are selected by default) are deselected. Simply select the file or directory objects you want to transfer and click OK to continue.

Hidden and system files are excluded from migration by default. Select the Transfer menu from the Files to Transfer dialog box to include hidden and system files.

**Figure 12.27.**
*You can designate individual files and directories to migrate.*

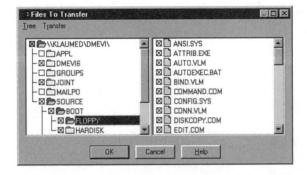

# 12.8. Translation Tables for NetWare and NT Permissions and Attributes

Tables 12.2, 12.3, and 12.4 elaborate on directory and file permission translation and file attribute equivalence between NT and NetWare. Translation occurs at the time of actual migration. With file attributes where no direct translation to NTFS attributes exists, the attributes are ignored.

**Table 12.2. Directory rights equivalence.**

| NetWare Rights | Windows NT 4.0 | (NTFS Permissions) |
| --- | --- | --- |
| Supervisor (S) | Full Control | (All) (All) |
| Read (R) | Read | (RX) (RX) |
| Create | Add | (WX) (Not Specified) |
| Erase (E) | Change | (RWXD) (RWXD) |
| Access Control (A) | Change | (P) (P) |
| Modify (M) | Change | (RWXD) (RWXD) |
| File Scan (F) | List | (RX) (Not Specified) |
| Write (W) | Change | (RWXD) (RWXD) |

**Table 12.3. File rights equivalence.**

| NetWare Rights | Windows NT 4.0 | (NTFS Permissions) |
| --- | --- | --- |
| Supervisor (S) | Full Control | (All) |
| Read (R) | Read | (RX) |
| Erase (E) | Change | (RWXD) |

*continues*

12

**Table 12.3. continued**

| NetWare Rights | Windows NT 4.0 | (NTFS Permissions) |
|---|---|---|
| Access Control (A) | Change | (P) |
| Modify (M) | Change | (RWXD) |
| Write (W) | Change | (RWXD) |

**Table 12.4. File attributes equivalence.**

| NetWare Attribute | Windows NT 4.0 | (NTFS Attributes) |
|---|---|---|
| Delete Inhibit | (None) | |
| Read Only (RO) | Read Only | (R) |
| Rename Inhibit (RI) | (None) | |
| Archive (A) | Archive | (A) |
| Hidden (H) | Hidden | (H) |
| System (S) | System | (S) |
| Copy Inhibit (CI) | (None) | |
| Read/Write (RW) | (None) | |
| Execute Only (EO) | (None) | |
| Shareable (SH) | (None) | |
| Transactional (T) | (None) | |
| Indexed (I) | (None) | |
| Purge (P) | (None) | |
| Read Audit (RA) | (None) | |
| Write Audit (WA) | (None) | |

# 12.9. Selecting Logging Options

Troubleshooting NWCONV is significantly easier with its built-in error-logging functions. As shown in Figure 12.28, you can set three levels of logging when you click the Logging options button on the main Migration Tool for NetWare dialog box:

- Popup on Errors: On each error during the migration process, a dialog box explains every error encountered.

- Verbose User/Group Logging: Summary-level information is captured for each user migrated. Information such as grace logons, password lengths, time restrictions, account expiration, and so on appears in the LOGFILE.LOG if you check this option.

- ■ Verbose File Logging: A detail for every directory and file migrated to the NTFS partition is generated.

**Figure 12.28.**

*Setting for verbose logging of users and groups.*

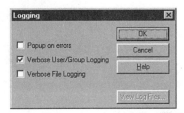

Three text-based log files are maintained automatically by NWCONV for the purposes of monitoring conversions. All three are available from the LOGVIEW applet after you perform a trial or actual migration:

- ■ ERROR.LOG: As the name implies, errors generated during the migration are recorded for administrative review. This option is excellent for zooming in on problems immediately after the process.

- ■ SUMMARY.LOG: A summary of the migration is recorded. Examples are the total number of groups migrated, total kilobytes of files transferred, and so on.

- ■ LOGFILE.LOG: Depending on the number of users and groups to be migrated and your logging level, this file can be very large or very small. It describes in painstaking detail every NetWare attribute with a Windows NT equivalent that was recognized by NWCONV. Because the LOGFILE.LOG provides more information than is functionally useful, it serves as support detail for the whole process.

**12**

# 12.10. Saving Migration Options

After specifying user and file options, you return to the Migration Tool for NetWare dialog box. Continue to add as many source and destination servers as you want, tailoring User, Group, and File Options where necessary. As shown in Figure 12.29, you can choose to save your configuration settings. Before continuing with a trial migration, it is a good idea to save your work.

**Figure 12.29.**

*You can save your configuration for later use.*

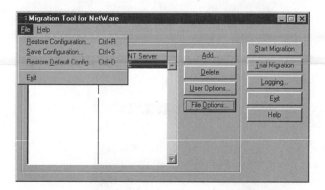

Migrating one NetWare 3.1*x* server at a time is highly recommended. This lets you spot errors in the migration process. Migrating one server at a time also eliminates the possibility of duplication snags. Take the time to run a trial migration after adding each server.

# 12.11. Starting the Trial Migration

After configuring User, Group, File, and Logging options, you are prepared to begin the migration. One of the more useful features of NWCONV is the capability to perform a harmless trial migration to isolate potential problems beforehand. It is recommended that you execute NWCONV using the trial migration feature several times until you address each error listed in the error log.

In the course of a trial migration, NWCONV reacts exactly as if it were a normal migration. The Converting dialog box shown in Figure 12.30 displays during the process, giving you real-time summaries of errors encountered, number of objects transferred, and total kilobytes of files copied.

**Figure 12.30.**

*A migration in progress.*

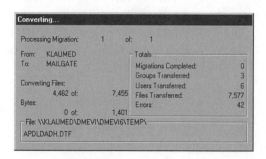

The Transfer Completed dialog box provides brief summary information about the migration (see Figure 12.31). Click the View Log Files button to view the *.LOG files inside the LOGVIEW applet (see Figure 12.32).

**Figure 12.31.**
*The summary informa-
tion of a completed
trial migration.*

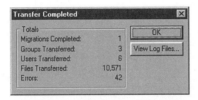

**Figure 12.32.**
*Three log files are
created as the result of
the trial migration.*

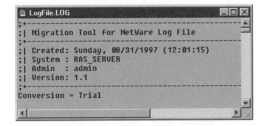

# 12.12. Starting the Live Migration

You should perform trial migrations several times and review the log files before performing the actual migration. As the administrator, you should feel comfortable with the results of your trials before you proceed with the actual migration. After all, you are responsible for solving any serious migration problems.

Select the Start Migration button on the main Migration Tool for NetWare dialog box to begin the migration. The duration of the migration depends upon the number of servers selected, the number of users to be converted, and the total kilobytes of files to be transferred.

12

There are two particularly interesting consequences to using NWCONV that you should be aware of:

■ All user and group object names are transferred in all uppercase letters; as you know, objects created in User Manager for Domains are usually generated in lowercase. Beyond being aesthetically unpleasing, all-uppercase usernames might have some significance in diverse computing environments.

*continues*

■ Deleting an imported username renders its SID obsolete in newly constructed Access Control Lists (ACLs) created when NetWare files were migrated, having some consequence for user and group permissions after migration.

Again, thoroughness counts big in performing a successful migration from NetWare.

# 12.13. Lab

This lab will aid you in your learning by testing you on the information presented in this chapter, as well as by giving you exercises to hone your skills. You will find answers to the review questions in Appendix B, "Answers to Review Questions."

## 12.13.1.  Review Questions

### Question 1

What must you install on a Windows NT server to let a user log on locally and access client/server applications installed on a Novell NetWare server? Choose all that apply. (See section 12.3.1.)

A.  File and Print Services for NetWare (FPNW)

B.  Gateway Services for NetWare (GSNW)

C.  Directory Service Manager for NetWare (DSMN)

D.  NWLink IPX/SPX protocol

### Question 2

What must you install on a Windows NT server to let a user log on locally and access file and print services on a Novell NetWare server? (See section 12.2.2.)

A.  File and Print Services for NetWare (FPNW)

B.  Gateway Services for NetWare (GSNW)

C.  Directory Service Manager for NetWare (DSMN)

D.  NWLink IPX/SPX protocol

### Question 3

What frame type does NWLink default to if no frame type is detected on an Ethernet network?

A.  802.2

B.  802.3

C.  Ethernet II

D.  SNAP

12

## Question 4

When installing a Windows NT computer on an Ethernet network with existing NetWare 4.1 servers, what frame type should be used?

A. 802.2

B. 802.3

C. Ethernet II

D. SNAP

## Question 5

What is the simplest explanation of what the Gateway Services for NetWare does at the network level?

A. It converts SAP to RIP.

B. It converts SMB to NCP.

C. It converts NBF to IPX.

D. It converts CNN to MTV.

## Question 6

The user that is used for the gateway of GSNW must be a member of what group on the NetWare server?

A. NTGWAY

B. GSNW group

C. NTGATEWAY

D. ADMIN

## Question 7

Microsoft SQL Server is installed on a Windows NT server. What must be installed on the Windows NT server to let NetWare clients access the SQL server? Choose all that apply.

A. File and Print Services for NetWare (FPNW)

B. Gateway Services for NetWare (GSNW)

C. Directory Service Manager for NetWare (DSMN)

D. NWLink IPX/SPX protocol

## Question 8

You successfully complete the NWCONV process. After tailoring your clients to log on to your local NT domain instead of NetWare, users in Engineering report that they no longer can access a network drive containing critical CAD files. You check to make sure the files migrated from the NetWare server; they did. What is the most likely cause of the problem?

A. NWCONV migrated directory permissions incorrectly, which prevents your users from accessing the network drive.

B. NWCONV changed the CAD file attributes to make them hidden system files.

C. NWCONV failed to migrate the logon script from the NetWare server. You should re-run NWCONV to fix the problem.

D. NWCONV does not migrate logon scripts. You must re-create them manually under Windows NT.

E. None of the above.

## Question 9

NWCONV reports four errors during a trial migration. Where can you quickly find out what happened?

A. `NWCONV.ERR`

B. `SUMMARY.LOG`

C. `NWCONV.LOG`

D. `ERROR.LOG`

E. `LOGFILE.LOG`

**12**

## Question 10

You are the administrator of four NetWare 3.1$x$ servers and three NetWare 4.1$x$ servers. You are implementing an NT server as an IPX RAS. You want any and all of your users to access the RAS remotely and are therefore considering using NWCONV to migrate your 700+ user base. Which server(s) will you identify for migration?

A. One NetWare 4.1$x$ server and one NetWare 3.1$x$ server.

B. Each NetWare 4.1$x$ server and each NetWare 3.1$x$ server.

C. One NetWare 4.1$x$ server and each NetWare 3.1$x$ server.

D. None. NetWare 4.1$x$ servers cannot be migrated simultaneously with NetWare 3.1$x$ servers.

## Question 11

When using NWCONV, which of the following conditions does not need to be true?

A.  You must be directly logged onto the NetWare server to run NWCONV.

B.  GSNW and NWLINK must be appropriately installed and configured.

C.  Files migrated to NT must be migrated to an NTFS partition.

D.  NWCONV must target a domain controller.

E.  You must be logged onto the NT server as an administrator.

## Question 12

You can modify destination share names and file paths on the NTFS volume by

A.  Building a mapping file.

B.  Modifying the file options.

C.  Manually renaming shares and directories after the migration is completed.

D.  Modifying the file options—but only the directory path can be changed.

E.  Share names and destination paths are inherited names from the NetWare volume and cannot be changed during the migration process.

## Question 13

True or False: You can successfully use NWCONV without supervisor rights to the source NetWare server.

## Question 14

True or False: If the Use Supervisor Defaults option is checked under the Defaults tab of the User and Group Options dialog box, NetWare time restrictions for all migrated accounts will supersede Windows NT account policy time restrictions.

# 12.13.2. Exercises

## Case Study: Urban Designs, Inc.

**Company:**

Urban Designs, Inc., a corporate interior decorating and art supply company with 89 employees in three offices: Baltimore, Dallas, and Seattle.

**Existing Network Operating System:**

Novell NetWare 4.10 installed at all three sites.

**Solution:**

- One mid-range server is installed per site; each site is connected by a T1 line.
- 1 AS/400 for back-office computing
    - 10BaseT Ethernet topology running IPX/SPX
    - 35 PC (486) clients, 20 Mac O/S, and 5 OS/2
    - Eight telecommuting clients via analog dial-up adapters
    - Five network (SAP) devices (laser printers)
    - Seven NetWare NPRINTERS

**Details:**

NDS replication between all three servers is active. Utilization averages 40 to 50 percent per server. Your third-party remote connectivity solution is reported too slow by users. Novell GroupWise is used for communications and everyone is very satisfied with the product. All buildings are wired CAT-5. The company has no commitment to the OS/2 platform. The company is projecting a 10 to 15 percent increase in PC-using staff next year. Its main competitor is on the Internet and experimenting with streaming video, VRML, and other bleeding-edge technologies with its customers.

**Situation:**

A network capital improvement project was given the green light by senior management. You are in charge of meeting the following expectations:

- Reduce network traffic and maximize available bandwidth.
- Upgrade clients to realistically support today's high-intensity design software packages and full multimedia.
- Prepare the network and clients for "Internet to the desktop."

Overall, what are your recommendations?

If your recommendation includes Windows NT, how do you handle NetWare integration? What audits, analysis, or studies do you perform?

Would you completely migrate to Windows NT and turn off the Novell servers? Why or why not? What would you have to address if you did?

What special steps are necessary to ensure migrated users could have remote access to the NT network after the migration?

**12**

# Day 13

# RAS Dial-In Solutions

## 13.1. Overview

Microsoft Remote Access Server, or RAS, provides a seamless integration of a remote user's system with the Windows NT network. After dialing up and connecting to the RAS Server, the remote user can access the company network exactly as if connected directly to the network cabling.

This chapter describes the steps for installing and configuring the RAS Server for various situations and details issues involving security and troubleshooting of the RAS Server. It also concentrates on helping you prepare for that part of the Windows NT Server 4.0 exam that pertains to the issue of dial-up networking.

Because the scope of the Windows NT Server 4.0 exam concerns only a single-domain LAN environment, RAS does not figure heavily into it. The primary uses of RAS provide for supporting a WAN environment, and it is of more importance in the Supporting Windows NT Server 4.0 in the Enterprise exam.

### 13.1.1. Objectives

Microsoft publishes preparation guides to use while studying for certification exams. The follow list points out the recommended guidelines from Microsoft concerning the RAS Server. You should be able to

- Configure RAS communications.
- Configure RAS protocols.
- Configure RAS security.

## 13.1.2. Fast Facts

The following list of facts is a concise picture of the information this chapter presents. It acts both as an overview for the chapter and as a study aid to help you do any last-minute cramming.

- RAS is a networking service that you can install during setup or through the Network Control Panel.

- Remote access protocols govern how information is transmitted over a WAN. RAS supports four types of remote access protocols: SLIP, PPP, RAS Protocol, and NetBIOS Gateway.

- Networking protocols govern how information is transmitted over a LAN. RAS supports three networking protocols: TCP/IP, NetBEUI, and IPX.

- TCP/IP is the networking protocol of choice in today's networks. RAS supports the use of a DHCP server for allocating IP addresses. RAS also enables you to specify a pool of IP addresses that you can assign to remote users.

- PPTP, or Point-to-Point Tunneling Protocol, is a relatively new protocol that can establish a connection using any supported protocol over a connection using TCP/IP. This is particularly useful for establishing secure links to a network LAN over the Internet.

- RAS supports multiple types of security. Windows NT authentication requires remote users to log on to the Windows NT network with a valid user ID and password. Call-back security enables RAS to hang up on a remote user and call her back. You also can use RAS to let remote users access only the RAS Server or the entire network.

- Remote Access Administrator is the program you will use to administer most features of RAS.

- You can grant users dial-in access on a user-by-user basis. You also can enable auditing for these users.

- You have two primary means of monitoring RAS performance. The Dial-Up-Networking Monitor enables you to view the current state of the RAS Server. The Performance Monitor enables you to collect and view information over time.

■ You can use RAS to route networks in several different ways. It enables dial-in users to access your LAN. It also enables users to access your company's Internet connection. You even can use RAS to connect two LANs to one another.

■ When troubleshooting RAS, problems tend to fall into two categories: A user either cannot connect to your RAS Server or, once connected, cannot access the resources she needs.

# 13.2. Installing the RAS Service

The Remote Access Server allows for 256 simultaneous dial-in connections by remote users, utilizing a bank of modems known as a *modem pool*. The RAS Service also can dial out to make a connection to another RAS Server or supported server type, but RAS only allows for one dial-out connection at a time.

> One important distinction for you to make is that RAS on Windows NT Server allows for 256 simultaneous dial-in connections, but Windows NT Workstation allows for only one dial-in connection at a time. This information may appear on both the Windows NT Server and Workstation exams.

RAS supports remote connections from various types of clients. Systems using Windows NT (Server or Workstation), Windows 95, and Windows for Workgroups 3.11 have a dial-up networking component that is included with the operating system that can connect to a RAS Server. RAS Server also supports dial-in PPP, or point-to-point, connections. This means that a client with a terminal application and the PPP protocol also can connect to a RAS Server.

The RAS Service installs as a networking service. You can install it either during the initial setup of Windows NT or through the Networking Control Panel after you already have set up Windows NT. This section details the latter option, but both methods are nearly identical.

## 13.2.1. Modem Setup

In order to use RAS, you must have at least one modem (or other telephony device) set up that can receive calls. If you do not have a modem set up when you attempt to install the RAS Service, Windows NT prompts you to configure one at that point.

13

When you choose, or are prompted, to install a new modem, the Windows NT Install New Modem wizard determines whether you want NT to attempt to detect your modem for you or if you would rather specify the manufacturer and model yourself. Either way, you must already have physically installed an NT-compatible device in your system.

After the drivers for your modem are installed, NT will ask you for your location information, including your country, area code, the number you must dial for an outside line, and whether you use tone or pulse dialing.

Now you are finished setting up your modem and may proceed with setting up the RAS service.

## 13.2.2. RAS Service Setup

Microsoft's Remote Access Server is a network service under Windows NT. As with any network service, you install the RAS service through the Services tab on the Network Control Panel shown in Figure 13.1.

**Figure 13.1.**

*Add the RAS Service via the Network Control Panel.*

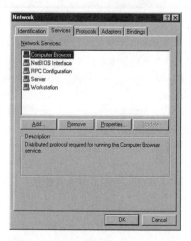

Simply select Add and choose the Remote Access Service from the list of available services that appears. After you have added the Remote Access Service, you are required to select at least one RAS-capable device from the modems you have configured on your system. Figure 13.2 shows this process.

When this is complete, you will be presented with the Remote Access Setup dialog box shown in Figure 13.3.

**Figure 13.2.**
*Add a RAS-capable device.*

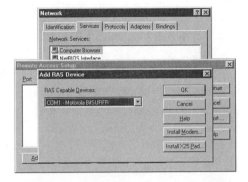

**Figure 13.3.**
*Remote Access Setup dialog box.*

From this window, select Configure to determine whether each device can receive calls, dial out only, or both (see Figure 13.4).

**Figure 13.4.**
*Configure Port Usage during the remote access setup.*

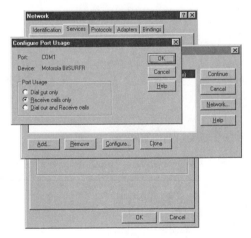

**13**

After you add the service, close the Network Control Panel and restart your machine when prompted. The RAS Service will start automatically when Windows NT starts.

Knowing that RAS is a network service and that it is installed through the Network Control Panel is about the level of detail that you will be expected to know for the NT Server exam. Knowing the details of each protocol by memory is not necessary. If you understand the concepts behind the details, are aware that the details exist, and know how to use them, you will do fine.

# 13.3. Selecting Protocols for Use with RAS

A *protocol* is simply a standard, accepted way of performing a task. In networking, protocols generally govern how information is transmitted from one computer to another. There are two general types of protocols with which you must be familiar to implement the RAS service: remote access (or line) protocols and LAN (or networking) protocols.

## 13.3.1. Choosing Remote Access Protocols

Remote access protocols, or line protocols, govern how information is broken up and transmitted over Wide Area Network (WAN) connections. The remote access protocols RAS supports include

- PPP (point-to-point protocol)
- SLIP (serial-line interface protocol)
- RAS protocol
- NetBIOS gateway

### PPP (Point-to-Point Protocol)

*PPP* is an industry-standard set of protocols governing data transmission over WANs using various types of LAN protocols or architectures. PPP is a robust, flexible protocol and has become the standard for most remote access situations. Most dial-in servers, including RAS, have some implementation of PPP, and it generally is considered to be the best choice for remote access situations.

### SLIP (Serial-Line Interface Protocol)

*SLIP* is an older protocol that was developed in UNIX and still is used as the remote access protocol on many UNIX networks. You can use Microsoft RAS to dial up a

SLIP server, and thus you can use it to connect NT networks to large UNIX-based installations. NT does not support dial-in access via SLIP.

> PPP is the standard protocol used in remote access. SLIP does not offer a secure, authorizable connection and is therefore not supported as a dial-in method in NT. This knowledge will be useful to you on your exam.

### RAS Protocol

The *RAS* protocol is used to support the NetBIOS naming convention and is a proprietary protocol, used only between Microsoft-based networks. It is required to support NetBIOS naming and is installed by default when you install the RAS Server.

### NetBIOS Gateway

Earlier versions of RAS supported only the NetBEUI LAN protocol and not IPX or TCP/IP. The NetBIOS gateway was used to translate data from the NetBEUI protocol to other protocols that the NT network might use. RAS still supports the NetBIOS gateway to maintain compatibility with older versions of the RAS Server.

## 13.3.2. Choosing LAN Protocols

LAN protocols, or networking protocols, govern how information is handled on Local Area Networks (LANs). RAS supports the use of three LAN protocol stacks:

- NetBEUI
- TCP/IP
- IPX

You must choose at least one LAN protocol to use, but RAS enables you to use all three simultaneously if necessary. Keep in mind that any remote client dialing in must support one of these protocols. RAS also supports the relatively new Point-to-Point Tunneling Protocol (PPTP), which you can use to establish a connection with one LAN protocol through another.

To configure the RAS protocol setup, you first must open the Network Control Panel. From the Services tab, highlight Remote Access Server and select Properties to display the Remote Access Setup dialog box shown in Figure 13.3. Choose Network, and the Network Configuration dialog box shown in Figure 13.5 will open.

**13**

**Figure 13.5.**

*Choose which protocols to use in the Network Configuration dialog box.*

This dialog box lets you choose which protocols you will use for both dial-out and dial-in access. To see the configuration options for each protocol, simply select the appropriate Configure button.

## NetBEUI

*NetBEUI* is a simple, efficient protocol that you would primarily use on small networks that consist only of Microsoft clients. Although easy to configure and manage, NetBEUI does not support routing and is therefore not suitable for use on large, varied networks.

Choose Configure for NetBEUI on the Network Configuration dialog box to open the RAS Server NetBEUI Configuration dialog box shown in Figure 13.6.

**Figure 13.6.**

*The RAS Server NetBEUI Configuration dialog box provides a single choice for the NetBEUI protocol.*

RAS Server provides only one choice for the NetBEUI protocol: whether to allow remote clients to access only the computer on which the RAS Server operates or to access the entire network.

## TCP/IP

*TCP/IP* (Transmission Control Protocol/Internet Protocol) is an extensive, robust protocol that is ideally suited for connecting different types of computers and operating systems. Thus, it is the standard choice of protocols for networks containing many different types of systems, such as Microsoft systems or those based on UNIX, and it is the standard protocol for the Internet.

Choose Configure for TCP/IP on the Network Configuration dialog box to open the RAS Server TCP/IP Configuration dialog box shown in Figure 13.7.

**Figure 13.7.**
*Determine how IP addresses will be governed in the RAS Server TCP/IP Configuration dialog box.*

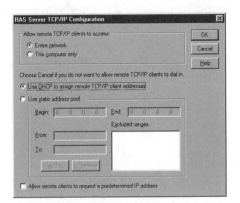

As with each protocol, you can choose whether remote clients have access to the Entire network or to This computer only.

The other section of this dialog box determines how the IP addresses of remote clients will be governed. There are three choices:

- Use DHCP to assign remote TCP/IP client IP addresses.
- Use static address pool.
- Allow remote clients to request a predetermined IP address.

**Use DHCP to Assign Remote TCP/IP Client Addresses**   If a Dynamic Host Configuration Protocol (or DHCP) server is running on your network, this option allows the RAS Server to pass client DHCP requests on to the DHCP server. This option enables your remote clients to be assigned IP addresses dynamically.

**Use Static Address Pool**   This option enables you to define a range of IP addresses from which your remote clients will be assigned an IP address. This also is dynamic, in that each time a user dials in, she is assigned a different IP address.

This option also gives you the choice of excluding ranges of addresses from the static address pool. This can be useful if you want all remote clients to use a certain range of IP addresses but want some of your remote clients to have a static, predetermined IP address.

**13**

**Note** If your network is using DHCP for IP address assignment, and you want to set up your static pool using addresses within the DHCP scope, you must exclude them from the scope on the DHCP server.

**Allow Remote Clients to Request a Predetermined IP Address**  Some of your remote clients might require a predefined IP address that does not change each time they connect to your network. This option enables the client to specify in her network settings what the IP address is, instead of having it assigned to her. Note that although the previous two options are mutually exclusive, this option can be used in conjunction either with DHCP or with a static pool of addresses.

**Test Tip** TCP/IP is the protocol of choice on just about any network today. It is also the protocol of the Internet. This is important, because is it the only protocol stressed in the NT exams. Although having a deep knowledge of the protocol for the NT Server exam is not too important, it becomes much more important in the Server Enterprise exam.

## IPX

IPX (Internetwork Packet Exchange) is the protocol of choice for networks using Novell's NetWare. If your network is using NetWare, and you need your remote clients to be able to access these resources, you must enable IPX.

Choose Configure for IPX on the Network Configuration dialog box to open the RAS Server IPX Configuration dialog box shown in Figure 13.8.

**Figure 13.8.**

*Enable IPX in the RAS Server IPX Configuration dialog box.*

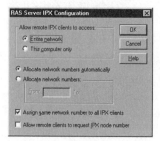

As with the other protocols, you can choose whether remote clients have access to the Entire network or to This computer only.

The other options available are similar to the options for TCP/IP. IPX requires that you assign all computers a network number. The default is to assign the numbers automatically and assign the same network number to all clients. If you choose the default options, no other configuration is necessary.

If you want, you can designate a pool of network numbers that will be assigned to all of your remote clients. You also have the option of letting remote clients choose their own network numbers.

> Allowing clients to choose their own network numbers represents a potential security violation, because it is possible for one client to impersonate another by using that client's network number.

> The only thing you really must know about IPX for the exam is that it is required for any network activity involving Novell's NetWare.

## PPTP (Point-to-Point Tunneling Protocol)

*PPTP* is basically a method for using one networking protocol through another protocol. For example, a remote client can be connected to a RAS Server via TCP/IP and tunnel through that protocol by using another protocol, such as IPX. The most common use of this scenario is to securely access a remote network over the Internet. If a RAS Server is connected to the Internet, the remote user can dial up an existing account with a local Internet service provider. After that connection is established using TCP/IP, a second connection (called a *tunnel*) is established between the RAS Server and the remote user using any protocol (including TCP/IP). This type of connection is illustrated in Figure 13.9. The primary advantage to PPTP is that a remote user can dial a local ISP instead of making a long distance call directly to her company's RAS Server.

13

**Figure 13.9.**
*Use PPTP to connect to a RAS Server over the Internet.*

The PPTP client software is included with Windows NT Server and Workstation. It also currently is available for Windows 95 with the version 1.2 upgrade to Microsoft Dial-Up Networking, which is available at `http://www.microsoft.com/windows95/info/updates.htm`.

# 13.4. Configuring RAS Security

Security is of major concern on any network, and it is an especially important issue if you choose to allow dial-up access to your network. RAS provides several different types of security. Note that this section includes information only about the security RAS provides. To ensure a secure networking environment, you should familiarize yourself with all aspects of Windows NT security.

## 13.4.1. NT Authentication

The RAS Server uses the same database to verify the user accounts, passwords, and permissions that NT Server uses. This ensures that the maintenance of users and administration of security is consistent and centralized. Whenever a remote user dials into your network, RAS server sends a challenge to the remote system requesting account information regarding that user. The client system sends an encrypted response to the RAS Server with the user account details. After RAS verifies that the account exists, RAS Server checks to see whether dial-in access has been granted to that user. If it has, the user then must successfully log on to Windows NT. This means that it is necessary for any remote user attempting to log on to have both a valid Windows NT account and the permission to dial in to the RAS Server.

With this in mind, it generally is recommended that you disable the built-in Guest account on any NT network. This especially is true if you are allowing dial-in access. This allows for better accountability because each remote user must log on with a different user account. If many users log on by using the single Guest account, associating any individual user with a particular action can be difficult or impossible. You can disable the Guest account by using User Manager for Domains.

**Test Tip**

How the Guest account affects various aspects of an NT network is a recurring theme in many of the exams you will take. Keep the preceding caution in mind as you study, because it applies to many different facets of NT.

## 13.4.2. Call-Back Security

RAS Server has the capability to automatically disconnect a remote user after he has connected and then call that user back. You can enable this feature with the Remote Access Administrator utility shown in Figure 13.10.

**Figure 13.10.**

*Enable call-back security with the Remote Access Administrator.*

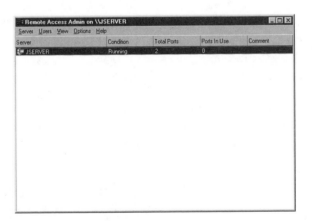

**13**

In this window, highlight the RAS Server you want to administer, and select Permissions from the Users menu. This will open the Remote Access Permissions dialog box shown in Figure 13.11.

**Figure 13.11.**

*Set user permissions in the Remote Access Permissions dialog box.*

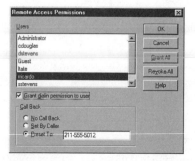

You set permissions on a user-by-user basis. You have a choice of two call-back methods to use. The first is Set By Caller. This option provides for a small amount of security because your company's phone bill should reflect the numbers dialed by the RAS Server.

 The Set By Caller option also is useful if you want your company rather than your remote users to bear any charges for long distance calls.

 Note that call-back security is within the scope of the NT Server exam. You must know how to enable it and what it is.

The second callback option available is Preset to:. This option provides a greater security advantage because it enables you to set a predetermined number at which a particular user will be called back. If you set this option, no one will be able to dial in to the network from a different location and impersonate that user.

## 13.4.3. Allowing Access to Your Network

As mentioned in the section "Choosing LAN Protocols," you can determine whether RAS Server enables remote users to access your entire network or only the machine on which RAS is installed (see Figures 13.6 through 13.8). Although you cannot select this option for each user, you can select it for each protocol, and thus you can allow different users access to different parts of your network. This option is discussed in more detail in the section titled "Routing via RAS."

### 13.4.4. Forcibly Disconnecting a Remote User

Using RAS Server, you also can forcibly disconnect a user who is connected to your network. You do this by using the Remote Access Administrator (refer to Figure 13.10). Choose the server for which you want to view the active users, and select Active Users from the Users menu. This brings up the Remote Access Users dialog box. From here you can disconnect users, view users' account information, and send messages to connected users.

### 13.4.5. Third-Party Solutions

You also can use various third-party security enhancements (such as encrypters/ decrypters and enhanced authentication devices) in conjunction with the RAS Server. These typically are installed between the connection device and the RAS Server.

## 13.5. Granting Dial-In Access

When you install the RAS service, two programs install with it: Dial-Up Networking Monitor and Remote Access Manager. Dial-Up Networking Monitor is discussed in detail in the section "RAS Performance Monitoring." Remote Access Administrator (refer to Figure 13.10) is the utility you use to grant dial-in permissions.

From the Users menu of Remote Access Administrator, choose Permissions. This brings up the Remote Access Permissions dialog box (refer to Figure 13.11). In the window titled Users, you see a list of users configured on your server. For each user, you can choose to Grant dial-in permission. You also may set the call-back procedure, if any, for each user for whom you grant dial-in permission. (This is discussed in detail in the section titled "Configuring RAS Security.") Note also the Grant All and Revoke All buttons to the right of the Users list. These buttons enable you to grant or revoke dial-in access to all users in the Users list.

13

You also may grant dial-in access by using User Manager for Domains. By viewing the User Account properties for any user and then selecting Dial-in, you can enable dial-in permissions for that user.

If you have not already enabled security auditing using the User Manager for Domains utility, you might consider doing so. Opening up your network to dial-in access dramatically increases the potential for security violations. Auditing, combined with the judicial granting of dial-in access, is a powerful step toward ensuring network security

Auditing your resources also can be a valuable troubleshooting tool because you can view a record of the successes and failures of certain resource access. Be careful, however, that when you enable auditing you enable auditing of only those items you really must track. Auditing increases the overhead on a system, thus slowing performance.

Although RAS security is not featured much in the NT Server exam, you must know a few points. Know that the RAS server allows encrypted NT authentication, thus allowing NT to extend its single logon feature to RAS clients. Know that you can audit a RAS client just as with any other user. Finally, know that you can set the call-back for particular users.

## 13.6. RAS Performance Monitoring

Monitoring the performance of your RAS Server provides two very important services. First, if you are familiar with the way in which your network normally operates, you can be more certain of spotting and correcting problems before they grow out of hand. Second, regular monitoring of your network also can help you identify the capacity of your current configuration and help you make an informed decision when you must increase this capacity. Two primary tools are available for monitoring the performance of your RAS Server:

- Dial-Up Networking Monitor
- Performance Monitor

### 13.6.1. Dial-Up Networking Monitor

The Dial-Up Networking Monitor utility runs automatically at any time there is a connection to the RAS Server. It usually runs in a minimized state, but double-clicking its icon in the taskbar brings up the window shown in Figure 13.12.

**Figure 13.12.**
*Quickly view the current connections to each device configured for your RAS server in the Dial-Up Networking Monitor.*

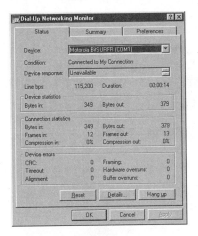

This window gives you a snapshot view of current connections to each device configured for your RAS server. This includes such information as the speed and duration of the connection, the statistics of the connection, and the accumulated errors since the connection was made. This tab also enables you to Reset the connection statistics, Hang up the device (disconnecting any users), and view the Details of the connection (see Figure 13.13)

**Figure 13.13.**
*View the details of a dial-up networking connection in this window.*

**13**

The Details view gives you protocol-specific information, such as the IP address for a TCP/IP connection, the network number for an IPX connection, and the NetBEUI name for a NetBEUI connection.

You can view a summary of all current dial-up connections and see which devices are associated with each by choosing the Summary tab on the Dial-Up Networking Monitor utility (see Figure 13.14).

**Figure 13.14.**

*View a summary of a dial-up networking connection in this window.*

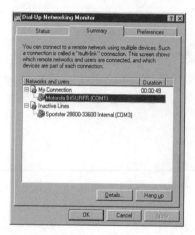

The only thing you really must know about the Dial-Up Networking Monitor is that it exists and can give you a current view of RAS activity.

## 13.6.2. Performance Monitor

Whereas the Dial-up Networking Monitor gives you a nice snapshot of what's going on with RAS Server at the moment, the Performance Monitor utility is a bit more powerful, giving you the ability to chart very detailed levels of performance over time and keep a log or make a report of this performance. A full discussion of Performance Monitor is beyond the scope of this chapter, but a few RAS-specific counters are available to you. Some of the important counters that the RAS service adds are summarized in Table 13.1.

**Table 13.1. RAS-specific counters in Performance Monitor.**

| Counter | Description |
|---|---|
| RAS Port:Bytes Received | The total number of bytes received for this connection. |
| RAS Port:Bytes Transmitted | The total number of bytes transmitted for this connection. |
| RAS Port:Total Errors | The total number of CRC, Timeout, Serial Overrun, Alignment, and Buffer Overrun Errors for this connection. |
| RAS Total:Bytes Received | The total number of bytes received for all connections. |
| RAS Total:Bytes Transmitted | The total number of bytes transmitted for all connections. |
| RAS Total:Total Errors | The total number of CRC, Timeout, Serial Overrun, Alignment, and Buffer Overrun Errors for all connections. |
| Telephony:Lines | The number of telephone lines serviced by this computer. |
| Telephony:Active Lines | The number of telephone lines serviced by this computer that are currently active. |
| Telephony:Incoming Calls/sec | The rate of incoming calls answered by this computer. |

Although there also are many other counters available for these three objects, the counters listed here should provide you with most of the information you need to track when monitoring your RAS service.

There also are many counters for monitoring the activities of your network in general and specific protocols that you might have configured on your RAS server. These also can be helpful to you in monitoring RAS performance.

**13**

Performance monitoring, especially in RAS, is another subject that the NT Server exam does not cover in much detail. Again, this subject is tested more heavily in the Enterprise exam.

# 13.7. Routing via RAS

Routers enable computers from one network (or individual computers) to communicate with computers on another network. You can configure any Windows NT Server with two or more network interfaces (including modems and ISDN adapters, as well as network adapter cards) as a router on your network. A computer with multiple network interfaces also is known as a multi-homed computer. There are several reasons for configuring your RAS server as a router, including allowing access to your network for remote clients, allowing access to the Internet from your network, and connecting two or more LANs across a distance to create a WAN.

> Because WANs are beyond the scope of the NT Server exam, you should not find any question on the NT Server exam that comes from the information in this section. Routing via RAS is more pertinent to the Enterprise exam.

## 13.7.1. Dial-Up Networking

You use the dial-out feature of the RAS Server via a utility called Dial-Up Networking, which you can use to access a RAS Server on another network, access the Internet, or access other types of networks by using various protocols. Dial-Up Networking is enabled by default when you install RAS. You configure this feature by opening the Dial-Up Networking utility found under My Computer (see Figure 13.15).

**Figure 13.15.**
*The Dial-Up Networking feature enables you to use the dial-out feature of the RAS Server.*

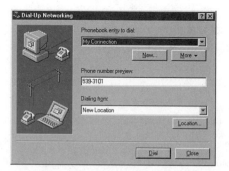

> RAS Server manages its connections intelligently. After a service has been dialed into using a particular phonebook entry, RAS remembers which entry was used and uses it automatically the next time.

### 13.7.2. Allowing Access to Your Network

The simplest form of routing with RAS is allowing remote users to dial in to your RAS Server and connect through that computer to the rest of your network (see Figure 13.16).

**Figure 13.16.**
*Allow remote users to connect to your network with RAS.*

You must do only two things to enable this form of routing:

■ Grant the remote user dial-in access.

■ Allow remote users to access the entire network using the appropriate protocol (refer to Figures 13.6 through 13.8).

> **Note**
>
> If you are using IPX or TCP/IP and want to enable dynamic routing, you also must add the appropriate RIP service, RIP for NWLink IPX/SPX compatible transport for IPX, and RIP for Internet Protocol for TCP/IP. These are network services, which you can install via the Networking Control Panel.

### 13.7.3. Internet Connectivity

You also can use RAS to allow users of your network, including your remote users, to access the Internet via your company's Internet service provider (see Figure 13.17).

**Figure 13.17.**
*Use RAS to allow Internet access.*

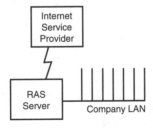

**13**

The first step in configuring Internet access is to ensure that the TCP/IP protocol is correctly configured on your RAS Server, using the address of your Internet service provider as the default gateway for accessing other networks. After you have configured the TCP/IP protocol, you must set up a dial-up networking connection from your RAS Server to your company's Internet service provider.

 Although you can allow users on your network to access the Internet by using just RAS, doing so is a security risk. It is much safer to use a product such as Microsoft Proxy Server because it gives you much more control over the connection.

### 13.7.4. Connecting Two (or More) LANs

Another common use of RAS as a router is to connect two networks that are separated by some distance (see Figure 13.18). In such an instance, RAS performs the task of routing packets of data from one LAN to the other.

**Figure 13.18.**
*Use RAS to connect two networks.*

In this example, two separate Microsoft-based LANs are connected by using RAS servers as routers. You only need to configure each RAS server with a dial-up networking connection to the RAS server on the other network and point to that server as the default gateway for connections to that network. Whenever a user on one network tries to connect to a resource on the other network, RAS automatically will dial in to the other network and negotiate the connection.

## 13.8. Troubleshooting RAS

Although many problems can occur when you are using the Remote Access Service, these problems tend to fall into two basic categories. Either the remote user cannot connect to your network at all or, once connected, the user cannot access the resources she needs. Although troubleshooting a remote connection can be quite frustrating, applying common troubleshooting methodology can help you assess the situation. If something does not work, was there a time when it did work? What has changed since then? Can none of your remote users connect or is just one having problems? Questions such as these, along with a thorough understanding of the principles behind the RAS Server, are your best tools for solving any problem.

Troubleshooting RAS is a topic you must know only in its most basic form for the NT Server exam. For example, if a user cannot access the network remotely, she might not have been granted access or the RAS service might not be running. You will not be expected to answer questions on protocol or modem troubleshooting.

## 13.8.1. Cannot Connect to RAS Server

Most of the time, the problem of not being able to connect to a RAS Server is a simple configuration problem in the client or server software. The following are the five main steps to take in making a remote connection (at least for the purposes of troubleshooting):

1. **The client machine attempts to make the connection by bringing up the dial-up networking interface.** If this step fails, it usually is because the remote user is not actually trying to log on to the RAS Server but rather is logging on locally.

2. **The client machine dials the number to the RAS Server. You actually should hear the dial tone and dialing of the modem.** If this step fails, it usually indicates an incorrect parameter in the setup of your modem or, possibly, a problem with the modem itself.

3. **A physical connection is made. You hear the squealing of the modem indicating this.** If this step fails, it usually is because the telephony information is incorrect. Double-check the phone number being dialed. Failure of this step also can indicate that the RAS service on the server is not running.

4. **The connection is verified.** If this step fails, it usually is because of a protocol or telephony configuration error. Double-check that you correctly installed the protocols and that dial-up networking is configured correctly to use this protocol.

5. **Logon is successful.** If this step fails, the problem most likely is a permissions or user account problem. Check that the remote user is using the correct account and password and that the account exists on your network or RAS Server. Check also that the user has been granted dial-in permission to the RAS Server.

**13**

The preceding list presents general guidelines based on a typical configuration of the RAS service. Note also that, although steps 2 and 3 indicate sounds or events specific to modems connecting over analog lines, the specific events may differ if you are using other communications technology, such as ISDN or X.25.

## 13.8.2. Cannot Access Needed Resources

If a remote client can dial and connect to the RAS Server but cannot access the resources that she needs, then a simple configuration error most likely is the source of the problem. The first thing to check is that the appropriate modem and networking protocols are configured on the client and server machines. After you have done this, make sure that you have chosen correctly whether the client has access to the Entire network or to This computer only (see Figures 13.6 through 13.8). If these are correct, you must verify the user's account settings and the permissions assigned to the needed resource.

# 13.9. Lab

This lab will aid in your learning by testing you on the information presented in this chapter, as well as by showing you how you could apply that knowledge in real-world situations. You can find answers to the review questions in Appendix B, "Answers to Review Questions."

## 13.9.1. Review Questions

### Question 1

How many simultaneous connections can a RAS server on a Windows NT Server support?

   A.  1

   B.  256

   C.  254

   D.  128

### Question 2

What remote access protocols are supported by RAS?

   A.  SLIP

   B.  PPP

   C.  PPTP

   D.  IPX/SPX

   E.  RAS Protocol

### Question 3

What networking protocols are supported by RAS?

   A.  NetBEUI

   B.  RAS Protocol

   C.  IPX

   D.  AppleTalk

**13**

## Question 4

You have decided to use TCP/IP as the protocol for direct dial-up access. Your company uses a DHCP server, but you want to assign static IP addresses to your remote users. How would you implement this?

A. Exclude the range of IP addresses you wish to assign to remote clients from the scope on the DHCP server.

B. fff.

C. Enter the values for the IP addresses you wish to assign with RAS Server.

## Question 5

Which of the following methods can you use to increase security when you allow dial-in access:

A. Use Dial-Up Networking Monitor to log calls into your RAS Server.

B. Set your RAS Server to call back remote clients who attempt access.

C. Enable auditing of the guest account.

D. Enable auditing of the remote users' accounts.

## Question 6

What should you do to allow remote users to connect to your company's main network securely over the Internet?

A. Configure the RAS Server and client to use PPTP.

B. Enable encrypted logon authentication to Windows NT.

C. Set the RAS Server so that it calls back remote users attempting to connect.

D. You cannot configure a secure connection over the Internet.

## Question 7

You suspect that remote users are logging on to your network and leaving their machines connected for long periods of idle time so that they will not be bothered to reconnect when they must use this system. You are worried that this might be consuming valuable server resources. What utility would you use to determine whether your supposition is true and how bad the problem actually is?

A. Dial-Up Networking Monitor.

B. Remote Access Administrator.

C.  Performance Monitor.

D.  Server Manager.

## Question 8

One of your users reports that he cannot connect to the company network. Upon further questioning, you determine that his modem does dial and physically connect to the RAS Server, but when he tries to log on to Windows NT, he is unsuccessful. What two things should you check first?

A.  Whether the proper protocol is installed on the client machine.

B.  Whether the user has been granted dial-in access.

C.  Whether the user is attempting to log on with a valid user account.

D.  Whether the RAS Server is set to call back remote users.

## 13.9.2. Exercises

The following exercises are each based on the scenario that is presented below. Each exercise presents a problem and asks you to determine what the proper course of action should be. There are many possible solutions to each problem, so don't worry about any particular "right" answer. The real purpose of these exercises is to get you to think about the information you have read in this chapter and how it might apply in a real-world situation.

### Scenario

You are the administrator of your company's main network. Your network consists of multiple servers and workstations configured with Windows NT 4.0. Your network is Ethernet and uses the TCP/IP protocol. One of your Windows NT Servers is configured with the RAS service and has a dial-up connection to the Internet (see Figure 13.19).

**13**

**Figure 13.19.**

*Your company's main network.*

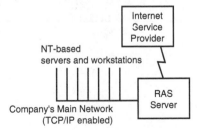

Your company has just acquired a smaller company, which also is networked. The new network consists of multiple servers and workstations configured with Windows NT 4.0, as well as a server and several clients configured with Novell's NetWare. This network is token-ring–based and uses an IPX/SPX-compatible protocol (see Figure 13.20).

**Figure 13.20.**
*The new company's network.*

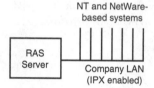

### Exercise 13.1

Your company wants to install a Windows NT Server on the new company's network and configure it as a RAS Server. This server and the RAS Server on your main network will be configured so that the two networks can communicate. Sketch out a map of the proposed new network. Determine how you would configure networking protocols between the two RAS Servers.

### Exercise 13.2

Your company also wants to configure the RAS Server on the main network to allow remote users to dial directly into the network. These remote users all will be using Windows 95 or Windows NT Workstation. How would you implement this? What protocols would the client machines need to be running? What steps would you take to ensure security? How would you determine the load that this is placing on your RAS Server?

### Exercise 13.3

Additionally, your company has several employees that travel regularly and must be able to connect to the main network. It has been decided to do this over the Internet, if it can be done securely. Can this be done securely? How would you implement this? How would these remote users differ from the users in the previous exercise?

# Day 14

# NT Server Troubleshooting Guidelines

*by Marcus Barton*

## 14.1. Overview

Troubleshooting is an art. For the most part, troubleshooting is something that you learn with experience. Humans are creatures of habit. Knowing this, you can surmise that humans learn things best through repetition and experience. You learn troubleshooting best by using a product and then seeing first hand what things might go wrong with it. You should spend some time in a chair sitting in front of a monitor and using Windows NT Server. Take what you learn in this chapter and apply it. It will prove invaluable at test time.

In this chapter, you learn some tools and techniques for troubleshooting Windows NT problems about which you might not have read in other chapters.

### 14.1.1. Objectives

The following list shows the Microsoft exam objectives for the topic of troubleshooting. Although other chapters covered many of these objectives, it is important that you know how to appropriately fix the troubleshooting problems you are required to understand for the exam.

- ■ Resolve installation failures.
- ■ Resolve boot failures.
- ■ Resolve configuration errors.

- Resolve printer problems.
- Resolve RAS problems.
- Resolve connectivity problems.
- Resolve resource access problems and permission problems.
- Resolve fault-tolerance failures. Fault-tolerance methods include
    - Tape backup
    - Mirroring
    - Stripe set with parity
    - Disk duplexing

## 14.1.2. Fast Facts

The following list of facts is a concise picture of the information presented in this chapter. It acts both as an overview for the chapter and as a study aid to help you do any last-minute cramming.

- The Emergency Repair Disk is computer-specific; the boot disk is not.
- To create a boot disk, you must format the floppy in Windows NT.
- The necessary files for a boot disk for an Intel-based computer are NTLDR, NTDETECT.COM, BOOT.INI, and NTBOOTDD.SYS (if the boot device is an SCSI).
- If the BOOT.INI is not present at bootup, NTLDR attempts to load Windows NT from the WINNT directory on the first partition of the first disk on the first controller.
- The default setting for a log file is a maximum size of 513KB with events that are older than seven days overwritten.
- The Last Known Good configuration is saved when a user successfully logs on to a system after bootup. Also, the boot must have been accomplished without any critical errors.
- Information dumped from the memory during an automatic recovery is saved as MEMORY.DMP by default.

# 14.2. Troubleshooting Methodology

You should develop a method for handling troubleshooting situations. After you find a method that works, stick to it. Creating a method is not easy, however, and so here are some guidelines to help you out. These guidelines are time-tested and work for most situations. Using these guidelines not only will help you determine your own method, but also will help you learn troubleshooting, should you not be experienced at it already.

## 14.2.1. Gathering the Facts

The first step in troubleshooting is gathering the facts. There is no way that you can troubleshoot a situation without having some facts. The more facts that you have, the more quickly and easily you can resolve the problem. Keep in mind that a fact only is something that you can verify as true. Often administrators let false guesses, which are nothing more than speculative fictions, lead them after much time-consuming effort to a dead end.

Symptoms, which are the end results of a problem, form part of these facts. By analyzing the symptoms, you can get closer to the problem that is causing them. After spending some time using a product, most administrators can resolve a problem by looking only at the symptoms. The infamous statement, "I've seen this before," can be invaluable when you are troubleshooting.

What has changed since the last time something that isn't working did work? Often you can resolve problems simply by asking that question. Quite possibly, whatever changed might be causing the problem. The fix usually is easy in this case: Change everything back to how it was before the problem.

Has what isn't working ever worked? I know you think I'm joking, but numerous help desks spend countless hours on the phone trying to resolve a problem that they think (because the user hasn't informed them otherwise) has worked at some time. If something has never worked, try starting it over (install a product a second time, begin a new process, and so on).

Was anything new installed or uninstalled? Installations sometimes can have detrimental effects on a server, especially if they replace that important DLL file with an older version. Equally as damaging is an uninstall that takes away files that other programs, especially the operating system, need.

Is all of the hardware working properly? No one likes a hardware failure; however, it does happen. Hardware doesn't live forever, and so you should expect hardware failures. Having a few extras on hand doesn't hurt anything, and if you think it hurts your wallet, think of how much it will cost you if the server is down until you can get a replacement part.

Who was the last person to touch what isn't working? This sounds like something a kid would say. However, knowing this can be invaluable. Usually, finding out who were

**14**

the last people to work with a malfunctioning server can save you time in diagnosing the problem. They will know what they have done to it, which is better than you trying to guess what they did. And let's face it, every network has at least one power user or administrator who knows just enough to be dangerous. Although they still are learning and can be an asset, they are at the stage that they also can be a liability.

These are just a few of the endless questions that you can ask yourself during the information-gathering phase of your troubleshooting process. The more facts you can collect, the closer you will be to solving the problem.

## 14.2.2. Formulating a Hypothesis

Troubleshooting is as much a science as it is an art. Any good scientist knows that before anything can be proven, a hypothesis must be formulated. My Webster's dictionary defines a hypothesis as, "a theory that explains a set of facts and can be tested by further examination."

So, you can see that the gathering of the facts in the previous step is necessary before you can hypothesize as to why a problem has occurred. With further investigation of the hypothesis, you can come to a conclusion about how to repair the problem.

This step is nothing more than taking the facts and making an educated guess about what caused the problem. The further testing comes next.

## 14.2.3. Testing and Documenting

The first part of this two-step phase is testing. Testing is taking your educated guess (hypothesis) and seeing whether it is correct. Your hypothesis is your judgment, based on the available evidence, of why the problem occurred. One way of testing is either reversing or attempting to repair the cause of the problem and then viewing the outcome.

Reversal is the undoing of what caused the problem. If the problem was in the setting of a configuration, then you should reset that configuration. If it was in the installation of something, then you should uninstall the program in question. Reversing a problem's cause is putting the computer back to the state it was in before the problem occurred.

Because reversal is not always feasible (you cannot, for example, uninstall a program you need), repairing the problem usually is more viable. This might mean installing the latest patch from the manufacturer, for example. Repairing is not changing the computer back to a previous state; it is the negation of the cause's negative effects.

During testing, you might change several things that do not resolve the problem. Be careful of domino situations, which are situations in which one thing has an effect on another, which in turn has an effect on something else, and so on. In most cases, when you are finished testing (and have resolved the problem), you will want to put the things that had nothing to do with the problem back to the way they were. Nothing is worse than resolving one problem only to create another.

The second part of this step is documentation. Documentation is something that most network administrators hate. However, it is a necessary evil. Documentation can help in several ways.

First, if you document what you do to the machine, you will have a better understanding of the problem should it arise again. Also, documentation can help others resolve a similar situation if they have access to the documentation but not to you. Finally, it can help you identify recurring problems with a particular server if you have an idea of what has gone wrong with it in the past.

## 14.3. Analyzing Boot Errors

Problems with Windows NT booting up can be the most frustrating troubleshooting cases you will have. If the server will not boot up, you not only are faced with a limited number of ways in which you can troubleshoot the machine, but you usually have a bunch of users breathing down your neck because they cannot access the server. You usually can attribute problems to one of the following:

- Corrupt files
- Missing files
- Incorrect BOOT.INI

The first two situations can consist of several files. Other than the many DLL files necessary to get Windows NT up and running, common boot files also are necessary. These files are listed in Table 14.1.

**Table 14.1. Common files needed at boot.**

| File | RISC | Intel | Description |
|------|------|-------|-------------|
| NTLDR | X | | The operating system loader for Intel-based machines. |
| OSLOADER.EXE | X | | The operating system loader for RISC-based machines. |

*continues*

**14**

## Table 14.1. continued

| File | RISC | Intel | Description |
|------|------|-------|-------------|
| BOOT.INI | X | | The boot loader operating system menu on Intel-based machines that enables you to choose to which OS to boot. |
| BOOTSECT.DOS | X | | This file contains boot sector information of any other operating system that was on the Intel-based computer when NT was installed. |
| NTDETECT.COM | X | | Builds a list of hardware at boot on Intel-based machines. |
| NTOSKRNL.EXE | X | X | The only file in this table not located on the root of the boot drive. This file is located in the Windows NT directory and is the Windows NT kernel. |
| NTBOOTDD.SYS | X | X | If your computer boots up to a SCSI hard drive for which the BIOS has been disabled, you will find this file. It is a device driver for just such a situation. |

Numerous error messages might pop up if any of these files are missing or corrupt. However, some of them can be misleading. The most common boot error is

```
Windows NT could not start because the following file is missing or corrupt:
\winnt root\system32\ntoskrnl.exe
Please reinstall a copy of the above file.
```

There actually are many causes for this error. The first is the obvious: NTOSKRNL.EXE is missing or corrupt. If this is the case, you should perform an emergency repair (discussed later in this chapter). Two other reasons are related to the BOOT.INI.

BOOT.INI points to the location of the NTOSKRNL.EXE. If it points to the wrong place, the computer thinks that the file is missing when it might not be. For this reason, you should modify the BOOT.INI to show the correct location of the NTOSKRL.EXE.

The last reason for the preceding error message would be in the absence of a BOOT.INI. If it is missing, NTLDR attempts to load Windows NT from the default location (in the WINNT directory on the first partition of the first disk on the first controller). If it does not find NTOSKRNL.EXE there, it once again pops up the preceding error message. The fix for this problem is to create a BOOT.INI with the correct path to the NTOSKRNL.EXE.

The next most common message is

```
BOOT: Couldn't find NTLDR
Please insert another disk.
```

This is the second most common error message not because the NTLDR file is missing, but because this is the message that appears if you leave in drive A a floppy disk that has been formatted in Windows NT. When you format a floppy in NT, the boot sector of that floppy is different than the standard Windows-formatted floppy. In Windows NT, the format process puts information on the boot sector of that floppy that points to the file NTLDR for booting (not COMMAND.COM).

If the NTLDR is missing or is corrupt, the proper way to replace it is through an emergency repair. Alternatively, copying an NTLDR file from another Windows NT server (same version) can repair this problem.

When the NTDETECT.COM file is missing, you receive a somewhat misleading message on your screen. The message will state

```
NTDETECT V1.0 Checking Hardware…
NTDETECT failed
```

It appears from the preceding message that NTDETECT.COM is present and attempting to load. However, NTLDR, not NTDETECT.COM, actually puts this message on the screen. The detection process fails if NTLDR is not present. Once again, copying another copy of this file to the server or performing an emergency repair is the appropriate course of action.

If you have a dual-boot configuration on your server and you attempt to boot the server to another operating system, the BOOTSECT.DOS file must be present. If it is not, the computer will not load the boot sector information from your previous operating system. If it is missing, the following message will appear:

```
I/O Error accessing boot sector file
multi(0)disk(0)rdisk(0)partition(1):\bootsect.dos
```

Do not attempt to copy this file from another Windows NT machine. The BOOTSECT.DOS file contains information specific to the computer on which it is located. You must perform an emergency repair by using the Emergency Repair Disk you created previously when repairing the machine.

## 14.3.1.  Bypassing the Boot Sector

If you can't start Windows NT because one or more of the files mentioned in the preceding section is missing or corrupt, you can start the server now and replace the files later. However, this takes a little planning ahead of time.

You can bypass the boot sector by creating a Windows NT boot disk. Use this boot disk to take the place of the missing or corrupted files discussed in the previous section. Unlike a typical MS-DOS boot disk, after the server boots up from the boot disk, you

14

then can remove the boot disk and the server will be operational. Think of it as jump-starting a car. After you have jump-started a car, you can remove the jumper cables and the car will continue to run. This basically is how a boot disk works under Windows NT. In MS-DOS, when you booted to floppy, that floppy had to remain there for reference to the COMMAND.COM. This is not so with Windows NT.

Creating a boot disk is a simple task. Take these steps:

- Format a floppy disk in Windows NT (not MS-DOS or Windows 95).
- Copy the files discussed in Table 14.1, with the exception of NTOSKRNL.EXE.
- Modify the BOOT.INI to reflect the proper path to the NTOSKRNL.EXE. (This is for Intel-based machines only.)

After you complete these steps, use the floppy to boot a Windows NT Server. Keep in mind that the NTOSKRNL.EXE file must reside on the hard disk where the Windows NT files are. If the NTOSKRNL.EXE file is missing, the boot disk won't do you any good.

 **Note** You should test your boot disk to make sure it works. Nothing is more frustrating than attempting to boot up to a boot disk and discover it is not working properly. Your main concern should be that the BOOT.INI is correct.

## 14.3.2. The BOOT.INI

The BOOT.INI file creates the menu at boot-up of Windows NT on Intel-based machines. It is a text-based file that points to the location of the NTOSKRNL.EXE. There may come a time when you must modify the BOOT.INI. You can use any text-based editor (such as Notepad or Edit) to do so.

However, most people are confused with the layout of the BOOT.INI file. It uses ARC (Advanced RISC Computing) naming conventions to specify the location of the NTOSKRNL.EXE. You must specify the correct ARC naming convention for the exam. Here is an example of a BOOT.INI file:

```
[boot loader]
timeout=10
default= multi(0)disk(0)rdisk(1)partition(1)\WINNT

[operating systems]
multi(0)disk(0)rdisk(1)partition(1)\WINNT="Windows NT Server Version 4.00"
multi(0)disk(0)rdisk(1)partition(1)\WINNT="Windows NT Server Version 4.00
➥[VGA mode]" /basevideo /sos
C:\="MS-DOS"
```

The BOOT.INI file contains two sections: boot loader and operating system. The boot loader portion specifies the timeout value, which is how long the computer will wait, in seconds, for you to make a choice. If the timer runs out, it will pick the default operating system, which also is specified in this portion of the BOOT.INI.

**Note**

If the timeout portion is set to 0, the default operating system specified will be booted without any action from you.

The operating system section specifies the different operating systems to which you can boot. In the preceding example, there are only two choices, Windows NT Server and MS-DOS. It specifies the operating systems through the use of ARC names. Here are two examples of ARC names:

```
multi(0)disk(0)rdisk(1)partition(1)
scsi(0)disk(1)rdisk(0)partition(1)
```

- ■ multi/scsi—Adapter. When the boot device is attached to a SCSI adapter with its BIOS disabled, use scsi. In all other situations, use multi.
- ■ disk—Hard disk assignment on the adapter, which is used when scsi is used in the ARC name. If multi is used, disk always will be 0.
- ■ rdisk—Hard disk assignment on the adapter, which is used when multi is used in the ARC name. If scsi is used, rdisk always will be 0.
- ■ partition—Partition in which the operating system resides.

Two basic situations play a big role in the ARC name. The first situation is one in which the boot device is a SCSI device without the built-in BIOS enabled. If this is the case, the first section of the ARC name will be scsi.

The second situation basically is all others. This includes IDE devices and SCSI devices with the BIOS enabled. When this situation arises, the first portion of the ARC name will be multi.

**Note**

Here is where I see some folks stray when they come across this topic on the exam. It may sound confusing, but actually it's simple. There must be a differentiation between scsi and multi so that Windows NT knows whether to load the NTBOOTDD.SYS necessary for SCSI devices.

**14**

*continues*

On standard SCSI adapters (without the BIOS enabled), Windows NT cannot access the device and must load the NTBOOTDD.SYS. You specify this situation by placing scsi at the beginning of the ARC name.

However, if the SCSI adapter has its BIOS enabled, it acts very similarly to an IDE device. In this case, the NTBOOTDD.SYS does not need to be loaded, so you specify multi in the ARC name.

So how does the numbering work? Well, take a look at a few examples, and it should become self-evident. The first example has a machine with two SCSI adapters (BIOS disabled). Both adapters have two hard drives. Windows NT is loaded on the first adapter, second disk, and first partition.

```
scsi(0)disk(1)rdisk(0)partition(1)
```

The next example is a hardware setup identical to the first. However, this time Windows NT is loaded on the second adapter, first disk, and second partition.

```
scsi(1)disk(0)rdisk(0)partition(2)
```

The last example is a different hardware layout. In this case, you have IDE drives. Windows NT is loaded on the first adapter, second disk, and second partition.

```
multi(0)disk(0)rdisk(1)partition(2)
```

Notice in all the examples that all hardware numbering begins at 0, with the exception of the partitions, which begin at 1. This might sound trivial, but it also can cause you to get the question wrong on the exam.

Several switches that you can use in the BOOT.INI can modify the way that Windows NT boots up. Even though the important part of the BOOT.INI when it comes to exam time is the ARC names, the switches still deserve a brief explanation. Here is a list of the possible switches and a brief description of each:

- /basevideo—Starts up Windows NT with a basic VGA video driver and a resolution of 640×480.

- /sos—Shows all drivers being loaded at boot up instead of showing progression dots (...).

- /noserialmice=[comn¦comx,y,z]—Disables checking for pointing devices attached to a serial port. If the com portion is not specified, no ports will be checked.

- /crashdebug—Enables automatic recovery and restart.

- `/nodebug`—Switches off monitoring of debugging information.
- `/maxmem:n`—Specifies the maximum amount of RAM to use. This can be handy in troubleshooting bad SIMMS.
- `/scsiordinal:n`—Specifies which SCSI adapter to use. This can come in handy when two identical adapters are used in the same machine.
- `/baudrate`—Specifies the baud rate to be used for debugging. If you do not set the baud rate, the default baud rate is 9600 if a modem is attached, and 19200 for a null-modem cable.
- `/debugport=comx`—Specifies the com port to use for debugging, where x is the communications port that you want to use.

### 14.3.3. The Last Known Good

Earlier in the chapter, I explained how to go about troubleshooting a machine. In that explanation, I talked about returning a computer to a previous state. However, if a configuration change is causing the server to have boot problems, you are presented with the problem of not being able to get the server up and running in order to return the configuration to its previous state. However, there is a way around this, and it is called Last Known Good.

You can use the Last Known Good configuration when a configuration change that you previously made causes the system not to boot properly.

So what will it change back? To understand the answer to that question you must understand what defines the Last Known Good configuration. Two things should happen before the configuration is saved as a good configuration:

- The configuration must not have caused any critical system errors.
- A user must log on successfully.

In other words, after you boot up the computer without any problems and log on, the configuration is saved as a good configuration. Then, say, for example, that you make a change to the system configuration that requires you to restart the computer. On restarting, the computer will not boot up properly. Invoking the Last Known Good configuration will take it back to the configuration that was in place when you last logged on successfully (without any errors).

With that in mind, you must consider when and when not to use the Last Known Good configuration. This is important for the exam. In a troubleshooting question, you might be asked what is the appropriate course of action to take, and the Last Known Good might be an option. However, the Last Known Good might not repair the problem.

**14**

One example of this type of problem is when you reboot the computer, log on, and then the system crashes. On restarting, the problem still will exist because the configuration was saved once you logged on to the server.

Another example of a situation in which the Last Known Good configuration might not solve the problem is when the configuration change is made after several reboots followed by someone logging on to the computer. Invoking the Last Known Good only changes the configuration back to the most recent successful configuration.

You invoke the Last Known Good configuration at bootup. Before you see the blue screen, you see a message that states, Press spacebar NOW to invoke Hardware Profile/Last Known Good menu.

Pressing the spacebar gives you three options. The first lets you have several hardware configurations for the server. The second is the Last Known Good configuration and the third is to exit. The top of the screen displays a brief message explaining the procedure along with a list of the different hardware configurations. The bottom of the screen displays three options.

- Use the up and down arrow keys to make the selection that you want. Then, press Enter.
- To switch to the Last Known Good configuration, press L.
- To Exit this menu and restart your computer, press F3.

The first option enables you to choose the hardware configuration with which you want to start the computer. The second option enables you to invoke the Last Known Good configuration. The last option is self-explanatory.

Note

Although you might not see the capability for multiple hardware configurations as a benefit for a server, you should be able to see the benefit for a workstation. Keep in mind that Windows NT Workstation was built around the concepts of Windows NT Server. NT Workstation can be extremely powerful on a laptop. However, because version 4.0 does not support plug-n-play, having the multiple configuration option can be beneficial. One example of the need for multiple configurations is the capability that enables you to place laptops into a docking station and remove them with relative ease. With the absence of plug-n-play, the capability to change the hardware configuration at bootup can be necessary in situations in which the change from docking station to an undocked status might cause the machine to lock up during boot.

Invoking the Last Known Good configuration by pressing L doesn't appear to change the screen at all. However, don't let this deceive you. If you look at the bottom of the screen, you see the following selections:

- Use the up and down arrow keys to make the selection that you want. Then press Enter.
- To switch to the Default configuration, press D.
- To Exit this menu and restart your computer, press F3.

Pressing Enter now will boot the machine to the Last Known Good configuration of the particular hardware profile that you specify. Press D to return to the previous screen.

If you made several configuration changes to the computer before restarting it, and you invoke the Last Known Good configuration, all changes you made since you saved the Last Known Good configuration will be lost.

## 14.4. Restoring a Corrupt Registry

There might be a time when one or more of the registry files becomes corrupt or missing. In this unlikely event, there are several ways that you can fix this situation.

The first and most obvious way to restore information to a server including the registry would be by restoring it from backup tape. Hopefully, you are backing up the registry as part of your regular backup routine. The Windows NT Backup program and many third-party backup utilities provide you with the capability to back up the registry. If your backup utility does not give you that capability, you should buy another program or use the Windows NT Backup utility.

Another way to restore the registry is through an *emergency repair*. The emergency repair process should be your last resort for fixing a server short of reinstalling Windows NT.

To perform an emergency repair, perform the same steps as if you were going to reinstall the server. After you see the Welcome to Setup screen, notice the option at the bottom to repair. After you press R for repair, a screen of repair options appears. You can choose any combination of the following options:

14

- Inspect registry files
- Inspect start-up environment
- Verify Windows NT system files (Windows NT setup files needed)
- Inspect boot sector

After you specify which options you want to perform and then continue the operation, you are prompted as to whether you want Windows NT to detect hard disk, floppy, and other controller hardware. (Remember, this is very similar to setting up Windows NT for the first time.)

After the hardware detection occurs, or you specify any additional devices, Windows NT setup asks whether you have the Emergency Repair Disk (ERD). If you specify that you do not, setup will attempt to perform the emergency repair from information in the Repair directory, which is located as a subdirectory of the Windows NT root directory.

> The information in the Repair directory is not updated automatically. You must update this information manually by using RDISK.EXE.
>
> Performing an emergency repair with outdated information returns the computer to the state it was in when the Repair directory or ERD last was updated.

After doing a quick disk check, Windows NT asks you what information in the registry you would like to restore. The choices are

- System (System configuration)
- Software (Software information)
- Default (Default user profile)
- NTUSER.DAT (New user profile)
- Security (Security accounts policy and SAM database)

Again, you can choose any combination of the choices depending on what information might be corrupt. After you make your choices and continue the operation, Windows NT replaces the information you specified and then prompts you to restart the computer.

# 14.5. The Event Viewer

The Event Viewer can be an invaluable tool during your troubleshooting process. An *event* is any significant occurrence in the operating system or in an application. If the event is critical, a message appears on-screen. However, any event that is significant appears in the Event Viewer log files. The Event Viewer logging starts automatically when you start Windows NT.

Additionally, the Event Viewer also keeps track of the auditing of security events. However, you must turn on auditing before the Event Viewer will log this information.

## 14.5.1. Interpreting Event Logs

The Event Viewer creates three log files: the system, application, and security event logs. The System log (see Figure 14.1) contains events created by any of the Windows NT system components. One example of these is a driver that failed to load at system bootup.

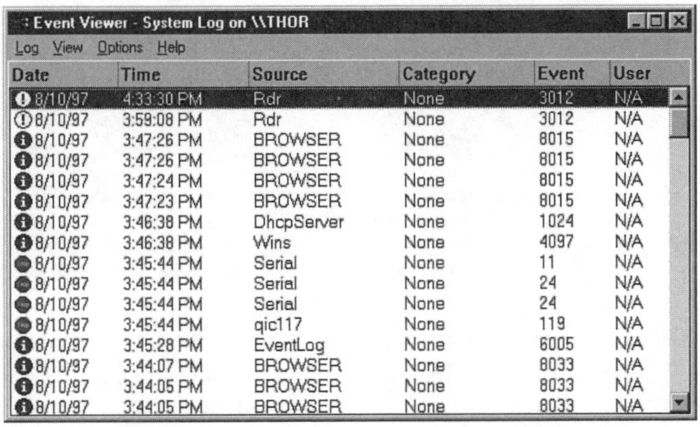

Event Viewer - System Log on \\THOR

Log View Options Help

| Date | Time | Source | Category | Event | User |
|---|---|---|---|---|---|
| 8/10/97 | 4:33:30 PM | Rdr | None | 3012 | N/A |
| 8/10/97 | 3:59:08 PM | Rdr | None | 3012 | N/A |
| 8/10/97 | 3:47:26 PM | BROWSER | None | 8015 | N/A |
| 8/10/97 | 3:47:26 PM | BROWSER | None | 8015 | N/A |
| 8/10/97 | 3:47:24 PM | BROWSER | None | 8015 | N/A |
| 8/10/97 | 3:47:23 PM | BROWSER | None | 8015 | N/A |
| 8/10/97 | 3:46:38 PM | DhcpServer | None | 1024 | N/A |
| 8/10/97 | 3:46:38 PM | Wins | None | 4097 | N/A |
| 8/10/97 | 3:45:44 PM | Serial | None | 11 | N/A |
| 8/10/97 | 3:45:44 PM | Serial | None | 24 | N/A |
| 8/10/97 | 3:45:44 PM | Serial | None | 24 | N/A |
| 8/10/97 | 3:45:44 PM | qic117 | None | 119 | N/A |
| 8/10/97 | 3:45:28 PM | EventLog | None | 6005 | N/A |
| 8/10/97 | 3:44:07 PM | BROWSER | None | 8033 | N/A |
| 8/10/97 | 3:44:05 PM | BROWSER | None | 8033 | N/A |
| 8/10/97 | 3:44:05 PM | BROWSER | None | 8033 | N/A |

**Figure 14.1.**
*The System log contains events the Windows NT system components create.*

The Application log contains events from applications, such as error or warning messages. In Figure 14.2, you see applications, such as the licensing service and Windows NT backup, place event information in the Application log.

The Security log contains events from a security auditing policy (see Figure 14.3). Unlike the System and Application logs, auditing is an option that a member of the administrators group must specify through the User Manager for Domains. Also, only administrators can access the Security log.

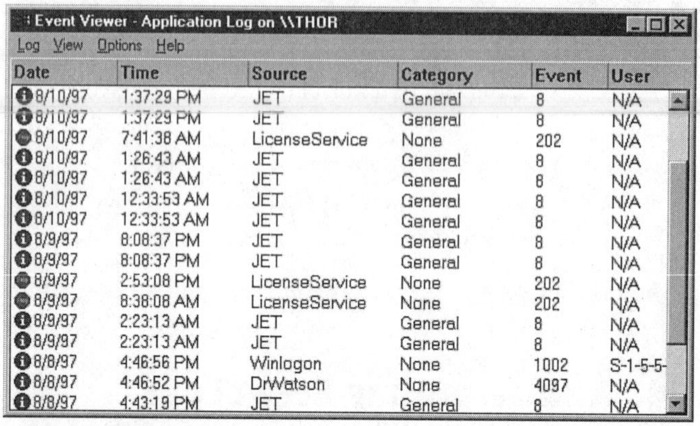

**Figure 14.2.**

*The Application log contains events from applications.*

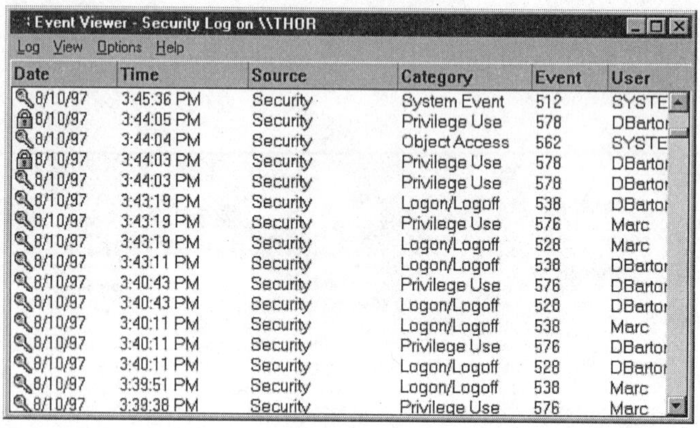

**Figure 14.3.**

*The Security log contains events from security audits.*

The information in the three log files is listed in order of occurrence by date and time. The most recent event appears at the top of the log. Using options in the View menu, you can change the order in which events are displayed. Each of the events in the log file has a corresponding icon that denotes what type of event it is. Table 14.2 lists the icons and their corresponding meanings.

**Table 14.2. Log file entries and their corresponding icons.**

| Icon | Description |
| --- | --- |
| i | A blue icon with a small letter i represents the information icon. This type of event usually is a successful operation of a major service. |
| ! | A yellow icon with an exclamation point represents the warning icon. These events aren't necessarily significant, but a problem could arise in the future because of this event. |

| Icon | Description |
| --- | --- |
| Stop | A stop sign icon represents an error. It usually is significant and means that data or some functionality of the server has been lost. |
| Key | When you audit the success of events, they appear as keys in the Security log. |
| Lock | A lock indicates a failure audit event in the Security log. |

Double-clicking an event in the System log produces a dialog box similar to that in Figure 14.4. If you look at the contents of this event, you see that it gives basic information at the top of the dialog box, such as date, time, computer, and so on. The description of this particular event is relatively straightforward. However, some events might not be so easy to understand.

**Figure 14.4.**
*This dialog box shows the details of an event.*

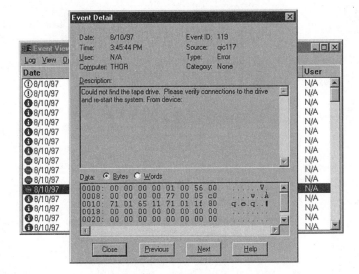

The Data portion at the bottom of the Event Detail dialog box contains any binary data the event generates. A support technician familiar with the application or part of Windows NT that generated the event can interpret this information.

## 14.5.2. Maintaining Log Files

The event logs are maintained separately from each other. You can change how large the event logs become, along with how they overwrite older information. You also can archive the event logs in several different formats.

You modify the behavior of the log files by clicking Log from the menu and then selecting Log Settings. You can maintain the event log settings (see Figure 14.5) for

14

each log file by selecting the log file settings, which you modify from the Change Settings For option.

**Figure 14.5.**

*The Event Log Settings dialog box enables you to modify the behavior of the log files.*

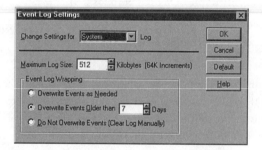

After you specify which log file to modify, you can change the maximum size of the log file in 64KB increments. The default size is 512KB. You should know the default size for the exam. It potentially could be an easy answer for you.

The other item that you can set for the log files is how information is overwritten. Here are the options:

- Overwrite Events as Needed—This overwrites events as necessary after the log file reaches the maximum size you specified for it.

- Overwrite Events Older than x Days—This enables you to specify that events are overwritten after an amount of days that you specify, regardless of the maximum file size. The default setting, as shown in Figure 14.5, is 7 days. The maximum amount of days is 365.

- Do Not Overwrite Events—This maintains all events without overwriting them. To clear the events, you must manually clear the log.

The first option clearly is obvious. However, the second and third options do not overwrite or clear the logs if they become full (reach their maximum size). If this should happen, a message appears on the screen that the event log is full. After this happens, you must clear the log events or you will continue to get this message as events attempt to write to the event log.

To clear the log file, click Log from the menu and select Clear all log events. This clears only the events to the log file that is currently being viewed. You then are prompted as to whether you want to save the current log events before you clear them.

All log information, if you do not save it, is irrecoverable after you clear the log.

You can archive event logs by saving them. You can save the log files by choosing the option you are given when you clear them or when you click Save As from the Log menu. Each log (whether system, application, or security) saves separately and must be the one you currently are viewing for you to save it. The following are three basic formats in which you can save log files:

- EVT files that allow for future viewing in the Event Viewer
- Basic text (TXT) files
- Comma-delimited files that you can use in other applications, such as spreadsheets or flat file databases

# 14.6. Memory Dumps

When a severe error (also known as a fatal error) occurs, it causes Windows NT to stop all processes and requires you to restart the computer. You can configure Windows NT to do different things if one of these unfortunate events occurs.

## 14.6.1. Capturing Memory Dumps

From the Control Panel, select the System applet. On the Startup/Shutdown tab, you will see two basic sections (see Figure 14.6), System Startup and Recovery. The upper portion, System Startup, enables you to set which operating system automatically starts at system bootup. You also can set the wait time of the startup menu.

In the lower half of the Startup/Shutdown tab you see Recovery options. Which of these options is selected depends on a Stop error event. The first two options are fairly basic. The third option, Write debugging information to, enables you to write whatever information that currently is loaded in memory to a file on the hard disk when the error occurs. This commonly is referred to as a *memory dump*. The last option automatically reboots the server when the Stop error event occurs. If you select the memory dump option, the server will not reboot until all information loaded in memory is dumped to the hard disk. The default location for the memory dump file is in the Windows NT root directory with a file name of MEMORY.DMP.

14

**Figure 14.6.**

*From the Startup/*
*Shutdown tab of the*
*System applet in the*
*Control Panel, you can*
*configure automatic*
*recovery options.*

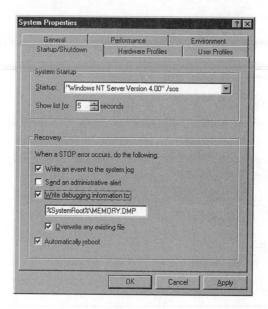

Because it dumps the entire contents of the memory onto the hard disk, there must be sufficient free disk space to receive the information. In other words, if you have 64MB of RAM installed on the server, a 64MB file is written in the event of a Stop error. If you do not have enough disk space for the file, you might lose information. Additionally, you must have a paging file on the computer's system partition that is equal to or larger than the amount of RAM that you have installed.

## 14.6.2. Dump Utilities

After you create this MEMORY.DMP file, you can use it in several ways to debug the problem that caused the Stop error. To do so, there are three command-line utilities on the Windows NT Server and Windows NT Workstation CD-ROMs. They are located in the support\debug directory. Of course, if you have Windows NT installed on a different platform, you should use the subdirectory that corresponds with your platform. For example, because I have Windows NT installed on an Intel-based machine, I use the support\debug\i386 directory.

You can use the first utility, dumpflop, to write the memory dump information to floppy disks. This can be handy if you must send the information to someone else for analysis. The information is compressed and spanned across several disks.

The correct syntax when you run the dumpflop command is

```
DUMPFLOP [opts] <CrashDumpFile> [<Drive>:]
```

The following line is an example of the application of this syntax:

```
DUMPFLOP -q c:\winnt\memory.dmp a:
```

There are a few command-line switches that you can use with dumpflop. Table 14.3 shows the available switches for dumpflop.

**Table 14.3. Dumpflop command-line switches.**

| Switch | Description |
| --- | --- |
| -? | Help |
| -p | Only print crash dump header on assemble operation |
| -v | Show compression statistics |
| -q | Format floppy when necessary during store operation |

After the persons who will debug the information receive the floppies, you retrieve the memory dump by running the dumpflop utility. However, the syntax here is slightly different. The syntax is

```
DUMPFLOP [opts] <Drive>: [<CrashDumpFile>]
```

If you run the dumpflop command without any options or other syntax, it attempts to write the memory dump information from the Windows NT root directory (default location) to floppies.

The second utility is dumpchk. It checks that the dump file was created and gives you some general information on the file if it indeed has been created. The correct syntax for dumpchk is

```
DUMPCHK [options] CrashDumpFile
```

As with the other utilities, you can use several command-line switches with dumpchk. They affect the information that dumpchk returns to you. The switches are listed in Table 14.4.

**14**

**Table 14.4. Dumpchk command-line switches.**

| Switch | Description |
| --- | --- |
| -? | Help |
| -v | Verbose mode |
| -p | Print header only, NO validation |
| -q | Perform a quick test |

Dumpexam is the last utility. It writes information from the dump file into a readable text-based file. Knowledgeable persons then can view the text file in an effort to determine what might have caused the stop error to occur. The file is called memory.txt and is located in the same directory as the dump file, unless you specify otherwise. The syntax for the dumpexam utility is

```
DUMPEXAM [options] [CrashDumpFile]
```

Table 14.5 shows the available switches for dumpexam.

**Table 14.5. Dumpexam command-line switches.**

| Switch | Description |
| --- | --- |
| -? | Help |
| -v | Verbose mode |
| -p | Print header only |
| -f Filename | Specify output filename |
| -y Path | Set the symbol search path |

# 14.7. NT 4.0 Resource Kit Utilities

The CD that accompanies the Windows NT Server Resource Kit contains utilities that apply to Windows NT Server and Windows NT Workstation. It includes a collection of information resources, tools, and utilities that can simplify tasks and give you some extra capabilities that you would not have otherwise. Even though it is not necessary to know about all of these utilities for the exam, using them will help you gain a better understanding of Windows NT and thus help you on the exam.

The following utilities are a few of those that are available after you install the resource kit. These are but a few of the applications and tools that come with the resource kit; numerous command-line utilities also are available.

## 14.7.1. Configuration

There are several configuration utilities. The first is an automatic logon utility (see Figure 14.7) that enables you to set up a certain account to log on automatically at system bootup. For security reasons, you should use this in an environment either where security is not important or the server physically is secure.

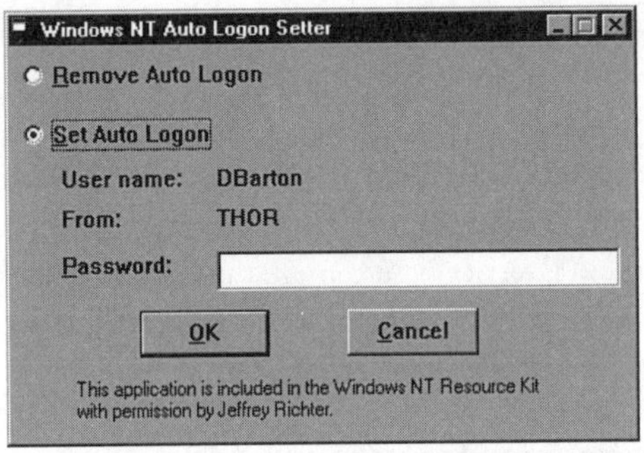

**Figure 14.7.**
*The Auto Logon utility enables you to set an account to log on automatically at startup.*

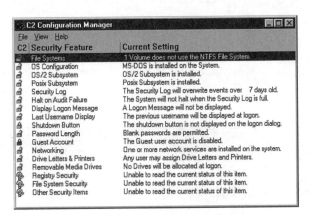

There also is a Class C2 security configuration utility that assists you in configuring the server with the proper requirements to classify the server as being C2-secure (see Figure 14.8).

**Figure 14.8.**
*The C2 Security utility points out what you properly must do to make the server C2-secure.*

Upgrading a computer from a single processor to multiple processors is not as simple as opening the case and installing the additional processor(s). You must make certain configuration changes to Windows NT. A utility to assist you in configuring a computer when you upgrade it from a single processor to multiple processors comes as a part of the resource kit.

**14**

**Note**
This has nothing to do with the exam, but I thought you might like to know. When using the uniprocessor to multiprocessor utility, you might run into a few problems.

Instead of explaining the problems here (which could take a couple of pages) you should see the Microsoft Knowledge Base article Q159564 available on TechNet and at Microsoft's web site (www.microsoft.com/kb).

If you want to schedule applications or other command-line options, such as a backup program, to run at a scheduled time, you can use the AT service in Windows NT. If you do not like the AT service, you can use the Command Scheduler that comes with the resource kit, as shown in Figure 14.9. It uses the AT service but gives you a graphical interface that is a little more intuitive.

**Figure 14.9.**
*The Command Scheduler automatically can run programs at scheduled times.*

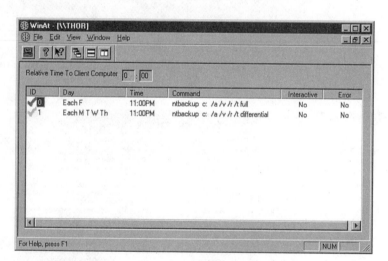

## 14.7.2. Desktop Tools

There are several desktop tools, such as 3D Paint, an animated cursor editor, and an image editor. Also, there is a utility called Microsoft Desktops that is a desktop switching program for Windows NT 4.0. It customizes the desktop wallpaper and colors and separates executing programs into new desk spaces.

### 14.7.3. Diagnostics

Probably the most important utilities are those that assist you in diagnosing problems with Windows NT. Two monitoring utilities, the Browser Monitor and Domain Monitor, are included. The Browser Monitor (see Figure 14.10) is a Windows-based utility that enables you to monitor the outcome of computer browser elections, including which computers are the master and backup browsers.

**Figure 14.10.**

*Viewing information about browsers is easy with the Browser Monitor.*

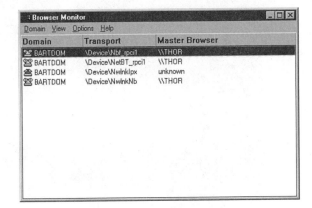

The Domain Monitor, also a Windows-based utility, gives you the status of domains, domain controllers, and any trust relationships, if these exist.

The Network Watcher enables you to view shared resources on the local or remote servers and which users are connected to them. Additionally, you can set up the Network Watcher to show you which files those users have opened (see Figure 14.11).

**Figure 14.11.**

*The Network Watcher can give you information about network shares, the users who are accessing them, and the files they have open.*

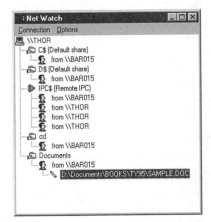

**14**

The Process Viewer (see Figure 14.12) enables you to view the processes running on a server. It also enables you to shut down any processes that you choose or boost the priority of those individual processes that are running.

**Figure 14.12.**

*Use the Process Viewer to see which processes are using the CPU.*

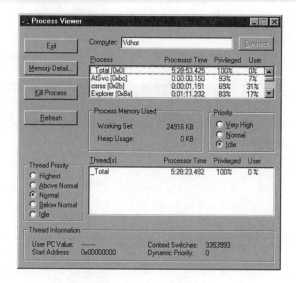

Quickslice, another diagnostic utility included in the resource kit, enables you to view CPU utilization by processes running on the server.

## 14.7.4. Disk Tools

DiskProbe is a sector editor for Windows NT Workstation and NT Server that enables a user with local Administrator rights to edit, save, and copy data directly on the physical hard drive that is not accessible in any other way. This can be helpful when you cannot read a disk by more usual means, such as with Explorer or from a command prompt.

The Fault Tolerance Editor in Figure 14.13 is a tool that gives you the capability to create, edit, and delete fault tolerance sets for disk drives and partitions of local and remote computers.

## 14.7.5. File Tools

There also is a tool called WinDiff that gives you the capability to compare files or complete directories. When you use this tool with mapped network drives, you can compare files or directories from one computer to another.

Another tool, the Expand for Windows (see Figure 14.14), gives you the same capability as EXPAND.EXE but with the ease of a graphical interface.

**Figure 14.13.**

*The Fault Tolerance editor enables you to create, edit, and delete fault tolerance sets on remote computers.*

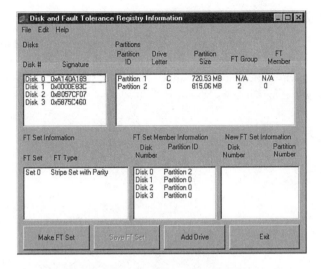

**Figure 14.14.**

*File expansion is a breeze with the Expand for Windows utility.*

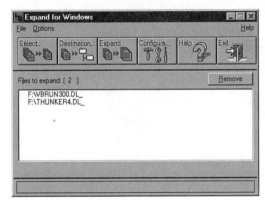

## 14.7.6. Internet Utilities

WebAdmin, which provides Web-based administration of Windows NT Server, is an ISAPI DLL that enables remote administration of Windows NT Server by means of HTML browsers, such as Internet Explorer 2.0 and later. This lets an administrator administer his server without physically being located on his network. The nice thing about WebAdmin is you can administer from Windows, Macintosh, and UNIX platforms. All you need is a Web browser.

DbWeb is a gateway between Microsoft Open Database Connectivity (ODBC) data sources and the Internet Information Server (IIS). You can use dbWeb to publish data from an ODBC data source and provide a familiar World Wide Web look and feel to your users. DbWeb enables users to create queries and enables you to filter the data and sources that users can access and display.

14

### 14.7.7. Online Documents

You can view numerous online documents pertaining to Windows NT Server and the resource kit. These documents can assist you in troubleshooting, using the utilities, or just learning more about Windows NT. With the look and feel of standard help programs in Windows NT, they are quick and easy to use.

# 14.8. Lab

This lab aids in your learning by testing you on the information you have learned in this chapter, as well as by giving you exercises to hone your skills. You can find answers to the review questions in Appendix B, "Answers to Review Questions."

## 14.8.1. Review Questions

### Question 1

Which of the following files do you need to boot an Intel-based computer using IDE hard disks to Windows NT? Pick all that apply.

    A. `BOOT.INI`

    B. `OSLOADER`

    C. `NTLDR`

    D. `NTDETECT.COM`

    E. `NTOSKRNL.EXE`

    F. `BOOTSECT.DOS`

    G. `NTBOOTDD.SYS`

### Question 2

Which of the following files do you need to boot a RISC-based computer using SCSI hard disks to Windows NT? Pick all that apply.

    A. `BOOT.INI`

    B. `OSLOADER`

    C. `NTLDR`

    D. `NTDETECT.COM`

    E. `NTOSKRNL.EXE`

    F. `BOOTSECT.DOS`

    G. `NTBOOTDD.SYS`

### Question 3

You have a Windows NT server that has a dual-boot configuration. You accidentally deleted the `BOOTSECT.DOS` file. What are your options to repair this problem? Choose all that apply.

**14**

A. Copy the file from another server.

B. Copy the file from a boot disk created for this server.

C. Copy the file from a boot disk created for another server.

D. Copy the file from the Emergency Repair Disk.

E. Perform an emergency repair.

## Question 4

You have a computer that has two SCSI hard disk controllers without BIOS. There are a total of four hard disks. Windows NT is on the first controller, first disk, and second partition. How would the correct ARC name look in the `BOOT.INI`?

A. `multi(0)disk(0)rdisk(0)partition(1)`

B. `multi(1)disk(1)rdisk(0)partition(2)`

C. `multi(0)disk(0)disk(0)partition(2)`

D. `scsi(0)disk(0)rdisk(0)partition(2)`

E. `scsi(1)disk(1)rdisk(0)partition(2)`

F. `scsi(1)disk(0)rdisk(1)partition(2)`

## Question 5

You have added a CD-ROM drive to a Windows NT server. After you install the drivers, Windows NT prompts you to restart the server in order for the changes to take effect. After you restart it, the computer hangs at the blue screen and will not boot. What is the easiest way to get the server back up and running?

A. Perform an emergency repair.

B. Boot up and invoke the Last Known Good Configuration.

C. Restore the registry from backup.

D. Use a boot disk.

## Question 6

You have added a tape drive to a Windows NT server. After you install the drivers, Windows NT prompts you to restart the server in order for the changes to take effect. After you restart it, the computer boots up and you log on. Shortly after you log on, the computer hangs, causing you to resort to resetting the computer. What is the easiest way to get the server back up and running?

A. Perform an emergency repair.

B. Boot up and invoke the Last Known Good Configuration.

C. Restore the registry from backup.

D. Use a boot disk.

## Question 7

You have a server that displays the following message:

```
BOOT: Couldn't find NTLDR
Please insert another disk.
```

What is the quickest way to get the server up and running?

A. Perform an emergency repair.

B. Boot up and invoke the Last Known Good Configuration.

C. Restore the registry from backup.

D. Use a boot disk.

## Question 8

You have a server that displays the following message:

```
NTDETECT V1.0 Checking Hardware...
NTDETECT failed
```

What is the quickest way to get the server up and running?

A. Perform an emergency repair.

B. Boot up and invoke the Last Known Good Configuration.

C. Restore the registry from backup.

D. Use a boot disk.

# 14.8.2. Exercises

## Exercise 14.1

In this exercise, you will create a boot disk for an Intel-based server.

1. Insert a 3.5-inch floppy into the A drive.

2. From the Windows NT Explorer, format the floppy.

3. Click on View from the menu and select Options.

4. Select Show all files.

**14**

5. Deselect Hide file extensions for known file types.

6. Click OK.

7. From the root of the C drive, copy the following files to the A drive:

   - `Ntldr`
   - `Ntdetect.com`
   - `Boot.ini`
   - `Bootsect.dos` (if it exists)
   - `Ntbootdd.sys` (if it exists)

8. Remove the floppy.

## Exercise 14.2

In this exercise, you will simulate missing boot files.

1. Select `Boot.ini`, `Ntldr`, and `Ntdetect.com` (hold the Ctrl key down while clicking them).

2. Right click while pointing to one of the files, and select Properties.

3. Clear the box marked Read Only, and delete the four files (leave them in the Recycle Bin).

4. Next, you must restart the computer. Make a note of the error message you receive.

5. Insert the boot disk, restart the computer, and then log on using an administrator account.

6. Open the Recycle Bin and restore the `Ntldr` file.

7. Remove the boot disk, restart the computer, and make a note of the error message that you receive.

8. Insert the boot disk and restart the computer and then log on using an administrator account.

9. Open the Recycle Bin and restore the `Boot.ini`.

10. Remove the boot disk, restart the computer, and make a note of the error message that you receive.

11. Insert the boot disk, restart the computer, and log on using an administrator account.

12. Open the Recycle Bin and restore the `Ntdetect.com`.

# Appendix A

# Glossary

**ACL (Access Control List)**   Every object in Windows NT has a list, called the Access Control List, which lists the Security IDs (SIDs) that have rights to that object, as well as which rights each SID has. See *SID*.

**ActiveX**   A Microsoft trademark for object services and interchangeable software controls, including COM and embedded Internet software components.

**Alpha**   A series of processors made by Digital Equipment Corporation that, at the time of this writing, held the distinction of being the fastest processors in the world. Alternatively, the first test cycle of an application in development.

**API (Application Programming Interface)**   A set of functions that gives application programmers access to common system functions. The native API in Windows NT is the Win32 API, although NT also supports subsets of the MS-DOS, Win16, OS/2, and POSIX.1 APIs through subsystems.

**AppleTalk**   A network protocol stack for Macintosh computers and printers. Originally designed to work only over Apple's serial cable technology (see *LocalTalk*), AppleTalk now is supported over EtherNet and Token Ring. Although it is traditionally a relatively chatty and inefficient protocol, most recently AppleTalk can be carried over TCP/IP, greatly improving its throughput. Windows NT's Services for Macintosh, however, does not yet support AppleTalk/IP.

**ARP (Address Resolution Protocol)**   A protocol TCP/IP hosts use to discover the hardware address of a destination node when only the IP address is known. Windows NT includes a command-line tool for examining the system's local ARP cache; for more information, type arp -? at a command prompt.

**ARPA (Advanced Research Projects Agency)**   A government agency responsible for the development of robust internetworking technologies that led to the ARPANET, a predecessor to today's Internet.

**ATM (Asynchronous Transfer Mode)**   An advanced packet-switching networking technology that provides phenomenal throughput for data traffic, particularly for the intense needs of videoconferencing and other multimedia tasks.

**auditing**   The process of tracking access to objects. Auditing can track success and failure on a per-object, per-user basis. Auditing most often is used to help trace security problems and breaches, although it also can be useful for tasks such as billing for printing services.

**authentication**   The process of identifying oneself to a security provider. NTLM (NT/LAN Manager) authentication, the current standard method supported by Windows NT, generally associates a user object's SID with a username and password.

**b-node**   Short for *broadcast node*, a method for NetBIOS name resolution over TCP/IP. B-node resolution uses NetBIOS broadcasts over TCP/IP to resolve names. See *h-node*, *m-node*, and *p-node*.

**b-tree**   Short for *balanced tree structure*, a b-tree is a data structure used to represent directories and files in file systems such as HPFS and the Macintosh HFS (Heirarchical File System).

**BDC (Backup Domain Controller)**   An NT Server that maintains a copy of the domain's SAM (Security Accounts Manager) database. BDCs provide an alternative source for authentication services in a domain, as well as a backup copy in case the domain's PDC (Primary Domain Controller) suffers catastrophic failure. See *PDC*, *SAM*.

**bindery**   The authentication database on a Novell NetWare 2.*x* or 3.*x* server. See *bindery emulation*.

**bindery emulation**   A NetWare Directory Services (NDS) server can use bindery emulation to allow non-NDS–aware NetWare clients to authenticate to the server.

**bridge**   A device that enables two or more networks, each using different types of data link protocols (such as Token Ring and EtherNet), to form a single logical network.

**browser**   A NetBIOS client that attempts to contact other NetBIOS resources on a network using the browse list maintained by one or more master browsers. The browse list contains a list of active systems, identified by their NetBIOS network names. See *master browser* and *network browser*.

**bus**   An architecture for communication between multiple devices, whether on a system board or across a network. A bus architecture is a shared medium in which all devices on the bus must contest for communication time, and all devices can hear all transmissions.

**bus mastering**   A process by which a device can gain temporary control of the bus to direct data transfer, thus reducing processor overhead during I/O operations.

**caching**   The process of storing commonly used data from one data storage medium in another, faster medium.

**CHAP (Challenge-Handshake Authentication Protocol)**   An encrypted password authentication protocol, for use with dial-up connection protocols such as RAS and PPP.

**CISC (Complex Instruction Set Computing)**   A philosophy for CPU design which states that the processor's instructions should be very powerful, allowing large tasks to be completed in fewer instructions. The Intel *x*86 family of processors is an example of a CISC architecture, although later models also have included RISC innovations. See *RISC*.

**Class (A, B, C)**   A type of IP address that determines the range of digits available to a particular installation. A Class A number is preallocated only the farthest-left octet of the dotted-decimal IP address, leaving the farthest-right three fields free for suballocation (for example, 110.0.0.0). Similarly, a Class B address is preallocated the farthest-left two octets (133.129.0.0), and a Class C address is preallocated the farthest-left three octets (205.122.89.0). A Class A number can have a maximum of 16,777,214 nodes, a Class B number 65,534, and a Class C 254. IP network numbers are currently assigned by the InterNIC.

**coaxial**   A type of cable used for data transmission and networking. Coaxial cable can support long lengths due to its shielding but is less cost-effective and harder to maintain than twisted-pair. See *STP*.

**collision**   On a CSMA/CD network, a collision is a jamming signal sent when multiple workstations attempt to access the transmission bus at the same time. When a collision occurs, all transmitting workstations wait a random amount of time before re-attempting transmission. See *CSMA/CD*.

**COM (Component Object Model)**   A model developed by Microsoft to develop, register, track, and use interchangeable software components on computer systems. COM is part of the larger product ActiveX. See *ActiveX*.

**connectionless**   A connectionless network protocol is responsible only for the transmission of data and has no role in the proper ordering, collection, or verification of data receipt. Data link protocols such as EtherNet and Token Ring, as well as transport protocols such as IP are examples of connectionless protocols. See *connection-oriented*.

**connection-oriented**   A connection-oriented protocol contains facilities for ordering, verifying, and retransmitting data to guarantee delivery (or report an error if delivery cannot take place). Transport protocols such as TCP are examples of connection-oriented protocols.

**console**   A console application runs from the command prompt and uses basic text input and output methods rather than the Windows Graphical User Interface. Alternatively, it is the physical location of a system.

**CSMA/CD (Carrier Sense-Multiple Access/Collision Detection)**   A bus contention communication method used by network technologies such as EtherNet. In a CSMA/CD network, workstations first attempt to determine whether a transmission is taking place (carrier sense) before trying to transmit. When the wire is free, any workstation can attempt to transmit packets (multiple access). If, however, multiple workstations attempt to transmit at the same time, a *collision* occurs (collision detection), and the workstations wait a random time to retry communication. CSMA/CD networks are not suitable for real-time data transmission because no workstation is guaranteed the capability to transmit its packets, but CSMA/CD networks have proven simple and reliable enough for most data transmission needs.

**CSNW (Client Service for NetWare)**   A network client included with Windows NT that enables the workstation to connect to NetWare resources. The client included with NT 4.0 enables the workstation to authenticate to NDS resources as well as bindery resources.

**data link layer**   The second level of the OSI network model, this layer is responsible for the formation and transmission of packets over layer one, the physical layer. The data link layer has no facility for connection-oriented communication. EtherNet and Token Ring are examples of data link layer protocols. See *OSI, connectionless,* and *connection-oriented.*

**DDE (Dynamic Data Exchange)**   A protocol for inter-process communication on Windows systems.

**debugger**   A tool for examining source code to determine the point of failure in an application, or to examine the status of a system to determine where a fatal system error has occurred.

**DHCP (Dynamic Host Configuration Protocol)**   A method for dynamically allocating IP addresses. DHCP can be run on servers such as Windows NT, UNIX, and NetWare, and can dynamically provide IP addresses and stack configuration to several different network clients, thus avoiding the process of manually configuring the stack on each workstation. DHCP supports the leasing of addresses to specific machines for set periods of time.

**A**

**differential backup**   A backup method whereby only the files modified since the last full backup are copied to tape.

**DirectX**   A series of services for providing high-performance access to video, network, input, sound, and other services. Primarily for game developers.

**DLC (Data Link Control)**   A non-routable network protocol used primarily by Hewlett-Packard JetDirect print servers, as well as IBM mainframes.

**DLL (Dynamic Link Library)**   A library file containing functions that can be used by many different programs, allowing those programs to be smaller and to load into memory only the shared execution code when needed.

**DMA (Direct Memory Access)**   A process that enables data to be moved from a device across the system bus to memory, or vice-versa, with minimal processor attention, thus greatly increasing system throughput.

**DNS (Domain Name Service)**   The standard for resolving IP addresses to canonical host names on TCP/IP systems. DNS relies on static tables that map addresses to host names, although standards for Dynamic DNS, designed to be used in conjunction with DHCP and NetBIOS naming, are under development. See *WINS*.

**domain**   A logical structure that allows for centralized administration of user and group objects and resources, as well as centralized authentication and rights management. A domain must have at least one Windows NT Server system serving as a domain controller. See *workgroup*.

**domain master browser**   A system that maintains a master NetBIOS browse list for an entire domain.

**dotted decimal**   The name for an IP address, rendered in four octets and represented in decimal form. For example, 123.14.5.115.

**driver**   An application or file that provides an abstracted interface to low-level hardware functions, allowing higher-level operating systems and application programs to use the same functionality independently across devices.

**duplexing**   The process of maintaining the same data on multiple disks across multiple disk controllers, protecting against data loss due to disk or controller failure. Alternatively, the process of printing on both sides of a sheet of paper. See *RAID*.

**EISA (Extended Industry Standard Architecture)**   An enhanced version of the ISA bus standard that uses a 32-bit bus with bus mastering to transfer data at up to 66MB per second while maintaining backward compatibility with ISA cards. EISA is a relatively rare bus standard, except in server-class systems, where it can still be commonly found. EISA bus devices can be configured automatically by using software utilities. See *ISA, micro channel, PCI.*

**election**    The process of determining, based on values such as operating system version and system response time, which system will serve as master browser. See *master browser, browser.*

**environmental subsystem**    A Win32 application that provides an emulated version of another operating system environment. Examples include the WOW (Windows-on-Windows) Win16 Subsystem, the OS/2 Subsystem, and the POSIX Subsystem.

**EtherNet**    A system for CSMA/CD networking, originally developed by Xerox in the 1970s and now adopted in many implementations as an industry standard data link layer networking protocol. See *CSMA/CD.*

**extent**    A portion of a file spread across a block or group of disk blocks. See *fragmentation.*

**FAT (File Allocation Table)**    A file system, originally developed for MS-DOS, that is still used by DOS, Windows 95, and Windows NT systems. FAT indexes all files and extents in a table called the FAT table. FAT requires little system overhead, making it simple and fast to implement, but it includes little fault tolerance, wastes disk space with inefficient block allocation, and suffers heavily from disk fragmentation. See *NTFS.*

**fault-tolerant**    A scheme that is not subject to data loss or system downtime due to the failure of one or more hardware devices.

**FDDI (Fiber Distributed Data Interface)**    A fiber-optic network technology for high-speed WAN interconnectivity that uses a token-based access method. FDDI is commonly used for high-speed, fault-tolerant interconnection between LANs in a Wide-Area Network.

**fiber**    A lightweight thread, lacking many thread features such as automatic processor scheduling. Fibers are provided by Windows NT to ease the porting of applications from other multitasking operating systems with weaker threading support. See *thread.*

**finger**    A protocol for checking to see whether a user is logged into a multiuser system over TCP/IP, as well as viewing some user-specified information (referred to as a *plan*). Finger can be a serious security hole on many shared-time network operating systems.

**FPNW (File and Print Services for NetWare)**    An add-on tool for Windows NT Server that enables the server to emulate a NetWare Bindery server in order to provide file and print services to NetWare Bindery client workstations. This tool now is included in the Services for NetWare package from Microsoft.

**fragmentation**   The process of spreading the extents of a file across the free space on a hard disk rather than placing them in contiguous blocks. Fragmentation generally occurs when a file system inefficiently plans space for file saves and the growth of existing files. Different file systems are affected differently by fragmentation. Fragmentation also can take place within the virtual memory address space of an operating system, but does not seriously affect operating systems with efficient memory managers.

**frame type**   One of several different standards for the layout of an EtherNet frame, based on the type of protocols the frame can carry. Examples of frame types are 802.2, 802.3, and Ethernet II.

**FTP (file transfer protocol)**   A protocol for performing file downloads and uploads over TCP/IP, supporting both raw binary and ASCII file transfer. See *TFTP*.

**gateway**   A device that provides access to outside networks. A gateway can be a dedicated hardware device, such as a network router; or a software service, such as an SMTP gateway for Microsoft Mail.

**GSNW (Gateway Service for NetWare)**   A service for Windows NT Server that enables NT clients to access remote NetWare hosts transparently, with all actual NetWare NCP traffic taking place only between the gateway server and the NetWare resources. GSNW can provide convenient access to NetWare resources without requiring NetWare client installation on NT clients but can act as a performance bottleneck, as well as making it simple to violate NetWare licensing restrictions.

**h-node**   Short for *hybrid node*, a method for NetBIOS name resolution over TCP/IP. A client configured to use h-node resolution first will attempt to use p-node resolution; if that fails, it then will attempt b-node resolution; finally, if all else fails, it will check the local LMHOSTS file for addressing information. See *b-node, p-node, m-node,* and *LMHOSTS*.

**HAL (hardware abstraction layer)**   A software interface that handles all hardware-specific programming code, allowing an operating system to be written in non-system–specific high-level languages, thus minimizing system dependency. This allows for simpler porting to other platforms, as well as better modularity and stability.

**hive**   A root-level subtree in the registry that contains keys and values.

**I/O port**   A unique memory address through which input and output to a hardware device takes place.

**IDE (integrated device electronics)**   A standard interface for mass storage drives on PC systems that is based on the original PC hard disk controller interface. EIDE (Enhanced IDE) improves still further on the IDE model.

**incremental backup**   A backup method that backs up all files that have been modified since the last backup. Unlike differential backup, however, an incremental backup sets the archive file for files it backs up.

**infinite loop**   A classic programming error in which a program enters a looping situation from which it cannot exit, causing the application to run in a loop until forced to quit by the user or operating system.   See *infinite loop*.

**interrupt**   A signal to the system's CPU to gain processor time to execute an I/O or other function. Operations that generate excessive interrupts can negatively impact system performance. Interrupts can be signaled either by hardware access or by software command.

**IPX/SPX (Internet Packet Exchange/Sequenced Packet Exchange)**   A LAN protocol designed by Novell Corporation for use with NetWare, IPX/SPX is a routable protocol that occupies the Transport and Network layers of the OSI model. IPX/SPX provides dynamic address configuration and high-speed networking, at the cost of chattiness and the incapability to route packets beyond a set hop limit. IPX/SPX can be used for NetBIOS communications.

**IRQ (Interrupt Request Queue)**   A dedicated queue over which a specific hardware device can interrupt the CPU.

**ISA (Industry Standard Interface)**   The bus designed for AT-class systems, still commonly in use today. ISA buses have a 16-bit data path, with a maximum theoretical transfer rate of 16MB/sec, without bus mastering. ISA buses do not, by default, have the capability to perform automatic adapter configuration, although the plug-and-play standard, on a system with a plug-and-play BIOS, does allow for automatic configuration of those devices that support the standard.

**ISDN (Integrated Services Digital Network)**   A high-speed service that can provide data rates much larger than those available over standard telephone lines, as well as the capability to use some bandwidth to support simultaneous phone and data connections. ISDN is slower than most LAN technologies but faster than standard modem communications.

**kernel**   The core of an operating system, the kernel provides essential services. Operating systems such as NT use a so-called microkernel, which provides only very basic services such as thread scheduling, for the sake of efficiency and stability.

**A**

**key**   A subfolder in the registry that can contain values. Also, a unique security token identifier.

**LAN (Local-Area Network)**   A network for allowing computers to communicate with one another. See *WAN*.

**LANMAN (LAN Manager)**   A term referring to network standards, such as Windows NT's current model, which are based on the LAN Manager product developed by Microsoft and IBM in the 1980s. LANMAN networking will be phased out in Windows NT 5.0, though it still will be supported.

**lease**   The period during which a client is associated with an IP address using DHCP. See *DHCP*.

**LMHOSTS (LAN Manager Hosts)**   A static list of NetBIOS names and their corresponding IP addresses. The use of LMHOSTS files predates the availability of the WINS service. See *WINS*.

**LocalTalk**   A standard for serial communications developed by Apple Computer. LocalTalk allows for simple network communications between Macintosh workstations and devices such as modems and printers; however, its slow data rate makes it unsuitable for LAN networking.

**LPC (Local Procedure Call)**   A facility for passing messages between client and server processes on a system. See *RPC*.

**LPD (Line Printer Daemon)**   A protocol for serving printers over TCP/IP originally developed for UNIX systems.

**LSL (Link Support Layer)**   Part of an ODI network stack, the LSL provides an interface between network device drivers and upper-layer networking protocols.

**m-node**   A method for NetBIOS name resolution over TCP/IP. A client configured to use m-node resolution first will attempt to use b-node resolution; if that fails, it will then attempt to use p-node resolution. See *b-node*, *h-node*, *p-node*, and *WINS*.

**MAC (Media Access Control)**   The unique hardware address of an Ethernet workstation; every Ethernet interface has a unique MAC address.

**master browser**   A system that maintains the list of all NetBIOS resources for a particular entity, whether a subnet or a domain. Browsers contact the master browser for the list of available NetBIOS resources, and master browsers are determined via the election process. See *domain master browser*, *election*, and *browser*.

**master domain**   A domain that provides user authentication services for subsidiary resource domains. See *domain*.

**micro channel**   A proprietary bus architecture designed by IBM that uses 32-bit width and automatic adapter configuration via software configuration files. Micro channel supports bus mastering and can support communication rates ranging from 10MB/sec to 160MB/sec. Micro channel no longer is common in PCs but can be found in other IBM computer systems.

**MIPS**   A series of processors made by the company MIPS (a subsidiary of Silicon Graphics) using RISC architecture. Future versions of Windows NT no longer will support MIPS systems. Also, an acronym for Millions of Instructions Per Second, a method of rating a processor's speed. MIPS measurements do not include data on how much work can be done in every instruction cycle, but merely list, theoretically, how many instructions the processor can perform each second.

**mirroring**   The process of maintaining multiple copies of data across multiple disks, thus reducing the risk of data loss due to a single disk's failure. See *RAID*.

**multihoming**   The process of placing a system on multiple subnets by using more than one network interface card. A multihomed system can perform services such as protocol routing.

**multitasking**   The process of switching system resources between processes and threads, thus seeming to allow multiple tasks to take place at once.

**NCP (NetWare Core Protocol)**   The protocol used for NetWare file, print, bindery, and NDS services.

**NDIS (Network Driver Interface Specification)**   The network driver model used by LANMAN and NT-based network clients, such as Windows for Workgroups, Windows 95, and Windows NT. See *ODI*.

**NDS (NetWare Directory Services)**   The replacement for the bindery, NDS uses an advanced X.500-based directory service to maintain a tree-hierarchy database of all network resources, including users, groups, servers, volumes, and printers, for ease of management and administration. NDS also provides distributed authentication and security management, as well as fault tolerance. NDS requires higher hardware and network overhead than other network implementations, but provides functionality not found in many other operating systems (although NT 5.0 promises the active directory, a similar service). NDS is based on pioneering directory services such as Banyan's StreetTalk, a part of its VINES UNIX-based network operating system, and acts as the model by which current and future directory services (such as the Active Directory) are judged.

A

**NetBEUI (NetBIOS Enhanced User Interface)**   Originally an enhanced version of the NetBIOS protocol designed by Microsoft and IBM, NetBEUI is now a highly efficient but unroutable protocol that replaces the original role of NetBIOS. NetBEUI can be used for NetBIOS networking in small, single-subnet workgroups, and provides efficient throughput and dynamic addressing. See *NetBIOS*.

**NetBIOS (Network Basic Input/Output System)**   Originally a subnet-only network protocol designed by IBM in the early 1980s, NetBIOS is now a standard for network APIs that can be transported over other protocols, such as NetBEUI, IPX/SPX, and TCP/IP. See *NetBEUI, IPX/SPX*, and *TCP/IP*.

**NetWare**   A Novell product for providing LAN file, print, and security services.

**network browser**   The service that implements NetBIOS browsing functionality on NT systems.

**NFS (Network File System)**   A UNIX standard that uses TCP/IP to mount remote file systems over the network as though they were local file systems.

**NIC (Network Interface Card)**   A generic term for any device, whether an actual adapter card or simply a port on a gateway device, which connects a computing system to a network.

**NOS (Network Operating System)**   An operating system with integrated support for networking services.

**NTFS**   The Windows NT File System. NTFS improves upon older file systems by providing highly efficient block sizing, file- and directory-level ACL security, fault tolerance via transaction logging, support for multiple streams within files, and advanced caching. NTFS uses more system overhead than FAT, but provides better reliability and higher performance on systems with enough resources to take advantage of its features. See *FAT*.

**NWLink**   Short for NetWare Link, the services and protocols provided by Microsoft to provide IPX/SPX support and communication with NetWare bindery services.

**ODI (Open Data Interface)**   A standard for implementing a network protocol stack that is used by NetWare and other network stacks.

**OLE**   Originally Object Linking and Embedding, OLE provides distributed object communication services. OLE is now a part of the larger service known as COM. See *COM* and *ActiveX*.

**OSI (Open Systems Interconnection)**   A reference model for implementing network protocol stacks. No real-world network stack is entirely OSI-compliant, although the OSI model remains a standard for describing how network stacks function.

**p-node**   Short for *point-to-point node*, a method for NetBIOS name resolution over TCP/IP. A client using p-node resolution will attempt to resolve NetBIOS names using a WINS server only. See *b-node, m-node, h-node,* and *WINS.*

**pagefile**   A file used by a virtual memory system to hold memory pages that temporarily are not being used by active processes, but which can be swapped back into RAM when called for. Also known as a swap file.

**PAP (Password Authentication Protocol)**   A password authentication protocol for use with dial-up connection protocols such as RAS and PPP.

**PCI (Peripheral Component Interconnect)**   A system bus designed by Intel but administered as a current industry standard, using 64-bit data width, with automatic adapter configuration and bus mastering. It supports data rates of up to 264MB/sec, although most PCs currently cannot transmit data across the bus at this rate.

**PDC (Primary Domain Controller)**   An NT Server that maintains the primary copy of a domain's SAM database. A PDC is required to create an NT domain, though some authentication services can be provided by backup domain controllers (BDCs). See *BDC.*

**physical layer**   The lowest layer of the OSI model, this layer refers to the actual physical cabling, as well as the method, whether electrical, optical, or otherwise, for transmitting digital data in a network.

**POSIX (Portable Systems Interface for Computing Environments)**   A standard for developing applications that can run across multiple operating systems without modification, needing only a recompilation of executable images. Windows NT supports the POSIX.1 standard, meaning that applications written to the POSIX.1 standard can run under Windows NT, requiring only a recompilation.

**PowerPC**   A series of processors made by IBM and Motorola that are used most commonly in Macintosh computers. Future versions of Windows NT no longer will support PowerPC systems.

**PPP (point-to-point protocol)**   A protocol designed to allow the encapsulation of other protocols, such as TCP/IP, over a modem connection.

**process**   A separate unit of application memory space, resources, and security access; each application has a process. A process consists of at least one thread of execution. See *thread.*

**protocol**   A standard for communication, defining rules for transmitting data in a fashion understandable to all parties supporting that protocol.

**RAID (Redundant Array of Inexpensive Disks)**   A system of standards for enhancing the performance and reliability of disk subsystems by using multiple disk drives or disk controllers.

**RAS (Remote Access Service)**   A dial-up server service that enables NT systems to serve connections over telephone lines, ISDN, or X.25 networks. RAS supports multiple dial-up protocols, including PPP, and can work using either multiport serial boards or via dedicated modem switching hardware.

**redirector**   A component that determines whether requests for mapped resources should be sent to the local file system or to the network stack, thus making access to those resources transparent to applications.

**registry**   A database that contains information used by the operating system and its applications, ranging from dynamic hardware configuration and system runtime information to application customization settings.

**replication**   The process of maintaining identical copies of a file system or parts of a file system on multiple NT systems to provide multiple access points and fault tolerance.

**RISC (Reduced Instruction Set Computing)**   A philosophy for CPU design which states that computing is best done by breaking up programs into small, efficient, low-functionality instructions that can be executed at very high clock rates. Examples of modern RISC chips include the DEC Alpha, the MIPS line of processors, and the PowerPC. See *CISC*.

**router**   A computing device designed to route network traffic from one subnet to its destinations. Any system with two or more NICs and the proper software can act as a router, though systems designed and dedicated to network routing are far more efficient and cost-effective.

**RPC (Remote Procedure Call)**   A facility for passing messages between client and server processes on systems over a network. See *LPC*.

**SAM (Security Accounts Manager)**   A component of Windows NT that maintains the list of security IDs for user and group objects and performs the authentication and verification for those objects. This term also refers to the database of users and groups for a system or a domain. See *SID*.

**SCSI (Small Computer Systems Interface)**   A bus architecture for mass storage and other devices, commonly used in servers and other systems where performance and extensibility are important.

**server** An NT (or other) system designed and tuned to provide centralized network services, such as network authentication, file and print, or application services. Alternatively, a version of the Windows NT product, which can act as a domain controller, designed specifically to provide these types of services. Alternatively, the service that enables clients to connect to an NT system's shared resources. See *workstation*.

**SID (Security ID)** A randomly generated number that represents a user, group, or other security object in a SAM database. See *SAM*.

**SMB (Server Message Block)** The protocol used by NT for file, print, and other services. See *NCP*.

**SMP (Symmetric Multiprocessing)** The capability of an operating system (such as Windows NT) to dynamically schedule individual threads on any processor on the system.

**SMTP (Simple Mail Transfer Protocol)** The protocol most commonly used for Internet e-mail transfer.

**SNMP (Simple Network Management Protocol)** A protocol used to allow network management of remote system and network resources.

**socket** A virtual connection using a network protocol such as TCP/IP. Alternatively, a standard for connecting a CPU to a mainboard.

**striping** The process of splitting data into chunks that are spread across multiple drives, thus increasing access speed. See *RAID*.

**STP (Shielded Twisted Pair)** A standard for cabling that uses a twisted pair of cable terminated with an RJ-45 connector. Similar to the RJ-11 standard used for telephone wiring, twisted pair is cheap and robust, and enhances the inherent interference-resistant qualities of a twisted wire pair by adding an external shielding wrapper. See *UTP*.

**subnet** A portion of a network separated by a router or other such device from the rest of the network. Alternatively, the addressing of that subnet in TCP/IP.

**TCP/IP (Transfer Control Protocol/Internet Protocol)** The standard protocol for communications over the Internet, TCP/IP is a protocol that supports efficient routing over large internetworks and generally requires static configuration of addressing information (although newer standards such as DHCP eliminate this need). See *DHCP*.

**Telnet** A protocol for terminal emulation communications over TCP/IP.

**TFTP (Trivial FTP)**   A protocol for file transfers over TCP/IP that is based on FTP. TFTP, however, provides no security.

**thread**   The smallest-possible unit of execution. Each process has at least one thread, but a process can have multiple threads to allow more efficient processing of complex tasks. See *process* and *fiber.*

**token passing**   A method for allowing each workstation on a network an equivalent number of opportunities to transmit on the wire, by using a "token" that is passed from workstation to workstation in sequential order. Contrast with CSMA/CD. See *Token Ring.*

**Token Ring**   A network standard developed by IBM that uses a token-passing method rather than competitive network access. Token Ring is more suitable for guaranteed workstation access to the network, though it can be less efficient under low-traffic situations. See *token passing.*

**trust relationship**   A secure connection established between two domains that enables the trusting domain to authenticate its resources to accounts existing in the trusted domain. Trust relationships can be two-way, but are not transitive in the current NTLM network model.

**UNC (Uniform Naming Convention)**   A standard for providing uniform resource names that are valid no matter where the resource is located or what type of resource it describes.

**unicode**   A standard for providing larger storage for characters, thus giving applications the capability to support multiple language sets much more easily than with ASCII.

**UPS (Uninterruptible Power Supply)**   A device designed to provide constant power to a workstation, thus allowing it to continue to function after a power failure. More advanced online UPS devices run on battery constantly, thus providing a steady source of power free of spikes and sags, and keep the batteries charged with the utility current supplied from the power jack.

**UTP (Unshielded Twisted Pair)**   A standard for cabling that uses a twisted pair of cable terminated with an RJ-45 connector. Similar to the RJ-11 standard used for telephone wiring, twisted pair is cheap and robust, and highly resistant to interference due to its twisted-pair configuration. See also *STP.*

**virtual memory**   A process for providing memory spaces that are not directly related to system RAM. This process allows memory spaces far larger than system RAM and removes the responsibility of an application to track its own memory addresses in RAM. See *pagefile.*

**WAN (Wide-Area Network)**   A series of interconnected LANs that provide networking services to a large campus or series of installations. See *LAN*.

**WINS (Windows Internet Name Service)**   A service for resolving NetBIOS names to TCP/IP addresses, WINS uses dynamic address configuration rather than static tables. See *DNS*.

**WINSOCK**   Short for Windows Sockets, a standard for network socketed communications over TCP/IP. The latest WINSOCK standard, Winsock 2.0, allows for socketed connections independent of network protocols.

**workgroup**   An organization of systems using peer-to-peer network resources. Workgroups lack centralized administration of accounts and access privileges. See *domain.*

**workstation**   An individual computer. Alternatively, the standard workstation product in the NT product line, capable of peer-to-peer networking as well as connection to larger, server-based networks and domains. Also the service that enables an NT system to act as a client to network resources on other NT systems. See *server.*

**WOW (Windows-on-Windows)**   The subsystem in Windows NT that provides an emulated DOS/Windows 3.*x* environment.

**x86**   Term for Intel's 80x86 line of processors, beginning with the 286 (though most system requirements that state an x86 processor actually require a 386 or higher). Later versions of these processors use names rather than numbers to enhance their trademarkability. The line includes the 286, 386, 486, Pentium, Pentium Pro, Pentium MMX, and Pentium II processors.

**zone**   A virtual organization of AppleTalk devices on a network. Also, in the context of DNS, a subtree of the domain name space. See *DNS*.

# Appendix B

# Answers to Review Questions

## Chapter 2, "Windows NT Architecture and Domain Design"

### Question 1

Answer: D

The server must be a primary domain controller to act as a security host. The only way for a stand-alone or member server to become a controller is to reinstall. (See section 2.6.1.)

### Question 2

Answer: A

The controller being available to validate the users is a byproduct of a poor solution. Because the links are not in place when the PDC is installed in Los Angeles, it has no way of knowing that there is already a PDC existing for the VALIDATE domain. The system administrator is successful in installing a PDC in a domain called VALIDATE; however, it is not the same VALIDATE domain the rest of the company is using. Because the unique security identifier (SID) for a domain is created when the PDC is installed, even after the links are up the systems will fail to communicate properly. (See section 2.6.5.)

### Question 3

Answer: D

Any account that is a member of the Domain Admins group on MASTERDOM could be used. (See section 2.6.4.)

## Question 4

Answer: A, B, C

Because each of the machines is running Microsoft NT they can act as an application server. It is true that the most likely choice on which to install SQL would be the member server because it does not have to validate domain logons. The question does not ask which is the best choice, only which systems are capable of performing the task. (See section 2.6.)

## Question 5

Answer: D

The PDC synchronizes its SAM database only with the backup domain controllers. Each BDC in a domain receives synchronization updates from the PDC to ensure that the SAM database held at the PDC is identical to that at each of the controllers. (See section 2.6.3.)

## Question 6

Answer: A, B

The system administrator has caused his own problem. When a domain account is modified, the change must first be recorded in the SAM database at the PDC. Over the course of time the update would be sent back to the BDC. Because of the excessive number of BDCs, synchronizing the accounts between all controllers will take a long time. When a BDC is requested to validate an account within the domain, it checks the account information against its copy of the SAM database. If the password is incorrect the BDC can pass the account information to the PDC for verification. If the PDC is too busy to respond, a delay or logon failure could result. (See section 2.6.3.)

## Question 7

Answer: D

The Security ID (SID) can be assigned only when an object is created. This is true of the SID assigned to controllers, users, and groups. When the system administrator installed the BDC to the wrong domain it was branded with the SID from that domain. Changing the name of the domain in the network properties would not replace the underlying SID. Unfortunately, reinstalling is the only way to move a BDC from one domain to another. (See section 2.6.5.)

## Question 8

Answer: True. Through the process of pass-through authentication, her validation request is passed from the PDC of Domain B to the PDC of Domain A, where her user account resides. (See section 2.7.1.)

### Question 9

Answer: B and D. Trust relationships require a permanent link between two NT servers that are PDCs. Trust relationships also require a common protocol. (See section 2.7.1.)

### Question 10

Answer: False. You cannot do this. Only a user account in a trusted domain can access a resource in a trusting domain, not the other way around. (See section 2.7.1.)

### Question 11

Answer: True. User accounts in a trusted domain can be put into a local group in a trusting domain. It is recommended, however, that the user account first be put into a global group and that the global group then be put into a local group. (See section 2.7.1.)

### Question 12

Answer: False. Remember that trusts are non-transitive. Just because Domain A trusts Domain B and Domain B trusts Domain C does not mean that Domain A trusts Domain C. (See section 2.7.1.)

### Question 13

Answer: True. Synchronization, however, may still occur. (See section 2.6.6.)

### Question 14

Answer: B. 40MB (See section 2.6.2.)

### Question 15

Answer: C. Seven. You need one domain controller for every 2,000 users. For 16,000 users, you need eight domain controllers: one PDC and seven BDCs. (See section 2.6.3.)

## Chapter 3, "Installing NT Server 4.0"

### Question 1

Answer: C

A RISC-based machine boots only from installed hardware. An NT installation is always done from the CD-ROM.

## Question 2

Answer: B

Because each machine supports standard VGA drivers, you need only one unattend answer file.

## Question 3

Answer: B

The NTHQ diagnostic disk is bootable and will confirm whether the hardware is NT compatible.

## Question 4

Answer: D

Because NetBEUI is not routable, the BDC and PDC would not be able to communicate over the router.

## Question 5

Answer: D

The repair disk utility enables you to update the repair information as well as create a new ERD.

## Question 6

Answer: A

Only one hard disk is required, although two partitions are necessary—one partition formatted with FAT and one formatted with NTFS.

## Question 7

Answer: B

In order to install a backup domain controller, it must be able to communicate with the primary domain controller.

## Question 8

Answer: A, B

Before TCP/IP can be initialized, both an IP address and subnet mask must be configured.

### Question 9

Answer: C

The DLC protocol is the protocol necessary to configure Hewlett-Packard JetDirect cards.

### Question 10

Answer: A, B

Both TCP/IP and NWLink are routable. DLC and NetBEUI are not.

### Question 11

Answer: All of the protocols can be forwarded by bridges.

### Question 12

Answer: D. NetBEUI

### Question 13

Answer: C

NWLink enables NetWare clients to communicate with NT servers.

### Question 14

Answer: A, B

The Gateway Services for NetWare provides client services on an NT server as well as Gateway services.

# Chapter 4, "Configuring the Environment"

### Question 1

Answer: B, C

The DependOnService entry lists the services that must be configured before the Messenger service starts.

A is incorrect. The Alerter service is not listed as a dependency. The Messenger service is not dependent on the Alerter service. The Alerter service is, however, dependent on the Messenger service to deliver the alerts it generates. The recipients of the alert also must be running the Messenger service.

B is correct. The LanmanWorkstation is synonymous with workstation. Because it is in the list of dependencies it would be required. (See section 4.4.)

C is correct. NetBIOS is listed in the list of dependencies. If the NetBIOS interface does not load properly, the Messenger service will fail.

D is incorrect. The Server service is not included in the dependency list.

## Question 2

Answer: E

The StartValue is used to categorize services.

Answer A is incorrect. A StartValue of 0x0 designates the service as one that will be activated at boot time. These services will be called by the NTLDR on x86-based machines.

Answer B is incorrect. A StartValue of 0x1 is used to represent a critical service that is called during the initialization phase.

Answer C is incorrect. A StartValue of 0x2 identifies services that are to be started automatically after NT has initialized. The Workstation and Server services receive a 0x2 StartValue by default.

Answer D is incorrect. A StartValue of 0x3 is assigned to services that must be started manually by the user or on demand by another process.

Answer E is correct. A StartValue of 0x4 is used to identify a service as disabled. (See section 4.5.)

## Question 3

Answer: C

Pausing the Server service often is done before sending a message to users to log off the server. Pausing the Server service guarantees that no new users will attach.

Answer A is incorrect. Pausing the Server service will not disconnect the current users. Stopping the Server service would disconnect the users.

Answer B is incorrect. The Alerter service would not generate a message based on the Server service being paused. In any case, the messages generated by the Alerter service are directed to individual people or computers, not to all connected users.

Answer C is correct. Pausing the Server service prevents additional users from attaching. (See section 4.6.3.)

Answer D is incorrect. The Workstation service is independent of the Server service.

## Question 4

Answer: A, B, D

Continuing the Server service will not disconnect the users.

Answers A, B, and D are all equally correct. (See section 4.6.3.)

Answer C is incorrect. The command issued in answer C would not work. Technically, the Server service does not need to be started because it was not stopped. The error message that would be received is shown in Figure B.1.

**Figure B.1.**

*Answer C would return an error message.*

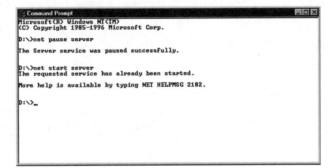

```
Command Prompt                                                      _ □ ✕
Microsoft(R) Windows NT(TM)
(C) Copyright 1985-1996 Microsoft Corp.

D:\>net pause server

The Server service was paused successfully.

D:\>net start server
The requested service has already been started.

More help is available by typing NET HELPMSG 2182.

D:\>_
```

## Question 5

Answer: C

The NT server is a member of DomainC. The account assigned to a service must come from the local SAM database of the member server, the SAM database of the local domain (DomainC), or the SAM database of a trusted domain.

Neither DomainA nor DomainB are trusted domains. They are referred to as trusting domains. (See section 4.2.)

## Question 6

Answer: D

NTBACKUP.EXE does not provide a scheduling function. It is quite common to create a batch file that contains the command-line parameters to execute NTBACKUP.EXE. To execute the batch file at specific times, the administrator creates a job to be carried out by the schedule service using either AT.EXE or WINAT.EXE. (See section 4.4.3.)

B

## Question 7

Answer: A, D

Answer A is correct. The Messenger service delivers the alert message. The alerts can be sent to either a user or a computer. (See section 4.4.4.)

Answer B is incorrect. The schedule service is used with AT.EXE or WINAT.EXE to run scheduled events.

Answer C is incorrect. The signal service does not exist as an NT service.

Answer D is correct. The Alerter service is of course required to generate the alert message.

## Question 8

Answer: C

By assigning the account to the directory replicator service through Server Manager or Control Panel, Services, the account would have been granted the right to log on as a service automatically. The right could also be granted to an account through User Manager, User Rights. (See section 4.6.2.)

When writing the question I thought it would be too much to expect people to be aware that an account is granted the right to log on as a service as a byproduct of being assigned to the Directory Replicator service. The question simply asks where one would go to confirm the right was assigned. This could only be done through User Manager, User Rights.

Answer A is incorrect. Server Manager could be used to assign the account to the Directory Replicator service but not to verify the right to log on as a service.

## Question 9

Answer: B

Answer A is incorrect. If a service is set to Disabled it cannot be started by the user or at the request of another service.

Answer B is correct. Because the service was set to Manual, the server did not attempt to start it after rebooting. A Manual service can be started by the user or at the request of another service. (See section 4.6.2.)

Answer C is incorrect. If the service were set to Automatic, the system would have attempted to start it upon reboot. If the service had simply failed to start, an error message most likely would have been displayed.

Answer D is incorrect. If the service account was not properly configured, the Net Start command would not have worked properly.

## Question 10

Answer: D

The Netlogon service is used to synchronize the SAM database between the PDC and BDCs. By pausing the Netlogon service, the PDC will not have to validate logon attempts to the domain but can concentrate on synchronizing the SAM database. (See section 4.6.3.)

Answer A is incorrect. Stopping the Server service also would stop the Netlogon service. This would prevent continued synchronization.

Answer B is incorrect. Pausing the Server service would not pause the Netlogon service. Although no additional users would be able to access the server, the PDC would continue to validate domain accounts.

Answer C is incorrect. Stopping the Netlogon service would stop synchronization.

Answer D is correct. The Netlogon service on the PDC can be paused to allow the system to concentrate on synchronizing the SAM database with the BDCs. The BDCs will continue to perform domain validation for the users.

## Question 11

Answer: D

An example would be when you double-click a text file and it is loaded automatically into Notepad.exe. This is based on the association of text files with Notepad. (See section 4.3.)

File associations and information regarding how applications interact via OLE is implemented in HKEY_CLASSES_ROOT.

HKEY_CURRENT_CONFIG contains the current hardware configuration profile loaded during the boot process.

HKEY_CURRENT_USER is the profile for the user presently logged on to the system.

HKEY_LOCAL_MACHINE contains information about the local computer system's hardware and operating system.

## Question 12

Answer: C

If the system is mistakenly configured in a way that prevents the system from starting properly, you can attempt to initialize NT using the LastKnownGood control set. The system automatically creates the LastKnownGood control set each time a user logs on to the system following a reboot of the system. This is updated every time a user logs on. (See section 4.3.)

## Question 13

Answer: D

The NT tape backup utility, NTBACKUP, can perform both online backups and restorations of the registry.

In almost all cases, the use of a tape backup utility will be more efficient than any means using disks. (See section 4.3.2.)

The Save Key feature in REGEDT32 will save only that key, not the entire registry.

Mirroring will not back up the entire registry because parts of it are stored in RAM.

The repair disk utility can be used to update the compressed copies of the registry databases in the %SYSTEMROOT%\repair directory, or create an emergency repair disk.

## Question 14

Answer: A

The HARDWARE hive or key is built dynamically during the boot process, which is why the HARDWARE key is often referred to as being volatile. The other keys have both a database file and a log file. (See section 4.3.)

On Intel-based systems the HARDWARE key is built from information provided by NTDETECT.COM; RISC-based machines retrieve the information from firmware.

## Question 15

Answer: B, D

Because the change involves modification of the physical hardware it will be recorded in HKEY_LOCAL_MACHINE and will affect all users. (See section 4.3.)

## Question 16

Answer: A, C

Swapping the mouse buttons is simply a preference that the administrator has. Because this option is applied when the administrator is logged on, the settings are placed in HKEY_CURRENT_USER (which at the time of making the changes would be the administrator's settings). The settings would be applied only when the administrator was logged on. (See section 4.3.)

## Question 17

Answer: B

The names NTUSER.DAT and NTUSER.DAT.LOG can be used by all users of the system, because the system can maintain a separate set of the files in a unique directory for each user below \%SYSTEM_ROOT%\PROFILES\%USERNAME%. (See section 4.3.)

Answer B is correct. The NTUSER.DAT and NTUSER.DAT.LOG files represent the local user's profile.

## Question 18

Answer: C

The key to the question is in the fact that the administrator logged on to the system before rebooting and using the LastKnownGood control set. Logging on to the system would have updated the LastKnownGood control set to contain the improper parameters. (See section 4.3.)

When the administrator logged on successfully at the server, the Last Known Good configuration was saved, regardless of the fact that the configuration was incorrect.

## Question 19

Answer: B

Although the emergency repair disk can be used to restore the configuration, and then only if it has been updated since the network card was installed, it is not the fastest method. The fastest and simplest method would be to simply boot using the Last Known Good configuration. (See section 4.3.)

## Question 20

Answer: C

The failure of one service or driver, such as the network card, could cause a chain of dependency service failures. User rights would not affect the start of services, because they start as part of the system. (See section 4.6.)

B

# Chapter 5, "Managing Local File Systems"

## Question 1

Answer: A, B

X86-based computers can use either FAT or NTFS partitions to house the system or boot files. Because the NTLDR file on x86-based systems initializes the mini-file system drivers for both FAT and NTFS, the file can reside on either a FAT or NTFS partition. System files, however, may not reside on a stripe set or volume set. (See section 5.7.3.)

## Question 2

Answer: A, B

The key is to first remember that the files will not be directly retrieved by the DOS-based clients. They simply make requests to the file server. Because the file server is running on top of NT all of these file systems can be accessed. The second issue is that only FAT and NTFS are file systems that can be applied to a hard disk; CDFS is for CD-ROMs. (See section 5.2.1.)

## Question 3

Answer: D

When a file or directory exceeds the standard 8.3 naming conventions it receives both a long and short filename. The filename 1997AC~1.doc was derived by taking the first six valid characters of the filename (1997AC), appending a unique ID (~1, ~2, and so on) and finally attaching the extension (.doc). (See section 5.2.)

## Question 4

Answer: A, C

Answer A is correct. A RISC-based computer does not utilize NTLDR and therefore does not initialize the mini-file system drivers required on boot to access NTFS as its system partition. Other partitions on a RISC-based computer can be either DOS or NTFS. (See section 5.2.1.)

Answer C is correct. Multi-booting into DOS and NT will require the system partition to be FAT. If the system partition were later converted to NTFS it would be inaccessible to DOS. (See section 5.2.1.)

## Question 5

Answer: A, B, C

When a folder is moved to a different partition it does not maintain its ACL. Also, the original share would no longer be valid because it would point to a location that no longer exists. (See section 5.4.)

Answer A is correct. A new ACL would have been generated based on the ACL of the folder on the new partition it was made a subdirectory of.

Answer B is correct. The move would delete the original folder and corresponding share, so it would need to be re-created.

Answer C is correct. Because the share is being re-created it will initially have permissions that allow Everyone Full Control.

## Question 6

Answer: C

Although the share has given administrators Full Control, the NTFS security will not allow the administrators access. If a user is a member of both the Administrators and Accounting groups, the effective rights would be Change. (See section 5.4.)

## Question 7

Answer: B

Full Control in a directory grants the hidden right File Delete Child, which enables you to delete files to which you otherwise would not have permission. This is required for POSIX compliance.

You might have Delete—or Change, which encompasses Delete—on a directory level, but this is the right to delete the directory itself, not the files within it. (See section 5.4.)

## Question 8

Answer: C, D

The question is testing your knowledge of the Take Ownership right. If you are the owner of a file or directory you have the ability to change the permissions. (See section 5.4.1.)

B

## Question 9

Answer: B

All users, including guests, are members of the group Everyone. It is not uncommon to have individual file rights that exceed the rights against the directory itself. (See section 5.4.1.)

## Question 10

Answer: C

The default ACL is designed to be most permissive. This is why it is often necessary to remove the Everyone group from the ACL when assigning restrictions. (See section 5.4.2.)

## Question 11

Answer: A

Only one partition can be marked as active at one time. The active partition will be the one from which the system will attempt to boot. Remember that the partition from which NT boots is called the system partition. (See section 5.7.)

## Question 12

Answer: A

A volume set requires from 2 to 32 segments; however, the segments do not need to all come from separate physical disks. A single volume set can span from 1 to 32 physical disks. (See section 5.7.3.)

## Question 13

Answer: D

An equal amount of space is taken from each of the areas making up the stripe set. You might think that the answer should be C, or 300MB, but a stripe set can be created from between 2 and 32 disks. By utilizing only the two disks with the largest common space between them you can create a stripe set of 400MB. (See section 5.7.4.)

## Question 14

Answer: A, D

A single physical drive can contain a maximum of four partitions. They can be either four primary partitions or three primaries and one extended. (See section 5.7.)

## Question 15

Answer: C

Either file system can be used when the volume set is created from free space. However, in order to extend the volume set it must be NTFS. (See section 5.7.3.)

## Question 16

Answer: B, C, D

When any disk that is a member of a volume set fails, the data across the entire volume set is lost. Because the scenario did not specify whether there was sufficient free space on the remaining drives on which to re-create the volume set it is necessary to replace the failed drive. The option to regenerate the volume set does not exist, so re-creating the volume set will be necessary. After the volume set has been re-created the data must be restored from backup. (See section 5.7.3.)

## Question 17

Answer: A

A cluster size can be specified up to 128KB when formatting a partition from the command prompt. If a cluster size of 64KB was specified, a 128KB file could be stored using only two clusters versus requiring 32 4KB clusters. (See section 5.7.4.)

## Question 18

Answer: A, C

The sole purpose of stripe sets without parity is to increase disk performance. Only NTFS volume sets can be extended. Watch out for answers like this one on the exam where the selection is offered in the negative. (See section 5.7.4.)

## Question 19

Answer: C

You can use the Disk Administrator to assign a different drive letter to a CD-ROM drive. The change is immediately put into effect unless the drive is in use. (See section 5.7.1.)

## Question 20

Answer: C

The existing 100MB FAT partition could be converted to NTFS. After the data partition is NTFS it could be extended over the two areas of free space to form a single volume set of 700MB. Because the 200MB NTFS partition contains system/boot files, it cannot become part of a volume set. (See section 5.7.2.)

B

# Chapter 6, "Data Protection: Fault Tolerance and NT Backup"

## Question 1

Answer: All of the above. Although not all of the levels provide fault tolerance, they can all be run on NT Server 4.0 regardless of the role they have in the domain. (See section 6.2.1.)

## Question 2

Answer: B, D

Disk duplexing gains additional fault tolerance over disk mirroring by having two controllers. (See section 6.3.)

## Question 3

Answer: C

You would need to restore the last full backup and then apply each of the successive incrementals. (See section 6.6.1.)

## Question 4

Answer: A, D

Stripe sets with parity provide excellent read capabilities along with fault tolerance. Although disk mirroring will increase the read capacity to a certain extent, the gain is offset by a decrease in write speed. (See sections 6.3 and 6.4.)

## Question 5

Answer: C

Stripe sets are the fastest disk configuration; however, they do not provide fault tolerance. (See section 6.4.2.)

## Question 6

Answer: A, B, C

These files are the only required files. NTOSKRNL.EXE is located on the BOOT partition and NTBOOTDD.SYS is only required in the case of having a SCSI controller where the BIOS is not enabled. (See section 6.5.1.)

### Question 7

Answer: C

In essence, the end result is the same as a copy. Because FAT does not support the permissions, they are lost. (See section 6.6.2.)

### Question 8

Answer: A

If more than one drive fails, the stripe set with parity cannot be regenerated. (See section 6.4.)

### Question 9

Answer: A

By restricting access to the owner or administrator, you limit the number of people who can restore the data, thereby increasing the security level. (See section 6.6.2.)

### Question 10

Answer: B

The last tape contains the tape catalog. If the last tape in a family set is damaged, the /missingtape option can be used to bypass the catalog. (See section 6.6.2.)

# Chapter 7, "Managing Users and Groups"

### Question 1

Answer: D

The NetLogon service provides the synchronization. The frequency of replication can be controlled through registry settings.

### Question 2

Answer: A, B

The administrator account is the only account that cannot be disabled. It is also not possible to rename the administrator account.

### Question 3

Answer: B

Unlike the administrator account, the guest account can be disabled; it cannot, however, be deleted.

B

## Question 4

Answer: True

The SID is a unique number that will not be regenerated based upon user name.

## Question 5

Answer: True

The SID remains with the user account until it is deleted. This is helpful if the person in a particular job function changes.

## Question 6

Answer: A

AGLP is designed around the ability to place global groups into local groups.

## Question 7

Answer: A, B

Both global groups and users from trusted domains can be made local group members.

## Question 8

Answer: D

A global group can contain only global users from the same domain.

## Question 9

Answer: A, B

Auditing of the printer requires auditing of file and object access to report print jobs.

## Question 10

Answer: A, D

Modifying the computer will affect HKEY_LOCAL_MACHINE, and modifying the user will change HKEY_CURRENT_USER.

## Question 11

Answer: C

Users can be restricted to selected Windows-based applications in the policy settings.

# Chapter 8, "Managing Network Resources"

## Question 1

Answer: B, C, D

Remember that members of the Domain Admins global group are empowered by being members of the Administrators local group. (See section 8.2.)

## Question 2

Answer: B

Only the Server service is required. (See section 8.2.2.)

## Question 3

Answer: B

Permissions applied to the Network group apply only when you are gaining access from across the network. (See section 8.2.3.)

## Question 4

Answer: A

The Server Manager allows an administrator to manage both local and remote share points. (See section 8.6.1.)

## Question 5

Answer: D

The user's effective rights can be blocked by NTFS settings. (See section 8.5.1.)

## Question 6

Answer: C

Pausing the Server service is the safest method because it will not disconnect currently attached users. (See section 8.6.1.)

## Question 7

Answer: B

Share names ending with a $ are always hidden; however, they do not necessarily imply that a share is for administrators only. (See section 8.6.1.)

## Question 8

Answer: C

Only users with the right to control shares will see directories as shared. (See section 8.6.)

## Question 9

Answer: C

Remember AGLP, which means Accounts go into Global groups, which go into Local groups, and Permissions are granted using the local groups. (See section 8.3.1.)

## Question 10

Answer: C

By keeping the documents in the spooler even after they have been printed, they can be reprinted if the printer jams from outside the client application. (See section 8.8.)

## Question 11

Answer: B

Although it is not required that each of the printer devices be physically identical, each of the print devices must support a common driver. (See section 8.8.)

## Question 12

Answer: C

Until the DLC protocol is installed on the print server, the option to print to the HP network port does not appear. (See section 8.8.2.)

## Question 13

Answer: B, C, D

The print server is the proper location to load the drivers for all clients that are capable of requesting the driver to be downloaded transparently. The Windows for Workgroups clients do not support the transparent download and so must be configured independently. (See section 8.8.4.)

## Question 14

Answer: A, C, D

After the printer is installed, it is necessary to remove the default permissions granted to the Everyone group and to grant permissions to the Accounting group. If No Access were granted to Everyone this would also prohibit members of the Accounting group from printing. (See section 8.9.1.)

## Question 15

Answer: A, B, C

When a printer is created, Full Control is granted to Administrators, Server Operators, and Print Managers.

## Question 16

Answer: C

An unavailable printer will still accept print jobs but will hold them until it is scheduled to print before sending them to the print device. (See section 8.9.2.)

## Question 17

Answer: C

By printing to a printer with a higher priority, jobs will be ordered ahead of those coming from a printer configured with default settings. (See section 8.9.2.)

## Question 18

Answer: C

By having the right to Manage Documents a user is capable of managing other persons' print jobs. (See section 8.9.2.)

## Question 19

Answer: D

The key is that the client is gaining access via the gateway. The client can use any protocol supported by the gateway. Finally, although the NetWare server will not pass the print driver to the client, the gateway will provide the proper driver; the driver on the gateway would have been already installed manually. (See section 8.10.1.)

# Chapter 9, "NT Server 4.0 Network Clients"

## Question 1

Answers: A, B, D

Both Windows 95 and Windows NT support both TCP/IP for Internet as well as NT Server 4.0 exchanges. They also support IPX/SPX compatibility to allow NetWare access. LAN Manager 2.2c client for MS-DOS comes with NetWare connection software. It is also TCP/IP compatible to connect with NT Server 4.0 and the Internet. (See section 9.2.)

### Question 2

Answer: C

The Pentium 133 can be configured for Windows NT 4.0 Workstation. Adding administration tools to the NT 4.0 Workstation will allow for management of DHCP and WINS, as well as Server Manager and User Manager for Domains. (See section 9.2.3.)

### Question 3

Answer: D

Only NTFS can provide support for Services for Macintosh. (See section 9.2.5.)

### Question 4

Answer: A

In Windows 95 with Server Tools, Windows Explorer is used to manage all file and print sharing assignments. (See section 9.2.4.)

### Question 5

Answer: A, B, C

To install Windows 95 you must have shared the Win95 subdirectory of the Clients directory. You then must create a Network Installation Disk and boot from that disk the computer on which you want to install Windows 95. There is no Windows 95 Setup Disks option in the Disk Administrator Tools. (See section 9.2.1.)

### Question 6

Answer: D

Network Client Administrator is used to create Network Installation Startup disks. (See section 9.2.1.)

# Chapter 10, "Optimizing Your Server"

### Question 1

Answer: A, C

By obtaining baseline information at nonpeak times, you can identify trends in network utilization. (See section 10.1.)

## Question 2

Answer: C

The chart view provides real-time data for a quick view of the health of your server. (See section 10.2.1.)

Answer A. The Log view is best for obtaining data over time to be used for the creation of a baseline. (See section 10.2.2.)

Answer B. The Alert view provides notification when threshold parameters are exceeded. (See section 10.2.3.)

Answer D. The Report view displays summary information that is updated periodically. This allows the identification of objects that you might need to monitor further. (See section 10.2.4.)

## Question 3

Answer: A

You must start DISKPERF before Performance Monitor can collect information on the physical disk. (See section 10.1.2.)

## Question 4

Answer: True

A short explanation of the purpose of each counter is available from the Explain button. (See section 10.3.)

## Question 5

Answer: C

After selecting the Processor object and the counter you are interested in monitoring, you must set this counter for each processor by selecting the appropriate instance. (See section 10.3.1.)

## Question 6

Answer: A

Excessive paging shows up as increased physical disk activity and increased processor usage. The solution to this problem is to add more memory. (See section 10.3.5.)

B

### Question 7

Answer: D

By setting a capture filter, you can acquire the information in which you are interested while keeping the size of the captured file small. Although you also can set a Display Filter to see the data in which you are interested, the size of your captured file would be considerably larger. (See section 10.4.1.)

### Question 8

Answer: D

Performance monitor allows for the monitoring of remote computers. By configuring the alert to send you a message when the threshold has been exceeded, you will be notified promptly. (See section 10.3.11.)

### Question 9

Answer: A, C, D

The Task Manager provides information on active applications and processes. In addition, it provides critical information on CPU and memory utilization. (See section 10.5.)

### Question 10

Answer: B

The Process Viewer provides you with detailed information on the memory allocation of any active processes. (See section 10.5.2.)

# Chapter 11, "Configuring and Optimizing NT 4.0 Services"

### Question 1

Answer: B

The Dynamic Host Configuration Protocol is used to dynamically assign IP addresses used by TCP/IP. Both A and C are different protocols. (See section 11.2.)

### Question 2

Answer: B

Your routers must be RFC-1542-compliant and be able to forward BOOTP packets. (See section 11.2.)

## Question 3

Answer: A

IPCONFIG displays the IP address, subnet mask, and default gateway for your computer. (See section 11.2.2.)

## Question 4

Answer: C

When providing redundancy, configure 75 percent of the local addresses on each DHCP server. The remaining 25 percent of the addresses can be configured on another DHCP server to provide backup address assignment. (See section 11.2.4.)

## Question 5

Answer: C

As pull partners. You can set a time interval for replication by using a pull partner. This would enable you to configure replication to occur during off-peak periods of network utilization. (See section 11.4.3.)

## Question 6

Answer: A

By using the WINS Manager, you could import the LMHOSTS file from the Static Mappings control dialog box. (See section 11.4.4.)

## Question 7

Answer: A and D

You could use a HOSTS file located on each of the non-WINS-enabled client or use DNS. (See section 11.4.4.)

## Question 8

Answer: A and B

It allows multiple computers on a network to have the same host name. It also places the responsibility for naming at the level of the organization controlling a particular domain level. (See section 11.5.)

## Question 9

Answer: B

From a master name server. (See section 11.5.1.)

**B**

## Question 10

Answer: D

A unique IP address for each of the virtual servers must be bound to your network adapter card. (See section 11.7.1.)

## Question 11

Answer: A

Directory replication is used primarily for the replication of logon scripts, system policy files, and other commonly used information. (See section 11.6.2.)

## Question 12

Answer: C

The Server Manager is used to configure directory replication. (See section 11.6.2.)

## Question 13

Answer: B

The parameters for synchronization are located in the `HKEY__LOCAL_MACHINE` hive under `System\CurrentControlSet\Service\Netlogon\Parameters`.

## Question 14

Answer: D

By comparing newly captured data with baseline data, you can determine the source of the traffic increase.

## Question 15

Answer: C

By pointing your clients to the DNS most likely to be capable of resolving its name queries, you would decrease the need for recursive lookups.

## Question 16

Answer: B

By limiting the amount of bandwidth that the IIS uses, you ensure the availability of adequate bandwidth for performing other network functions, including logon authentication.

### Question 17

Answer: C

By lengthening the time between WINS replication, you reduce the amount of traffic on the WAN link.

### Question 18

Answer: C

By lengthening the `Interval` parameter on the export server and the `Pulse` parameter on the import workstation, you decrease the frequency of replication resulting in decreased traffic across the WAN link.

### Question 19

Answer: C

The Replication Governor determines the amount of bandwidth that can be utilized for synchronization, whereas the Pulse Concurrency determines the number of BDCs that can be simultaneously synchronized. By adjusting these two parameters, you would decrease the amount of bandwidth utilized for synchronization at any one time. However, you would lengthen the amount of time it takes to synchronize your entire domain.

### Question 20

Answer: B

Generally, if NT servers or workstations are available to act as browsers, you should exclude Windows 95 clients from being master or backup browsers.

### Question 21

Answer: C

Stopping unnecessary services decreases the number of registrations each computer must make with the WINS server.

# Chapter 12, "Managing a Heterogeneous Environment"

### Question 1

Answer: D

Installing the NWLink protocol is the only thing you must install for Windows NT machines to access client/server applications on a NetWare server.

## Question 2

Answer: B

When you install Gateway Services for NetWare, NWLink is also installed.

Installing the GSNW also gives you client capabilities to the NetWare server. For this service to work, you must also install NWLink. Note that if you install the GSNW, NWLink is installed automatically.

## Question 3

Answer: A

802.2 is the default protocol. (See section 12.3.3.)

## Question 4

Answer: A

802.2 is the standard frame type for NetWare 3.12 and later versions. For NetWare 3.11 and earlier versions, 802.3 is the standard. (See section 12.3.3.)

## Question 5

Answer: B

The GSNW acts as a translator between the SMBs used by Microsoft networks and the NCPs used on NetWare networks. (See section 12.2.)

## Question 6

Answer: C

There must be a group called NTGATEWAY on the NetWare server, of which the gateway user must be a member. All security can then be set on the NTGATEWAY group. (See section 12.2.2.)

## Question 7

Answer: D

Installing the NWLink protocol is the only thing you must do for NetWare clients to access client/server applications on a Windows NT server. Expect to see client/server applications listed on the exam rather than the words "client/server." (See section 12.3.1.)

## Question 8

Answer: D

In this example, the NetWare logon script was constructed to identify the Engineering group and map a virtual drive to its files. NWCONV does not migrate logon scripts.

The conditional MAP instruction was overlooked by the administrator and must be reconstructed as either a logon script or profile under Windows NT. (See section 12.7.1.)

## Question 9

Answer: D

The ERROR.LOG file is generated each time NWCONV is executed and explicitly lists the errors encountered while performing a migration. (See section 12.9.)

## Question 10

Answer: C

The 3.1x servers have a separate and individual bindery and therefore each server has its own user and group information. Each must be identified for migration under this situation. Meanwhile, only one 4.1x server must be accessed because all user objects are specified in the NDS. (See section 12.6.)

## Question 11

Answer: A

You do not need to be directly logged onto the NetWare server; the administrator simply requires the supervisor account for access. As long as NT can see the NetWare server on the network and the administrator has supervisor access, you can execute NWCONV. (See section 12.4.)

## Question 12

Answer: B

The Modify button on the File Options dialog box allows the administrator to define new paths and share names. Mapping files are not constructed or used during file migration. (See section 12.7.1.)

## Question 13

Answer: False. Supervisor access is required.

## Question 14

Answer: True. If NetWare defaults are migrated, they are expressed as individual restrictions to Windows NT and thus supersede the domain account policy. (See section 12.2.2.)

# Chapter 13, "RAS Dial-In Solutions"

## Question 1

Answer: B

NT Server can support up to 256 simultaneous questions. NT Workstation can support only one. (See section 13.2.)

## Question 2

Answer: A, B, and E

Serial Line Interface Protocol (SLIP), Point-to-Point Protocol (PPP), RAS Protocol, and NetBIOS Gateway are the supported remote access protocols. (See section 13.3.1.)

## Question 3

Answer: A and C

NetBEUI, TCP/IP, and IPX are supported networking protocols. (See section 13.3.2.)

## Question 4

Answer: A and C

There are two steps to this. First, you must decide the range of IP addresses you want to assign and enter the values in the RAS Server TCP/IP Configuration dialog box (see Figure 13.7). You must also exclude this range of addresses from the scope on the DHCP server, if the ranges you selected fall within that scope. (See section 13.3.2.)

## Question 5

Answer: B and D

The two best things you can do to increase the security of dial-in access are to set predetermined callback numbers and enable auditing of your resources. Note that the unified Windows NT logon authentication provides the best security. This feature is enabled by default. (See section 13.4.)

## Question 6

Answer: A

You must configure both the RAS Server and the remote client machine with the Point-to-Point Tunneling Protocol. This creates a secure connection by using one protocol to tunnel through the TCP/IP protocol of the Internet. (See section 13.3.2.)

### Question 7

Answer: C

Although you could use the Dial-Up Networking Monitor utility to see a snapshot of the current connections and connection times, it probably is better to create a log by using Performance Monitor. This will enable you to see specifically how many of your incoming lines are utilized and how much each is being used. (See section 13.6.2.)

### Question 8

Answer: B and C

The most likely problem is that this user's user account has not been granted dial-in access. It also is possible that there is a problem with the user account itself, such as an incorrect password or invalid logon times set. (See section 13.8.1.)

**B**

# Chapter 14, "NT Server Troubleshooting Guidelines"

### Question 1

Answer: A, C, D, E

These four files are necessary for you to boot up Windows NT. You do not need the others because either they are not necessary or pertain only to RISC-based machines. Read the question carefully. (See section 14.3.)

### Question 2

Answer: B, E, G

You need these three files to boot up Windows NT. The rest of the files pertain only to Intel-based machines. (See section 14.3.)

### Question 3

Answer: B, E

You can copy the file from a boot disk created for this server or you can replace it by performing an emergency repair. The BOOTSECT.DOS file is computer-specific, so you cannot copy it from another server. (See section 14.3.)

## Question 4

Answer: D

BIOS is not on the SCSI adapters, and so the ARC name begins with scsi. Windows NT is on the first controller. Numbering starts with 0, and so scsi is (0). Because it is on the first hard disk and the disk is SCSI, disk is (0). The rdisk only pertains when you use multi, so you don't need it, and thus it is (0). Partition numbering begins with 1, not 0. Because Windows NT is on the second partition, it is (2). (See section 14.3.2.)

## Question 5

Answer: B

Although an emergency repair would fix the problem (if you did not update after you installed the drive), the easiest way is to use the Last Known Configuration option, which would have removed the CD-ROM configuration. (See section 14.3.3.)

## Question 6

Answer: A

The Last Known Good was saved when you logged on. Therefore, it will not remove the new configuration information. You can't get the computer to run long enough to run the backup utility, and so your only resort is to perform an emergency repair. (See section 14.3.3.)

## Question 7

Answer: D

Using a boot disk is the fastest way to bypass missing boot files. (See section 14.3.)

## Question 8

Answer: D

Using a boot disk is the fastest way to bypass missing boot files. (See section 14.3.)

# Appendix C

# The Employable MCSE

Having an MCSE is not quite the same as having a Harvard MBA, but it certainly will open some doors. The trick is to know which doors to go through and which to shut. Applying the principles laid out in this guide will help you identify prospective employment opportunities and prepare yourself for overcoming the technical interview.

There are countless opportunities open to MCSEs worldwide. Only you can determine in the end which to pursue in order to attain your personal goals.

## C.1. Valuing Your Certification

No doubt, achieving your MCSE certification was or will be a significant milestone in your life. Only a small fraction of those who claim to be IS professionals are certified. This alone sets you and your certification apart. In the jungle of employability, having an MCSE certification puts you a little "higher on the food chain." Remember that your certification belongs to you.

**Note**
If you want a more quantitative valuation of your certification, look at *MCP Magazine's* Annual Salary Survey. You can find the survey at http:// www.mcpmag.com.

## C.1.1. Giving the Most, Getting the Most

The greater your degree of flexibility, the more valuable you can make yourself to your current or future employer. Your MCSE certification confirms to others that you have a set of quality skills. However, those skills themselves won't do the work for you. The more willing you are to travel, work as part of a team, and go the extra mile, the more opportunities you will have.

# C.2. Specializing in Your Field

Not many years ago it would have been possible to be skilled in most, if not all, of the items in the Microsoft product line. Today, however, there are over 10 electives to choose from in the MCSE program alone.

No one is expecting you to be an expert in every aspect of every application. To be truly employable you must have not only a breadth of understanding on a wide range of topics but also a depth of knowledge in a specific field.

## C.2.1. Focusing Your Skills

By specializing in a specific field you can set yourself apart not only from the uncertified, but also from the certified individuals who don't know how to focus their skills. Focusing your skills does not mean resting on your laurels. If, for example, you decide to focus on Internet solutions, this easily could require detailed knowledge of Microsoft Proxy Server, IIS, Index Server, SQL Server, VBScript, and Visual J++. Regardless of the area of expertise you pursue, achieving and maintaining your knowledge base will require continued perseverance.

The employable MCSE won't even stop there. Microsoft might be your bread and butter, but that doesn't mean you can ignore other industry solutions, complementary products, and certifications.

## C.2.2. Maintaining Your Certifications

You must maintain your certifications. As Microsoft updates its products, there is always a chance that a test you have used to achieve your certification will be retired. Although Microsoft will inform you if you must take a specific exam to maintain your certification, it is better to be proactive, which means monitoring the MCSE forum for details regarding certification revisions. You can find the latest requirements at www.microsoft.com/mcse.

When a test is being retired a beta exam is often offered in advance of the final replacement. Beta exams are a great way to maintain or increase your certifications, often at a reduced cost.

## C.2.3. Increasing Your Certifications

Saying that you have too many certifications is like saying you have too many trump cards. Multiple certifications let you stack the playing field in your favor.

> I currently maintain certifications as a Microsoft MCSE and MCT, and Novell MCNE and CNI. Currently, I am pursuing my Microsoft MCSD status and Cisco CCIE certification.

Keep in mind that the certifications you pursue should not be merely for the sake of quantity, but focused on your area of specialty. Choosing which certifications to pursue is largely a matter of the direction that you choose to take in the industry. A programmer might find that simply an MCSD certification is all that is required to gain and maintain employment. Network engineers often benefit from showing that they are cross-trained in other industry-standard network operating systems such as Novell NetWare and SCO UNIX.

An obvious cost factor is associated with pursuing and maintaining any of these certifications. You should analyze your marketplace to determine whether the certifications on which you plan to focus will give you a sufficient return on investment (ROI). The ROI might not always be so much a direct monetary increase but often helps you establish a firmer foothold on your existing employment.

Many companies are required to maintain a certain number of staff employees with certain certifications. For example, Microsoft Certified Solution Providers must maintain a minimum of two Microsoft Certified Product Specialists.

## C.2.4. Corporate Views on Certification

Companies realize that the certifications belong to the individual, not the company. Because of this, many organizations, both public and private, are often hesitant to invest too much in a single individual. Some management too often feels it is spreading the risk of key individuals leaving by employing more minimally certified individuals than a select few highly qualified persons.

This attitude can often be overcome by committing a minimum number of months to a company following the company's investment in your certifications. It is not uncommon to see people even sign a promissory note for the cost of any training they receive. The balance due on the note is reduced automatically for each subsequent month of employment. If the employee leaves before the agreed-upon term, he or she would be responsible for the balance of the note.

### C.2.5. Low-Cost Certification Preparation

If your company is unwilling or unable to pay for instructor-led classroom training, it would be wise to consider alternative methods of certification preparation. One of the foremost ways to prepare for examinations is by using certification prep guides.

Somewhere in between instructor-led classroom training and self-study comes online training. The Internet is becoming an excellent tool for providing quality low-cost training from numerous suppliers. Search for MCSE using your favorite search engine and check out the various options. Before enrolling in one, get details of the type of training. Also, ask for student comments. Not all offerings are of equal quality.

# C.3. Maintaining Your Technical Edge

Keeping up with the ever advancing technological changes is a nearly impossible task. The employable MCSE must be able to absorb, comprehend, and retain information on a wide variety of topics. Fortunately, several excellent resources are available, such as newsfeeds, forums, conferences, user groups, online magazines, and newsletters to help you keep abreast of new developments and maintain your technical edge.

## C.3.1. Newsfeeds

Newsfeeds are one of your best resources for keeping up to date with current industry developments. Newsfeeds are excellent sources of summarized information on all of the major technology companies.

I start each day by launching PointCast and reading every summarized article on what I consider to be the 10 most influential computer-related companies. Although I might not own stock in each of the companies, I still watch for fluctuations in the stock value. Whenever I note a major variation in the stock price, I review all the referenced articles watching for mergers, licensing agreements, new releases, and anything else that could directly or indirectly affect the direction I will need to head in the upcoming months.

Your MCSE certification also will open the door to several private news servers. Focus only on the newsfeeds that give specific, factual information. Hearing other peoples' personal predictions might be interesting, but if they are not based on fact they can prove destructive to your knowledge base.

## C.3.2. Forums

A forum is different than a newsfeed in that you can take on an active role. Make sure that the forum in which you participate is made up of people with similar qualifications and certifications; avoid becoming the big fish in the small pond. Several newsgroups also exist as an excellent tool for soliciting and providing information.

Both questions and answers on forums and newsgroups should be concise. Post only questions that are within the realm of the forum's purpose. Although your goal is to maintain and increase your employability, you will do yourself a disservice by soliciting work on support forums or in inappropriate newsgroups.

One additional resource is a mailing list. There are mailing lists aimed at just about any product and any subject with new ones being added daily. By selecting the right mailing lists you can find excellent resources for technical information or career advancement.

C

It is a bad, albeit common, practice to solicit work on support forums. Several employment forums and newsgroups exist specifically for posting job opportunities and resumes.

## C.3.3. Networking with Your Peers

Many Microsoft Authorized Technical Education Centers (ATEC) worldwide host technical user groups. As with forums and newsfeeds, the content of user group meetings can vary greatly. User groups offer an excellent platform for increasing your technical abilities. Presentations and demonstrations are normally geared toward the implementation of networking products from Microsoft and other vendors. User groups often can bring you the opportunity to get hands-on exposure to beta software and the latest developments in networking hardware.

You can find the latest Microsoft events near you at `http://www.microsoft.com/isapi/events/default.asp` and information on user groups at `http://www.bhs.com`.

As you meet new people in the industry, be sure to get their business cards. These same people might be capable of getting you the real-world experience you'll need later when you are preparing for your technical interviews.

### C.3.4. Technical Conferences

Nothing keeps your technical edge honed like a conference. Conferences can range from a single-day event to a week-long series. Conferences are an excellent occasion to associate yourself with other MCSEs.

For an MCSE there is no doubt that Microsoft's annual TechEd conference is the single most important technical event. TechEd provides an opportunity to meet and speak with many of Microsoft's premier developers, along with MCSEs from around the world. To ensure that you get the most from the conference, review the conference details well in advance. You can find information on TechEd and other Microsoft events at `http://www.microsoft.com/events/`.

If you have increased your certifications to include being a Novell CNE, you also might consider attending BrainShare. BrainShare is the Novell equivalent of Microsoft's TechEd. You can find details on BrainShare and other Novell events at `http://www.novell.com/events/`.

## C.4. Increasing Your Opportunities

Whether your goal is to gain employment as an MCSE or simply to keep abreast of new opportunities, there are several avenues to pursue. You can find employment for MCSEs online, through a recruiter, or even create it by yourself. No single path is better than another for an MCSE to take, as we each are pursuing our own goals.

### C.4.1. Finding a Job Online

You can find some of the best opportunities for employment online. If you know which employer you want to pursue, you can probably find a listing of potential jobs by visiting that employer's Web site.

As search engines become more sophisticated, performing simple searches with excellent results becomes possible. A simple query of the World Wide Web using any of the major search engines can result in screen after screen of opportunities.

Note

At the time of writing the search +MCSE +Jobs returned over 500 hits. Of course, not all the hits are necessarily offers for employment, and not all employment opportunities are listed on the Web.

Several Web sites are dedicated to nothing but the advertisement of technical jobs and the posting of related resumes.

## C.4.2. High-Tech Recruiters

Many companies employ the services of professional recruiters to assist them in hiring MCSEs. Make it easy for them to find you by posting your resume online.

## C.4.3. Self-Employed MCSEs

You might decide that the best company to work for is one you own. Many MCSEs are self-employed. In order to be successful as a self-employed MCSE it is very important to form a close relationship with Microsoft. Microsoft has several programs geared specifically toward the small business and independent consultant.

I normally recommend gaining experience as a member of an organization before you attempt self-employment.

Remember that your MCSE certification is not like the proverbial dentist's shingle. Hanging an MCSE logo on your business card does not in itself guarantee employment.

# C.5. Overcoming the Technical Interview

The last step in becoming an employed MCSE is to receive and pass the technical interview process. Before the technical interview you must ensure that you have fully researched your prospective employer and developed both the conceptual and real-world knowledge to be successful. Don't rush into an interview unprepared. People often will say you can try again, but in reality you usually have only one chance in a technical interview.

## C.5.1. Researching Potential Employers

Many people tend to take a shotgun approach to employment. They simply generate a decent resume listing their skills, education, and accomplishments, and then send it off to as many companies as they can. This is the approach of minimal effort and usually meets with minimal response.

A better approach is to identify and focus on the companies with which you want to be employed, and then pursue them. Remember that many of the best positions are not even advertised; they might not even exist until you create them. You might even be able to take this same approach within your existing company and find new avenues to pursue. After you have identified the companies you want to work with, the next step is to help them understand the benefit of working with you.

Finding the right position begins with identifying the companies with which you want to work. Remember that as an MCSE you possess a valuable set of skills. Locate the organization that will enable you to exercise your capabilities to the fullest.

**Note**

It is your responsibility to show that you meet the needs of the organization, not vice-versa. Although you might have the best skills for a position, no one is going to work with you if you come across like a prima donna.

The more information that you research on your potential employer the more prepared you will be for the technical interview. The best place to start is at the employer's Web site. By examining its Web site you can easily learn in what areas the company is involved. Make a list of the general areas, such as network installation, training, programming, and Web site development. Although you might be pursuing a position in a specific vertical area, you will want to identify as many of your complementary skills as possible.

After you have created a general list of areas in which the company is involved, it is time to explore the details of the areas that you are most qualified for. For example, if you are pursuing a position as a network engineer you will want to list all the network operating systems that the company implements. The list that you create will comprise the areas that you will pursue for both breadth and depth.

## C.5.2. Breadth and Depth

A good technical interview will ask questions on a wide range of topics, often well beyond the scope of the job requirements. The breadth of questioning is used to establish your range of knowledge. After the range of knowledge is established the subjects will become more focused on the areas that directly relate to the job function. You must demonstrate a depth of knowledge in the focused questions.

Think of breadth and depth like language fluency. If you were to move to France you would want to be fluent in French; this would represent a depth of knowledge. Because

France borders on other countries, it also would be reasonable that you would want to develop basic skills, such as how to ask directions or order food in perhaps German or Italian; this would represent a breadth of knowledge.

Use the list of areas that you compiled while researching the companies as a guideline in researching topics of breadth and depth.

## C.5.3. Developing a Breadth of Knowledge

A breadth of knowledge must go beyond simply understanding that a certain technology exists. You must know enough about various technologies to understand how they interrelate. For example, a position might state that a person with Microsoft Exchange Server experience is required; this should tell you that you should have a depth of knowledge in Microsoft Exchange Server and, at a minimum, fundamental knowledge of Novell GroupWise and IBM/Lotus Notes. The information you gather on GroupWise and Notes will add to your breadth of knowledge.

Because a breadth of knowledge often is little more than basic awareness, the best sources are the white papers developed by the manufacturers. This is true whether you are developing a breadth of knowledge on software or on hardware.

If you have properly researched the position, you will be able to identify the areas in which only a breadth of knowledge is required for a given position. By showing a breadth of knowledge, you differentiate yourself from other candidates who might appear to have tunnel vision on the industry.

Of course, you will be required to have a depth of knowledge in certain key areas. The following section will help you develop your depth.

## C.5.4. Developing a Depth of Knowledge

You must develop a full depth of knowledge systematically. Although hands-on experience is definitely the best way to get hands-on knowledge, it is not the only means. In fact, people who rely simply on their personal use with a product as the sole means of generating depth are often brought to the harsh realization that their product knowledge is too focused.

Reading definitely is the doorway to knowledge. Regardless of whether you prefer to read online documents or printed technical guides, being a voracious reader is imperative. Focus your reading on specific areas of study. If you over-generalize in your selection of topics you will build your breadth but will not quickly develop a depth of knowledge.

Choose a single area of study at a time, and then dedicate enough time to fully comprehend the topic. A good place to start is with the topics that Microsoft lists for each of the MCSE exams. The fact that you have already passed the exam on the topic has no bearing here. To be an employable MCSE you want to go further in depth than is typical.

For example, assume that one of the companies you are targeting has included the requirement for a strong knowledge of TCP/IP. You might have already passed the Microsoft TCP/IP exam, but don't stop there. Research topics referenced in the exam topics to a greater depth and using a viewpoint that is not Microsoft-centric. You might start by downloading RFCs on common topics from the InterNIC. Next, gather information on related topics from manufacturers. It's almost inevitable that you will be asked opinions on various routers, so be prepared by having read up on Cisco, Bay Networks, and others. As you identify topics of importance, it often is good to see what technical guides are available for subjects in which your knowledge is limited.

By this point, you will have developed both strong breadth and depth of knowledge, but there is one more step to ensuring your employability. You must gain real-world experience.

## C.5.5. Developing Real-World Experience

Stating that you need real-world experience to become an employable MCSE might seem like the chicken and the egg. On one hand you need real-world knowledge to gain employment, and on the other you can't seem to get it without being employed.

This is where you will benefit most from the effort you've made to network with your peers. You might not personally have access to routers, mainframes, multiprocessor systems, FDDI-based networks and the like, but from among your peers you can certainly find someone who does.

You will find that many of your associates will be glad to mentor you on a product that they have mastered. Don't feel at all like you are imposing by asking to be shown how something works. Most of the time people are flattered that you view them as an expert in a particular subject. Remember, though, that this works both ways.

If possible, spend a full day as an apprentice to someone who has a position similar to the one you wish to pursue.

## C.5.6. Anticipating Interview Questions

Anticipating interview questions serves two purposes. The first is to ensure that when asked a question you have an intelligent and well-thought-out response. Second, in the event that the interviewer is prepared with only cursory questions, it will be your responsibility to raise the level of the interview to differentiate your abilities from those of others pursuing the same position.

Write out 10 questions that you would ask if you were the one holding the interview. As you come up with answers to the questions, make sure to base your responses on what you have learned about the company's infrastructure.

## C.5.7. Sample Questions

Below are some examples of the kind of questions you should be prepared to answer during an interview.

### A Question of Breadth

Which do you think is easier to manage, a Microsoft NT Server-based or Novell NetWare-based network?

**Response Advice**

Opinion questions are the most common of the questions that I categorize as *questions of breadth*.

Before the interview you already should have determined the mix between Microsoft and Novell products installed at the potential employer. This is a good opportunity to demonstrate to the interviewer that at a minimum you have a solid conceptual understanding of how each of the systems functions.

Additionally, the question was left intentionally vague. The ease of management may vary greatly given differing network topologies, applications in use, and versions of the software being used. This brings an additional opportunity to show the breadth of your knowledge.

Because the question is one of breadth the response should not be overly detailed.

**Sample Response**

Each of the products has its advantages. In an environment like this where both products are coexisting, I feel that a systems administrator would need to be comfortable with both. The actual ease of management would vary depending on the task and, of course, the version of NT or NetWare being used.

### A Question of Depth

When would it be advantageous to set the method of NetBIOS name resolution on a client to MIXED?

**Response Advice**

Make sure that your response to questions of depth includes the basis for your response.

The question implies that your potential employer has a WINS server in place on a routed network. Choosing MIXED will cause the client to attempt resolution using a broadcast before contacting the WINS server. Broadcast traffic normally is acceptable with few clients.

The degree of depth is high and deserves a response at the same level or greater.

**Sample Response**

Because this would generate broadcast traffic, this would be the best method to choose when you have a small group of clients that are located remotely from a WINS server, perhaps across a slow link, but are local to the resources they most commonly require.

By choosing MIXED, name resolution traffic to the WINS server only would be generated across the router when the clients attempt to access a remote server.

# C.6. Summary

When you have your certification, what do you want to do with it? The opportunities that lie before you are limited only by your imagination. This Appendix has given you some pointers; however, do not consider yourself limited by the suggestions here. By becoming an MCSE you have set yourself above the crowd. Take advantage of it.

# Index

## O